CHRISTIAN PHILOSOPHICAL THEOLOGY

CHRISTIAN PHILOSOPHICAL THEOLOGY

by
STEPHEN T. DAVIS

OXFORD
UNIVERSITY PRESS

OXFORD
UNIVERSITY PRESS

Great Clarendon Street, Oxford OX2 6DP
United Kingdom

Oxford University Press is a department of the University of Oxford.
It furthers the University's objective of excellence in research, scholarship,
and education by publishing worldwide. Oxford is a registered trade mark of
Oxford University Press in the UK and in certain other countries

First published 2006
Reprinted 2013

Published in the United States of America by Oxford University Press
198 Madison Avenue, New York, NY 10016, United States of America

British Library Cataloguing in Publication Data
Data available

Library of Congress Cataloging in Publication Data
Data available

ISBN 978-0-19-928459-7

Acknowledgements

I wish to thank several friends and colleagues who helped me in the process of producing this book. Professors Alan Padgett, Susan Peppers-Bates, Gerald O'Collins, S.J., Marguerite Shuster, and Dale Tuggy read and helpfully commented on the entire manuscript. I am exceedingly grateful to them for their generosity and helpful suggestions. I also wish to thank three anonymous referees for Oxford University Press for their useful comments and criticisms. Very many people also commented on those individual chapters that have appeared, in earlier versions, in different settings. Most of them are mentioned in the footnotes of the relevant chapters.

Several of the chapters of this book originally appeared in other forms in other venues. Let me accordingly thank the relevant publishers and periodicals. I thank Oxford University Press for permission to use in this book much of Chapter 6 of *The Resurrection* (1997), edited by Stephen T. Davis, Daniel Kendall, S.J., and Gerald O'Collins, S.J., much of Chapter 10 of *The Incarnation* (2002), edited by the same team, and much of Chapter 10 of *The Redemption* (2004), also edited by the same team. I thank William B. Eerdmans Publishing Company for permission to use in this book much of Chapters 3 and 5 of my *Risen Indeed: Making Sense of the Resurrection* (1993). I thank Paulist Press for permission to use in this book much of Chapter 15 of *The Convergence of Theology*, edited by Daniel Kendall, S.J. and Stephen T. Davis. I thank Westminster John Knox Press for permission to use in this book much of my contributions to *Encountering Jesus: Live Options in Christology* (1988). I thank Macmillan Press and St. Martin's Press for permission to use in this book much of Chapter 3 of Stephen T. Davis (ed.), *Philosophy and Theological Discourse* (1997). And I thank Kluwer Academic Publishers for permission to use much of my contribution (Chapter 6) to *The Trinity: East/West Dialogue*, edited by Melville Y. Stewart (2003).

Let me also thank the editors of *Philosophia Christi*, for permission to use much of my 'The Cosmological Argument and the Epistemological Nature of Religious Faith' (1 January 1999), as well as the editors of *Theology News and Notes*, for permission to use parts of my essay 'Why the Historical Jesus Matters' (June 1999).

All quotations from the Bible, unless otherwise indicated, are from the New Revised Standard Version, copyright 1989, National Council of the Churches of Christ in the U.S.A.

Contents

Introduction

A book called *Christian Philosophical Theology* requires explanation. My own professional discipline is philosophy, and most of my publications have been in the field of the philosophy of religion. But from time to time, throughout my career, I have addressed in print various issues in Christian theology, such as the nature of God, resurrection, incarnation, Trinity, and scripture, among others.

In those writings I have tried to be sensitive to biblical issues, as well as to the great tradition of Christian theology. But I have also approached the topics with my own training and experience as a philosopher in place. For example, I have tried to write with clarity and argue rigorously. (Doubtless I have not always achieved those goals.) I have also had a preference for dealing with those theological issues which would be of interest to Christian philosophers.

All of those writings were influenced by my own professional location, which is that of a Reformed Protestant Christian of a fairly traditional theological orientation whose career has been spent almost entirely at secular institutions. This location means that I have often found myself in conversation with people of other religious traditions or of no religion at all, as well as with people whose understanding of Christianity is much at variance with mine, usually far to the left of it. Having these sorts of conversation partners has affected both the topics that I have addressed and the ways in which I have approached them. So if there is a slight apologetic bent to much of this book, that is perhaps understandable.

The possibility of writing this book occurred to me in the spring of 2001. My notion was to revise slightly some of my published theological essays (some of which had appeared in fairly obscure places), substantially revise others, and write several new chapters, in order to form a coherent whole. What I wanted, and hope to have achieved, is not a book of discrete essays but a unified, sustained argument. My aim was to write a coherent statement and defence of certain central claims of the Christian world-view.

Arranged in a certain order, some of those central claims constitute the logic of the argument of this book. I have in mind such assertions as: God exists; human beings ought to believe that God exists; God, the creator of the heavens and the earth, reveals himself to human beings, and does so pre-eminently in his Son Jesus Christ; God is Trinitarian in nature; Christ was bodily raised from the dead and his resurrection constitutes a promise of our resurrection; Jesus Christ is God incarnate; human beings are separated from God owing to their sinfulness and need to be reconciled to God; redemption is offered as a free gift to human beings on the basis of the life, death, and resurrection of Jesus; it is received by faith; and redeemed human beings will one day 'see God'.

In recent years I have co-edited (along with my friends, Gerald O'Collins, S.J. and Daniel Kendall, S.J.) four different Oxford University Press books on theological topics. They include *The Resurrection: An Interdisciplinary Symposium on the Resurrection of Jesus* (1997); *The Trinity: An Interdisciplinary Symposium on the Trinity* (1999); *The Incarnation: An Interdisciplinary Symposium on the Incarnation of the Son of God* (2002); and *The Redemption: An Interdisciplinary Symposium on Redemption* (2004). I have no doubt that the process of helping to edit, as well as contributing to, those volumes helped prepare me for the present book. I have in mind specifically the notion of sticking to essential and central theological topics and trying, as much as possible, to speak from the broad centre of the Christian theological tradition.

As I consider these and other theological topics in the book, three concerns are pre-eminent in the discussion. The first is logical coherence. Since critics have charged that certain crucial Christian claims are internally inconsistent, in places it will be important for me to ask whether such charges are true. The second is evidential considerations. In other places—especially where historical claims are at issue—we shall have to consider matters of evidence and probability. The third is fit with Christian orthodoxy, as I see it. In some chapters, one of these concerns will be the main focus; in other places two or even all three will be considered.

The 'philosophy of religion', as I understand that term, deals with philosophical issues that relate to general theism, which is belief in the God of traditional monotheism. Such issues as arguments for and against the existence of God, the rationality or irrationality of religious faith, the problem of evil, the possibility of miracles, and the prospects for survival of death, as well as others, are dealt with under this rubric. 'Philosophical theology' is sometimes used as a synonym for 'philosophy of religion', but, as noted, I will use it simply to mean the kind of approach that a believing philosopher would make to Christian theological topics.

There are many other ways to approach theology: biblical theology, history of doctrine, and practical theology, for example. And of course there is systematic theology. I am not anxious for this book to be seen as an effort in that genre. I am not a professional theologian, and there are many important topics in systematic theology—for example, sacramental theology, ecclesiology, eschatology, social ethics—about which I know little, and that I do not address in this book. Moreover, although my knowledge of some theological topics and thinkers in the Christian tradition is probably fairly deep, my overall knowledge of the history of doctrine is rather uneven.

I just used the term 'Christian world-view'. This usage reflects my opinion that the Christian faith (like, I suppose, most other religions) is a system, an intellectual whole, a coherent way of understanding all of life, history, and the world. This point first strongly occurred to me decades ago, a few years after my conversion to Christianity, when I read Calvin's *Institutes of the Christian Religion*. The fact that Christianity is a world-view is important in an age that discourages intellectual systems, and that encourages at least some theologians to exercise enormous freedom in picking and choosing certain Christian notions and not others. There are even some theologians today who try syncretistically to combine Christian ideas with notions from other religions.

It is inevitable that my own Reformed or Calvinist approach to Christian thought will emerge in this book. But I want to be clear that my aim has been to write something that is generically or 'merely' Christian, to adapt slightly a usage of C. S. Lewis.[1] I cannot claim to have avoided controversial theological issues in this book, and some Christians will dispute some or even many of the claims that I make, but I have not intentionally pushed private or denominational stances.

There are 'boundary' or 'turf' issues whenever philosophers try to do theology. In the 1980s, several Christian philosophers in the United States and Great Britain, some Catholic and some Protestant, most of them members of the Society of Christian Philosophers, seemed almost simultaneously to tire of writing about generic theism, and started venturing into theology. Since then the trend has continued and has even grown. In a way, this movement is surprising. Those of us who were trained as philosophers in the 1960s can remember well the days when, as graduate students, we were scarcely allowed even to mention the word 'theology'.

I offer no apology for philosophers doing theology. Indeed, Christian history is full of philosophical theologians, from Justin Martyr to Søren Kierkegaard. I believe that every thinking Christian is a theologian and has every right to communicate theological thoughts both to fellow Christians and to the world. The only caveat is that those who want to do serious theology must be versed both in biblical studies and in the history of doctrine.

---

[1] C. S. Lewis, *Mere Christianity* (New York: Macmillan, 1960).

Sound Christian theology cannot be done without a foundation in both disciplines.

Although it will cause pain to some, another reason for the move of philosophers into theology must be mentioned, namely, dissatisfaction with the current state of the discipline. There are of course contemporary theologians whom Christian philosophers read with respect and gratitude. But in connection with their professional work, especially in the philosophy of religion, Christian philosophers occasionally find themselves reading theological texts from classical authors like Anselm, Aquinas, or Calvin or recent authors like Barth or Rahner. And it seems that many Christian philosophers, including me, find the work of such thinkers typically to be more careful, stimulating, rigorous, and faithful to the Christian tradition than the work of many contemporary theologians, especially the more radical ones. Much recent theology strikes many of us interested outsiders as extraordinarily faddish. (In slight defence of theology at this point, however, I must admit that most disciplines studied in the university these days—including philosophy—are easily captivated by whatever seems new and different.)

This book revolves around certain crucial questions. Part I deals with the question, Why believe? or rather, Why believe in God? Chapter 1 asks why, from a theological perspective, there is so much religious unbelief. Chapter 2 uses a theistic proof—what I call 'the generic cosmological argument'—to argue that God exists and accordingly that belief in the existence of God is warranted. Chapter 3 uses the concept of divine sovereignty to answer the questions: What is God like? How is God related to creation? How is God revealed? Chapter 4 develops a new and, I hope, plausible version of the so-called Social Theory of the Trinity; I call it Perichoretic Monotheism.

Part II deals with various aspects of christology and is understandably the longest section of the book. Christianity is, after all, the religion of Jesus Christ. Chapter 5 deals with the some two-century-old 'quest for the historical Jesus', and argues (contrary to the views of some scholars who write about Jesus) that, when properly done, the quest supports rather than refutes orthodox views of Jesus. Chapter 6 continues the conversation about Jesus and tries to connect the earthly Jesus with what Christian theology has typically said that he was and with what he did. Chapters 7 and 8 deal with different aspects of the vital Christian claim that Jesus Christ really and truly died, and then was really and truly brought back to life by God. They ask—and try to answer—the question why we should believe that this is so. Chapter 7 considers the Christian claim—sometimes disputed by recent and contemporary theologians—that Jesus was *bodily* raised from the dead. Chapter 8 asks how we are to understand the New Testament assertion that various witnesses to the resurrection—for example, Mary Magdalene, Peter,

Thomas—'saw' the risen Jesus. Chapter 9 considers in detail an apologetic trilemma argument popularized by C. S. Lewis and widely dismissed since then, namely, the argument that Jesus was either 'mad, bad, or God'. The chapter amounts to a qualified defence of the argument. Chapter 10 deals with christology and constitutes a defence of a broadly kenotic way of understanding the divinity and humanity of Christ.

In Part III I turn to the Christian understanding of sin and redemption. The question here is how human beings are redeemed from sin, death, and suffering. Chapter 11 considers the strength and weaknesses, on the basis of natural theology alone, of two systems of salvation—what I call 'Karma' and 'Grace'—and argues in favour of the second. Chapter 12 deals in a limited way with atonement; it is an attempt to rehabilitate two traditional theological themes that in recent times are either completely ignored or else rudely scorned, the themes of the wrath of God and the blood of Christ. Chapter 13 deals with the Christian notion of redemption. It emphasizes the bodily aspect of redemption and discusses Catholic–Protestant differences on the notion of justification. Chapter 14 lays out what I take to be Christian belief about the general resurrection, that is, the future resurrection of all people.

Finally, in a partial and sketchy way, Part IV asks how Christian theology ought to be done. Chapter 15 deals with the relationship between two sources of Christian theological authority, namely scripture and tradition. Although I will argue that much can be said in favour of the Roman Catholic emphasis on tradition, I end up embracing a version of the Protestant principle, 'scripture alone.' And in Chapter 16 I try to answer the question of how Christians ought to view the Bible and what we might mean when we say, 'The Bible is true.'

Part I

Why Believe? God and Belief in God

1

Religious Belief and Unbelief

I

Let me raise two questions that puzzle me. Both have to do with the phenomenon of religious unbelief. First, why do certain people who hear and understand the Christian message not accept it? This question poses a problem for me for three reasons: (1) I think the Christian message is true; (2) I think it is in the interest of all persons to accept it; and (3) scripture, as I read it, claims that at least in some sense all people know certain crucial aspects of the Christian message.

This last point constitutes my second puzzle. In Romans 1: 19, Paul says of unbelievers:

What can be known about God is plain to them because he has shown it to them.

My puzzle is this: What exactly did Paul mean? Let us begin to answer that question by asking what is it that we Christians think 'can be known about God'. That of course can be disputed. But in order to keep things relatively simple, we'll call it proposition (1):

(1) God exists, and is the all-powerful, all-knowing, and loving creator of the heavens and the earth; and God is worthy of worship and obedience.[1]

But in what sense is this truth about God (as well as other things, of course) 'plain' to non-believers? There certainly appear to be sincere atheists, agnostics, and members of non-theistic religions who do not know proposition (1) at all. They don't even *believe* it. It would be odd, maybe even insulting, if I were to say to one of my atheist colleagues at the Claremont Colleges, 'The existence of God is plain to you; indeed, you *know* that God exists.' So again my second puzzle is this: What can Paul possibly have meant?

---

[1] Some Christians would argue that natural revelation is inadequate to reveal God's love and mercy, and that Paul was not claiming otherwise. That may well be true, and, if it is true, the word 'loving' should be removed from (1). This point will not affect the argument of the present chapter.

One clue is that Paul seems to have thought that the problem of religious unbelief is a spiritual, rather than an intellectual, problem. He goes on to say (Rom. 1: 20–2):

Ever since the creation of the world his eternal and divine nature, invisible though they are, have been understood and seen through the things he has made. So they are without excuse: for though they knew God, they did not honor him as God or give thanks to him, but they became futile in their thinking, and their senseless minds were darkened.

Let us say that an *intellectual problem* is one that is solvable by learning, by the right application of human reason and experience. And let us say that a *spiritual problem* is one that is solvable by being rightly related to God. Paul seems to have thought that religious unbelief is a matter of being wrongly related to God. To borrow Pascal's distinction, it is more a matter of the heart than of the mind.

II

We are trying to understand Paul's claim that 'what can be known about God is plain to them'. To put it bluntly, the problem is that such a claim seems plainly false. Let us then see if we can figure out how it might nevertheless be true. Now, it is a truism in philosophy that there are different senses of the word 'know'. Let us call all those uses of the expression 'A knows p' that entail 'A believes p' *strong senses* of 'know'. There are also *weak senses* of the word 'know', that is, senses where knowing p does not entail believing p, or at least not consciously believing p.

If I may speak personally, I am quite sure that, before my conversion to Christianity years ago, I knew (in the weak sense) certain things about myself that I was then quite unwilling to believe. These were things that I was afraid might be true about my own inherent pride, self-centredness, and propensity for violence and lust. Sometimes in life we see what we want to see. Only after my conversion did I come to know, in the strong sense, these truths about myself.[2]

---

[2] This phenomenon of both believing and not believing a proposition can be variously described. Perhaps it is a matter of rejecting it consciously and believing it unconsciously. Perhaps it is a matter of wavering back and forth—believing it some of the time and rejecting it at other times. Perhaps it is a matter of believing with part of one's brain or even personality and rejecting it with another. However it is described, I am quite sure that the phenomenon occurs.

Is it, then, possible for the following three claims to be true for some person A and claim p:

(2) A knows p (in the weak sense);
(3) A does not know p (in the strong sense);

and

(4) A *ought* to know p (in the strong sense), that is, A is culpable for not knowing p (in the strong sense)?

Yes, I think such a situation is quite possible. I once knew a young man who was, frankly, a malicious person. But his mother, whom I also knew, was unwilling to face the truth about him. I think she knew (in the weak sense) the truth about her son, but not in the strong sense. She was always making excuses for him, overlooking his misdeeds, claiming that his behaviour was just a phase that he would soon outgrow. Her unwillingness consciously to face the truth was, I think, at least somewhat culpable. In the weak sense, she knew that he was a bad person; but she did not (consciously) believe it; and she *should* have believed it.

This tension between knowing and not knowing is evident even in the Psalms. Psalm 19 begins as follows:

> The heavens are telling the glory of God;
>   and the firmament proclaims his handiwork.
> Day to day pours forth speech,
>   and night to night declares knowledge.

But then the Psalm seems to go in quite the opposite direction:

> There is no speech, nor are there words;
>   their voice is not heard.

And then it returns to the original affirmation:

> Yet their voice goes out through all the earth,
>   and their words to the end of the earth.

The psalmist seems to be saying that the heavens, God's handiwork, speak. Indeed, they speak constantly, day to day and night to night. What they speak about is the glory of God. The voice of the heavens goes out 'through all the earth'. This is an odd claim in and of itself. How can the stars *tell* anything? Yet, as we have seen, the next claim seems almost to contradict the first. 'Their voice is not heard,' the psalmist says; it is almost as if 'there is no speech, nor are there words.'

I read these lines as follows: the voice of the stars and of other created things declaring the glory of God is or should be clear to everyone. Given our created natures, they should be natural signs that produce in us certain concepts and beliefs. But if some people are unwilling to listen to that voice, they will hear no other voice. It will be for them as if there is no evidence of the glory of God at all.

The Bible has a metaphor for the phenomenon of culpable disbelief. The metaphor is 'hardening of the heart'. In other words, the truth is this:

(1) God exists, and is the all-powerful, all-knowing, and loving creator of the heavens and the earth; and God is worthy of worship and obedience;

(5) Everybody knows (in the weak sense) that (1) is true;

and

(6) Those who do not know (1) in the strong sense are culpable for their ignorance.

Proposition (1) is a truth that unbelievers do not want to admit, so they refuse to accept it. They harden their hearts against it. Again, the problem is essentially spiritual rather than intellectual. It exists not in the state of the evidence, but rather with us. We have a *defect* that prevents us from seeing the truth, from knowing (1) in the strong sense.

That defect is called *pride*. This includes the desire to control one's own life, and the firm setting of the will against someone else being in charge, even if that person has a right to be in charge. Those who accept the truth about God and know it (in the strong sense) must do several things that humans do not naturally want to do. First, they must believe what they cannot see or touch or prove. Secondly, they must humble themselves and admit that they owe their lives to the one who created them. Thirdly, they must submit themselves to worship and obey the commands of the one who created them. Pride works to prevent all three.

III

My claim, then, is that spiritual considerations prevent people from knowing (in the strong sense) certain truths that would otherwise be clear to them. Notice that visual metaphors naturally come into play here. The non-believer says of the existence and glory of God, 'I just don't see it.' The believer says, 'Your eyes need to be opened.' Non-believers who convert and become believers frequently says things like, 'It was as if blinkers were removed from my eyes; I can now see what I didn't see.'

Having taught virtually my entire academic career at secular institutions, I think I have seen culpable disbelief in some of my religiously sceptical colleagues (doubtless it exists in myself, as well). Some of them, so far as I can tell, would be unwilling to accept

(1) God exists, and is the all-powerful, all-knowing, and loving creator of the heavens and the earth; and God is worthy of worship and obedience,

even if it were as obvious as the noses in front of their faces. Indeed, I have a name for a certain atheological argument that nobody verbalizes, but by which many people today live. I call it the Lifestyle Argument Against the Existence of God. It is a simple argument, a two-step proof. It goes like this:

(7) I am not living and don't want to live the kind of life that God would want me to live if God existed;
(8) Therefore, God does not exist.

Of course what we have here is absurdly fallacious as an argument, but that does not prevent people from being influenced by it. That is why the Lifestyle Argument is not necessarily indicative of logical inability in those who accept it, but rather of moral and spiritual dysfunction. It seems to me that *the* most dogmatically anti-Christian folk in academia today are those who are intentionally following lifestyle choices that they know are not approved by Christianity.

Let me illustrate. I will describe a certain philosophy of life that I call 'Meism'. The essence of Meism is the notion that everything that I want in life is rightfully mine. Meism has a motto or, perhaps, mantra. It is the words, 'I deserve it.' This is what Meists always say when they think of something that they want. If I want to be wealthy, then wealth is something that I deserve. If I want to be physically attractive, then good looks are something that I deserve. If I want to have complete freedom of choice, then power over other people and the ability to invent my own moral rules is something that I deserve. If I want to have perfect relationships with others, especially with members of the opposite sex, then that too is something that I deserve.

Meism is the dominant personal philosophy of our time. If I am a Meist, then I believe that *I* am the centre of the universe. My only moral duties are to myself. I can be as self-indulgent as I want, because, after all, I deserve it. If other people prevent me from getting what I want, then I have the right to complain loudly, because, after all, they are standing in the way of my getting what is rightfully mine. I even have the right to elbow them aside if that is necessary to my achieving wealth or good looks or power over people or perfect relationships or whatever I want.

Dedicated Meists, knowing as they do that Meism and Christianity are incompatible, tend to be insistent anti-Christians. The deepest reason that they are non-believers is not intellectual, but spiritual. Certain commitments that they have made render them incapable of seeing reality as it genuinely is. It is as if there were blinkers over their eyes. They can't see things—like the presence of God in their lives—which they ought to see.

IV

What is it that is ultimately real? What is the centre, the core, the heart of the universe? If we could see reality as it genuinely is, what would we see?

There are various intellectual options on this question. Most atheists would say that ultimate reality consists of atoms in motion; what is real is matter, in its various configurations. Another option: I know a person, a devout Vishnu-ite Hindu, who would insist that what is ultimately real is the karmic cycle of life, death, and rebirth. A third option: some who embrace postmodernism hold, so far as I can tell, that there is no such thing as a unified whole that might be called 'reality' and thus no unifying centre of reality.

To Christians, what is at the centre of reality is *a personal relationship*. At its deepest level, this claim points to something that we will explore in Chapter 4—namely, the loving, open, and interpenetrating relationships among the Trinitarian persons—the Father, the Son, and the Holy Spirit. But God created us human beings in God's image. One aspect of that image is that we too are essentially involved in a personal relationship. The Christian claim that a personal relationship is at the heart of reality refers not just to the Trinity. It also means that we human beings were created for the sake of a relationship with God (as well as with each other).

Well then, what is the nature of that relationship? It is a *covenant* between God and human beings. A covenant is simply a two-part agreement between persons: 'I will do this if you will do that.' The covenant that is at the heart of reality is tersely but sublimely summed up by the prophet Jeremiah: 'I will be your God and you will be my people' (Jer. 7: 23). In this case, God, the superior party, initiates the covenant and remains faithful to it, despite human betrayal of it. So at the centre of the universe is a loving, covenantal relationship between persons and a God who acts on behalf of that relationship. This is what unbelievers ought to see but cannot see.

The relationship between God and human beings was cosmically and morally severed with the entrance of sin and spiritual blindness into the universe. So far as individual persons are concerned, that relationship is broken whenever we separate ourselves from God by our pride, anger, lust, and self-centredness. All of God's actions in salvation history are done for the sake of restoring human beings to the pristine splendour of that relationship. Christians believe that the relationship is fully restored through the action of God in the world and pre-eminently through God's actions in the world in Jesus Christ.

V

Precisely how do people come to believe in God or in the truth of the Christian message (which of course includes (1) and much else)? This question is ambiguous: there are at least two ways in which it might be understood. First, it might be a question about the *origin* or initial cause of a belief. Suppose we ask a theist, 'Why do you believe in God?' If the answer is something like, 'I believe in God because as a child my parents taught me to believe in God,' that answer would normally be taken to explain the origin or genesis of the belief. Secondly, sometimes we wonder about the *warrant* or evidence for or justification of a belief, that is, we wonder whether the belief is rational or can be intellectually justified. If the theist were to appeal, say, to some version of the cosmological argument for the existence of God, like the one to be discussed in Chapter 2, that would normally be taken as an attempt to provide warrant or justification for the belief.

We are asking how a person moves from the state of not seeing God, that is, being an unbeliever, to the state of seeing God. Suppose that we are interested in the first question, the question of origin or initial cause. Then, in my opinion, the answer is: people come to believe because of (1) private evidence, and (2) the illumination or inward testimony of the Holy Spirit. (I will explain both terms momentarily.) God changes their minds, turns on the lights, causes them to see things that they were not able to see before.

Private evidence is my technical term[3] for considerations in favour of (or against) a given claim that are probative or convincing to a given person but not to others. 'Public evidence' (what we normally just call 'evidence') ought to be open to the awareness and inspection of anyone and transpersonal in its appeal. If I claim to know that God exists because of some sort of theistic

---

[3] I first used the term years ago in my *Faith, Skepticism, and Evidence* (Lewisburg, PA: Bucknell University Press, 1978), pp. 26–30, 58–9, 62–6, 74–86, 214–26. In that work, I attempted to answer a question that I will not tackle here: when is it epistemologically justified to base belief (in part) on private evidence, and when is it not? I also tried to show that being influenced by private evidence is unavoidable for rational people.

proof or body of scientific facts, that would be public evidence. If I claim to know that God exists because my parents told me that God exists or because I strongly sense that God has acted in my life (say, forgiving my sins, rescuing me from harm, etc.), that would be private evidence. (I should note that the term 'private' here does not mean 'logically private', in the sense in which some philosophers used to argue sense-data are private.)

Powerful public evidence in favour of some claim ought to convince anybody of its truth. Private evidence in its favour is probative only to the person to whom the evidence is private, not necessarily to anybody else. Such a person finds certain considerations convincing that most rational people would not find convincing. Private evidence or private reasons are, as we might say, subjective or person-relative. The cognitive aspect of faith, and certainly religious faith, can in part be understood as conviction based on private evidence. What convinces one person that a given claim that is accepted 'on faith' is true will not necessarily convince another person.

But what then about natural theology? Is it ever the origin of anybody's belief? This is not an artificial question for me to ask, since one of my recent books is on the proofs for the existence of God.[4] Natural theology or apologetic arguments definitely have value in providing warrant for the Christian message, but for most believers natural theology has little to do with the origin of belief. There are exceptions, of course. But most Christians do not seem particularly interested in natural theology. The origin of their belief lies elsewhere.

Notice that most Christians are *certain* that the Christian message is true, while most arguments in natural theology only produce, at best, more or less probability. And the force of any powerful argument can be resisted if one especially wants to do so; one need only find its weakest premiss and then call it into question. Arguments against that premiss, or arguments that undercut justification for it, will not be hard to find—not if one is familiar with the literature in the philosophy of religion, anyway. Especially in situations where self-centredness, pride, and the desire to resist any call from God are involved, it seems that objections can always be found and that, accordingly, apologetic arguments will produce few conversions.

As Paul says, 'even if our gospel is veiled, it is veiled to those who are perishing. In their case the god of this world has blinded the minds of the unbelievers, to keep them from seeing the light of the gospel of the glory of Christ' (2 Cor. 4: 3–4). To people whose 'senseless minds were darkened' (Rom. 1: 21), even sound arguments in favour of the existence of God or the resurrection of Christ will seem like foolishness. Nor does it seem that the

---

[4] Stephen T. Davis, *God, Reason, and Theistic Proofs* (Edinburgh: Edinburgh University Press, 1997).

learned are more sensitive at detecting the religious truth than the unlearned. Otherwise, scholars would rank above ordinary believers in religious certainty and maybe even religiosity, and I see no reason to think that they do.

John Calvin argued as follows: 'Credibility of doctrine is not established until we are persuaded beyond doubt that God is its Author.'[5] Natural theology, as well as the testimony of the church, Calvin said, are both valuable, but do not protect us from 'the instability of doubt' or from boggling 'at the smallest quibbles'. 'The word of God will not find acceptance in men's hearts', he said, 'before it is sealed by the inward testimony of the Holy Spirit.'[6] This testimony produces a certainty that each believer experiences; it is an illumination that opens the sinful heart to the message of the word of God and gives assurance of its truth. 'Indeed,' Calvin declared, 'the Word of God is like the sun, shining upon all those to whom it is proclaimed, but with no effect among the blind. Now, all of us are blind by nature in this respect. Accordingly, it cannot penetrate into our minds unless the Spirit, as the inner teacher, through his illumination makes entry for it.'[7]

What exactly is *the inward testimony of the Holy Spirit*? Let me define it as follows: it is *that influence of the Holy Spirit on the minds of believers that causes them to believe firmly that the Christian message, or some aspect of it, is true.* This is the origin of Christian certainty. The inward testimony is a species of persuasion, not of evidence. It is an illumination that opens eyes that are closed to the truth.

As we have seen, one of the effects of sin is that it prevents people from recognizing truths that we strongly wish not to be true, for example, that we owe our lives to God; that we don't deserve everything that we desire; that we need a saviour. Thus Paul says: 'Those who are unspiritual do not receive the gifts of God's spirit, for they are foolishness to them, and they are unable to understand them because they are spiritually discerned' (1 Cor. 2: 14; see also 2: 10). The Spirit's testimony does not supply new evidence of the truth of the Christian message; it illuminates or renders convincing evidence that is already there. It is not a question of propaganda or brainwashing or of making feeble evidence appear powerful. It is a question of removing blinkers and helping us to grasp the epistemic situation correctly.

As philosophers know, Descartes was shocked and horrified when Gassendi argued that Descartes' famous *Cogito, ergo sum* was a deductive argument, a syllogism with a suppressed middle premiss that said something like, *Omnia cogitantia sunt* ('Everything that thinks exists'). Descartes' reply was that the

[5] John Calvin, *The Institutes of the Christian Religion*, ed. John T. McNeil, (trans. Ford Lewis Buttles), 2 vols (Philadelphia: Westminster Press, 1960), (hereinafter *Institutes*) I, vii, 4.

[6] Calvin, *Institutes* (n. 5 above), I, vii, 4.

[7] Calvin, *Institutes* (n. 5 above), III, ii, 34.

cogito was not an inference of any sort, but rather a direct intuition of truth.[8] I want to say the same thing about the inward testimony of the Holy Spirit. It is not a process of reasoning or weighing evidence, but a direct intuition of truth. It is like the opening of blind eyes, the unplugging of deaf ears, the removal of a veil. How does it work, phenomenologically? We do not know. Bernard Ramm says that it is

no audible voice; no sudden exclamation that 'the Bible is the word of God;' no miracle removing us out of our normal routine of creaturely existence; no revelation with flashing lights and new ideas; no religious experience as such; no creation of some new or special organ of spiritual vision; but rather, it is the touch of the Holy Spirit upon native and resident powers of the soul which had been rendered ineffectual through sin.[9]

Notice that the inward testimony is private or secret. The assurance that it provides cannot be passed on through communication or proved. This is why non-believers typically take the Christian message to be sheer foolishness and the Bible to be a book like any other book. Those of us who have friends in departments of religious studies can speak authoritatively on this matter; we know people who have spent their professional careers teaching and writing about the Bible, but who do not believe what it says. Since the inward testimony is essentially private, it is not (so to speak) directly communicable. Just because you claim that the Spirit has told *you* that p is true, that does not mean *I* must accept p. Of course, if you are a person whom I respect, especially in religious matters, your testimony will doubtless impress me and may even cause me to look at p in a new light. I may even become convinced that you are correct. But the point is that your testimony will not constitute for me the inner witness of the Holy Spirit. It will not be normative for me. On any topic a mere appeal to the Spirit is insufficient to carry conviction; the Bible itself recognizes that many who are in error will try to validate their claims by appealing to the Spirit. Thus the expressed need to 'test the Spirits to see whether they are of God' (1 John 4: 1; cf. 1 Cor. 12: 10).

It might be objected that the inward testimony is too subjective to warrant any religious beliefs at all. Muslims can claim what might be called in Inward Testimony of Allah on behalf of the claim that the words of the *Koran* are from God; members of Christian Science can claim something similar for *Science and Health With Keys to the Scriptures*. But surely the mere fact that people disagree with one of my beliefs does not *by itself* cast doubt on that belief. More importantly, as I have stressed, the inward testimony of the Holy Spirit

---

[8] René Descartes, *Philosophical Writings*, vol. II (ed. John Cottingham, Robert Stoothoff, and Dugald Murdoch) (Cambridge: Cambridge University Press, 1984), p. 100.
[9] Bernard Ramm, *The Witness of the Spirit* (Grand Rapids, MI: Eerdmans, 1959), p. 84.

is not to be understood as an argument, and certainly not as an argument directed at those who doubt or deny the Christian message. The inward testimony constitutes the central reason why I (and presumably other Christians) accept proposition (1) and the other aspects of the Christian message. It is not meant as a vehicle for convincing others.

It is important to note that the inward testimony is not a source of new truth or revelation. It is not an 'inner light' or mystical oracle or private vision that provides extra-biblical answers to theological questions. It is a witness to the truth of scripture and of the Christian message. As Jesus said: 'When the Advocate comes, whom I will send to you from the Father, the Spirit of Truth who comes from the Father, he will testify on my behalf' (John 15: 26; cf. also 1 Cor. 2: 10). If this were not so—if the inward testimony provided new truths—the shape of the Christian gospel would be perennially dependent on private revelations and visions.[10]

In an article entitled 'Is Faith Infused into Man by God?'[11] Aquinas argued that the assent or belief aspect of faith is not adequately explained by external inducements, such as being persuaded by someone or seeing a miracle. Such influences obviously do not constitute sufficient explanation, because some people are exposed to the same sermon or even see the same miracle, yet do not believe. There must, then, be an internal cause of assent. Aquinas rejected the suggestion that our own free will is the cause; he thought the idea smacked of Pelagianism. Thus, he concluded, the cause must be 'some supernatural principle' that moves us inwardly by grace, and that (he says) is God.

Aquinas did not use any phrase like 'the inward testimony of the Holy Spirit', but his central point was similar to Calvin's. A properly disposed heart (or, if you will, an illumined mind) is necessary to weigh the evidence properly. Those who have not been illumined by the Spirit are in an inferior epistemic position. They do not see everything that must be seen.

VI

What about the question of warrant or justification for belief in the Christian message? Can the inward testimony provide it? In one sense, yes it can. The belief of a Christian that the Christian message is true does not need anything

---

[10] Moreover, it goes without saying that the inward testimony is not a vehicle for solving scholarly problems, e.g. about the biblical text, canon, authenticity, geography, archaeology, history, etc.

[11] Thomas Aquinas, *Summa Theologica* (trans. Fathers of the English Dominican Province) (New York: Benzinger Brothers, Inc., 1947), II-II, 6, 1.

more than the inward testimony. It does not stand in need of public verification, for example, by arguments from natural theology, for it to be sensible, rational, defensible.

Who gets to decide which beliefs are warranted and which are not? Who gets to decide whether private evidence or (something equally private) the inward testimony warrants certain Christian beliefs? Are atheists and agnostics the privileged few who get to decide? Some people seem to think so; they seem to hold that acceptance of the Christian message is irrational or unwarranted until Christians can prove that message to the satisfaction of sceptics. But why should any Christian accept such a claim?

My argument, then, is this: if I accept the Christian message because of private evidence and the inward testimony, and if that message has not been refuted or rendered improbable, then my acceptance of the Christian message is fully rational. Of course if there exists evidence or a powerful argument *against* the truth of the Christian message—a disproof of (1), for example— that would be another matter. My belief would not then be warranted. But in my opinion no such evidence or argument exists.

But here is a point where natural theology can enter in. Many sceptics have strongly argued against the Christian message—against (1), among other items—and apologetic arguments can be used to respond to those objections. In order to answer critics outside the Christian community (or indeed, to convince anyone other than oneself), appeal to the inward testimony will not usually suffice. But one certainly can appeal to rational arguments in favour of the truth of the Christian message.

The reason that natural theology alone rarely suffices to produce a conversion is not hard to find. Suppose that some clever philosopher were to produce a proof of the existence of some being B, a proof that no one is able to refute. That is, suppose the premises of the argument are clearly true, the argument is clearly formally valid, and it clearly commits no informal fallacy like equivocation or question-begging. But now let us suppose that B is something that you have very good reason to believe does not exist, like, say, your thirteenth daughter. Your reaction to the proof probably would and indeed should be something like this: 'Something is wrong here; the proof of B *must* be fallacious in some way that I did not see earlier; for example, one of its premises must be false after all.' This, I think, is quite parallel to the attitude many atheists have towards theistic proofs—since they are firmly convinced that God does not exist, no piece of natural theology can possibly prove the existence of God. Even if at some level they recognize that a certain theistic proof amounts to a good argument, it will not persuade them.

Of course there are some arguments that virtually everyone would accept— the Pythagorean theorem, for example. I have never heard of any rational person who both understood and rejected the claim that the square on the hypotenuse of a right triangle is equal to the sum of the squares on the other sides. But it is hard to think of any arguments for substantive philosophical conclusions, let alone theological ones, that everybody would accept as successful arguments. Unlike truth, rationality is in part person-relative. That is, belief in a certain proposition might be rational for one person and irrational for another. Accordingly, as noted above, no matter how logically impeccable a given piece of natural theology may be, a religious sceptic who wants to resist its conclusions can always find reason to do so.[12]

So natural theology is probably not best looked at as a vehicle for producing conversions. There are some things it can do, however. For some folk it can remove intellectual blockages that stand in the way of faith. For others it can cause them to consider the possibility of God more seriously than they had done previously. For some open-minded people, it might just move them to embrace bare theism, as a kind of halfway house to Christianity. But that is about all. Natural theology presumably has other jobs in the Christian community that it does much better, for example, strengthening believers by replying to sceptical attacks on the faith. So to the extent that natural theologians hope to produce spiritual and not just intellectual results by their efforts, probably their best strategy is (1) to present arguments that are as powerful as possible; (2) to hope and pray that religious sceptics will come to believe; and (3) to leave the rest up to the mercy of God.

VII

We began with two questions: Why do some people not accept the Christian message? and What did Paul mean when he said of unbelievers, 'What can be known about God is plain to them'? My answer to the first question is spiritual blindness. Sin has the pandemic effect of hardening the heart against the truth. People do not want to hear that they must live godly lives, that they have a moral defect called pride that has epistemological consequences, that they cannot save themselves, that they need to repent, that salvation is to be found only in Jesus Christ. If the heart is not right, both the mind and the eyes will be affected. People will not know what they should know. They will not see what ought to be plain.

---

[12] This sort of thing is true not just of religious sceptics. If someone were to publish an apparently impeccable proof of the non-existence of God in the next issue of the *Journal of Philosophy*, I'm sure I would try to find a rational way to reject one of its premises.

So my answer to the second question is that the truth about God, which I have summarized by

(1) God exists, and is the all-powerful, all-knowing, and loving creator of the heavens and the earth; and God is worthy of worship and obedience,

is indeed 'plain' to those who are not blinded by sin, those who have been graciously illuminated by the Holy Spirit. It is seen to be warranted, and accepted as true. But what about unbelievers? Since like all people they are morally responsible for their sinful acts, they are also morally responsible for the epistemological consequences of their sinful acts. They morally *ought* to see that (1) is true. They ought to *know* (1) (and of course other truths) in the strong sense. What non-believers pre-eminently ought to see, but cannot see, is that we human beings are in relationship with God, a relationship that will culminate in the eschaton when we will see God.[13]

VIII

In the passion story in Mark's gospel, there is a curious verse that records an event that occurred immediately upon Jesus' death: 'And the curtain of the Temple was torn in two, from top to bottom' (Mark 15: 38). The curtain, of course, was the heavy laminated veil that separated the Holy of Holies from the Holy Place. Only the high priest could enter the Holy of Holies, and only once a year, on *Yom Kippur*, to make atonement for the sins of Israel. Christian theology has always interpreted this verse as a signal from God (note that the tear in the curtain was from the top down) of the close of the Jewish sacrificial system. The final and perfect sacrifice for sin had just been made; no other sacrifice would ever be needed.

I have no wish to quarrel with that aspect of what the Church Fathers called the rule of faith. I only wish to add that perhaps the evangelist was also saying something like this: before the passion of Jesus, God was hidden; no one was allowed to see God. God and humans could only meet once a year;

[13] Although I do not pursue his line of argument, my own indebtedness in this chapter to Alvin Plantinga's pioneering work in the epistemology of religious belief needs to be acknowledged. I intend the chapter in part as a proposal for bridging a gap that currently exists between two groups of Christian philosophers—those who embrace epistemological internalism and natural theology and those who embrace the epistemological externalism of Reformed Epistemology and eschew natural theology. My hope is to provide an important role for natural theology, and thus a way of doing apologetics aimed at non-believers, within an epistemological framework that is in sympathy with the aims and orientation of the Reformed Epistemologists.

at all other times, there was a curtain separating them. Since the curtain is now torn in two, we human beings can enter into God's presence. We have access to God. God no longer hides behind a curtain. We can now see God (cf. John 1: 18).[14]

---

[14] Mark uses the strong verb *schizo* only here (15: 38) and in 1: 10 (at Jesus' baptism). In that text, the heavens are 'torn asunder', the Spirit descends, and the revealing voice is heard. In Matthew and Luke the verb is softer, and the heavens are merely 'opened'. God is revealed in all three stories. God is no longer hidden.

2

The Epistemic Status of Belief in God

I

In the previous chapter I offered an interpretation of Paul's claim that 'what can be known about God is plain to them [i.e. unbelievers] because he has shown it to them.' I argued that what ultimately prevents unbelievers from seeing the truth is spiritual blindness. I do not deny, of course, that there are unbelievers for whom other factors—perceived lack of evidence, the existence of great suffering in the world, damages brought about by religious believers—constitute genuine reasons for their unbelief. But in such cases I would argue that spiritual blindness influences the way that they evaluate those considerations. I also argued in Chapter 1 that religious belief—belief, for example, in what I called proposition (1)—can be warranted. But I also argued that exercises in natural theology such as the Cosmological Argument for the existence of God can provide additional warrant. It is to that argument that we now turn.

First we must note that very few people who believe in God do so because of a theistic proof. So far as the origin of religious belief is concerned, for most people natural theology plays little role. Nevertheless, even for religious believers, a powerful theistic proof might serve a useful purpose. It could certainly contribute to the confidence of religious believers, so to speak, if it were possible to prove the existence of God by natural reason. It would increase the warrant of their belief. It would be possible to show that belief in God has a rational basis, that to believe in God is not necessarily—as religious sceptics often charge—to be gullible, credulous, or superstitious.

The cosmological argument for the existence of God (CA) is a venerable and frequently debated theistic proof. It has been discussed by philosophers at least since the fourth century BC, when a version of it appeared in Plato.[1] Since then it has been both attacked and defended throughout the history of philosophy. There have been important discussions of it in the ancient,

---

[1] See Edith Hamilton and Huntington Cairns (eds.), *The Collected Dialogues of Plato* (New York: Pantheon, 1961), pp. 1455–79 (*Laws* 894A–899C).

medieval, modern, and contemporary periods.[2] However, there is no one 'cosmological argument'; what we refer to by that name is a whole cluster of related arguments that revolve around certain common and recognizable themes. Virtually every author who discusses the CA has a favourite version.

In the present chapter I will focus on what I will call the 'generic cosmological argument' (GCA). I can find no philosopher to whom to attribute this precise version, although it clearly has affinities with eighteenth-century versions of the CA, especially those of Leibniz and Clarke.[3] Moreover, the GCA contains several themes that we associate with Aquinas' versions of the CA, especially the 'Third Way'.[4] Here, then, is what I am calling the GCA:

(1) If the universe can be explained, then God exists.
(2) Everything can be explained.
(3) The universe is a thing.
(4) Therefore, the universe can be explained.
(5) Therefore, God exists.

Let me now set out to clarify the argument. First, three terms need definition. By the term 'the universe' (or 'the world'), I simply mean the sum total of everything that has ever existed or will exist (minus God, if God exists). By the term 'God', I mean some sort of divine reality or divine realities. I do not think the CGA, even if it is an entirely successful theistic proof, necessarily proves the existence of the God of theism—a being that is unique, all-powerful, all-knowing, loving, and so on. But if the GCA is successful, it certainly does prove the existence of some sort of divine reality or necessary being[5] (which of course could possibly be the God of theism). So whenever I use the word 'God' in this chapter I mean it as shorthand for the more

---

[2] There are several good surveys of the literature. See, for example, William L. Craig (ed.), *The Cosmological Argument from Plato to Leibniz* (New York: Barnes and Noble, 1980). See also the essays collected in Donald R. Burrill (ed.), *The Cosmological Arguments* (Garden City, NY: Anchor Books, 1967).

[3] See Gottfried Leibniz, 'On the Ultimate Origin of Things', in Philip P. Wiener (ed.), *Leibniz: Selections* (New York: Scribner's, 1951), pp. 345–55, and the selections from Samuel Clarke's *A Demonstration of the Being and Attributes of God* in D. Raphael (ed.), *British Moralists 1650–1800* (Oxford: Oxford University Press, 1969).

[4] Thomas Aquinas, *Summa Theologica* (trans. Fathers of the English Dominican Province) (New York: Benzinger Brothers Inc., 1947), 1, 2, 3 (pp. 13–14).

[5] Let us say that a necessary being (NB) is a being that (1) is everlasting; there is no moment when it does not exist; and (2) depends for its existence on no other being. In some strong sense of the word 'cannot', an NB cannot not exist. A contingent being (CB), on the other hand, is a being that can either exist or not exist; if it exists it (1) has a finite lifespan (it does not exist, and then exists for a time, and then ceases existing (unless there are CBs that, after coming to exist, God everlastingly preserves in existence)); and (2) depends for its existence, as long as it exists, on another being or other beings. Some CBs exist (e.g. horses) and some do not (e.g. unicorns). Thus CBs, unlike NBs, can fail to exist.

complex set of possibilities just noted. By the term 'thing' I simply mean a being or entity ('substance', as earlier philosophers would have called it)— something that has an identity distinct from other things and is a property-bearer.

Secondly, let me briefly discuss the premisses of the GCA. Premiss (1) simply claims that if there is any explanation of the existence of the universe, then God must exist and provide that explanation. This premiss seems perfectly sensible because if God exists, then the explanation for the existence of the universe is just this: 'God created it.' And this seems to be about the only sort of explanation that could be given. If no God or god-like creator of the universe exists, it seems that the universe will have no explanation whatsoever for its existence. Its existence will be what we might call a 'brute fact'. It is just there, and that is all that can be said. (If the universe is a necessary being—a point that I will consider below—it will require no explanation for its existence.)

Premiss (2) is a version of a principle that philosophers call the 'principle of sufficient reason' (PSR). There are many versions of the PSR; I will interpret it to mean simply this: *everything that exists has a reason for its existence.*[6] That is, if something x exists, there must be a reason or explanation why x exists. Defenders of the PSR usually admit that the PSR cannot be proven, since it constitutes one of the basic axioms of rational thought against which all other claims or statements are measured. That is, we normally try to argue for the truth of a proposition by means of other propositions that are more evident or certain than it; but in the case of the PSR (so this argument goes), there are no propositions more certain or evident than it that can be used in this way.

But the PSR—so its defenders claim—is rationally indispensable in that it is presupposed in all rational thought. Richard Taylor says that you cannot argue for the PSR without assuming it; he calls the PSR 'a presupposition of reason itself'.[7] We encounter thousands of existing things every day, and we always assume that there is some reason or explanation why they exist. Suppose one day you were to encounter something unusual—a strange animal, or an automobile completely unknown to you. You would dismiss as absurd any such statement as 'There is no reason why it exists; it's just

---

[6] A slightly weaker version of the PSR says this: everything that comes into existence has a reason for its existence. I opt for the stronger version so that the PSR will apply to the universe even if it turns out that the universe is everlasting (if there is no moment of time when it does not exist) and thus did not come into existence. This is because even if the universe is eternal, the question, 'Why should it exist instead of not exist?' is still a legitimate question. One problem with the stronger version of the PSR is that it requires that even NBs (if there are any) have a reason for their existence. But then we will say that the reason for the existence of a given NB is simply that it is an NB.

[7] Richard Taylor, *Metaphysics*, 4th edn. (Englewood Cliffs, NJ: Prentice-Hall, 1992), p. 101.

there—that's all.' That is, your commitment to the truth of the PSR would make you reject out of hand any suggestion that the existence of the thing is entirely random or inexplicable, a brute fact. Moreover, it needs to be pointed out that there are *no* existing things about which we know that they have no explanation for their existence.

Premiss (3) represents what we might call the 'lumping together' strategy that we see in many versions of the CA. The typical move is to lump together all the existing things, or all the contingent things that have ever existed or will exist, and call it 'reality' or 'the world' or 'the universe'. Then causal questions are asked about this huge aggregate—questions like, 'Who made it?' or 'Where did it come from?' or 'Why is it here?' or 'What is its cause?' Premiss (3) simply says that the huge aggregate that we call 'the universe' is itself a thing about which such causal questions can coherently be asked.

Suppose a critic of the GCA wanted to deny premiss (3). If so, the response to the critic would be to point out that the universe has the two essential characteristics of 'things'. First, it has an identity apart from other things; the universe is not the same thing as the earth or as my computer, for example. Secondly, the universe is a property-bearer. That is, it has certain unique properties like a certain pressure, density, temperature, space–time curvature, and so on. In its very early history everything was so smashed together that there wasn't even atomic structure, so that the only thing there was the universe itself. Accordingly, premiss (3) seems highly plausible.

But a critic might still argue that not every collection of things is a thing. Notice for example that the set that includes my left shoe, the planet Mars, and Bill Clinton does not constitute a 'thing'. Nor does a set that includes the tail of every cocker spaniel in Claremont. These sets are not 'things'—so it might be said—because the sets we are talking about are diffuse; their parts are not connected; once each member of the set is explained, there is no 'set' left unexplained; there is no unifying principle. They, like the universe, are mere aggregates.

These are controversial issues, much discussed in contemporary metaphysics. There is no denying that the universe is an aggregate, that is, a huge collection of everything that has ever existed, is existing, or will exist. But it is hardly a *mere* aggregate, precisely because it is *not* diffuse. All its members are causally connected, and the totality (as just noted) has certain properties. Nor would it be true to say that every property of the universe is a property of its parts. The universe began to exist at the Big Bang, but no part of the universe did. They began to exist later. It is true that if the existence of every member of the universe is explained, there is nothing called 'the universe' left to explain. But for logical reasons we *cannot* explain the existence of every member of the universe: its temporally first existing member will always remain unexplained.

Finally, there *is* a unifying principle to the set of things that we are calling the universe, and that is the origin of all its members in some prior existing thing or things. Every member of the universe other than God can ultimately be explained by some such sentence as, 'God made it.' Accordingly, premiss (3) is plausible.

Premiss (4) is entailed by (2) and (3). That is, if it is true, as premiss (3) says, that the universe is a thing; and if it is true, as premiss (2) says, that everything can be explained; then it strictly follows, as premiss (4) says, that the universe can be explained. It is impossible for (2) and (3) to be true and (4) false. The conclusion of the GCA follows from (1) and (4). If it is true, as (1) says, that, if the universe can be explained, then God exists; and if it is true, as (4) says, that the universe can in fact be explained; then it strictly follows, as (5) says, that God exists. Because of the argument form known as *modus ponens*, it is impossible for (1) and (4) to be true and (5) false.

II

Now the GCA looks at first glance to have promise as a theistic proof. But some have argued that it commits the fallacy of begging the question, and accordingly fails.[8] (There are, of course, other objections that are often raised against the CA,[9] but with one exception—an objection we will consider in Section IV—we will focus here just on the 'question begging' objection.)

In order to clarify this objection to the GCA (it also constitutes an objection to most versions of the CA), let me refer to the transcript of a famous debate in 1948 on BBC radio. The debaters were Bertrand Russell, the famous atheist philosopher, and Frederick Copleston S.J., the eminent historian of philosophy; the debate topic was the existence of God. In a discussion of the CA, Copleston remarked, 'Well, my point is that what we call the world is intrinsically unintelligible, apart from the existence of God.'[10]

Copleston thus in effect endorsed premiss (1) of the GCA. But Russell consistently took the position that the world has no explanation, and that it is illegitimate to ask for an explanation of the world. Russell thus in effect insisted on denying premiss (2) of the GCA, which is the PSR. 'I should say

---

[8] As indeed I argued in my *God, Reason, and Theistic Proofs* (Edinburgh: Edinburgh University Press, 1997), pp. 144–6. The present chapter represents a correction of the argument presented there. John Hick has also argued that the CA begs the question. See John Hick (ed.), *The Existence of God* (New York: Macmillan, 1964), pp. 6–7.

[9] For discussion of them, see *God, Reason, and Theistic Proofs* (n. 8 above), pp. 70–6.

[10] See Hick, *The Existence of God* (n. 8 above), pp. 174–7.

that the universe is there, and that's all,' Russell said; 'the notion of the world having an explanation is a mistake.'[11]

The debate over the CA then ground to an inconclusive halt, with Russell unwilling to grant the PSR and Copleston unable to convince him of its truth. As Copleston wrote at the end of his own discussion of Aquinas' Five Ways, 'If one does not wish to embark on the path which leads to the affirmation of transcendent being..., one has to deny the reality of the problem, assert that things "just are" and that the existential problem in question is a pseudo-problem. And if one refuses even to sit down at the chess-board and make a move, one cannot, of course, be checkmated.'[12]

What the Russell–Copleston debate shows, according to some critics, is that at least some versions of the CA, doubtless including the GCA, fail as theistic proofs because they commit the fallacy of begging the question. Now, there are many ways in which an argument can beg the question. At issue here is the question-begging that is engaged in when one's argument contains a premiss or premisses that will only be acceptable to those who already accept the conclusion. As an illustration, notice this theistic proof:

(6) Either God exists or $7 + 5 = 13$;
(7) $7 + 5$ does not $= 13$;
(8) Therefore, God exists.[13]

This argument is certainly formally valid; it is impossible for (6) and (7) to be true and (8) false. And for theists (those who believe in the existence of God), it is also sound; that is, they hold both its premises (i.e. (6) and (7)) to be true. Now, nearly everybody will grant the truth of (7), and theists are happy also to grant the truth of (6). But the problem here is that no sensible person who denies or doubts the conclusion of the argument (i.e. no sensible atheist or agnostic) will grant the truth of (6). There is no reason to grant (6) apart from a prior commitment to the existence of God. Thus the (6)–(8) theistic proof is an unsuccessful theistic proof because it begs the question.

Returning to the GCA, the criticism we are discussing argues that it begs the question at the point of premiss

(2) Everything can be explained,

that is, at the point where the PSR is introduced. Let me explain the objection in this way: it is clear to all concerned that the GCA is formally valid; so the deepest question we can ask about it is whether its premisses are true. Now

---

[11] Ibid., pp. 175, 177.   [12] Reprinted in Hick, *The Existence of God* (ibid.), p. 93.
[13] This argument is discussed by Alvin Plantinga in *The Nature of Necessity* (Oxford: Oxford University Press, 1974), pp. 217–18.

premises (1) and (3) appear to be beyond reproach, and can be accepted by any sensible person. But what about (2)? Well, there is a certain set of rational persons who will be much inclined to consider premiss (2) true as well, that is, inclined to accept the truth of the PSR. These people may accordingly consider the GCA to be both valid and sound (again, we are ignoring other possible objections to the GCA). That is, these folk might well consider the GCA a successful proof of the existence of God.

The people whom I have in mind are of course theists: people who already believe in the existence of God. Those folk quite naturally accept the suggestion that everything can be explained. They do so because they hold that the universe and everything in it (the whole of reality minus God) can be explained in some such terms as 'God created it.' But here is the crucial point: there is also a certain set of rational persons who will be much inclined to reject premiss (2). These folk are atheists. No atheist like Bertrand Russell will have much inclination to grant the truth of premiss (2). Such persons will hold that the PSR is false because there is at least one existing thing—the universe itself—that has always existed and cannot be explained. Its existence is simply a brute fact.

If the defender of the GCA can find a way of arguing convincingly for the truth of the PSR that does not appeal to or presuppose the existence of God, then the GCA might well constitute a successful theistic proof (depending of course on whether other objections to it can also be answered). In the absence of such an argument, the GCA, according to the objection that we are considering, fails because it requires a premiss that should not be granted by those at whom the GCA is aimed, namely, atheists and agnostics. Thus, since even defenders of the PSR admit that it cannot be proved, the GCA fails as a theistic proof. One of its crucial premisses will only be acceptable to those who already accept its conclusion.

The point is not that only theists accept the PSR. Some atheists affirm it. The point is, as Bertrand Russell saw, that atheists *should not* affirm the PSR. In order to be consistent, they must insist that there is no explanation of why there is any reality at all. Accordingly—so the objection we are considering concludes—the GCA begs the question.

III

But perhaps the objection that the GCA fails as a theistic proof because it begs the question is too hasty. It seems correct to say that rational theists quite naturally accept the PSR and that rational atheists and agnostics do not, or should not, do so. But does it follow that the GCA, or indeed any version of the CA that relies on the PSR, accordingly begs the question? Perhaps the answer to that question will depend on the aim, goal, or purpose of the GCA.

Suppose the goal of the GCA is *to convince all atheists and agnostics to believe in the existence of God* or *to constitute an argument that rationally should convince all atheists and agnostics to believe in the existence of God*. Then, of course, the objection to the GCA that we are considering would appear to stand. The GCA would be a failure as a theistic proof. It would achieve neither purpose because rational and thoroughly convinced atheists and agnostics will reject its second premiss.

But suppose the goal of the GCA is instead *to strengthen the belief of theists in the existence of God* or *to show theists that they can know that God exists*. If something like this is the purpose or goal of the GCA (which is a view that I do not hold), then the objection to the GCA that we are considering appears to fail. It will not matter that atheists and agnostics rationally should reject the GCA's second premiss. Since the theists at whom the argument is aimed all accept its second premiss, the GCA might well (again depending on what is to be said about other objections that might be raised against it) constitute a successful proof of the existence of God.

But it seems that most theistic proofs in the history of philosophy, including the many versions of the CA that we find there, are offered with at least some sort of apologetic purpose in mind, that is, with some such goal in the mind of the theistic prover like showing to any rational person that belief in God can be rational. Theistic proofs have rarely been offered, so far as I can see, for intramural use only, for believers only. I will take it, then, that the actual aim or goal of the GCA is to *demonstrate the existence of God* and thus to *demonstrate the rationality of belief in the existence of God*. That is, what a successful theistic proof aims to do is substantiate the theist's belief in God, give a convincing reason for it, show that it is credible, show that it is *true*. But to whom is it to be demonstrated? Let me suggest that theistic proofs aim to demonstrate the rationality of theistic belief to all rational persons (whoever exactly they are), theists *or* atheists.

One way to do this is to convince folk that the premisses of the theistic proof under consideration are more plausible than their denials. The premiss with which we are concerned is premiss (2) of the GCA:

(2) Everything can be explained.

And its denial is

(2′) It is false that everything can be explained.

Which then is more plausible: (2) or (2′)? And that question, in the context of the current discussion, amounts to this: Is it possible to argue convincingly for the truth of the PSR in such a way as not to appeal to or presuppose the existence of God?[14]

It is surely possible to argue for the truth of the PSR without invoking or presupposing God. The question is whether it is possible to do so convincingly. The argument normally used by defenders of the PSR is the one briefly suggested above, namely, that the PSR is an indispensable requirement of reason. That is, it is an intuition shared by all rational folk (except perhaps atheists and agnostics when they are objecting to the CA) about the way reality operates. It is a kind of natural belief or basic assumption that all rational people quite normally make. In this way—so defenders of the PSR say—it is not unlike the belief that

(9) My epistemic faculties do not systematically mislead me.

Clearly our faculties for gaining true beliefs about and even knowledge of the world (faculties like memory, perception, reasoning, etc.) sometimes mislead us; but any attempt to argue that they systematically mislead us would involve assuming the reliability of our epistemic faculties. So no rational person can deny (9).

The point can be made in a slightly different way: just as it is necessary for our survival as living organisms on the earth that we accept (9), so it is necessary for our survival that we accept the PSR. Imagine the life of someone who seriously doubted the PSR. Such a person would—so it seems—live in constant fear that no matter what precautions she took, dangerous things might always pop into existence in her vicinity uncaused—things like hungry lions or speeding trains or deep chasms or armed terrorists. Thus—so the argument concludes—human nature compels us to accept the PSR.

Is this a convincing argument? Perhaps it is to theists, who will say: 'The PSR seems true to me; the arguments against it seem to me to fail; and it is rational for me to trust my faculties.' But it will surely not convince the

---

[14] It should be noted that attempts have been made to argue against the PSR, but they are not convincing. (1) Some have argued that since quantum physics, at least on some interpretations, allows for undetermined and inexplicable *events*, it can also allow for *things* to come into existence uncaused. But even if indeterministic interpretations of certain quantum events are correct, the conservation laws in physics still rule out things coming into existence uncaused. (2) Others argue that the uncaused and totally random coming-into-existence of something is not logically contradictory, and indeed is perfectly conceivable. Both points are true, but prove nothing. There are lots of reasons why a given proposition might be intellectually unacceptable besides its being logically contradictory. And in some sense of the word 'conceive', I can surely conceive of, say, a poodle popping into existence in my office for no cause or reason. But that does nothing to show that belief that such an event can occur is plausible.

Bertrand Russells of this world. Such folk will happily grant that (9) is not rationally deniable, but they will deny that the PSR has that same status. They will happily deny that tigers, lions, chasms, and terrorists pop into existence uncaused; but they will still insist on the rationality of holding the *whole* of reality, that is, the universe itself, to be uncaused. Moreover—so they will ask—who says that the demands of human reason are all satisfied? Is reality bound to agree with our presuppositions, even presuppositions that otherwise seem rational? In short, as J. L. Mackie argues, even if it is true that reason demands that we hold that the PSR is true, that does not show that the PSR is true.[15]

Mackie is surely correct in allowing that the universe need not comply with what he calls our 'intellectual preferences'. I have an intellectual preference that the mathematics of quantum theory be much simpler than they in fact are. Perhaps many people share that preference. But even if I am right about what people would prefer, that shows nothing about the way reality is. However, it is a long way from this undeniable point to the claim that a conclusion that we cannot rationally deny or cannot help believing is false. If in some sense we cannot help but accept the PSR and have no good reason to think it nonetheless false, it is otiose to suggest that we take seriously the possibility that it is false.

IV

As noted earlier, there are several objections that are often raised against the CA beside the begging-the-question criticism with which we have been principally concerned. Although I am ignoring most of them for present purposes, there is one that seems highly relevant to our discussion and should be considered. The objection is this: if GCA is a successful argument, the 'god' or necessary being that it proves to exist is not the God of theism or even any lesser god-like sentient being, but rather the universe, or physical matter itself. And an argument that proves the existence, or indeed the necessary existence, of the universe itself hardly does much to bolster the epistemic status of belief in God.

But it does not seem sensible to consider the universe, or physical reality, to be a necessary being. I cannot quite prove this by arguing that 'Everything in the universe is a contingent thing; ergo the universe is a contingent thing,' for that argument might well commit the fallacy of composition. Sometimes such

[15] See J. L. Mackie, *The Miracle of Theism* (Oxford: Oxford University Press, 1982), pp. 82–7.

arguments are clearly fallacious ('Every member of the human race has a mother; ergo the human race has a mother'); although at other times they are perfectly acceptable ('All the tiles in this mosaic are blue; ergo the whole mosaic is blue'). Whether or not the inference goes through in the case of the world's contingency, it is still a meaningful fact about the universe that none of its members is necessary.

That fact strongly suggests that there is no telling reason to consider the universe a necessary being. If we knew that the universe were everlasting, that might suggest it is a necessary thing. But those who would so argue would still have to overcome the obstacle of Richard Taylor's trenchant argument to the effect that something can be both everlasting and contingent. He says: Suppose, contrary to fact, that the sun and the moon are both everlasting. Then moonlight would also be everlasting but still contingent, because it would (everlastingly) depend for its existence on sunlight.[16] Moreover, we do not know that the universe—physical reality—is everlasting. Indeed, all indications are that it began at the Big Bang some 6.5 billion years ago (or whenever it occurred). And we have no basis whatsoever—no physics—for suggesting that anything existed before the Big Bang.[17]

A telling point against the objection to the GCA that we are considering is this: even if the universe were everlasting, it would still make sense to ask about it: Why should it exist at all? That is, why is there a cosmos or space-time reality at all? Why is there anything and not nothing? There is no absurdity at all in the idea of there being nothing at all, no universe. (No one would be there to notice that state of affairs, of course, but that does nothing to rule out the possibility.) It follows that nothing about the universe implies or even suggests that it is a necessary being. Accordingly, the objection to the GCA that we are considering fails.

Where, then, have we arrived? What does our discussion imply about the epistemic status of belief in God? If the purpose of the GCA is *to demonstrate to any rational person that belief in the existence of God is rational*, then our conclusion ought to be that the GCA (assuming it emerges unscathed by other criticisms) *can* constitute a successful theistic proof. This is because defenders of the GCA, as we have seen, are perfectly capable of making a rational case for its truth that does not invoke or presuppose God. It seems that even atheists will be able to understand (though they might not agree with or be convinced by) the argument that the PSR is a demand of rational

---

[16] Taylor, *Metaphysics* (n. 7 above), p. 101.

[17] As William L. Craig argues. See his 'Scientific Confirmation of the Cosmological Argument', in Louis P. Pojman, *Philosophy of Religion*, 4th edn. (Belmont, CA: Wadsworth, 2002), p. 32.

thought. A strong case can be made—a case that any sensible person can understand—that belief in the PSR is rational.

But theists can also understand (though they might not agree with or be convinced by) the argument that while the PSR applies well to existing items like animals, automobiles, and houses (things that have finite lifespans, things that come into and later pass out of existence), it does not apply to the mega-thing of the universe itself. Bertrand Russell might be right that it is a mistake to expect that reality itself has an explanation.

But which then is more plausible,

(2) Everything can be explained,

or

(2′) It is false that everything can be explained?

Since, as we have seen, commitment to (2′) does not entail commitment to the absurd notion that things like animals, automobiles, and houses can come into existence uncaused (one can consistently hold that the universe itself is the only exception to the PSR), it does not seem possible to show which is more plausible.[18] We appear to be left with the possibility that the theist's belief in the existence of God might well be rational (given the theist's rational acceptance of (2)) and that the atheist's disbelief in the existence of God might well also be rational (given the atheist's rational acceptance of (2′)).

But it is important to note that even this relatively irenical conclusion—that both atheists and theists can be rational—has an important consequence. If the conclusion of this chapter is correct (and again if the GCA can withstand other objections that might be raised against it), then belief in God (or some God-like being or beings who is or are responsible for the existence of the universe) is rational. Hence, it is rational to hold that naturalism and physicalism are false.

This is not a trivial conclusion. Why? Because no objection to theism is more common than the objection that in believing in God, theists are being soft-headed, gullible, and credulous; they are violating the ethics of belief; they are setting a poor epistemic example. For example, Kai Nielsen (I could have quoted almost a host of others) says: 'For someone living in the

---

[18] There is a problem with the atheist's theory that I will note but not explore. It was originally pointed out by A. N. Prior: it cannot be the case that only certain things and not others come into existence uncaused because, before they exist, there is simply nothing that would determine that only things of that kind can come into existence uncaused. Why then is it that animals, automobiles, and houses cannot come into existence uncaused, but the universe can? See A. N. Prior, 'Limited Indeterminism', in A. N. Prior, *Papers on Time and Tense* (Oxford: Clarendon Press, 1968), p. 65.

twentieth century with a good philosophical and a good scientific education, who thinks carefully about the matter . . . for such a person it is irrational to believe in God.'[19] In the light of the GCA, this objection to theism collapses.[20]

[19] J. P. Moreland and Kai Nielsen (eds.), *Does God Exist? The Great Debate* (Nashville, TN: Thomas Nelson, 1990), p. 48.

[20] I would like to thank William Lane Craig for his helpful comments on an earlier version of this chapter.

3

God, Creation, and Revelation

I

Part of the argument of Chapter 1 was that belief in the existence of God, even if it is based on private evidence, can be rational as long as, among other things, that belief has not been refuted. In Chapter 2 I used a piece of natural theology, the GCA, to demonstrate or at least come close to demonstrating that God exists. But even if we know or rationally believe that God exists, it is still an open question what God is like, that is, what God's attributes are. There are many sorts of Gods, gods, and divine beings in the various religions of the world. What is God like? That is the question to which the present chapter is meant to constitute a partial answer.

The Christian notion of God contrasts markedly to many views of the divine. One difference has to do with the Christian insistence that God is *sovereign*. There are many aspects of divine sovereignty that can be highlighted, but I am going to emphasize two points: that God is sovereign in creation, and that God is sovereign in revelation. But first I will sketch out what Christians believe to be the main characteristics of God.[1]

First, contrary to all versions of polytheism, Christianity insists that God is *one* (Deut. 6: 4–6; 1 Cor. 8: 4–6); God is absolutely unique (Isa. 40: 13–28); there is no other like God (Pss. 113: 4–6; Isa. 43: 10; 44: 6–8; 45: 21–2). Secondly, unlike the limited gods of some religions, God is *transcendent* over all existing things, including human beings (Num. 23: 19; Pss. 50: 21; Hos. 11: 9; Rom. 9: 20). Thirdly, contrary to all views that make God a physical object, like rocks and trees and human beings, God is a *spirit* (2 Chr. 6: 18; Jer. 23: 24; John 1: 18; 4: 24; 1 Tim. 1: 17; 6: 16). Fourthly, contrary to all views that make God limited or dependent on other beings, God is *eternal, uncreated* and (in God's essential nature) *changeless* (Pss. 90: 1–4; 102: 25–7; Mal. 3: 6; Jas. 1: 17; Rev. 22: 13); there is no moment when God does not exist or is not God.

---

[1] The scriptural references in the next two paragraphs beg many hermeneutical questions. I list them not as strict proofs that God possesses the properties in question but rather as texts to which Christian theologians have traditionally turned in order to buttress the theological claims in question.

Fifthly, contrary to all views in which an impersonal absolute (e.g. Brahman, the Dharma, the Tao, emptiness) is ultimate reality, God is *personal*. This means that God, like humans, is a person, that is, a being who has beliefs, has desires, formulates intentions, and works to achieve them. It also means that (unlike the absentee God of the Deists) God lovingly cares about the creation, and works to achieve God's good purposes for it. Sixthly, unlike theologies which posit realities that God did not create, God is the *creator* of the heavens and the earth and of all existing things apart from God (Gen. 1: 1; 2: 4; Pss. 33: 6, 9; 100: 3; Isa. 41: 4; 44: 24; 64: 8; Rom. 4: 17; Heb. 11: 3; Rev. 4: 11), including human beings and the spirit of human beings (Pss. 8: 3–5; Zech. 12: 1). Seventhly, contrary to all limited gods, God is *omnipotent* (Gen. 18: 14; Job 42: 2; Pss. 115: 3; 135: 6; Jer. 32: 17, 27; Dan. 4: 35; Matt. 19: 26; Eph. 1: 19) and *omniscient* (Pss. 139: 1–6; 147: 5; Heb. 4: 13; 1 John 3: 20). God is all-powerful; unlike humans, God has the ability to bring about any state of affairs that is logically possible for God. And God is all-knowing; in the case of any proposition whatsoever, even propositions about the future, that proposition is true if and only if God believes it. Finally, contrary to the semi-demonic divinities of some religions, God is *perfectly good* and *loving* (Pss. 100: 5; 107: 1; Mark 10: 18); there is no evil in God, and God graciously and mercifully works for the salvation of human beings.

II

That God is sovereign is the clear teaching of the whole of scripture. Note the following texts:

Heaven and the heaven of heavens belong to the Lord your God, the earth with all that is in it. (Deut. 10: 14)

I am the LORD, and there is no other; besides me there is no god. I arm you, though you do not know me, so that they may know, from the rising of the sun and from the west, that there is no one beside me; I am the LORD, and there is no other. I form light and create darkness, I make weal and create woe; I the LORD do all these things. (Isa. 45: 5–7)

Remember this and consider, recall it to mind, you transgressors, remember the former things of old; for I am God, and there is no other; I am God, and there is no one like me, declaring the end from the beginning and from ancient times things not yet done, saying, 'My purpose shall stand, and I will fulfill my intention,' calling a bird of prey from the east, the man for my purpose from a far country. I have spoken, and I will bring it to pass; I have planned, and I will do it. (Isa. 46: 8–11)

There is none like you, O LORD; you are great, and your name is great in might. Who would not fear you, O King of the nations? For that is your due; among all the wise ones of the nations and in all their kingdoms there is no one like you. (Jer. 10: 6–7)

In these texts several points are made about God. First, God is absolutely unique; there is no other like God; God has no rivals. Secondly, the whole of the created order belongs to God, and God can do with it whatever God pleases. God has the right to impose the divine will—whatever it is—on the world and on human beings. Thirdly, God has complete knowledge of what occurs in the created order. Fourthly, God is in control of events both in the natural order and in the sphere of human affairs; God has certain purposes in mind and will bring them to fruition. Fifthly, God is great and is to be feared.

The notion of the greatness of God was crucial to the philosophical theology of Anselm of Canterbury. He famously referred to God as 'that than which nothing greater can be conceived'.[2] Philosophers abbreviate that long phrase by the term 'the greatest conceivable being' (or GCB). Although I will not discuss Anselm's 'ontological' argument for the existence of the GCB,[3] I consider his term to be an appropriate way of referring to God. What then exactly is 'the greatest conceivable being'?

Notice first that greatness seems to come in degrees; some things are greater than others. Notice also that some properties of things increase (or decrease) the thing's greatness or degree of greatness, and others do not. The property of *being red-headed*, for example, is not (as we might say) a great-making property because a red-headed thing is not (other things being equal) necessarily greater than a non-red-headed thing. But other properties clearly *are* relevant to the greatness of the things that have them (or fail to have them). The property of *being all-powerful*, for example, is a great-making property. This is because, other things being equal, an all-powerful thing *is* necessarily greater than a thing that is not all-powerful. Let us call these properties—properties that make things that have them greater—'G-properties'.

Next we notice that some properties admit of degree or increments and others do not. For example, the property of *being a prime number* admits of no degrees—a thing either possesses that property or it does not. The same would be true of properties like *being pregnant* and *being six feet tall*, for example. But some properties *do* admit of degrees—*being tall*, for example. Some tall people are taller than other tall people. The same would be true of *being wise*, *being polite*, and *being learned*.

---

[2] M. J. Charlesworth (ed.), *St. Anselm's Proslogion* (Notre Dame, IN: Notre Dame University Press, 1979), p. 117 (*Proslogion* II). Charlesworth actually translates Anselm's *alquid quo nihil maius cogitari posit* as 'something than which nothing greater can be thought'.

[3] I do consider the argument in some detail in Chapter 2 of my *God, Reason, and Theistic Proofs* (Edinburgh: Edinburgh University Press, 1997).

Now, of the properties that admit of degrees, some of them possess, so to speak, a conceivable or intrinsic maximum, and others do not. The property of *being tall*, for example, possesses no intrinsic maximum. This is because of the fact that no matter how tall we imagine a tall person as being, we can always imagine one that is taller. But some properties do possess an intrinsic maximum. The property for a football team of 'winning as many of its games as possible' has an intrinsic maximum, and a team that is undefeated and untied possesses it. And the property of *being powerful* is such a property. A thing that is omni-powerful or omnipotent at a given time is a thing that can bring about any state of affairs that is logically possible at that time. I am not omnipotent because there are things that it is logically possible for me to do—for example, leap over a two-storey house—that I cannot in fact do. Omnipotence is a degree of power that cannot be surpassed, and I believe God possesses it.

We are now in a position to understand what a GCB is. The GCB is a thing (1) that possesses all the compossible G-properties that it is possible for a thing to possess; (2) that possesses all of its G-properties that admit of an intrinsic maximum to the maximal degree (e.g. being omnipotent); and (3) that possesses all of its G-properties that admit of no intrinsic maximum (if there are any) to a degree unsurpassed by any other thing. (This might include properties like being benevolent or loving; if so, then God is more loving than all other things.)

I hold that God is the GCB in some such sense as this. We noted above that imbedded in the biblical concept of the sovereignty of God is the notion that God is great. Accordingly, I suggest that calling God the GCB captures much of what is meant by saying that God is sovereign.

III

Let us now turn to creation, and to my point that God is sovereign in creation. I will discuss two main points under this heading.

First, let me here consider briefly the denial in Process Theology of the traditional Christian claim that God's creation of the world was *ex nihilo* or 'out of nothing'. Following A. N. Whitehead, Process theologians argue that existing eternally alongside God was the chaotic 'stuff' that God fashioned or 'lured' into a cosmos, and that God could not change the somewhat recalcitrant properties of that stuff. So in creation God did not have complete freedom of choice; God is not (as this word is traditionally understood) 'omnipotent'. God's power is limited both by the properties of the uncreated material out of which God fashioned the world and by the power over against God that every existing thing must possess. These sorts of assumption, Process thinkers claim, form a more plausible metaphysical theory and make solving the problem of evil easier. Process thinkers also argue that, rightly understood, the Bible does not teach creation out of nothing.[4]

But the idea of creation out of nothing is a virtually unanimous aspect of the Christian tradition from the early theologians (Hermas, Theophilus of Antioch, Irenaeus, Origen[5]) until today. And while I agree that creation *ex nihilo* is not unambiguously taught in Genesis or anywhere else in the Bible, this should not surprise us: the biblical writers were not doing metaphysics or philosophical theology. But despite the protestations of Process thinkers, the doctrine does seem to be strongly suggested in several biblical texts, for example, John 1: 3; Romans 4: 17; 11: 36; Colossians 1: 16; Hebrews 11: 3. Moreover, it is implied in two biblical concepts: the power of God (for whom 'all things are possible' and 'nothing is impossible') and the absolute dependence of the world on God.[6]

Moreover, there is no suggestion in Genesis 1: 1 (however the verb *bara* is to be translated) of a pre-existent 'stuff' that was not created by God and that God partially depends on. Nor is this notion taught anywhere else in the Bible. My argument from Genesis 1 in favour of creation *ex nihilo* does not concern lexical issues, but the fact that God seems to create the cosmos with a kind of effortless ease, that is, merely by speaking the word (see Pss. 33: 6–9). There is no hint of any laborious struggle to construct the world out of pre-existing and somewhat intractable material.[7]

Secondly, the very decision to create a universe, as well as the decision about what it is to be like, is God's and God's alone. Let us perform a thought-experiment. Suppose God's central aims in creation were to create a world (1) in which there is as much moral goodness (or balance of moral goodness over moral evil) as possible; (2) in which as many rational creatures as possible

---

[4] See David Griffin's contributions to Stephen T. Davis, *Encountering Evil: Live Options in Theodicy*, 2nd edn. (Louisville, KY: Westminster John Knox Press, 2001).

[5] I say 'virtually unanimous' because there are exceptions among early theologians, e.g. Justin Martyr.

[6] For a thorough and compelling case for creation out of nothing, see Paul Copan and William Lane Craig, *Creation Out of Nothing* (Grand Rapids, MI: Baker Book House, 2004). I read a pre-publication copy of this book too late to be of use in the present work, but recommend the book highly.

[7] In *Encountering Evil* (n. 4 above) (p. 138), Griffin points to Psalm 74: 12–17 and Isaiah 51: 9–11 as suggesting 'a real battle with chaos in creation'. But I cannot understand how Griffin sees anything like that in these texts. They do enumerate many of the things that God did in creating the world, but I see nothing of what Griffin suggests. These texts seem to me to support my side of the argument, not his.

come to worship, love, and obey God rather than hate and curse God; and (3) in which they do so freely. If that is so, we can ask this question: Given those aims, what sort of world would we expect God to create?

1. We would expect that the world would be a *rational* and *coherent* world. That is, the world will contain enough regularities to make human knowledge possible, as well as achievement of at least some human projects. If the universe is brought into being by the word of God and the wisdom of God, then the world will reflect the very coherence and rationality of God's nature. If spiritual lessons are to be learnable, so must be lessons in areas such as morality, human relations, and science (by which I mean the broad area of learning how the world works and how we can survive and thrive in it).

2. We would also expect the world to contain evidence that God exists and has the attributes that God has. But God does not want to coerce belief. Accordingly, it will be a world in which it is possible to detect and act upon that evidence, but where it is not obvious to every rational person that God exists and wants us to behave in certain ways. Suppose we define a 'theoretical atheist' as someone who believes that God does not exist. And suppose we define a 'practical atheist' as someone who (whether a theoretical atheist or not) lives as if God does not exist. Then we would expect God to create a world in which theoretical and practical atheism can be, or at least can widely seem to be, rational. In our normal experience, certain statements are obviously true, for example, '2 + 2 = 4,' 'Grass is green,' and 'Alaska is larger than Rhode Island.' No one is rationally free to deny them. We will expect God to create a world in which 'God exists' is not obviously true. In other words, God must hide, but not too well. God must be, to a certain extent, incognito in the world. When we decide to worship and obey God, God wants us to be rational and free in so deciding.

3. Similarly, we will expect God to create a world of *moral ambiguity* and even *suffering*. This means two things. First, it will be a world of problems, challenges, risks, and dangers. There will be a certain degree of at least apparent randomness. Evil events will strike for no apparent reason. Certain events will seem inexplicable. Disasters as well as successes will be possible, and they will strike good and evil people alike. Secondly, it will be a world in which wrongdoing is not immediately followed by punishment and virtuous acts are not immediately rewarded. It is sometimes possible to sin with impunity (or so it will seem).

Why should we expect that God would create such a world? Because, prior to the eschaton, a pleasurable utopia, entirely plastic to our wishes, would not be an optimal world from God's point of view. In such a world, there would be little sense of right and wrong (the concept of moral wrongness is closely tied to causing people pain), no possibility of moral growth (which is usually achieved through painful experiences that count as lessons), courage, and determination, and little felt need for God.

4. It will be a world in which human beings sense in themselves *a longing for God*. This longing can be ignored and can even be made to disappear, if we work hard enough at it. It will be vague and resistible, but real. It will be like 'a still small voice'.[8]

In running through this thought-experiment, it clearly sounds like a rough description of our world, the world that God actually created. In other words, *this* world is just the sort of world we would expect God to create, if God exists. The one part of our world which might be totally unexpected (if we were not already inured to the idea) is the notion of grace. Christianity says that God not only provided a way in which we can be forgiven and saved, but also took the initiative and, so to speak, did the work in carrying out the method he provided for our salvation.[9]

In Romans 5: 6–8, Paul says:

For while we were still weak, at the right time Christ died for the ungodly. Indeed, rarely will anyone die for a righteous person—though perhaps for a good person someone might actually dare to die. But God proves his love for us in that while we were still sinners Christ died for us.

Here Paul makes a distinction between a 'righteous person' and a 'good person'. Perhaps he means this: a righteous person is one who always does her duty, one who is always upright, strict, and stern, one who never compromises her integrity. And perhaps a good person is one who is righteous, as just defined, but who is also compassionate, loving, kindly, and forgiving. Perhaps he meant something like this when he said that rarely would anyone die for a person of the first sort, thought it might happen that somebody might give her life for a person of the second sort.

But notice Paul's implicit point: *nobody* would ever die for a person who is sinful, for someone who is despicable, for someone who is unlovable. But— according to Paul—God does this very thing. We are neither righteous nor good. But God's free and sovereign decision is to act to bring about our reconciliation to God.

---

[8] It will also be a world in which God and goodness triumph in the end. I do not list this as a separate point since at this time in history it is not evident to any but the eye of faith.

[9] One admitted exception to the claim that the sort of world we are envisioning is like the actual world is the huge magnitude of moral evil in the world. Its existence must be explained in another way. For my own attempt, see Stephen T. Davis (ed.), *Encountering Evil: Live Options in Theodicy*, 2nd edn. (Louisville, KY: Westminster John Knox Press, 2001).

IV

Let us now turn to the sovereignty of God in revelation. It is important that we get clear on what it is for God to *reveal*, that is, what the term *revelation* means.

One way to stress the importance of revelation is to consider a God who does not reveal (or at least does not engage in *special* revelation), namely, the God of Deism. Deism was a loosely defined philosophical and religious movement that thrived in Europe in the seventeenth and eighteenth centuries and in America in the eighteenth. The Deists believed in the existence of God, and held that God created the universe, with its immutable natural laws. They were also defenders of religion, although they tended to view it as entirely rational and ethical. They had confidence in the power of human reason to reach proper conclusions about God and religion, which for the Deists consisted of a few simple truths about God, the creation, morality, and perhaps immortality.

The Deists crucially differed from traditional Christian thought in their rejection of all robust notions of divine revelation (except what is called 'natural revelation', i.e. conclusions about God and religion reached by unaided human reason). Indeed, they rejected as superstitious any and all claims of direct interaction or relation between God and the world—not only acts of special revelation but also miracles, epiphanies, and incarnations were ruled out. God is something like an absentee landlord, or like someone who winds a clock and then lets it run on its own without interference. Religious institutions, supplicatory prayers, and mysterious dogmas were also looked upon with great suspicion by the Deists.

Oddly, Deism has made a comeback, although its defenders do not use that term. Despite some differences, there are striking commonalities between the seventeenth- and eighteenth-century Deists and those recent and contemporary religious thinkers who affirm God but deny divine intervention in the world. I will not discuss this movement here.[10] Let me simply note the fact that some contemporary Deists retain the notion of revelation, although the concept ends up being quite unlike traditional notions of God speaking or being supernaturally manifested in the world.[11] Their operative notion of revelation is more like (1) insight into religious mysteries by those blessed

---

[10] But it is helpfully discussed in Richard Sturch, *The New Deism: Divine Intervention and the Human Condition* (New York: St. Martin's Press, 1990).

[11] Notice the interesting discussion in Basil Mitchell and Maurice Wiles, 'Does Christianity Need a Revelation?', *Theology*, LXXXIII/692 (March, 1980), pp. 103–14.

with the relevant sort of spiritual wisdom; (2) enlightenment gained from a turning point in personal or communal history; or (3) new truth arrived at through dialogue in interpersonal or inter-religious communication, truth that the participants would not have discovered independently. In short, God is 'revealed' through ordinary historical, cultural, intellectual, or scientific processes.

In contrast to such claims, traditional Christians believe in a God some of whose revelatory acts constitute interventions in the ordinary events of history. The idea is that God chooses to reveal himself to human beings by being involved in human life. But it must be emphasized that human beings have no moral right to receive divine revelation, no claim on God that God must reveal himself. So Christians must still—if they understand matters correctly—feel a degree of awe when they grasp the fact that God has chosen to reveal himself to us. God did not need to do so. To put the point radically, the Deists hold a *possible* view of God, a way God might have been. No necessity causes God to reveal himself. God could have chosen to remain silent.

What would have been the salvific consequences for human beings if God had remained unrevealed? After all, the psalmist cries: 'To you, O Lord, I call; my rock, do not refuse to hear me, for if you are silent to me, I shall be like those who go down to the Pit' (Pss. 28: 1). Suppose the Deists were correct— suppose that God does not particularly care about the affairs of the earth, that there is no special divine revelation, and that God never gave us a law or sent us prophets or a Son. What would follow?

Of course human beings would still be interested in ultimate religious questions: Does God exist? If so, how ought we to worship? How ought we to live our lives? What happens to us after we die? The most important religious question of all is the one posed with elegant simplicity by the Philippian jailer in the book of Acts (16: 30): 'Sirs, what must I do to be saved?' If God were silent, we would be left to our own resources when we tried to answer questions like these.

What answers to these questions might we come up with? One possibility is some sort of *legalism*. This would be a religious system containing a series of rules that human beings must obey. Obey them and you'll be saved; disobey them and you'll be lost. Another possibility would be *ritualism*. If you follow the prescribed ceremonials, the gods will be placated and you'll be saved; fail to follow them and you'll be lost. Another possibility, much in the spirit of our age, is *relativism*. This would be the answer which says that it doesn't really matter a great deal what you believe or how you behave; what matters is whether you sincerely believe what you believe and whether you give your best effort to behave according to your best lights. A fourth possibility might be some version of *nihilism*: there is no answer; even if God exists, there is no way of knowing God or anything else for sure; there are no ultimate values; there is no justice; death ends everything. All we can do is try to endure the pain of life, and try as best we can to make it a bit more endurable.

In short, if God were silent it is most probable that human beings would come up with wrong answers to the ultimate religious questions. All human schemes would ultimately fail; there would be no sure answer, based on human wisdom alone, to the question of the Philippian jailer. If God were silent there would be little hope of salvation. We would be like those who 'go down to the Pit'.

The purpose of divine revelation is to achieve God's aims in creation. Pre-eminently God desires that human beings come freely to love, worship, and obey God. Revelation, then, is not just for the purpose of imparting information, issuing commands, engendering sentiments, or initiating ceremonies. It is for the purpose of establishing a personal and loving relationship between God and human beings.

To reveal is to unveil, show, or disclose something that was hidden or unknown. Divine revelation is God unveiling, showing, or disclosing to human beings things that were hidden from them or unknown to them. Revelation is a way for God to leap, so to speak, across the gap that separates God from human beings. More precisely, there are three gaps—an *ontological* gap, an *epistemological* gap, and a *moral* gap. The first is due to the difference between a non-contingent, eternal, all-powerful creator and a contingent, temporal, feeble creature. The second is due to the difference between an omniscient being and a largely ignorant being. The third is due to the difference between a holy and morally perfect being and a depraved, self-centred, sinful being.

Because of these gaps, human beings naturally know little of God and God's requirements. And even what they do know or can come to know quite on their own (e.g. that God exists, that murder is morally wrong) can be denied, forgotten, or ignored. We are ignorant of much that we need to know in order to be saved, and we cannot save ourselves. If we are to attain saving knowledge of God and God's will, that knowledge must come from God. It must be revealed. The initiative of revelation comes, as a gift, from God.

Some theologians, wishing to emphasize the transcendence of God, have argued that there is an absolute or infinite difference between God and human beings.[12] But that seems an ill-advised theological position. How could revelation leap across an absolute gap? The creation story in Genesis insists

---

[12] See Søren Kierkegaard, *On Authority and Revelation* (trans. Walter Lowrie) (New York: Harper and Row, 1966), p. 112.

that human beings were created 'in God's image' (Gen. 1: 26), which suggests that God and human beings are in some ways similar. Indeed, since 'being similar to' is a symmetrical relationship (if A is similar to B, then B is similar to A), then if we are (in some ways) similar to God, it follows that God is (in some ways) similar to us. That similarity—whatever exactly it is—is doubtless the ontological basis of revelation. Unless God and human beings were related in some such way, revelation would be impossible. Our relationship to God, then, makes revelation possible. God has created us to be receivers of revelation.[13]

Again, what God pre-eminently wants is for human beings to come to love, worship, and obey God. (For convenience we'll lump these three together and say that God wants us to 'glorify God'.) Let us also suppose that what God wants is a free or unforced choice on the part of human beings to glorify God. As Justin Martyr said: 'For not like other things, as trees and quadrupeds, which did not act by choice, did God make man: for [man would not be] worthy of reward or praise did he not of himself choose the good.'[14] And the central obstacle that God faces in achieving these ends—so the Christian 'story' runs—is that human beings are both ignorant and sinful. They need to be taught and they need to be redeemed.

There are many areas in which humans are ignorant. Human beings who are asked to glorify God will need answers to at least the following questions:

- Does God exist?
- If God exists, what is God like?
- Exactly how do human beings 'glorify God', that is, how do they go about loving, worshipping, and obeying God? What exactly are they required to do?
- What are the consequences of glorifying God, and what are the consequences of not doing so?

In other words, there are many things that human beings do not know and that they must know, if God's aims in creating human beings are to be realized (1 Cor. 15: 1–4; Heb. 11: 6; 1 John 1: 1–3). It seems, then, that if God's aims are to be realized, one of the things that God must do is find a way to answer these and other questions.

Accordingly, 'revelation' means God's actions to answer for our benefit the questions listed above and others like them. As noted, the claim that God

---

[13] This point is rightly insisted on by Kern R. Trembath in his *Divine Revelation: Our Moral Relation With God* (New York: Oxford University Press, 1991), pp. 4, 114–15, 136, 168–9.

[14] Justin Martyr, *First Apology*, XLIII, Alexander Roberts and James Davidson (eds.), *The Ante-Nicene Fathers*, vol. I (Edinburgh: T. and T. Clark, 1989), p. 177.

reveals himself is one of the theological distinctives of Christian faith—as an act of sovereign grace, God reveals God to us. Thus the prophet Amos says:

For lo, the one who forms the mountains, creates the wind, *reveals his thoughts to mortals*, makes the morning darkness, and treads on the heights of the earth—The Lord, the God of hosts, is his name! (Amos 4: 13; italics added)

Moreover, in Christian theology, human ignorance and sinfulness are connected. As was noted in Chapter 1, sin has the effect of darkening the eyes to the truth, especially uncomfortable truths. Thus, as noted, God's revelatory words and acts all have a redemptive purpose: God does not just reveal interesting information to human beings. God uses revelation as a means of achieving God's redemptive ends. Revelation is God's action aimed at creating a new relationship between God and human beings.

Whatever revelatory methods God uses, the aim will be to answer human questions in ways that are clear, lasting, and convincing. A revelation is *clear* if it is unambiguous, if its meaning is not easily mistakable. Now, any communication from one person to another, whether in word or deed, can be misinterpreted. But obviously God will want the divine acts of revelation to be as clear as possible. (As noted above, I believe that God intends a certain degree of ambiguity in order to preserve our cognitive freedom.) A revelation is *lasting* if its content can be fairly easily passed on from one person to another or even from one generation to another. Now any revelatory act can be forgotten or garbled through time, but God will obviously want the divine acts of revelation to be as lasting as possible. A revelation is *convincing* if it is powerful and tends to produce conviction. Now, any revelatory act, no matter how convincing, can be rejected, even if that rejection results from sheer stupidity or stubbornness. Nevertheless, God will obviously want the divine acts of revelation to be convincing.

There are many possible ways in which God can choose to impart or reveal a given message (let us call it M) to some human being (let us say Jones). One way of revealing or imparting M to Jones would be to create Jones in such a way as to be naturally disposed to believe M. Another would be telepathically to cause Jones to think or come to believe or at least cognitively entertain M. Another would be to appoint someone as a spokesperson and cause that person to say or write M to Jones. Another would be to cause Jones to dream M. Another would be miraculously to bring it about that Jones sees M written on a wall. Another would be to do some non-linguistic deed or action whose proper interpretation or deep meaning is M.

Of these possible modes of revelation, some are linguistic (i.e. primarily involve words and sentences) and some are non-linguistic (i.e. primarily involve persons or actions). God's revelatory action of rescuing Israel at the Red Sea was primarily non-linguistic; it was a deed or act that spoke mightily to Israel about the character of God. The Decalogue that God gave to Israel was primarily linguistic; it consists of words. This raises the theological question—much discussed in the previous century—whether divine revelation is by words or deeds. Some theologians denied that God reveals propositions: such things are timeless, static, impersonal, and cold. God's primary mode of revelation, they insisted, was through dynamic personal encounters; God is revealed in deeds or persons or events rather than words.[15]

It does seem, a priori, that there are values, as well as problems, in both approaches. Actions are often more impressive, powerful, gripping, and graphic than words. Just saying that you love your spouse or child is typically much less convincing than showing it. Yet the problem with revelatory actions is that they can be interpreted variously, can easily be changed in the retelling of them, and unless they are written down can easily be forgotten over time. Words are sometimes less powerful than deeds, as noted; but perhaps revelatory words are valuable because they are not quite so easily misinterpreted, are easier to preserve and pass on in their original form, and once preserved are not quite so easily forgotten. These last two points seem to be important considerations given God's redemptive aims, that is, given the assumption that God would intend at least some revelations to be for the benefit of other folk beside the original receivers or witnesses (see Pss. 22: 29–31).

It is clear that God has used both modes of revelation. And typically God's great revelatory actions have been accompanied by authoritative verbal interpretations.[16] Indeed, it is hard to see how a bare event, action, or encounter could be revelatory in any strong sense without interpretation or explanation. Events do not interpret themselves. And when an interpretation is offered, then we are talking about words and sentences. A pure encounter with God (e.g. in the Exodus) will only be recognized as such if it is explained or at least conceptualized as an encounter with God. Both the fact that conceptualization is possible and the claim that there is truth here logically entail that the revelatory act be expressible in propositions.

[15] See, for example, John Baillie, *The Idea of Revelation in Recent Thought* (New York: Columbia University Press, 1956), p. 49: 'what is fundamentally revealed is God Himself, not propositions about God.' See also pp. 28, 32–3, 50, 62–4. See also John K. S. Reid, *The Authority of Scripture* (London: Methuen and Co., 1957), p. 180, Emil Brunner, *Revelation and Reason* (trans. Olive Wyon) (Philadelphia: Westminster Press, 1946), pp. 4, 118, and H. R. Niebuhr, *The Meaning of Revelation* (New York: Macmillan, 1962), p. 112. The view that revelation is not propositional is still very much alive. See Trembath, *Divine Revelation* (n. 13 above), pp. viii, 92–4.

[16] This point was emphasized in the Neo-Orthodox period by (among others) James D. Smart. See his *The Interpretation of Scripture* (Philadelphia: Westminster Press, 1961), pp. 172–3.

But a comment about earlier debates about propositional versus non-propositional revelation is in order. Certainly God is revealed in deeds and persons and human experiences (see 2 Cor. 12: 1–4), but it seems absurd to deny—as some theologians did—that God reveals words. To experience a genuine encounter with God logically presupposes the possession of at least some knowledge about God.[17] Thus Avery Dulles says: 'If we had no confidence in the propositional teaching of the Bible, we could hardly put our trust in the persons or events of biblical history, or even in the God to whom the Bible bears witness.'[18] And William Abraham says: 'It is only because God has spoken His word that we can have any assurance about what He has done in creation and history and about His intentions and purposes in acting in creation and history.'[19]

The enemies of 'propositional revelation' argued that Christian faith is trust in the person of God or Christ rather than in any proposition. Propositions are too abstract, impersonal, non-relational, static, and timeless to constitute the proper objects of religious faith; they elicit or call for no genuine response. There is truth here, but also a great deal of confusion. The kernel of truth is that Christian faith—or at least that crucial aspect of it that involves trust (*fiducia* (faith *in*))—is in God rather than any proposition. But of course the belief aspect of faith (*fides* (faith *that*)), does essentially involve acceptance of certain propositions as true. And believing the truth of a proposition is inextricably tied to trusting a person in those cases where the person trusted takes responsibility for the proposition, for example, by saying or writing it.[20] My trust in (*fiducia*) my mother makes no sense unless it involves willingness to believe (*fides*) what she says to me. Thus traditional Christians would argue that their faith as trust in God entails acceptance of the things God has revealed to us.

It is quite misleading, then, to argue (as enemies of propositional revelation did) that propositions are too static and invoke no genuine response. Christians would make no response to God at all unless they accepted as true propositions like: *God loves us*; *Christ died for our sins*; *We should thank and praise God*, and the like.

Furthermore, the Bible itself insists that God reveals words. For example, God is revealed in the words of the Decalogue, in the words that constitute the

---

[17] This point is made convincingly by Ronald H. Nash. See his *The Word of God and the Mind of Man* (Grand Rapids, MI: Zondervan, 1982), pp. 43–54.

[18] Avery Dulles, S.J., *Models of Revelation* (Garden City, NY: Doubleday, 1983), p. 205.

[19] William Abraham, *Divine Revelation and the Limits of Historical Criticism* (New York: Oxford University Press, 1982), p. 21.

[20] This point is made by Paul Helm, *The Divine Revelation* (Westchester, IL: Crossway Books, 1982), p. 26.

oracles of the prophets, in the words of the parables and other teachings of Jesus, and in the words of the epistles of Paul. And very many of those words were grammatically configured as propositions. They conveyed cognitive information; they contained truths. I should like to suggest that those theologians who denied that revelation was propositional believed (in fact, if not officially) in propositional revelation. They simply did not like the propositions that more conservative interpreters of the Bible claimed to find there, and so (in effect, if not by admission) they looked for and—not surprisingly—found other propositions.

V

I have mentioned some ways in which God might have chosen to be revealed to humans. But how did God actually choose to be revealed? A distinction is usually made between general and special revelation. *General revelation* consists of those things about God, human beings, morality, and religion that human beings can come to know on their own, that is, without any direct (or 'special') assistance from God. These would be things we can know as a result of using our own reasoning faculties. The scriptures assert that some such things can be learned in this way (cf. Pss. 19: 1; Acts 17: 22–9; Rom. 1: 18–23). It is possible to see evidence for them in thinking about the beauty and grandeur of creation, in examining our own consciences, and perhaps even by considering the beliefs and practices of other religions and cultures. Such naturally revealed things can form, for some folk, a foundation for morality and religion. But, as we saw in Chapter 1, they are incomplete, hazy, and easily confused. They are in need of supplementation.

Special revelation consists of those things about God, human beings, morality, and religion that we can come to know only as the result of some direct or special act of assistance by God. Typically these would consist of things revealed to some person or group through dreams, visions, epiphanies, prophecies, miracles, or (supremely) through the life, death, and resurrection of Jesus Christ. The scriptures equally assert that there are such acts (cf. Matt. 16: 17; Luke 4: 18–19; John 1: 14; Gal. 1: 11–12; Heb. 1: 1–4). I believe that reading scripture can also, through the illumination of the Spirit, constitute revelation.

Under the heading of special revelation, then, let me distinguish among three sorts of revelatory acts on the part of God. (Maybe these are really three different stages of one and the same revelatory act. From our viewpoint, perhaps the first is the better way of describing matters; from God's, perhaps the second is better.) I will call them *original revelation, recorded revelation*, and *appropriated revelation*.

Original revelation consists of God's revelatory actions in history, some in the form of events and some in the form of words. Pre-eminently, this sort of revelation would include: the Exodus, the giving of the Decalogue, the oracles of the prophets, the teachings and miracles of Jesus, and the crucifixion and resurrection of Jesus. These are divine deeds or words that appear, by God's initiative, in the history of the people of God. Although God is still at work in history, Christian tradition holds that original revelation ceased with the death of the last apostle. Thus the Westminster Confession includes a phrase that reads (having discussed what I am calling original and recorded revelation): 'these former ways of God's revealing his will unto his people now being ceased'.[21] Christians celebrate the fact that God still speaks to people, moves them, and works in various ways in their lives. But these divine actions are not theologically normative for all Christians, and so do not count as original revelation.

But original revelation will most likely be ephemeral and unstable unless it is written down. This is not to deny that oral traditions can endure, with amazing accuracy, for long periods of time. Nor is it to deny that written records can be corrupted or be lost and forgotten. Still, if it is God's will that as many human beings as possible know about God's acts of original revelation, those acts must be recorded and interpreted in some sort of authoritative written document. And that is what I mean by *recorded revelation*. The Bible is in part a record and interpretation of original revelation. By reading the Bible it is possible to find out something of what God has done in the past. This 'finding out' need not be, in any direct sense, supernatural. It just involves reading and learning. Furthermore, at least some of what the biblical writers recorded need not have been supernaturally revealed to them—possibly they learned about some of the events and words that they recorded by quite ordinary means. Recorded revelation, too, ceased long ago—when the last book of the Bible was completed. Presumably since then other Christian writings—sermons, hymns, liturgies, and perhaps even theology books— were written under God's influence. Pronouncements of some early ecumenical councils have, in my view, a certain degree of normativity. But none is theologically authoritative for all Christians in the sense that the Bible is. (I will return to this point in more detail in Chapter 15.)

But the Bible is not *merely* (as is often claimed) a record of previous divine revelation. The Bible in itself is revelatory. Through the illumination of the

[21] See the Westminster Confession, I, 1 in John H. Leith (ed.), *Creeds of the Churches* (Garden City, NY: Doubleday, 1963), p. 193.

Holy Spirit, God speaks to us in the Bible. When correctly interpreted, the Bible itself constitutes a unique and authoritative divine revelation. As Paul Helm points out, it is possible that some things that were not necessarily revealed to the biblical writers, things they learned quite naturally, do constitute revelation to us as we read them in the Bible.[22] When God does speak to us in scripture, then we are speaking of what I call *appropriated revelation*. It is simply recorded revelation speaking to the reader in God's voice. As noted, this adds nothing to original and recorded revelation, nor did it cease with the death of the apostles, nor are its deliverances theologically authoritative for all Christians. No post-apostolic vision, prophecy, exegesis, creed, pronouncement, sense of discernment, decision, or conviction is normative for all Christians. It is normative only to the person to whom the revelation is appropriated, to whom the Holy Spirit is speaking. Appropriated revelation is a supernatural act of God; when I correctly sense that God is speaking to me in scripture, that is a supernatural act of the Spirit of God.

Suppose God wanted to be revealed to as many people as possible, and to as many sorts of people as possible—young and old, black and white, men and women, Eskimos and Hottentots, scholars and peasants. If so, it would seem appropriate for God to decide that at least part of divine revelation would consist of a book. That is, one way in which God would be revealed to human beings would be through a book. Presumably God's motivation in doing so would be to make the content of revelation available to as wide a population as possible, and not just, say, to those present at the appropriate time, to an elite of scholars, or to those initiated into mysteries. This population would include people in generations and centuries after the book was completed. God's redemptive purposes would presumably include wide distribution of the revelation, and a book seems particularly well suited to accomplish that end.

It is inevitable that such a book would appear in a certain historical, national, cultural, and linguistic context, and that those who belonged in that context would at least initially have the easiest access to the book. Why God would choose a certain human group rather than another to be the original home of the book we are envisioning is unanswerable. Note ancient Israel's puzzlement over its election as God's beloved people: 'It was not because you were more numerous than any other people that the Lord set his heart on you and chose you—for you were the fewest of all people. It was because the Lord loved you...' (Deut. 7: 7–8a). In other words, God loved Israel because God loved Israel. Still, if the revelatory book that first appeared

---

[22] Helm, *The Divine Revelation* (n. 20 above), p. 70.

in a given context were readily translatable into other contexts, that is, if the revelation were communicable, God's aims could still be achieved.

If this were God's decision, it would seem that God would then superintend the process of the writing of the various documents of which the book would ultimately consist, ensuring that they contained, at least in large part, what God wanted them to contain. That is, enough of their content would have to correspond to God's revelatory aims that people could read them and be reasonably sure of learning what God wanted them to learn. It would also seem that God would superintend the process of copying, reproducing, and preserving the book, again so that those who read it could be reasonably sure that what they read corresponded reliably, even if not perfectly, to what was originally intended. There would have to be ways for the errors of copyists and printers to be detected and corrected.

According to Christians, this is precisely what occurred. God actually did choose to be revealed in a book, and that book is the Bible. God did supervise the creation, production, transmission, and preservation of the book in the indicated ways. The fact of God's providential guidance of the history of the Bible makes it unique among all the books that have ever been written. It reveals God in a unique way.

But the Bible by itself is not enough to accomplish God's redemptive goals. Among other things, a community is needed in order to provide authoritative texts, translations, and interpretations of the Bible. In this way, the original revelation can be preserved and communicated.[23] The notion, sometimes heard in Protestant circles, that the 'Bible alone' is sufficient to accomplish God's aims is quite mistaken. (I will discuss this point further in Chapter 15.)

VI

Is revelation 'progressive'? Are later divine revelations more sophisticated and accurate than earlier ones? The concept of progressive revelation has been used by defenders of revelation to solve problems caused by the fact that some earlier revelations seem crude, and perhaps even immoral, when compared

---

[23] I entirely agree with the emphasis placed on this point by Richard Swinburne in his *Revelation: From Metaphor to Analogy* (Oxford: Oxford University Press, 1992), pp. 81–4, 113, 119, 178, 183–4. But I believe Swinburne is led to his emphasis on the church for the wrong reason. He concedes too much, I believe, to historical-critical biblical scholarship, and concludes that on historical grounds alone (that is, apart from authoritative church teaching) there is little that we can know, for example, of the life of Jesus. Note this telling remark: 'The task of discovering some vague outlines of what Jesus said and did and what happened to him is not, I suggest, an impossible one' (p. 105).

with later ones. Some have felt, for instance, that this notion might be a way to reconcile (1) the insistence of the books of Deuteronomy (see 2: 31–5; 3: 1–8; 7: 2) and Joshua (see 6: 15–21; 8: 25–6; 11: 12) that it was God's will that the Israelites kill every Canaanite man, woman, and child with (2) the law of love of the New Testament. The argument would go like this: the earlier revelation was the best God could do at the time, the most God could reveal, given the level of theological and moral sophistication of the post-Exodus Israelites; they would not have been able to understand the more complete revelation of God as found in the New Testament. But by the time of the first century, people were ready to hear and receive that fuller revelation of the divine nature and so were ready for the teachings of Jesus.

There is both something right and something wrong here. What is right is that all revelation, both the earlier and the later, involves accommodation or even condescension on the part of God. To borrow Calvin's apt metaphors, God must 'stoop' and even 'lisp' (i.e. must engage in a sort of baby talk) to speak to us.[24] All revelation meets us where we are. The ontological, epistemological, and moral gaps between God and human beings ensure that we will not be able to grasp the fullness of God's nature. So all revelation is partial. We now know only 'in part', not 'face to face' (1 Cor. 13: 12). What God has revealed is trustworthy; we do indeed have knowledge of God. But it is only provisional and inchoate. Even as revealed, much of God remains mysterious to us.

What is false in the concept of progressive revelation is the hint that the ancient Israelites were too morally or intellectually primitive to grasp the fuller revelation of God that appears in the New Testament—a revelation that the much more enlightened folk of the first century (as well as, of course, those of us in the twenty-first) are clever and moral enough to grasp. That is not a particularly convincing argument. There is a sense in which revelation is progressive, but it has nothing to do with God's inability to teach certain folk things that they were too dumb to understand.

Revelation is progressive in that (1) God has sovereignly chosen to be revealed over time rather than all at once, and in earlier times did make concessions to then prevalent views, allowing such things as slavery, polygamy, or divorce (Matt. 19: 3–9); (2) God has sovereignly chosen to be revealed in such a way that earlier revelations are interpreted by, are incorporated within, and are sometimes superseded by, later ones (see Matt. 5: 21–48); and (3) God has sovereignly chosen that normative revelation occurs only for a time and then ceases. Thus the picture of God and of God's will for us is

---

[24] See John Calvin, *Corpus Reformatorum* (Calvin's Works, ed. Baum, Cunitz, and Reuss (Braunschweig, 1865)), vol. 26, pp. 35, 312, 387.

indeed more complete at the end than it is at the beginning. All three points are contingent, however; God could have chosen otherwise. God could have chosen to be revealed all at once. God could have chosen to be revealed over time but in such a way that all acts of revelations were hermeneutically on a par, or even in such a way that later fragmentary revelations were interpreted in the light of the more complete earlier ones. God could have chosen to make normative revelation continue indefinitely.

To accept a revelation from God is to be subject to a radical paradigm shift. Revelation calls for a response, a response of repentance, commitment, and trust. But it is possible to receive a revelation from God, or to have reliable evidence of one, and remain unmoved. Even the 'signs and wonders' that accompany some revelatory acts—for example, the Exodus—can be explained away by those who are hard-hearted or spiritually blind. God structures all God's revelatory acts—even the Christ event—in such a way as to ensure our cognitive and moral freedom to say no. God does not coerce our response.

Again, revelation is not just for the purpose of imparting information or ensuring obedience—those results could be caused or coerced. The purpose of revelation is to bring it about that human beings come into a personal relationship with God, one that involves freely chosen love (which cannot be coerced) as well as worship and obedience. I argued earlier in this chapter that God's aim would be to make all acts of divine revelation clear, lasting, and convincing. But they cannot be so overwhelmingly convincing as to coerce consent—as, say, the existence of my computer is to me now. The evidence for its presence with me here is so overwhelming that no sensible person in my shoes could reject it. God's acts of revelation cannot be so convincing that no sensible person could reject them.[25]

But when revelation is accepted, there will be change. A whole new notion of God is provided, as well as a whole new notion of what we owe God, what we 'must do to be saved', and how our religious questions are to be answered. Indeed, there is typically a radically new way of looking at everything—at all of human experience and all of reality. The one who accepts revelation now interprets everything in terms of God and in the light of what has been revealed. When this occurs in someone's life, as noted in Chapter 1, it is the work of the inward testimony of the Holy Spirit. That work marks the difference between merely receiving a new bit of information or a new command or a new ritual, on the one hand, and receiving a divine revelation, on the other.[26]

---

[25] This point is well argued in W. S. Anglin, *Free Will and Christian Faith* (Oxford: Oxford University Press, 1990), pp. 187–92.

[26] See George Mavrodes, *Revelation in Religious Belief* (Philadelphia: Temple University Press, 1988), p. 150.

How, then, can human spiritual questions be answered? How can we—to borrow Justin Martyr's apt phrase—learn to 'choose the good'? How can we learn how to glorify God and thus satisfy God's redemptive aims in creation? The answer I am suggesting is: pre-eminently by attending to the revelation of God in scripture. All Christians affirm that Jesus Christ is the supreme revelation of God. They should also affirm that the Bible is the primary appointed place where Christians meet Jesus Christ and learn the divine will.

VII

Talk about God, creation, and revelation can sometimes seem overly theoretical. So let me close this chapter by pointing to three religious implications of the high view of the divine sovereignty sketched out here.

1. *The freedom of God's grace.* God had no obligation to create the world. Having created the world, and having watched human beings in their pride and disobedience mar the harmony of creation and ruin their own lives, God had no obligation to redeem the world. Accordingly, both creation and redemption must be seen as free acts of divine grace. 'I will be gracious to whom I will be gracious, and I will show mercy on whom I will show mercy' (Exod. 33: 19). When we recognize this fact, it ought to have the effect of heightening our gratitude to God. In the Heidelberg Catechism of 1563, Part III, which is about the Christian life, is entitled 'Thankfulness'. I believe that title is exactly right. The motivation for Christian worship of God and service to God is nothing other than sheer thanksgiving for what God has done.

Given God's grace, we can add a fifth point to our earlier four about what kind of world we should expect God to create. It will surely be a world in which redemption is possible. God will make provision for reconciliation with disobedient human beings. There will be a way for us to be rescued, forgiven, and placed on the right path. God will make a way for this to happen, but then God will allow us freedom to accept God's path or not. And God will reward those who say yes and punish those who say no.

2. *The freedom of God in response to prayer.*[27] God is free to answer our petitionary prayers in the ways that we want them answered, or not to do so. I fear that those who do not recognize the sovereignty of God can lose their way at this point. They can easily slip into the idea that whether or not God

---

[27] I am not going to enter into current debates in Christian philosophy about petitionary prayer. For a helpful essay on the subject, see Eleonore Stump, 'Petitionary Prayer', Eleonore Stump and Michael J. Murray (eds.), *Philosophy of Religion: The Big Questions* (Oxford: Blackwell, 1999), pp. 353–66.

answers our prayers—say, that some friend or loved one be healed of cancer—
depends on us. If the friend or loved one dies, such folk can easily suspect it is
their fault: they did not pray enough times, or they did not pray earnestly
enough, or not enough people were convinced to pray. The truth is that God
has his own purposes, some of which we understand and some of which we do
not; accordingly, the fact that our petitionary prayers sometimes go unanswered (unanswered, that is, as we want them to be answered) is exactly
what we should expect.

But let me return to the notion of divine omnipotence. I do so in order to
raise a different criticism of all 'limited Gods', including the God of Process
Theology. In order to be religiously adequate, to be a being who is worthy of
worship, God must be the sort of being to whom it makes sense to address
petitions in the first place. That is, God must be able to hear our petitions and
have the power to grant them, if God so chooses. But what sorts of petitions?
I would argue that no God is worthy of worship and is religiously adequate
unless granting the following sorts of petitions is within God's power:

- petitions for healing from disease (not just psychosomatic disease);
- petitions for forgiveness from sins (even heinous sins);
- petitions for deliverance from death (that is, for eternal life); and
- petitions for prevention of the world's destruction.

Naturally, I do not argue that in order to be sovereign, God must actually
grant all such requests. My point is that God must be *able* to do so. Otherwise,
God is not God, or at least is not worthy of the love, worship, and obedience
that Christians believe that we owe God. Limited Gods are not able to grant
some of the petitions that Christians have always considered essential.

A larger point follows: in order to be religiously adequate, God must be able
to accomplish God's purposes. But if God is limited in power, then quite
possibly there are prayers that God cannot answer, creatures that God cannot
control (and not just creatures whom God has decided not to control), and
divine purposes that God cannot bring to fruition. If God is limited in power,
then neither God nor humans know whether God's aims for the world will be
achieved. To put the point bluntly: there is no good news in the news that God
is trying hard to bring about the divine purposes for the world and may (or
may not) succeed.

3. *Friends of God.* There is a long biblical tradition that those who love
God and obey God become 'friends of God' (Jas. 2: 23). Nothing I say here
should be taken as denying or denigrating that important tradition. But I fear
that the heavy emphasis on friendship with God in some theological circles
today can lead people to lose their way. God becomes a friend almost as one's
bosom buddy is a friend. That is, this notion de-emphasizes the sovereignty of

God. The truth is that God and human beings can be friends only in a limited sense. We certainly can be friends with God in the sense that (1) we can love God; (2) in prayer we can share our deepest hopes, aspirations, doubts, and fears with God; (3) we can choose to be in alignment with God's purposes; and (4) we can trust in God's protection and guidance. But we are not friends with God in any sense that implies equality with God or that implies that we can presume to tell God what to do or even negotiate with God.

The sovereignty of God entails that our main responsibility as human beings is to honour and glorify God. As Paul says: 'So...whatever you do, do everything for the glory of God' (1 Cor. 10: 31). And as the Westminster Shorter Catechism of 1647 beautifully says: 'Man's chief end is to glorify God, and to enjoy him forever.'

4

Perichoretic Monotheism

I

Suppose it is rational to believe in God based on private evidence, as long as that belief is not refuted by public evidence. And suppose one's belief in God is supported by the GCA, or some other theistic proof. As noted, that immediately raises the question of what God is like. We discussed some of the attributes of God in Chapter 3. But we have yet to consider one fundamental Christian claim about God, namely, that God is a Trinity. That will be the topic of the present chapter. In a sense, the chapter presupposes topics that will come up later. In Chapters 6, 9, and 10, for example, I will argue, among other things, that Jesus Christ is the incarnate Son of God; he is 'truly divine and truly human'. The Christian church has always recognized that that claim has implications for our understanding of the nature of God. The result—together with other points, of course—is the doctrine of the Blessed Trinity.

So this chapter is a defence of Christian Trinitarianism. But it also defends the so-called Social Theory of the Trinity (ST), or at least a certain version of it. Let me begin with an overview of the chapter's structure. After dealing with introductory issues, I define ST, contrasting it with the so-called Latin Theory of the Trinity (LT). I then present an a priori argument in favour of ST and defend that argument against objections. Next I explain in more detail the version of ST that I wish to defend. Finally, I reply to objections that have recently been raised against ST by Brian Leftow.[1]

I consider ST to be a valid option for Christians. That is, I believe the theory can be shown to be both defensible and orthodox. To try to establish this point is one of this chapter's two central aims. The other is to show that, despite appearances, LT and ST (or at least the version of ST that I defend) end up differing only slightly.

---

[1] Brian Leftow, 'Anti Social Trinitarianism', in Stephen T. Davis, Daniel Kendall, S.J., and Gerald O'Collins, S.J. (eds.), *The Trinity: An Interdisciplinary Symposium on the Trinity* (Oxford: Oxford University Press, 1999), (hereinafter *The Trinity*) pp. 203–49.

The belief that the one and only God exists as three distinct and co-equal Persons—Father, Son, and Holy Spirit—is one of the defining doctrines of the Christian faith. Christians are not polytheists—we do not believe in three Gods. Nor do we believe, as Moslems do, in a simple, undifferentiated monotheism. We are Trinitarians. We believe that God is three-in-one. To borrow the classical terminology, we hold that God is three Persons in one essence.

Here is a brief statement of the doctrine from one of its more powerful ancient defenders, namely, Augustine of Hippo:

> There are the Father, the Son, and the Holy Spirit, and each is God, and at the same time all are one God; and each of them is a full substance, and at the same time all are one substance. The Father is neither the Son nor the Holy Spirit; the Son is neither the Father nor the Holy Spirit; the Holy Spirit is neither the Father nor the Son. But the Father is the Father uniquely; the Son is the Son uniquely; and the Holy Spirit is the Holy Spirit uniquely. All three have the same eternity, the same immutability, the same majesty, and the same power.[2]

The doctrine says in sum that the one God exists in three distinct and co-equal Persons—Father, Son, and Holy Spirit. The three Persons are not three Gods, or even three actions or aspects of God, but one God. No Person is subordinate to any other; all are co-equally and co-eternally divine.

Contemporary people face several problems in trying to appreciate the doctrine of the Trinity. One obstacle is the venerable metaphysical terminology traditionally used to express it. This terminology is all the more confusing because it was used somewhat fluidly until the end of the fourth century, when the various technical christological and Trinitarian formulas were largely fixed, although the meanings of some crucial terms were still debated (especially 'person') and developed further. The *oneness* of God has traditionally been expressed either by means of the Greek word *ousia* (substance, essence, in this case deity or Godhead) or the Latin word *substantia* (which is the Latin equivalent to *ousia*). These terms are usually translated into English (in this context) as 'substance'. That is, Christians claim that the members of the Trinity have or constitute one substance or essential divine nature. (Augustine, who waffles in Trinitarian terminology from one context to another, expresses himself differently in the passage cited above; he there uses the word 'substance' to describe the threeness as well as the oneness.) The *threeness* of God was expressed by the Greek fathers by means of the term *hypostasis* (sometimes *prosopon*) and by the Latin fathers by means

---

[2] Augustine, *On Christian Doctrine* (trans. D. W Robertson, Jr.) (Indianapolis, IN: Bobbs-Merrill, 1958), p. 10.

of the term *persona*. So the Trinity is described in Eastern Christianity by the phrase 'three hypostases in one ousia',[3] and in Latin Christianity by the phrase 'three Persons in one substance'. Both East and West agree that there are three Persons in the Trinity, and that the Trinity is one God.

The Christian doctrine of the Blessed Trinity is often called a mystery. Christian theologians virtually with one voice have stressed this point. Accordingly, we can explain what the doctrine of the Trinity is (as I just briefly tried to do), but we cannot ever fully explain the Trinity. This inability should not surprise us. Even when we study beings like pigeons, *e. coli*, or humans, there are always things about them that we do not know or understand. But when we study God—whom theologians insist is transcendent—the problem is far worse. Divine transcendence does not mean that God cannot be coherently described in human language; it means, I believe, that we never fully understand (certain of the) true statements that can be made about God. Thus Paul exclaims: 'O the depth of the riches and wisdom and knowledge of God! How unsearchable are his judgments and how inscrutable his ways!' (Rom. 11: 33).

Given that the Trinity is a mystery, the words we use to describe it—including the words I just used—are signposts or pointers more than explanations. Our Trinitarian language does make claims, of course; it is not just pictures or metaphors. Indeed, in this chapter I will try to make true and explanatorily helpful statements about the Trinity. But given the mystery, it is best to see orthodox Trinitarian language as aiming us in the right direction by showing what can and cannot be said about God. No human explanation and no analogy drawn from human experience can ever fully capture the reality of God's being.

Orthodox Trinitarianism faces theological dangers in either direction. Pushing too hard on the oneness of God can lead to modalism, which is the theory that God is truly one, but only seems to us or appears to us to be three; as God relates to human beings, God plays three roles. Pushing too hard on the threeness of God can lead to tritheism, which is the theory that the Trinity is three Gods who are perhaps unified in some ways. Both modalism and tritheism have been condemned as heretical, and are to be avoided.

ST is one way of understanding the Trinity. In what I will call the 'standard picture' of the early Trinitarian controversies, it is often associated with the Eastern Orthodox churches, and especially with the Cappadocian fathers,

---

[3] This despite the fact—as Joseph T. Lienhard has demonstrated—that the phrase 'three *hypostases* in one *ousia*' is rare in the writings of the Cappadocians. See his '*Ousia* and *Hypostasis*: The Cappadocian Settlement and the Theology of "One *Hypostasis*"', in *The Trinity* (n. 1 above), pp. 99–121.

Gregory of Nyssa, Gregory of Nazianzus, and Basil of Caesarea.[4] It logically begins with and takes as basic the *threeness* of the Blessed Trinity. It also emphasizes the primacy of the Father as the 'fount of divinity'. The word 'God' or 'the Godhead' names the triune reality itself. So God is in some ways like a community or society. The three Persons each possess the generic divine nature as an attribute, and so are all fully divine. In most versions of ST, they have distinct minds and wills. Indeed, something like this seems essential if the Persons are to be in loving relationship with each other, which is one of the central *desiderata* of ST. It is important to note that ST is not a claim merely about what we now call the economic Trinity (e.g. that God *in God's relations to us* is three); the claim is that God in God's inner life is like a loving community. The great challenge facing ST is to make room for and explain the oneness of God, that is, to ensure that Christianity is monotheistic.

Although we will return to the question of whether ST is safely monotheistic in more detail below, I should say a word here about its usual strategy for coping with that question. The issue is this. Suppose that God is like a community, that is, that there are three Persons or subsistent centres of consciousness, will, and action in God. (Again, something like this seems to be required if God's inner life is to be relational, although later in the chapter I will back away considerably from the visual image of three individuals that naturally springs to mind here.) If so, then how is it that God is *one* (as of course orthodoxy requires)? How is the Trinity an individual? The answer, according to ST, is threefold: (1) Each of the Persons equally possesses the divine essence in its totality. (2) The three necessarily share a marvellous unity of purpose, will, and action; that is, it is not possible for them to disagree or to be in conflict. (3) They exist in *perichoresis* (circumincession, co-inherence, permeation). That is, each is 'in' the others; each ontologically embraces the others; to be a divine Person is by nature to be in relation to the other two; the boundaries between them are transparent; their love for and communion with each other is such that they can be said to 'interpenetrate' each other. (I will say more about perichoresis in Section III below.)

It is important to note that the affirmation is: God is something *like* a community. Some more radical defenders of ST claim that God *is* a community, but in my view that statement swings too dangerously close to tritheism for comfort. Three Gods who are unified in will and purpose is not orthodox Trinitarianism.

---

[4] Although Sarah Coakley convincingly disassociates Gregory of Nyssa from ST, or at least from the way ST has been understood by contemporary analytic philosophers. See her ' "Persons" in the "Social" Doctrine of the Trinity,' in *The Trinity* (n. 1 above), pp. 123–44.

As noted, according to the standard picture, ST contrasts with the Western theory of the Trinity, which we are calling LT. This theory is associated most closely with Augustine, and especially his great work, *De Trinitate*. (I do not want to be seen as interpreting Augustine in the following brief summary of LT, however.) LT logically begins with and takes as basic the *oneness* of the Blessed Trinity. LT stresses the claim that there is but one divine being or substance, and it is God. God does exist in three Persons, but the three Persons have the same divine individual nature. All three are simply God; there is one and only one case or instance of God. While on ST (as Leftow would have it[5]) the Persons are both distinct and discrete, on LT the Persons are distinct but not discrete. The great challenge for LT (which we will not explore in any detail in this chapter) is to make room for and explain the threeness of God, that is, avoid modalism.

It should be noted that the way in which I have just distinguished between the East and the West—the 'standard picture'—has recently been called into question.[6] The Cappadocians stressed the oneness as much as did Augustine—so the revisionists claim—and Augustine stressed the threeness as much as did the Cappadocians. The East and West continued to have mutually fertilizing contacts and conversations; right up until the Photian schism of AD 863 it was entirely possible to see their Trinitarian views as compatible. But whether the disjunctive paradigm of the standard picture is historically accurate will not ultimately matter for the purposes of this chapter. There definitely is a disjunction in contemporary theological and philosophical discussions of the Trinity, with people like Richard Swinburne, Cornelius Plantinga, and Edward Wierenga[7] defending ST and people like Kelly James Clark and Brian Leftow[8] defending LT. However, part of my aim here is to show how the two emphases captured by what I am calling ST and LT can be unified, or at least nearly so.

I should close this section by explaining exactly how LT and ST differ. As I see it, there are three central differences: (1) As noted, LT begins with, and

⁵ Leftow (n. 1 above), p. 204. I do not claim to know precisely what Leftow intends with this distinction.

⁶ See, for example, Yves Congar, *I Believe in the Holy Spirit*, I (London: Geoffrey Chapman, 1983); Michel Rene Barnes, 'Rereading Augustine's Theology of the Trinity', and Sarah Coakley, ' "Persons" in the "Social" Doctrine of the Trinity', both in *The Trinity* (n. 1 above).

⁷ See Richard Swinburne, *The Christian God* (Oxford: Oxford University Press, 1994), pp. 170–91; Cornelius Plantinga, 'Social Trinity and Tritheism', in Ronald J. Feenstra and Cornelius Plantinga (eds.), *Trinity, Incarnation, and Atonement* (Notre Dame, IN: Notre Dame University Press, 1989), pp. 21–47; Edward Wierenga, 'Trinity and Polytheism', *Faith and Philosophy* (forthcoming).

⁸ Kelly James Clark, 'Trinity or Tritheism', *Religious Studies*, 32/4 (December, 1996), pp. 463–76; Leftow, 'Anti Social Trinitarianism' (n. 1 above).

takes as basic, the oneness of God, while ST begins with, and takes as basic, the threeness of God. (2) On ST the Persons are robust—robust enough to constitute a genuine 'other'. They are three centres of consciousness, will, and action. (God is like a community, but because of *perichoresis* cannot be said to *be* a community, as we will see.) On LT the Persons are not robust; they are not three separate centres of consciousness, will, and action; God is not like a community at all. (3) On ST the Persons share a universal nature (which we can call 'divinity'), while on LT they share an individual nature ('God'). In other words, in ST the three Persons are all one kind of being, namely, God (of which there is but one instance), and so each is divine; while on LT the three Persons are all one individual being.

II

Here I offer a proof of ST. It is an a priori proof, based on the concept of love. There are seven steps. I will first state the argument by way of summary. Then I will distinguish my proof from three other related arguments in the history of theology. Finally, I will discuss each premiss in turn. Here then is the argument:

(1) Necessarily, God is perfect, and perfect in love (1 John 4: 8).
(2) Necessarily, if God does not experience love of another, God is imperfect.
(3) Therefore, necessarily, God experiences love of another. ((1), (2))
(4) Necessarily, it is possible that only God exists (i.e. that God does not create).
(5) Necessarily, if ST is false, there is no 'other' in the Godhead.
(6) Necessarily, if God alone exists, and if ST is false, then God does not experience love of another, and thus is not perfect. ((2), (4), (5))
(7) Therefore, necessarily, ST is true. ((4), (6))

I make very little claim to originality with this proof. Indeed, in the tradition there are several a priori proofs based on the concept of love in favour of the divine threeness. For example, in book 9 of *De Trinitate*,[9] Augustine argued that God is necessarily triune, since God is love. This is because love—consisting, as it must, of that which loves, that which is loved, and love itself—is necessarily triune. And in his own *De Trinitate*,[10] Richard of

---

[9] Augustine, *On The Trinity* (Grand Rapids, MI: Eerdmans, 1956), book 9.

[10] Richard of St. Victor, *De Trinitate* (NY: Paulist Press, 1979), III, 1–25. Perhaps Richard's real concern—placed, as he was, in a monastic setting—was not that there could not be any sharing in love with two alone, but rather that that sharing would or could be selfish, to the exclusion of others, like the 'particular friendships' monks were encouraged to avoid.

St. Victor defined God as absolute love, power, and beatitude. If God were one Person alone, God would have no fitting object of the divine love; if God were two Persons, that too would be insufficient, because there would be no sharing of love; there must then be three divine Persons mutually to share the bliss of their love and so to complete their beatitude. Now since God is omnipotent, God can bring about whatever is necessary for divine beatitude, and so God is three Persons.

And in our own day, Richard Swinburne similarly argues that God must be triune. Love is a supreme good, Swinburne says, and necessarily involves sharing, cooperating, and benefiting another. Two persons makes sharing possible, but only three or more allows cooperation in sharing. More than three is unnecessary, because it is not essential to the fullest manifestation of love.[11] (The three arguments just noted are arguments in favour of divine threeness; my own argument in the present section of the chapter is an argument in favour of divine plurality or robust differentiation ('otherness') among the Persons.[12] It is an argument to the effect that God is something like a community.)

The premises of the proof require discussion.[13] To begin, I take it that the first premiss:

(1) Necessarily, God is perfect, and perfect in love (1 John 4: 8)

must be acceptable to all Christians, both because of its scriptural warrant and because virtually every theologian takes lovingness and perfection to be central defining characteristics of God. As such, I need not argue for its truth.

Premiss (2) says:

(2) Necessarily, if God does not experience love of another, God is imperfect.

Now love of oneself is surely a good. Jesus' words, 'Love your neighbor as yourself' (Mark 12: 31), seem to imply or at least assume as much. And certainly Christians want to affirm that God loves himself. Still, it seems obvious (at least to me) that love of *another person* is also a very great good. It seems that a God who does not and cannot love another has missed out on something high and wonderful; there would be a deficiency in God. God

[11] Richard Swinburne, *The Christian God* (Oxford: Oxford University Press, 1994), pp. 177–80.

[12] For an argument somewhat similar to mine, see C. J. F. Williams, 'Neither Confounding the Persons Nor Dividing the Substance', in Alan Padgett (ed.), *Reason and the Christian Religion* (New York: Oxford University Press, 1994).

[13] I develop a version of this proof much more briefly and tentatively in Stephen T. Davis, 'A Somewhat Playful Proof of the Social Trinity in Five Easy Steps', *Philosophia Christi*, Series 2, 1/2 (1999), pp. 103–6.

would be less than perfect. (The same would be true of any great good that can logically be experienced by an omnipotent and perfectly good being: if God were not to experience beauty or justice, that would be a deficiency in God.) And so premiss (2) is true. Premiss (3) says:

(3) Therefore, necessarily, God experiences love of another.

This premiss follows immediately from (1) and (2). If they are necessarily true, it is necessarily true.

Now let us turn to a different point. A question: Was God in God's timeless eternity or pre-creation state free *not* to create the heavens and the earth and the sentient creatures that would one day populate it? Some theologians in effect have said no. Following the 'principle of plenitude' notion (as it was called by Arthur Lovejoy, in his classic *The Great Chain of Being*),[14] they argue that God is essentially perfectly good, and that goodness is necessarily generous rather than jealous, and allows all sorts of things and types of things to exist. Accordingly, God necessarily expresses himself in the act of creation. This principle originated with Plato (see *Timaeus* 29E), was developed further by Plotinus, and entered Christian theology through Augustine. Some theologians took the principle not only as an explanation of the existence of the creation itself, but also as an explanation of its great variety of living things. A universe containing an immense variety of kinds of creatures, from the least to the most complex, was taken to be a better universe than one that is sparse, barren, and bereft of various sorts of creatures. A full, abundant, overflowing world is morally better than an empty or barren one. So a good God will create and will bestow the gift of existence as widely as possible.

The principle of plenitude is rarely invoked in Christian theology any more, and for good reason. For one thing, it is difficult to state precisely. Does it concern merely *kinds* of creatures, sheer *numbers* of creatures, or both? For another, no matter which way the principle is understood, we do not seem to inhabit a universe that exemplifies it. Both the number of things and the kinds of things in existence (or that have been or ever will be in existence) seem limited. It is easy to imagine all sorts of possible creatures who have never existed and doubtless never will—mermaids, unicorns, green tigers, seventy-foot tall moles. And we have no reason whatsoever to think that all such creatures do indeed exist somewhere else in the universe.

More importantly, most Christian traditions have stressed the notion that creation is an unnecessitated act of grace on God's part. My own Reformed tradition—wanting, as it always does, to preserve the freedom of God—

---

[14] Arthur Lovejoy, *The Great Chain of Being* (Cambridge, MA: Harvard University Press, 1936).

argues that God was indeed free not to create a world at all. That is, the question, 'Why is there anything and not nothing?' (which is at the heart of all cosmological arguments for the existence of God) envisions a possibility—there eternally existing *only* God and nothing else—that was, until the moment of creation, a genuine possibility. God is totally self-sufficient, and does not need to create. Accordingly, God *could* (in some strong sense of the word 'could') have decided not to create at all. Thus

(4) Necessarily, it is possible that only God exists (i.e. that God does not create).

Now had God actually chosen not to create, and were ST false, then God would have had no experience of 'another', no 'other' (in the sense of a distinct centre of conscious, will, and action) to love. Accordingly, God would not have experienced the great good of love of another, perhaps the highest form of love. This point follows because of premiss (5), which says:

(5) Necessarily, if ST is false, there is no 'other' in the Godhead.

That is, given premiss (4) it is quite possible that there might not have been any 'other' for God to love ('other' in the sense of a separate centre of consciousness, will, and action), and thus God would not be perfect, contrary to premiss (1). Thus premiss (6) explicitly says:

(6) Necessarily, if God alone exists, and if ST is false, then God does not experience love of another, and thus is not perfect.

A possible objection looms here: perhaps the high status that we grant to the notion of 'loving another' depends on the envisioned 'other' not being identical to the lover or not being metaphysically 'within' the lover in some sense. That is, it depends on the lover and the one loved being both distinct and discrete. But that is precisely what we do not have (so the objection continues) with ST's 'Persons'. There the love among the members of the Trinity is at least a sort of self-love. But this point does not appear decisive. The 'Persons' in ST *are* robust; that, indeed, is the essence of the theory. It is true that the three Persons are not 'other than God', but they are 'other than each other'. The intuited importance of love of another is accordingly relevant to ST.
    Thus

(8) Therefore, necessarily, ST is true.

This premiss follows because ST, however unpacked, entails, as noted, that there are eternally differing robust individuals (possible objects of love) within the Godhead. QED.[15]

---

[15] The argument, as it stands, is far from formally valid, but could easily be made so with the addition of a few sub-premisses and with the use of standard predicate calculus plus modal operators.

III

Before turning to Leftow's criticisms of ST, I will explain in more detail the version of ST that I wish to defend. There are three versions that Leftow criticizes—what he calls Trinity Monotheism (the one God is the Trinity itself), Group Mind Monotheism (the one God is the conscious sum of the three Persons), and Functional Monotheism (the Persons are one functionally). But my own version of ST, which I am calling Perichoretic Monotheism, differs from these three at important points.

Perichoretic Monotheism rests upon six claims, many of which are shared by other versions of ST (and indeed by other versions of Christian Trinitarianism). There will be little that is particularly new or surprising here.

1. *God is like a community.* The three Persons are three distinct centres of consciousness, will, and action. There are three instances or cases of divinity. (This language might be taken to sound like tritheism, but points 1–6, taken together, ensure that it is not tritheism.)

It would be best if I explain what I mean by the word 'person', especially since this word is often left undefined and has been used variously in the history of theology (let alone philosophy). But let me first point out that in defining this term, I am not trying to exegete the work of any particular Trinitarian theologian, defender of ST or not. 'Person' is one of those words that we use frequently, but which defy rigorous definition. I will loosely define a person as 'a conscious purposive agent'. *Conscious* means that persons are things that engage in 'mental' or 'conscious' acts like thinking, feeling, loving, willing, believing, remembering, and knowing. *Purposive* means that persons are things that have desires, intentions, and aims; and they frequently set out to achieve them. *Agent* means that persons are things that have the ability to act, to do or achieve things. So a 'person', whether divine or human, is a property-bearer that is conscious, and has intellect, will, and the ability to be an agent.

Other notions could be added as well: persons are moral things, that is, things that can be held morally responsible for causing harm or benefit; persons are things that exist in social relations with other things; and persons are members of linguistic communities. (I intentionally exclude from my definition any such notions as autonomy (in my view God is autonomous but humans are not), privacy, individual rights, or individualism.) So far as the Trinity is concerned, you can talk about Father, Son, and Holy Spirit as persons. You can also talk in an extended sense about God (where this means the Godhead or Trinity) as a person, although this has not been the usual language of theology (it is better to say that God is 'personal'). But these are simply different ways of talking about the same three-in-one reality. You cannot say that there are four divine persons.

2. *Each of the three Persons equally possesses the divine essence.* Thus all three are fully divine, no one of them any more or less so than any of the others. If, *per impossibile*, the three Persons were not related trinitarianly (i.e. if they did not share the divine essence, necessarily agree, and relate to each other perichoretically), there would exist three Gods. There is one and only one God *because* the Persons are related to each other trinitarianly.

3. *The three Persons are all equally and essentially divine, metaphysically necessary, eternal (or everlasting), uncreated, omnipotent, omniscient, and perfectly good.* These are essential properties; the Persons could not be the things that they are without them. No one divine Person caused any other divine Person to exist in any important sense. It is possible for Christians coherently to say things like 'The Father is omnipotent' or 'The Son is omnipotent' or 'The Spirit is omnipotent'. It is also possible for Christians coherently to say, 'God (where this means the Godhead) is omnipotent.' But there are not four omnipotent things. Again, these are simply different ways of talking about the same three-in-one reality. In no sense is there any fourth mind, fourth being, or fourth God. (The notion of 'different ways of speaking of the same reality' is meant to apply only to the oneness and threeness of the Trinity; it does not apply to immanent relations among the Persons, let alone to their economic activities.)

There exists a powerful argument against this last claim. Suppose it is true, as I affirm, that the Father is omnipotent, the Son is omnipotent, and the Holy Spirit is omnipotent. Suppose it is also true, as I affirm, both that the Godhead is omnipotent and that 'Father', 'Son', 'Holy Spirit', and 'the Godhead' are all numerically distinct from each other. Then it seems rigorously to follow that there are indeed four omnipotent things. But what blocks this inference is the fact that the three Persons are related to each other perichoretically (to be explained further below).

4. *In the immanent Trinity (i.e. the Trinity as it is in itself), the logical basis of all differentiation among Father, Son, and Holy Spirit is their relations to each other.* The Father has the relation of 'begetting' to the Son, and the Father and (possibly) the Son (depending on which Christian communion you belong to) have the relationship of 'spirating' or 'sending' to the Spirit. The Spirit proceeds (as it is often said) 'from the Father through the Son'.[16] Indeed, if, as I claim, the Persons immanently differ primarily and pre-eminently in their

---

[16] As Gregory of Nyssa himself said. Cited in James Stevenson, *Creeds, Councils, and Controversies*, rev. edn. (London: SPCK, 1989).

relations to each other, something like the *Filioque* clause is necessary; otherwise there could conceivably be no way to distinguish the Son from the Spirit.[17] I am of course affirming that the Persons are different centres of consciousness, will, and action; but those differences among the three exist precisely because of the relations among the Persons, which are (so to speak) logically prior.

However, 'begetting' here does not mean the normal biological act of producing offspring (whereby Abraham begets Isaac, etc.). The Father's relation to the Son (and the Spirit) is non-causal and non-temporal. The priority had by the Father as the 'fount of divinity' is entirely logical in nature. In my view, the Father's priority has to do only with the proper place to begin an explanation. That the Father is first in the order of explanation is taken by Christians as a matter of revealed truth (see, among other texts, John 6: 46; 8: 42; 13: 3; 15: 26; 16: 27–8). The inter-Trinitarian relationships of begetting and so on have nothing whatever to do with bringing something non-existent into existence. In the traditional language, what differentiates the Persons is paternity for the Father, filiality for the Son, and procession for the Spirit.

The phrase 'of one substance' (*homoousias*) was first used to protect Christ's full divinity. Later it was used to protect the unity of the three Persons of the Trinity, that is, to ensure that the Christian view of God is monotheistic. I would say that X and Y are definitely not 'of one substance' if X created Y (or vice versa), or if X has existed longer than Y (or vice versa), or if X has existed as God longer than Y (or vice versa). In other words, I hold that an essential aspect of the doctrine of the Trinity is to deny that the Father is God in any stronger or different sense than the Son or the Holy Spirit is God. As we have seen, a robust notion of ontological oneness among the Persons is mandatory for Christians. This is because Christianity accepts monotheism from its parent Judaism as a defining characteristic. Christianity is essentially monotheistic (Deut. 6: 4; 1 Cor. 8: 5); without divine ontological oneness, a theology is not Christian.

5. *All three Persons are involved in all extra-Trinitarian acts.* Thus Augustine's principle, *Omnia opera Trinitatis ad extra indivisa sunt* ('All the actions of the Trinity outside itself are indivisible'), which is everywhere attributed to him, but is not locatable in his extant writings. For example, only the Son is God incarnate, but the incarnation is the work of all three.

---

[17] This point is made by David Brown in his essay, 'Trinity', in Philip L. Quinn and Charles Taliaferro (eds.), *A Companion to the Philosophy of Religion* (Cambridge, MA: Blackwell, 1997), p. 528.

6. *The Persons are related to each other by perichoresis.* As noted, this Greek word, first formally used in this context by John of Damascus, means co-inherence, mutual indwelling, interpenetrating, merging. It reaches towards the truth that the core of God's inner being is the highest degree of self-giving love. The Persons are fully open to each other, their actions *ad extra* are actions in common, they 'see with each other's eyes', the boundaries between them are transparent to each other, and each ontologically embraces the others. But (so someone might ask) doesn't a core of unshared personal status (Son-ness, let's say) remain, even in *perichoresis*, even if this core is something like a mere (non-spatial) Euclidian point? Yes, it does; these are the Persons; this is the threeness of the Trinity. Again, none of this is to be taken as true only of the Trinity as it appears to us. The Persons are related to each other perichoretically in the inner being of the Blessed Trinity. But do not these 'cores of unshared personal status' constitute another way in which the Persons immanently differ (besides in relationship, that is)? Not at all. Since there can be no relationships without things that are related, this is a logical implication of their relationships; this is simply another way of saying that the basis of all immanent differentiation among the Persons is their relationships.

I am unable to provide a rigorous or precise explication of the concept of perichoresis. Since perichoretically related things are not part of our ordinary experience, we are reduced to vagueness or to metaphors when we try to explain the notion. We do of course know of gaseous or liquid substances that in some circumstances can fully permeate ('interpenetrate') each other. But for at least three reasons that sort of thing hardly helps. (1) Perichoresis, a relationship of love, can only obtain between persons, not between gaseous or liquid substances. (2) Such substances, when fully permeated, do not retain their integrity as discrete things; the perichoretically related Trinitarian Persons do. (3) When two or more gaseous or liquid substances permeate each other, that is a contingent fact about them; but that the three Trinitarian Persons are related to each other perichoretically is a necessary fact about them.

It is a venerable tradition in theology to give analogies of the Trinity. All are ultimately recognized as inadequate, as this one admittedly is. Imagine three circles, which we will call Circles 1, 2, and 3. (Although Christians have often used circles to illustrate the Trinity—a habit that apparently began with Joachim of Fiori (1135–1202)—I am not aware that the use I will make of such figures appears anywhere in the tradition as a Trinitarian analogy; if it does, so much the better.) In State A, the circles border on each other, that is, the circumference of each circle touches the circumferences of the two others.

State A:

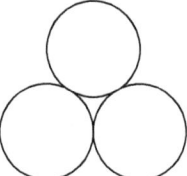

In State B, the circles overlap each other, but not entirely; there is an area that is enclosed by all three circles; there are three areas enclosed by two and only two circles; and there are areas enclosed by one circle only.

State B:

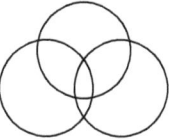

In State C, the circles have wholly merged; they circumscribe the same area.

State C:

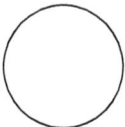

Now imagine something that is impossible with geometrical objects like circles and physical objects like human persons. Imagine that the three circles are simultaneously in State A and State C. Then you could legitimately say, of any property p possessed by all three, that Circle 1 is p, that Circle 2 is p, and that Circle 3 is p. You could even speak of the one circle that exists in State C—call it Circle 123—and say that it is p. But you cannot say that there are four things that are p; that would simply be false. When we imagine that the circles are simultaneously in State A and State C, there are either three circles or one circle (or the circles are three-in-one)—you decide which way you want to talk—but don't try to say there are four.

Perichoresis blocks this improper inference. It will be said: 'If Circle 1 is p, Circle 2 is p, Circle 3 is p, and Circle 123 is p, then, obviously, there are four things that are p.' Not so, I say, since Circle 123 just *is* (in my illustration) Circles 1, 2, and 3 in perichoresis. Similarly, the Godhead just *is* the Father, the Son, and the Holy Spirit in perichoresis. Again, there is either one omnipotent thing or three omnipotent things—you can sensibly talk either way—but not four.

'What!', so a critic might respond at this point. 'With the circles you are illustrating the Trinity by what you admit is a logical impossibility; how can that possibly help?' But this analogy is not an attempt to solve the logical problem of the Trinity, that is, demonstrate the logical coherence of the dogma. At the moment I am simply trying to explain *perichoresis*. But my claim is that perichoretically related persons *can be* or indeed *are* simultaneously in something like State A and State C, that is, are simultaneously one and three.

I have admitted that the Trinity is at bottom mysterious, and that all the anthropomorphic illustrations of the Trinity fail (including this one). But it is important for Christians to note the essential location of the mystery of the Trinity. It has to do with perichoresis: How are the three Persons related to each other in such a way as to retain their threeness while being one God?

If a *riddle* can be solved and a *mystery* continues to puzzle no matter how much we learn or think about it, then my own view is that only in the eschaton will the Christian doctrine of the Blessed Trinity become a riddle. Still, I claim that what my story about the circles illustrates—God simultaneously being three-in-one—*is* logically possible (for perichoretically related Persons). Indeed, Christians believe that it is actual.

IV

How can Perichoretic Monotheism, thus described, be brought to bear upon Leftow's objections to ST? In the course of his paper Leftow raises many objections to ST. Some of them, as he admits, are not relevant to versions of ST that stress perichoresis, and some of them are aimed specifically at the other versions of ST that he considers. I will focus on four of his objections.

1. *ST amounts to tritheism rather than monotheism.* This is Leftow's central worry about all versions of ST. And he is surely correct that any version of Christian Trinitarianism that departs from monotheism is theologically unacceptable; if ST amounts to tritheism, it should be rejected. The way Leftow formulates the objection is this: If God is a discrete personal being with the full divine nature, then, because ST says that all three Persons are discrete personal beings with the full divine nature, ST posits three Gods. Comparing the Christian God to the Greek pantheon, Leftow says: 'So on the functional-monotheist account, the reason the Persons are one God and the Olympians are not is that the Persons are far more alike than Zeus and his brood, far more cooperative, and linked by procession. But it is hardly plausible that Greek paganism would have been a form of monotheism had Zeus & Co. been more alike, better behaved, and linked by the right causal relations.'[18]

---

[18] Leftow (n. 1 above), p. 232; cf. also p. 208.

Now I am defending Perichoretic Monotheism rather than the functional monotheism against which Leftow is here training his guns. Yet that point does not suffice by itself to answer the objection; perhaps Leftow's criticism applies equally well to my preferred version of ST. But I hold that it does not. The crucial point is that the Greek gods were not related to each other perichoretically. Leftow is correct that even if they were better organized, better behaved, of one essence, and so on, they would still constitute a plurality of gods rather than one God. Hence, I hold that ST is monotheistic not only because of the Persons' shared divine essence and their necessary agreement and cooperation, but also because of their loving, interpermeating, boundaryless relations with each other.

But Leftow also raises the polytheism issue in a different way. He argues that on ST there must be more than one God, because according to ST there is more than one way to *be* God. One way to be God is to be one of the three divine Persons, which ST insists are all fully divine. The other way to be God is to be the Godhead itself, which ST also insists is fully divine. Because there is more than one way to be divine, there is more than one divine being. That is, Leftow insists that if we say of all four members of the set consisting of (a) the Godhead, (b) the Father, (c) the Son, and (d) the Holy Spirit that they 'are God', then there are two different ways to be God, and thus four Gods. He says: 'Either the Trinity is a fourth case of the divine nature, in addition to the Persons, or it is not. If it is, we have too many cases of deity for orthodoxy. If it is not, and yet is divine, there are two ways to be divine—by being a case of deity, and by being a Trinity of such cases.'[19]

But this does not follow. We must notice that the predicate '... is God' is being used in two different ways here. The Godhead 'is God' in the sense of strict numerical identity. The Godhead (which consists of Father, Son, and Holy Spirit), as we might say, *exhausts* God. Here the word 'God' in the predicate '... is God' refers to an individual. But when we say that the Father 'is God', the Son 'is God', and the Holy Spirit 'is God', we are not talking about strict numerical identity; it would be false to say that 'the Father exhausts God.' Here the predicate '... is God' does not refer to an individual but is a property meaning something close to 'is divine'.

Accordingly, as noted above, it is possible coherently to talk on the one hand of the Godhead as being God, and it is possible on the other to talk of the Father as God, the Son as God, and the Holy Spirit as God. But these are simply two different ways of talking about one and the same reality. There are not four Gods or even two ways of 'being God'.

[19] Ibid., p. 221.

2. *How many Gods are compatible with monotheism?* In the light of the various attempts by defenders of ST to reconcile the threeness that they emphasize with monotheism, Leftow asks whether there is a maximum allowable number of Gods that could be treated in the way that friends of ST treat the three Persons. 'It does not seem that we can make a religion monotheist merely by altering its gods' *nature*,' he insists.[20] And he is surely right about that. Leftow also asks why, on ST, the number is *three*. Why not two or five or a million persons in the Godhead? He says: 'The question "why does deity have the number of cases it has?" is live for ST in a way it is not for LT. For LT, there is just one case of deity.'[21]

I would reply that the maximum allowable number of Gods is one. Any religion that posits more than that is polytheist. Perichoretic Monotheism posits—and ends up with—one and only one God. As to the 'Why three?' question, there is no reason for, or explanation of, there being three Persons rather than some other number. Three is the number that has been revealed to us; that is the way reality is. But it is not quite true to imply, as Leftow does,[22] that advocates of LT are excused from facing this same question. To put the point in Leftow's terms, the friends of LT still face the question, 'Why are there three and not two or a million distinct but not discrete divine Persons?'

3. *All versions of ST raise the spectre of inequality among the Persons.* Much of what Leftow says on this point is not relevant to the version of ST that I have been defending. Perichoretic Monotheism denies that the Son and the Spirit were created by the Father. All versions of Trinitarianism admit that there are inequities in the economy—the Son but not the Father or the Spirit dies for our sins; the Spirit but not the Father or the Son indwells us, and so on. Leftow thinks that this creates more of a problem for ST than for LT, since ST holds that the Persons are discrete things or (as he says) substances. The Son did more for us than the other Persons, since they did not bleed and die for us; ergo, the Persons are unequal. But it is difficult to see how these admitted inequities in the economy constitute any theologically untoward inequity among the Persons. They certainly entail no inequities in the immanent Trinity.

To return to a point discussed earlier, Leftow thinks there are problems of inequity related to his point (which I deny) that on ST there are two ways to be divine—by being one of the Persons and by being the Godhead. The Trinity itself is not the same sort of thing that the Persons are, Leftow says. Doesn't that mean the Trinity has *more of what it takes to be divine* than the Persons do? Doesn't it mean that the Trinity is *more divine* than any of the

---

[20] Leftow (n. 1 above), p. 233. [21] Ibid., p. 239. [22] Ibid., p. 241.

Persons? But again, it is hard to see how this conclusion follows. For one thing, I have already denied that on ST there is more than one way to be God; what we have are two ways of talking about 'being divine'. For another, why say that the Godhead is more divine than the Persons? As I have insisted all along, you can say that 'The Father, the Son, and the Spirit are all divine' and you can say that 'The Godhead is divine.' Yet these are simply two different ways of talking about the same thing.

4. *How can co-mingled divine minds be distinct?* I have stipulated that on Perichoretic Monotheism, all three Persons are omniscient. If that is true, then the Son knows all that the Father knows, and so on, unless there exist logically private truths like 'I am the Father' (when said by the Father) or 'I am the spirated one' (when said by the Spirit). The contents of their minds are wholly open to one another. Perhaps something like telepathy is at work. But Leftow's worry is this: We can make sense of co-mingled but distinct human minds, because we can associate them with different groupings of brain hemispheres. But—he asks—what would keep discarnate divine minds distinct? It would have to be a non-mental state, he says, since all their mental states would presumably be shared among the three by telepathy (or whatever mechanism they use).[23]

But surely the non-mental states that Leftow is looking for are simply states like *being the unbegotten one* or *being the begotten one* or *being the one who is sent*, and so on. If the three Persons are omniscient, the three minds will know not only truths like '2 + 2 = 4' and 'Abraham Lincoln was shot by John Wilkes Booth in 1865,' but also truths like 'The Person who says, "I am the unbegotten one" is the Father.'

As far as the reference of the word 'I' (when said by God) is concerned, I have been emphasizing that Perichoretic Monotheism is an attempt to describe the immanent Trinity. In some cases it is clear who is talking when the divine 'I' is used. 'I and the Father are one,' very much sounds like the voice of the Son. 'This is my beloved Son,' sounds like the Father. But there are many cases where the reference is not clear. In such cases it will not matter whether the divine 'I' is taken as the voice of one of the Persons or as the voice of the Trinity.[24]

It has not been part of this chapter's aim to explore the difficulties faced by LT. Nevertheless, I will express the opinion that the problems ST has with the oneness of God are exactly paralleled by difficulties LT has with the threeness. We see this even in Leftow's paper. The spectre of modalism looms when Leftow says of LT, 'for the Son to be in the forefront of an act is just for God to

---

[23] Ibid., p. 225.

[24] I note here, but do not discuss, a fifth criticism that Leftow raises against ST: that it raises the possibility of conflict among the Persons. I will not reply to this objection because Leftow admits that it does not apply to versions of ST that stress *perichoresis*.

be more prominent in one role (or state, etc.) than he is in others.'[25] Still, in Leftow's defence, I suspect that there has been a tacit consensus in the tradition that modalism is the least egregious of the Trinitarian heresies, preferable by far to tritheism.[26]

V

In the end, however, LT and Perichoretic Monotheism nearly, but not quite, come together. They end up in my view being two quite appropriate ways of talking about the same reality, differing mainly in emphasis. If my analysis is correct, both theories are moved slightly towards the other—ST is edged towards LT by perichoresis; and LT is edged towards ST by the point that the Persons are not *just* relations. The theories virtually (but not quite) merge, because on Perichoretic Monotheism the three are virtually as robustly one as on LT. The remaining differences have to do either with emphasis (e.g. the proper place to begin Trinitarian explanations) or with the question of how robust the Persons are.

It has been the aim of this chapter to defend Christian Trinitarianism and, more specifically, the Social Theory of the Trinity. I have claimed that ST can be defended against Leftow's criticisms. Indeed, I believe it does a better job of avoiding the twin dangers of modalism and tritheism than either LT or more radical versions of ST. It amounts to a viable option for theologians and worshippers of the Blessed Trinity. And interpreted along the lines of Perichoretic Monotheism, ST ends up differing from LT mainly in emphasis.[27]

[25] Leftow (n. 1 above), p. 238.

[26] This despite the fact that modalism endangers several important theological points: Christ's full humanity, the loving relationships among the Persons, and the salvific role of Christ as mediator.

[27] I would like to thank Sarah Coakley, Christine Helmer, Brian Leftow, Gerald O'Collins, Susan Peppers-Bates, Michael Rea, and Dale Tuggy for their very helpful comments on earlier drafts of this chapter.

Part II

Why Believe in Jesus? Resurrection and Incarnation

5

Why the Historical Jesus Matters

If we know or rationally believe that the Trinitarian God exists and reveals himself to us in order to accomplish our salvation, the natural question is: How does God go about accomplishing it? The book of Hebrews makes it clear that God has used many methods: 'Long ago God spoke to our ancestors in many and various ways by the prophets,' it begins. Those various ways surely include God's dealings with the Patriarchs, God's rescue of Israel from Egyptian slavery, God's revelation of the Decalogue and the rest of the Law, as well as the oracles of the prophets. 'But in these last days,' so Hebrews continues, 'he has spoken to us by a Son' (Heb. 1: 1–2a). The Christian message is that God's supreme revelation of himself to human beings and the pre-eminent vehicle for achieving our salvation is Jesus Christ. Accordingly, Chapters 5 to 10 of this book all deal, in one way or other, with Jesus Christ.

Let us begin with a thought-experiment. Suppose one day an astronaut from some far-off galaxy entered my office. Suppose our space traveller was interested in the cultures and religions of the earth, and asked me, 'What is this thing called Christianity? Could you tell me, please, what it is?' I don't know all that I would say in response, but I know what my opening line would be: 'Let me tell you about a person whose name is Jesus.'

This thought-experiment has theological implications. Christian faith begins with Jesus, with stories about who he was and what he did. This same impulse caused the early church, beginning some thirty to forty years after its founding, to write Gospels. Christian thinking, worship, and practice must be rightly related to Jesus. If our beliefs and practices are out of touch with the Jesus who actually lived in Palestine centuries ago, Christian faith is in serious trouble. It has no plausible foundation.

Accordingly, questions about who Jesus was and what he said and did are crucial for Christians. Our faith is not a dropped-from-the-sky code of behaviour or a set of timeless teachings from a guru. Ours is a religion of history, a faith whose vital essence consists of great revelatory actions of God in human history, pre-eminently the life, teachings, death, and resurrection of the Son of God (Heb. 1: 1).

So we need to know about Jesus: Who was he? How did he view himself and his mission? What did he do and say? Why was he crucified? Was he really raised from the dead? What was it about Jesus that brought the Christian church into existence? For most of Christian history, these questions were answered by simply accepting uncritically what the four canonical Gospels said about Jesus. No major differences were expected or detected between the Jesus of the Gospels and the Jesus who actually lived—or, indeed, between the historian's 'Jesus of history' and the church's 'Christ of faith'.

II

A German scholar, H. S. Reimarus (1694–1768), often considered the founder of 'the search for the historical Jesus', brought this long era to a close. Reimarus wanted to discover who Jesus was by entirely rational means, that is, by historical research unfettered by dogmatic considerations or ecclesiastical control. Other notables in what has come to be called the 'Old Quest' were David Friedrich Strauss, author of *The Life of Jesus Critically Examined* (1835), and Ernest Renan, who wrote *Life of Jesus* (1863). The culmination of the Old Quest was Albert Schweitzer's famous *Quest of the Historical Jesus* (1909). Schweitzer's own proposals about Jesus no longer command assent, but his lasting contribution was his critique of his predecessors. He showed conclusively that their 'Jesus' was largely a fantasy made in their own image.

The next period in the 'quest' is sometimes called 'No Quest', largely because of the influence of Rudolf Bultmann. In *The History of the Synoptic Tradition* (1921), *Jesus and the Word* (1926), and other influential works, he argued that it is impossible for scholars to come to know much about Jesus. Accordingly, the main object of study for Bultmann and his disciples was not so much Jesus as the early church.[1] Indeed, Bultmann stressed the importance for his own day of the preached kerygma of the early church, although many believe that the way he interpreted that message had more to do with existential philosophy than it did with Christianity.

Then in the 1950s a much heralded 'New Quest' for the historical Jesus began, under the influence of such scholars as Ernst Kasemann, Gunther Bornkamm, my own Claremont colleague James M. Robinson, and (a few

---

[1] Rudolf Bultmann, *Jesus* (Tübingen: J. C. B. Mohr, 1951), p. 11. This despite the fact that Bultmann said a great deal about Jesus in *Jesus*.

years later) Edward Schillebeeckx. The contemporary continuers of the tradition of the New Quest are such figures as Marcus Borg, John Dominic
Crossan, Burton Mack, and the members of the Jesus Seminar. What seems
to unite these contemporary scholars is (1) the fact that their 'Jesus'—not
always for the same reasons—largely seems to float above his own Jewish
background; (2) their insistence that Jesus was not an apocalyptic or eschatological teacher; and (3) their eager willingness to entertain almost any ideas
about Jesus, however bizarre, except orthodox ones.

But another group of contemporary scholars, sometimes called the 'Third
Quest', is also at work: people like Martin Hengel, John Meier, E. P. Sanders,
Ben Witherington, Larry Hurtado, and N. T. Wright.[2] They emphasize the
Jewishness of Jesus and consider him an apocalyptic prophet who announced
the coming of the Kingdom of God. These folk have no unified theological
agenda—they include Catholics and Protestants, liberals and evangelicals—
but they all emphasize the importance of the death of Jesus. They ask: What
was it about Jesus that caused him to be crucified?

Jesus is now a 'hot topic'. Many Jesus books have been written in the past
twenty years, including at least one by a journalist in effect reporting on the
current state of Jesus studies.[3] This explosion of publicity about Jesus, at least
in the United States, may be partly due to the media-savvy work of the Jesus
Seminar. Indeed, one of the reasons I decided to write about Jesus, despite not
being a professional New Testament scholar, is a conversation I had several
years ago with a retired Presbyterian high school teacher. A highly intelligent
person, but with little theological education, she had seen Robert Funk, co-
chair of the Jesus Seminar, on television. She was deeply worried by what he
said and in effect was asking me whether it was still intellectually possible to
be a believer in Jesus.

It is obvious that there has sometimes been an adversarial relationship
between many of those who engage in the 'Search for the Historical Jesus', on
the one hand, and the Jesus that we find in the New Testament and in the
church, on the other. Indeed, as noted, in Reimarus this point was quite

---

[2] I see my own conclusions about Jesus in this section of the book as influenced by, and in
keeping with the central conclusions of, people like Wright, Witherington, and Hurtado. See, for
example, N. T. Wright, *Jesus and the Victory of God* (Minneapolis, MN: Fortress Press, 1996), p.
xiv. See also three books by Ben Witherington: *The Christology of Jesus* (Minneapolis, MN:
Fortress Press, 1990); *The Jesus Question* (Downers Grove, IL: Inter-Varsity Press, 1995); and *The
Many Faces of the Christ* (New York: Crossroad, 1998). See also Larry W. Hurtado, *Lord Jesus
Christ: Devotion to Jesus in Earliest Christianity* (Grand Rapids, MI: Eerdmans, 2003). (This last
book came to my attention long after largely finishing Part II of the present work, but I was
helped by several of Hurtado's earlier scholarly articles.)

[3] Charlotte Allen, *The Human Christ: The Search for the Historical Jesus* (New York: Free
Press, 1998).

explicit: he wanted to discover who Jesus was by entirely historical means. This ideal continues to the present day; the Jesus Seminar makes much of its total freedom from church teachings. Its members, so it insists, are 'just scholars'; that is, they are 'free of ecclesiastical and religious control'.[4]

The assumption of some Jesus scholarship has been, and continues to be, that the New Testament and certainly the church largely got it wrong about Jesus. And at certain points it is doubtless true that New Testament scholarship for the first seventeen centuries was deficient. How so? It simply assumed uncritically that the historical Jesus is the incarnate Son of God, the Second Person of the Blessed Trinity. Its knowledge of the first-century Roman and Jewish milieu of the New Testament was far less complete than ours (think of the Dead Sea Scrolls and the Nag Hammadi library). It knew little of comparative studies with other sacred texts of the era. And its uncritical assumption of biblical unity caused it to miss much of the rich variety of theologies in the New Testament.

Nevertheless, I want to argue that the New Testament and the church, at least in broad outline, got Jesus right. I believe this conviction can be substantiated via the historical-critical method itself. And in a brief and sketchy way, I will try to do so in this chapter.

So let me ask these sorts of questions: What if Jesus really believed himself to be the Messiah and Son of God? What if he really did heal people and turn water into wine? What if he really did say, 'I and the Father are one' (John 10: 30) and, 'Whoever has seen me has seen the Father' (John 14: 9)? What if he really did die believing that his death was an atoning sacrifice 'for our sins'? What if he really was alive after his death by crucifixion? What if he really did intend to found a church? (Note that these are items that in principle could be demonstrated by historical-critical scholarship as currently practised in academia. I have avoided claims like, 'God raised Jesus from the dead' or 'Jesus was God incarnate', which could not.)

III

There are many ways of being religious in the world. The various religions of humankind seem so diverse as to have little in common with each other aside from what Wittgenstein called 'family resemblances'. Zen Buddhism has little in common with Islam; Advaita Vedanta Hinduism is not strikingly similar to Christianity.

---

[4] Robert W. Funk et al. (eds.), *The Five Gospels: The Search for the Authentic Words of Jesus* (New York: Macmillan, 1993), p. xviii.

Let me distinguish between two sorts of religions: historical religions and non-historical religions. The historical religions are those that essentially depend on God or divinity acting in human history in certain ways. The crucial idea is that our salvation or liberation or enlightenment (or whatever term is preferred) essentially depends on the truth of certain claims about events that happened in the past. Certain events, brought about by God, must have occurred. The discipline that we call history is crucial for these sorts of religions. If historians could prove, for example, that Mohammed never lived (and thus was not God's final prophet and thus did not receive the Koran from God), Islam would be in some difficulty.

The non-historical religions are simply those that do not essentially depend on divine activity in history. Typically, they would be religions that revolve around a group of wise teachings to be followed, a pattern of life to be emulated, a set of rituals to be observed, a code of rules to be obeyed, or a level of spirituality to be achieved. There may or may not exist stories that anchor these teachings or patterns in history (like, say, a founder who produced the wise sayings). However, the soundness or validity of the religious way of life being recommended stands on its own; it does not essentially depend on those stories being true.

The distinction between the historical and the non-historical religions is not hard and fast. Indeed, we can observe tendencies on the part of some adherents of historical religions to try to move them towards being non-historical. A rabbi friend once told me that he had no strong feelings about whether the children of Israel were ever actually rescued from Egyptian slavery or even whether Moses ever existed. What did greatly concern him was that Jews live according to the Torah. (I do not claim, of course, that this sort of sentiment is shared by all Jews.) One obvious motivation for this sort of move is clear: historical religions are vulnerable to potential falsification in ways in which non-historical religions are not. If Christianity depends upon the New Testament picture of Jesus being essentially correct, then Christianity is vulnerable to the results of historical scholarship in ways in which, say, Taoism is not.

If Christianity is a historical religion, then the study of its history matters crucially to it. We can see this insight at work in all shades of the theological spectrum. It is obvious with those on the conservative side; they frequently argue (as I do here) that historical-critical scholarship, when practised aright, supports the New Testament and church picture of Jesus. But it is also true on the liberal side. John Hick, in his book on christology, *The Metaphor of God Incarnate*,[5] argues that proper historical research supports the picture of Jesus

---

[5] John Hick, *The Metaphor of God Incarnate: Christology in a Pluralistic Age* (Louisville, KY: Westminster John Knox Press, 1993).

that he paints. To Hick, Jesus was 'God incarnate' only metaphorically. Literally, he was a man who was acutely aware of and extraordinarily responsive to God; he was an agent of God's activity on earth; he embodied in his life the divine ideal of self-giving love; and his teachings make God real to us and challenge us to live in God's presence. Similarly, the Jesus Seminar argues that authentic historical-critical scholarship establishes its view of Jesus. He was, the Seminar says, something like an itinerant teacher of religious philosophy; he was full of provocative and pithy sayings and parables, and he had almost no connection to Jewish apocalypticism, and no big controversy with the religious leaders.

My point, then, is that almost everybody who paints a picture of Jesus—conservative or liberal—tries to anchor it in history. Bultmann was, of course, something of an exception to this point. In some of his writings, one gets the impression that he gives up on finding Jesus and moves directly to the church's Christ.[6] But most scholars paint a picture of Jesus and then try to show that '*this* is the actual Jesus'. So in one sense almost everybody looks for Jesus and finds Christ, where 'Christ' broadly means the object of one's religious devotion or emulation. Almost everybody struggles mightily to connect the 'Christ' they believe in or follow or at least admire with the 'Jesus' who lived. This is a natural and understandable strategy.

Here are two theses on the matter of faith and history:

Thesis 1: *It is important for the church that its message, and especially its christology, be solidly anchored in history.* Without any firm historical basis for its claims about Christ, Christian teachings devolve to the level of myth. Indeed, we use the word 'myth' precisely for those stories about the past that cannot be anchored in history. Now the word 'history' can mean either something like *what actually occurred in the past* or it can mean something like *the best accounts historians can give about what actually occurred in the past.* Here I am using the word 'history' in the first sense.

Note, for example, that Paul anchors Christian belief and practice in past events—not in myth, philosophy, poetry, or ideology, but in the actual life and teachings of Jesus. Note his careful distinction between his own teachings and Jesus' teachings (1 Cor. 7: 10–12). Note the institution of the Eucharist, with its remembrance of the Lord's Supper (1 Cor. 11: 23–6). Note the phrase 'as of first importance', followed by a list of people who saw the risen Lord (1 Cor. 15: 3–8). Paul apparently believed that salvation depends upon certain claims about the life, death, and resurrection of Jesus being true claims.

---

[6] Perhaps at this point Bultmann was being influenced by Martin Kahler (1835–1912), who argued that we cannot get behind the data and find the historical Jesus, and that 'The real Christ is the preached Christ.' Martin Kahler, *The So-Called Historical Jesus and the Historic, Biblical Christ* (trans. Carl Braaten) (Philadelphia: Fortress Press, 1964), p. 66.

Note also 1 Corinthians 15: 6: 'Then he appeared to more than five hundred brothers and sisters at one time, most of whom are still alive, though some have died.' The phrase 'most of whom are still alive' is intriguing for several reasons. I will mention but one reason: it seems clear that Paul is in effect saying, 'If you do not believe me, go and ask one of them.' That is, he seems to be opening up his own theological reflections on the resurrection of Jesus to historical verification or falsification. (Note also Luke 1: 1–4.)

Of course Christian faith is not exhausted by, nor can it be totally reduced to, the historical credibility of the Bible. But there are some historical claims made by the Bible—for example, that Jesus was raised from the dead—that in my judgement Christian faith cannot do without. We will discuss that claim in Chapters 7 and 8. The credibility of the Bible's claims on this point (and others) is crucial. We still have to do historical research.

Thesis 2: *If our only source of knowledge of Jesus were the historical-critical method, the life and teachings of Jesus would have little religious significance, and Christianity would be in deep trouble.* If Christianity has religious significance—is, in some important sense, 'from God', and does have the power to save us—we would expect a priori that God would find ways of communicating and passing on information about it quite apart from the historical-critical method. Indeed, it is almost ridiculous to suppose, on these assumptions, that the truth about Jesus would be unknown until a small group of scholars discovered it nearly twenty centuries afterwards. As noted in Chapter 3, it seems that God would have taken steps to ensure the protection and preservation of that message (say, by stating it in a text), would have taken steps to ensure that it would be properly interpreted (say, by creating a tradition of interpretation like that which the Church Fathers called 'the rule of faith'), and would have taken steps to ensure its authoritative interpretation and application by creating an institution (the church) designed to do that very thing.[7]

I have been presupposing, and I am prepared to argue, that past events can be understood from the perspective of the present and that texts from the past can be properly interpreted. Who am I arguing against here? It is the view, espoused by some folk who describe themselves as postmodern, that texts—especially texts from the ancient past—have no stable meaning, and accordingly that meaning is something that is created by the reader rather than intended by the author or established by the text itself. To put it crudely, my own view is that the past may be alien (as postmodernists are apt to say), but it's not that alien.

---

[7] C. Stephen Evans has argued similarly in his 'Methodological Naturalism in Historical Biblical Scholarship', in Carey C. Newman (ed.), *Jesus and the Restoration of Israel* (Downers Grove, IL: Inter-Varsity Press, 1999), p. 202.

Texts from the first-century Jewish milieu are alien in that they were written in a language that is different from ours, were produced in a culture different from ours, and at points presuppose knowledge of events and persons (as well as perhaps a world-view) that we lack. This 'alienness' creates a barrier to understanding, but the barrier is not impenetrable. As someone who has taught ancient philosophy for years, I am convinced that teachers and students alike can come to understand texts like Plato's *Phaedo* and Aristotle's *Nichomachean Ethics*. Sometimes it takes great effort, not the least of which is expended in learning to read the Greek language, but it can be done.

IV

Is the picture of Jesus painted in the canonical Gospels an accurate one? Obviously, this is a difficult and complicated question. As noted, I believe this picture is a reliable one. I will argue for that point in two ways. The first has to do with the Gospel of Mark, which by virtually unanimous consent was the first Gospel written and the primary source for the other Synoptic Gospels.

Is there reason to consider Mark historically reliable? Of course Mark was not writing neutral, facts-only history. He had a theological purpose in mind and shaped his material accordingly. But that does not entail that he was not also trying to write true claims about the past, for example, that Jesus died on a cross.

Many Christians accept a doctrine of scripture that entails a presupposition of historical reliability at least as to central points. I take it that most mainstream Protestants and Catholics do, let alone Fundamentalists and Evangelicals (who would of course make the point even more strongly). And I certainly do. But belief in the general trustworthiness of the Bible will not carry much weight with those who do not hold such a presupposition. So the question is: Are there historical-critical reasons for holding that Mark is, in the main, historically reliable?

I believe there are two such reasons.

1. *Agreement with Paul.* It is often said that the apostle Paul knew and cared little about the life of Jesus. But that is far from the truth. What is correct is that as far as we know Paul never wrote a gospel; his extant letters were all occasional pieces that responded to various needs that he saw in the churches and individuals to whom he wrote.

But clearly the life and teachings of Jesus were important to Paul. This fact is not difficult to establish. He stressed the need for believers to obey and even imitate Jesus (1 Cor. 11: 1; 4: 10–12; 10: 5; 1 Thess. 1: 6), as he himself did. But it is difficult to see how that could be done or even attempted without at least some knowledge of Jesus' life. Moreover, as noted, Paul made a careful distinction between Jesus' teachings and his own teachings (1 Cor. 7: 7–16; cf. 2 Cor. 11: 17; 1 Thess. 4: 2, 15). Again, it is hard to see how Paul could do that without knowing what Jesus' teachings were. Note also that Paul accused his enemies of preaching 'another Jesus' (2 Cor. 11: 4), as though knowledge of the real Jesus were crucial.

In broad outline, we can piece together a credible 'life of Jesus' by noting scattered references in the eight letters that most New Testament scholars accept as authentically Pauline (Romans, 1 and 2 Corinthians, Galatians, Philippians, 1 and 2 Thessalonians, and Philemon). This broad outline largely confirms what is said in Mark.

Here is what we can find. His name was Jesus (1 Cor. 1: 1); he was a man (Rom. 5: 15), born of a woman (Gal. 4: 4); he was Jewish, a descendent of Abraham (Gal. 3: 16) and David (Rom. 1: 3); he had brothers (1 Cor. 9: 5); and he was brought up under the Law (Gal. 4: 4). He was sent by God to take on human form (Rom. 8: 3; Phil. 2: 6–11); he was poor (2 Cor. 8: 9) and humble (Phil. 2: 6–11); he suffered (Rom. 8: 17); he was loving and compassionate (Phil. 1: 8); and he lived an exemplary life, aiming to please God rather than himself (Rom. 15: 3, 8; 2 Cor. 8: 9; Phil. 2: 6–8).

Jesus gathered disciples, including Cephas and John (Gal. 1: 19; 2: 9), and taught people on various religious subjects (1 Thess. 4: 2), including marriage and divorce (1 Cor. 7: 10), the way in which those who preach the gospel should make their living (1 Cor. 9: 14), and his own ultimate triumphal return (1 Thess. 4: 15–17). On the night Jesus was betrayed he took bread, broke it, gave thanks, and said, 'This is my body that is for you. Do this in remembrance of me.' Then he took a cup and said, 'This cup is the new covenant in my blood. Do this, as often as you drink it, in remembrance of me' (1 Cor. 11: 23–6).

There are many other echoes in Paul of Jesus' teachings in the Gospels. For example, Romans 12: 17–20 contains several phrases that seem to be taken from what we now call the Sermon on the Mount (Matt. 5–7). Indeed, the topics are listed in the same order in both places: not to return evil for evil, to live at peace with everyone, to avoid revenge, and to love one's enemy. Paul's teaching in Romans 12: 14—about blessing those who persecute you—seems to echo Jesus' teachings (Luke 6: 27b–8a) in Luke's Sermon on the Plain (Luke 6: 17–49).[8]

Jesus was betrayed (1 Cor. 11: 23), was killed by 'the Jews' (1 Thess. 2: 14) by crucifixion (1 Cor. 1: 18, 23; 2: 2), and was buried (1 Cor. 15: 4). On the

---

[8] Notice, for example, the apparent parallels between Rom. 13: 7 and Mark 12: 17; Rom. 13: 9 and Mark 12: 31; Rom. 14: 10 and Matt. 7: 1–2a; Rom. 14: 14 and Luke 11: 41 (Mark 7: 19b); Rom. 16: 19 and Matt. 10: 16b; 1 Cor. 13: 2 and Mark 11: 23; and 1 Thess. 2: 14–16 and Matt. 23: 29–38.

third day (1 Cor. 15: 4) God raised him from the dead (Rom. 1: 4; 4: 25; 6: 4; 8: 34; 1 Cor. 15: 4; 2 Cor. 4: 14 Gal. 1: 1; 1 Thess. 4: 14). He appeared to Peter, then to 'the twelve', then to more than five hundred people, then to James, and then to all the apostles (1 Cor. 15: 5–7). Finally, as the Gospel writers do, Paul insists that Jesus will one day return (1 Thess. 4: 16–17) to be revealed (1 Cor. 1: 7) and to judge all people (Rom. 2: 16). Indeed, this last point constitutes a major theological innovation shared by Mark and Paul: the idea of a suffering messiah who dies on a cross and will one day return in victory over his enemies.

I do not claim that the canonical Gospels or even Mark are simply *repro-duced* in Paul; indeed, some items just mentioned are not in Mark at all (e.g. resurrection appearances only occur in that Gospel's inauthentic 'long end-ing'); and many items from the Gospels (e.g. miracle stories, parables) are not mentioned in the Pauline letters. But the basic outline is there.

The importance of this point about agreement with Paul is obvious: the authentically Pauline epistles were all written well before Mark, well before the Jewish war, and indeed within twenty to thirty years of the death of Jesus. Thus what Paul said about the life of Jesus is much more likely to be reliable on purely historical-critical grounds than something written, say, after the Jewish war. And this reliably confirms the accuracy of later texts (like Mark) that largely agree with Paul on the life of Jesus. Mark does not appear to be myth or fable or fiction.

2. *The ring of truth.* This is hardly the place for a major apologetic effort in favour of the reliability of Mark's picture of Jesus. But I will make a gesture towards two reasons for considering Mark generally historically trustworthy, for considering his 'life of Jesus' to have 'the ring of truth'. It needs to be remembered that virtually whatever sensible date is accepted for the Gospel of Mark, it was written at a time when the events it records were within the living memory of at least some individuals.[9]

(a) One obvious but seldom remarked-upon point is that Mark's Gospel was convincing to the first-century church and to the other synoptic evan-gelists. Luke, who claimed to have consulted sources carefully (Luke 1: 1–4), simply adopted Mark's outline of the life of Jesus, as well as almost every specific event that Mark recorded. He added a great deal to Mark from other sources, and consistent with his own theological purposes, he worded, ordered, and interpreted certain events differently from the way Mark did. But it cannot be gainsaid that Luke basically accepted Mark. Matthew too simply adopted Mark's outline and most of the events Mark records.

---

[9] Although opinions differ widely, Raymond Brown notes that 'there is wide scholarly agreement that Mark was written in the late 60s or just after 70.' Raymond E. Brown, *An Introduction to the New Testament* (New York: Doubleday, 1996), p. 164.

(b) A second point: certain aspects of the Gospel of Mark indicate trust-worthiness. I will mention just one of them,[10] a point that was recognized early in the history of the church. Notice, for example, these lines from Eusebius:

Mark writes these things, and through him Peter bears witness, for the whole of Mark is said to be a record of Peter's teaching. Note how scrupulously the disciples refused to record those things that might have given the impression of their own fame. Note how they handed down in writing numerous charges against themselves ... which no one in later years would ever have known about unless hearing it from their own voice. By thus honestly reporting their own faults, it is reasonable to view them as relatively void of false speaking and egoism. This habit gives plain and clear proof of their truth-loving disposition. ... If it was their aim to deceive, and to adorn their master with false words, they would never have written these demeaning accounts of his pain and agony and that he was disturbed in spirit, that they themselves forsook him and fled, or that Peter the apostle and disciple who was chief of the apostles denied him three times, unless they had an extraordinarily high standard of truth-telling.[11]

Few scholars now hold, as Eusebius did, that the Gospel writers were all members of 'the twelve', and some doubt that Peter was Mark's main source. Still, Eusebius' central argument holds: unless the evangelists had determined to tell the truth, they would never have recorded events that must have been embarrassing to Peter and the other disciples who were, at the time Mark was written, pillars or recently deceased former pillars of the church. Even if you think (as I do not) that the story in Mark of Peter's denial of Jesus was largely copied or borrowed from earlier sources,[12] it would still constitute an acute embarrassment for the church in the 70s to hear that its leaders behaved as Mark says they did behave before and during passion week.

V

A second way of approaching the question of the reliability of the picture of Jesus painted in the four Gospels is to ask: What did Jesus think of himself? The traditional way of answering this question, especially in the period before

---

[10] Another point, which I do not have space to explore and thus must relegate to a footnote, is that Mark's Jesus says little that seems relevant to many of the burning issues that were facing the Christian churches in the 70s and 80s, which is not what we would expect if Mark were an unreliable product of that period. For example, there is little or nothing in the Gospels about whether male Gentile converts to Christianity should be circumcised, the proper use of charismatic gifts, and Docetic or proto-Gnostic christologies.

[11] Eusebius, *The Proof of the Gospel* (ed. W. J. Ferrer), vol. I (New York: Macmillan, 1920), 3.5.

[12] As Dennis MacDonald apparently argues. See *The Homeric Epics and the Gospel of Mark* (New Haven, CT: Yale University Press, 2000), pp. 22–3.

Reimarus, was simply to quote the christological statements in John's Gospel, for example, 'I and the Father are one' (John 10: 30), or 'Whoever has seen me has seen the Father' (John 14: 9). But many biblical scholars deny that these words constitute the *ipsissima verba* of Jesus. These statements, and the many other high christological statements made about Jesus throughout the Gospels (they say), tell us more about the faith of the early church at the time the Gospels were written than they do about the actual teachings of Jesus.

Is that true? Well, it is clear that the Gospels are statements of faith rather than strictly neutral 'facts-only' biographies of Jesus. (The writer of John even admits as much; see John 20: 31.) It is also true that John's Gospel was the last canonical Gospel written, and thus was the furthest removed from the events it describes. As even the early church recognized, it is a more overtly theological interpretation of Jesus than were the Synoptics. Moreover, if Jesus spoke and taught in Aramaic, then since the New Testament was written in Greek, almost none of the sayings attributed to Jesus in the Gospels constitute his *ipsissima verba*.

Still, a convincing case can be made that much of the material in the Gospels that implies a high christology can in some form be traced back to Jesus. That is, Jesus implicitly claimed the high status that the church attributed to him. That is, he viewed himself as more than a prophet, as more even than the Messiah, or even as more than a 'son of God' (in the sense in which that term was applied to kings and other special men). He was, in some robust sense, conscious of himself as divine, or became conscious of it at some point during his career. I will briefly sketch an argument to this effect in Chapter 6, and try to complete the job in Chapter 9.

It is important to note that Jesus' lofty view of his own aims and vocation best explains why he was crucified. It cannot sensibly be denied that there existed a man Jesus who was crucified, and that he was crucified primarily because of things that he did and said during his public ministry, especially during the last week of his life. It may well be that thinking about that fact is one good way of figuring out what his aims and vocation were. I mention this point because on some current views of Jesus it is not easy to see why some of his contemporaries would get worked up enough about him to want to kill him, let alone succeed. This certainly seems to be to be a problem for the slightly counter-cultural Jesus of the Jesus Seminar who produces pithy religious aphorisms. People might well have taken such a Jesus as something of an eccentric, maybe even as an oddball, but hardly as the kind of person who must be killed.

It can also be argued that the view of Jesus found in the New Testament and the church does a better job than current non-orthodox views of Jesus in explaining the rise of the church. It is obvious that there is a phenomenon called first-century Judaism. There is also a phenomenon called first-century Christianity. Now, how do we get from the one to the other? What exactly is it that explains the rise of faith in Jesus and the existence of the Christian movement? On some contemporary views of Jesus, this constitutes a puzzle in the extreme. But if Jesus really performed miracles, claimed to be divine, and was raised from the dead, an explanation seems close at hand. In other words, perhaps the New Testament does a better job of explaining first-century phenomena than, say, the Gospel of Thomas or Q.

So the argument can be advanced that the best explanation of early Christian worship of Jesus and the propensity to make lofty claims about Jesus is that Jesus himself was at least implicitly conscious of being divine and communicated his awareness of his own vocation and status to his followers. This, at least, is what I will argue in Chapter 9. (I do not claim, of course, that Jesus thought of himself in the creedal terms arrived at centuries later—terms like 'hypostatic union', 'Second Person of the Trinity', etc.) To anticipate: on the basis of arguments like those that I will advance, I believe it can be shown that the view of Jesus found in the New Testament and in the church is largely the correct view of Jesus.

But to return to a point made above, I do not want Christians and non-Christians to get the impression that the historical-critical method is our only source of information about Jesus Christ. There are, of course, many people who hold this view. But for Christians to hold it would spell disaster. What about the teachings of the church? What about the phenomenon that Calvin called the illumination of the Holy Spirit? What about the teachings of one's own mother or pastor? What about one's own experience of Jesus in, say, the Eucharist? I would argue that unless and until somebody shows that those teachings are mistaken, it is rational for Christians to accept them, even if they are not confirmed by historical-critical research.

This indeed would be my solution to a conundrum posed by Rowan Williams.[13] Does the history of Jesus have significance for Christian faith? He and I both reject the roughly Bultmannian line that it has no importance. But, Williams asks, 'If we give to Jesus' history a specific significance for the shaping of belief, how do we avoid the situation where Christians are dependent on the rather chaotic world of New Testament scholarship for guidance on what they must believe and do?' The answer (from the point of view of the believer) is that we have other sources of information about Jesus than the currently assured results of historical scholarship.

---

[13] Rowan Williams, 'Looking for Jesus and Finding Christ', in D. Z. Phillips and Mario von der Ruhr (eds.), *Biblical Concepts and Our World* (London: Palgrave, 2004), p. 146.

As noted above, Christianity is a historical religion. As such, it cannot avoid the messy and imprecise world of history. It must contend with historical issues, and with historians, whether they agree or disagree with Christians. To try to establish Christian claims through historical research alone is futile. Historical-critical research is a very valuable tool; and for historical-critical scholars, it's the only tool they've got, or will allow. Christians claim to have others: communal satisfaction in reading, coherence with tradition, and fit with religious experience. Combine historical research with those three, and you have got a powerful instrument. It might just allow you to look for Jesus and find Christ.

VI

The question of the status or person of Jesus pushes us inevitably towards the resurrection. As I argue later in this book, theologically orthodox scholars have made a powerful case in recent years for the reality of Jesus' resurrection from the dead—indeed, his bodily resurrection.[14] Once it is established that Christians rationally presuppose a world-view called supernaturalism—God exists, created the world, and has the power and interest occasionally to intervene in human history—a strong case can be made for the resurrection. (Supernaturalism is opposed to the naturalism or Deism that many critics of the resurrection presuppose.)

It is important to note that the earliest Christians unanimously and passionately believed that Jesus was alive. This belief sustained the Jesus movement and allowed it to survive and thrive (unlike, say, that of John the Baptist or even Bar-Kochba a century later). This conviction allowed Christians to overcome both the discouragement of their leader's death and their later persecution. Further, the criticisms of the empty tomb tradition and of the appearance stories that are typically given by critics can, in my view, be answered. Finally, opponents of the resurrection face one huge embarrassment: no one has ever produced a plausible naturalistic explanation of what happened after the crucifixion that accounts for all the accepted facts (e.g.

---

[14] See George E. Ladd, *I Believe in the Resurrection of Jesus* (Grand Rapids, MI: Eerdmans, 1975); Gerald O'Collins, S.J., *Jesus Risen* (New York: Paulist Press, 1987); William L. Craig, *Assessing the New Testament Evidence for the Historicity of the Resurrection of Jesus* (Lewiston, NY: The Edwin Mellen Press, 1989), and Stephen T. Davis, *Risen Indeed: Making Sense of the Resurrection* (Grand Rapids, MI: Eerdmans, 1993). More recently, see Richard Swinburne, *The Resurrection of God Incarnate* (Oxford: Oxford University Press, 2003), and N. T. Wright, *The Resurrection of the Son of God* (Minneapolis, MN: Fortress Press, 2003).

Jesus was crucified and died; early Christians believed in the resurrection). None of the explanations that have been suggested—wrong tomb, swoon, hallucination, mistaken identity, myth—have any compelling evidence in their favour, and many are so weak as to collapse of their own weight once spelled out.

So the claim that Jesus really was raised from the dead by God looks to be, for supernaturalists, by far the best explanation of the evidence. (I am not claiming that the resurrection by itself proves authentic all Jesus' words and deeds in the Gospels; this is a separate issue.)

VII

Now, I have discussed only a few out of many important issues that are relevant to the historical Jesus, and them only briefly. But my point is that the study of Jesus, carefully done, can provide a plausible basis for Christian teaching and worship. It is crucial that it do so, since one's views about Jesus Christ are at the heart of the Christianity that one holds. They influence what one will say about virtually every other theological topic—the Trinity, creation, providence, sin, redemption, ethics, ecclesiology, and the sacraments.

Although theologically orthodox Christians must keep their critical faculties alive, they also approach scripture with a hermeneutic of trust. This trust irritates non-believers and radical critics, who see no reason to treat the Bible differently from any other book. But (as Thomas Oden argues[15]) if God decides to offer salvation to human beings through Jesus Christ, and if Jesus Christ is primarily mediated to people of later generations via written texts, then it follows that God will not allow the testimony of those texts to be massively misleading or false. There needs to be, and in fact is, a strong link between the Jesus whom we find in the Gospels and the Christ whom we Christians worship.

Let us return to our imaginary astronaut who visits me in my office and wants to know about Christianity. Again, I would begin my part of the conversation as follows: 'Let me tell you about a person whose name is Jesus.' That is, I would begin by telling stories about Jesus, the same stories that the apostles and their followers told and that have come down to us today. To tell anyone what Christianity is, we must begin with Jesus—with the Jesus who lived in our midst, with the historical Jesus.

---

[15] Thomas Oden, *The Word of Truth* (San Francisco: Harper, 1992), p. 212.

6

·

Jesus Christ: Saviour or Guru?

If my argument thus far has been convincing, we have reason to believe that God exists, that God reveals himself to us, that God is a Trinity, that part of what God reveals is that he wants to reconcile us to him, and that it is pre-eminently through a person named Jesus that he accomplishes our salvation. But Christians want to say more about Jesus than that it is through him that we are reconciled to God. Christians want to say that Jesus is Jesus Christ, the incarnate Son of God. And so we must move on to that part of Christian theology called christology.

One of the most striking texts from the fourth Gospel tells of an encounter between Jesus and a Samaritan woman at a well. It ends with the villagers of Sychar declaring of Jesus: 'we have heard for ourselves, and we know that this is indeed the Saviour of the world' (John 4: 42). I believe these villagers were correct; I too hold that Jesus is the Saviour of the world. I will now try to show why.

Although I remember as a child hearing some of the stories about Jesus, I first saw myself as one who believed that he was the Saviour of the world after I, as a teenager, encountered Jesus in a conversion experience. As I began to read the Bible, listen to sermons, and speak with other Christians, I remember forming the definite impression that Jesus must have been an extraordinary person. There were several reasons for this impression.

First, I remember being convinced that Jesus must have been an attractive person who had a flair for leadership and an aura of charisma. Like most strong leaders, he must have been a great polarizer of people—they seem in the Gospels either to love him and follow him loyally or else to hate him and plot against him. He does not seem to have been the sort to inspire neutrality.

Secondly, I remember thinking that Jesus must have been an enigma to many of his contemporaries. He must have struck people as being strangely different from other folk; they could not figure him out or place him in a category. Once, when some hardened temple officers were sent by the authorities to arrest him, they were dumbfounded by his words. They returned to their superiors, gasping, 'No man ever spoke like this man!' (John 7: 32–46).

Thirdly, I remember noting that Jesus seemed a loving, concerned, compassionate person. The story of Jesus and Zacchaeus (Luke 19: 1–10) is one of the earliest that I remember hearing about Jesus, and it made a deep impression on me, even as a child, that the Son of God would make friends with an ostracized tax collector. Jesus' love extended to all sorts of people, rich and poor, educated and ignorant, righteous and sinful, sophisticated and crude. I remember feeling how strange and unexpected it was that the Lord seemed to love and accept all the people he met, just the way they were, even his deepest enemies.

Fourthly, I remember being impressed with Jesus' apparent facility for changing people. Almost nobody met Jesus and remained the same as before. Some changed for the better: Peter, an ignorant fisherman, became the courageous leader of the church. Saul, a persecutor of Christianity, met Jesus in a vision on the road to Damascus and became Paul, the greatest missionary and theologian the church has known. Others changed for the worse: the man whom we call the rich young ruler came to Jesus anxiously seeking salvation, but left him rejecting salvation when he learned how dearly it would cost (Matt. 19: 16–22). An obscure man named Judas, who would otherwise be long forgotten today, met Jesus, made a decision, and became infamous for an act of betrayal that history will never forget.

I count myself as one of those whom Jesus has changed. I am convinced that I was once on a wrong path that was leading nowhere and that in Christ I found the right path. I have a strong sense of having been created, guided, forgiven, and redeemed by God in Christ; that, I suppose, is much of what makes me a Christian and engenders my interest in christology.

Soon after my conversion, I joined a church of a mainline Protestant denomination. (I am now an ordained minister in the direct historical descendant of that same denomination.) As a member of that denomination, broad and inclusive as it was and is, I soon became aware of theological pluralism. Lots of theological options were available. People interpreted the Bible differently. How should one decide what to believe?

II

Even more than in those innocent days, we live today in a time of theological pluralism. Many Christian theologies are available today, and many christologies. However, it seems to me that all the available christological options can be divided into two categories, what I will call maximal and minimal christologies. A maximal christology accepts and presupposes (even though it may struggle with) the classical doctrine of the incarnation from Nicaea and Chalcedon (i.e. Christ is 'truly divine and truly human' and 'two natures in one person'). A minimal christology does not presuppose or accept this notion and indeed is usually offered as an alternative to it.

Many (not all) minimal christologies seem to me to revolve around at least some of the following six points.[1]

(1) The Bible is a wholly, or at least primarily, human book. No doctrine of biblical inspiration or trustworthiness is accepted; the Bible (it is said) should be treated like any other ancient text.

(2) A great variety of distinct and inconsistent christologies can be found in the New Testament, but the classical doctrine of the incarnation is not one of them. In addition, some sort of quasi-evolutionary explanation is given of the rise of 'high' Johannine christology and of the classical doctrine.

(3) The classical doctrine of the incarnation is incoherent. On purely logical grounds it is to be rejected.

(4) There never has been a universally accepted christology in the church. What we find in the history of the church is the same kind of christological pluralism that exists in the New Testament. As John Hick says, 'there is nothing that can be called the Christian doctrine of the incarnation.'[2]

(5) The classical doctrine of the incarnation should be rejected not only because of its logical incoherence, but also because it has had dire pragmatic consequences; it has, for example, helped foster Christian exclusivism vis-à-vis other religions, or male domination of women, or anti-Semitic attitudes.

(6) Accordingly, what the New Testament writers say or were trying to say about Jesus can best be captured via a minimal christology.

Naturally, the christology proposed can take many shapes, but nearly always the humanity and the teachings of Jesus are stressed. In fact, some minimal christologists like to claim ownership, as it were, over the humanity of Jesus;

---

[1] I do not claim that all contemporary minimal christologists accept all six of these points or even that any one minimal christologist accepts all of them exactly as stated. Naturally, each minimal christology has its own themes and emphases and differs from the others in striking ways.

[2] John Hick, 'Is There a Doctrine of the Incarnation?', in Michael Goulder (ed.), *Incarnation and Myth: The Debate Continued* (Grand Rapids, MI: Eerdmans, 1979) (hereinafter *Incarnation and Myth*), p. 48.

maximal christologies, they sometimes imply, always entail some form of Docetism. Jesus is said to be a man who perfectly reflects the presence of God, or a man who is uniquely chosen by God to express and symbolize God's love for us, or a man gifted by God with love and wisdom and self-sacrifice, or a man whose exemplary life and unparalleled teachings still inspire men and women to live godly lives and to alter oppressive structures of society.

In sketching my own christology, I try to reply to many (but, for lack of space, not all) of the criticisms that minimal christologists have raised against the classical doctrine of the incarnation. In the concluding section of this chapter, I mention the deepest reason I have for rejecting minimal christology.

III

In AD 451 the Council of Chalcedon declared that Jesus Christ is

at once complete in Godhead and complete in manhood, truly God and truly man, consisting also of a rational soul and body; of one substance with the Father as regards his Godhead, and at the same time of one substance with us as regards his manhood; like us in all respects, apart from sin; ... one and the same Christ, Son, Lord, Only-begotten, recognized in two natures, without confusion, without change, without division, without separation; the distinction of natures being in no way annulled by the union, but rather the characteristics of each nature being preserved and coming together to form one person and subsistence.[3]

This is the dogma I have been calling the classical doctrine of the incarnation. It constituted something of a consensus in Christendom from the time of Chalcedon until recently. Some aspects of what the fathers were trying to say are difficult to grasp, especially for us today. The concepts from Greek ontology that form the metaphysical underpinnings of the doctrine are particularly intractable. Few people today have any idea what a 'hypostatic union' is (this is the term that is typically used for the unity of divinity and humanity in Christ); the many subtle ancient uses of the word 'substance' are now almost impossible to sort out and explain to non-experts; and even the one important metaphysical term that we recognize, 'person', was used by the fathers in a different way from the way we use it.

Nevertheless, the main idea that the fathers were driving at is quite simple. It is that Jesus Christ is one person who is truly divine and truly human. That

---

[3] Henry Bettenson (ed.), *Documents of the Christian Church*, 2nd edn. (London: Oxford University Press, 1960), p. 73.

is, Jesus Christ is one person with two natures, a divine nature and a human nature. The natures are neither confused nor separated in him. Nor are they merged or amalgamated—divinity and humanity are far too different for that. Nor are the two joined so as to convert the one into the other—that cannot happen either. Nor are they fused so as to produce a third, or hybrid, nature. The two are united in the person of Jesus Christ 'without confusion, without change, without division, without separation'.

Notice that the classical doctrine is primarily negative. It makes no attempt to explain, for example, how one person can have two natures (let alone a divine and a human nature); it merely insists that this characterizes Jesus Christ. The mystery, the paradox, of the incarnation stands unresolved. What the fathers did, I believe, was set a boundary. Certain heresies and errors (adoptionism, Docetism, Ebionism, Arianism) are ruled out; any christology that affirms that Jesus Christ is 'truly divine and truly human' and has 'two natures in one person' is allowed.

Should the classical doctrine still be believed by Christians today? I believe it should. Of course, like any exercise in theology (which is, after all, a human discipline), the words of the fathers at Chalcedon are fallible. They can never have scriptural authority for Christians. Thus, we must leave open the possibility that some theologian will find a doctrine superior to the classical doctrine. As for me, however, I do not believe any past theologian has done so, and I doubt that any current or future theologian will do so either. I confess to believing that the church was led to the classical doctrine by the Holy Spirit. As I argue later, the theological costs are far too high if we deny either the divinity or the humanity of Christ's person.

IV

My early impressions of Jesus (mentioned earlier) and the classical doctrine of the incarnation defined at Chalcedon were based upon what we might call a pre-critical reading of the four Gospels. But one of the facts of our age is that the Gospels are subject to rigorous and searching historical-critical scholarship. Surely this fact is the single most important factor distinguishing Christian faith in the twentieth century from Christian faith in, say, the fifth or the sixteenth century. All those who intend to do christology today must first make their peace with the historical-critical study of the New Testament.

My own view is that the historical-critical study of the Bible is to be strongly encouraged. I have no problem with the various methods New Testament scholars have been using to illuminate biblical texts—source criticism, form criticism, redaction criticism, canonical criticism, and so on. I have no doubt that such methods are both helpful and necessary. I am not a defender of the theory that the Bible is 'inerrant'; the Gospels contain inconsistencies that I am quite unable to harmonize sensibly. I do, however, hold a 'high' view of scriptural authority and reliability.[4] Accordingly, I am suspicious of many of the more radical conclusions some historical-critical scholars have been reaching about the Gospels.

1. One of the reasons for my disquiet concerns what appears to be a near axiom of contemporary Gospel scholarship. It can be expressed like this: what we encounter in the Gospels is not Jesus himself (i.e. the actual events as they occurred, say, in AD 29 or 30), but the Christian church's understanding of Jesus, say, in the 70s or 80s or 90s, when these books were receiving final form; ergo, many of the events recorded in these books did not occur as described. Is this axiom worthy of belief? Well, part of it surely is. I have no difficulty accepting the idea that the Gospels are indeed expressions of the faith of the Christian church and that accordingly we do indeed come into contact there with the consciousness of the church at the time they were written. But what I do not see is how that fact entails that in the Gospels we do not also come into contact with Jesus himself, with events that occurred in AD 29 or 30.

The point can be generalized. In reading any historian's work about any figure or period of history, we do naturally enough come into contact with the consciousness of the historian at the time the work was written. But surely if the historian has done a worthwhile job of writing history, we also come into contact with the person or period written about. I do not wish to be interpreted as claiming that the Gospels are entirely or even primarily works of history. Nevertheless, I believe these books bring us into contact with Jesus himself, that is, with what he said and did.

2. A second reason for my disquiet about some of the more radical conclusions of contemporary New Testament scholarship concerns the unity of the New Testament. Reacting against an almost a priori assumption of biblical unity in the so-called 'biblical theology' movement of a few decades ago, some contemporary biblical scholars seem to me to have gone overboard in the other direction. They seek contradictions in the Bible with inquisitorial zeal; they label as laughably unsophisticated any attempt at harmonization of two apparently inconsistent texts; one sometimes feels it is considered almost *uncouth* to use a text, for example, from the fourth Gospel to illuminate a Pauline text, or vice versa; and it seems to be assumed that there is almost no such thing as 'the New Testament view' of this or that.

---

[4] For details see Stephen T. Davis, *The Debate About the Bible: Inerrancy Versus Infallibility* (Philadelphia: Westminster Press, 1977). But see also Chapters 15 and 16 of the present book.

The issue of biblical unity and disunity becomes relevant to my concerns in this chapter at the point of the contemporary insistence that many christologies exist in the New Testament. It is now frequently held that the New Testament contains many competing and mutually inconsistent interpretations of Jesus, that harmonization is impossible, and that accordingly no one orthodox biblical christology is normative for all believers.

Once again (in my opinion), some of this is right and some is wrong. Surely there are different christological emphases in various New Testament texts, and facile harmonization should be avoided because it can cause us to miss the richness and variety of christology in the New Testament. We need to respect the differences among the portraits and interpretations of Jesus. However, I believe that the various interpretations are mutually consistent, are best seen as related insights that developed about Jesus among different persons and communities, and are best expressed in terms of the classical doctrine of the incarnation. It is, I think, a telling fact that many theologians from the second century (e.g. Ignatius) onward, most of whom were presumably not obtuse, were sufficiently impressed by the unity of the various New Testament pictures of Jesus to claim strongly that they can be synthesized in the notion of incarnation.

Furthermore, it seems to me evident that what might be called a 'New Testament picture of Jesus' does exist. Despite differences of emphasis, all the New Testament texts seem to agree on various crucial points about Jesus. As Arthur Wainwright has convincingly argued, the Gospels agree (a) that Jesus is uniquely related to God; (b) that Jesus is the unique revealer of God; (c) that Jesus is Saviour; (d) that Jesus has certain personal characteristics (e.g. strength of purpose, compassion, obedience to God); (e) that Jesus is teacher; and (f) that Jesus is identical with the risen Christ.[5]

3. A third reason for my disquiet about some of the conclusions of contemporary New Testament scholarship concerns the life of Jesus. A rough and fuzzy, but nevertheless real, consensus about the life of Jesus seems to emerge among the more radical New Testament scholars. Here are the main facts many of them would claim we can know about Jesus: he was a first-century Palestinian Jew from Nazareth who conducted a ministry of preaching, teaching, and healing; he became a public figure; under the influence of Jewish apocalyptic thinking he preached the kingdom of God and came into conflict with leading Jewish groups such as the Pharisees and Sadducees; though ministering mainly in Galilee, he eventually came to Jerusalem, where he was arrested, tried, and crucified; some time later his disciples began preaching that he had been raised from the dead and was alive.

---

[5] Arthur Wainwright, *Beyond Biblical Criticism: Encountering Jesus in Scripture* (Atlanta: John Knox Press, 1960), pp. 22–33.

I have no difficulty accepting that these are facts; I am quite prepared to do so. My difficulty comes in seeing how anybody can claim that this is *all* (or almost all) that we can know about Jesus. I have never been able to understand how these minimum facts can be sufficient to explain the existence of the Christian church and the traditions about Jesus that we find in the New Testament and in the early church. Why, for example, would anyone hold that the relatively innocuous figure described here was God incarnate? Surely scholars are rationally obligated to posit a 'life of Jesus' that would go at least some way towards explaining why the church so quickly arrived at notions such as sinlessness, pre-existence, divine sonship, and unity with God. Surely more needs to be said about Jesus than what is said in the consensus just described.

4. A fourth reason for my disquiet follows immediately from the third. It concerns the intense speculation about the sources of and influences on New Testament christology. Some scholars seem strongly committed to the assumption that Jesus was an entirely human figure and that notions such as pre-existence and divinity were arrived at years later through a long and complicated quasi-evolutionary process primarily involving embellishments in the tradition due to the influence of other cultures and religions. A mere Jewish prophetic teacher who was deeply committed to God eventually became a pre-existent being, ontologically one with God.

The minimum point to be made here is that those who argue for some such scenario have yet to make a compelling case. Despite the best efforts of certain scholars to find pre-Christian parallels to and influences on the classical doctrine (and some such efforts surely merit high marks for imaginativeness), no assured parallels and influences have been found. Even if parallels were located, the assumption of extensive pagan syncretistic influence on pre-Pauline christology seems to me implausible in the extreme.

Keep in mind that I am trying to criticize not the current state of New Testament scholarship on christology but its extremes. One need only read some of the attempts to explain how the church so quickly arrived at the high christology of the kenosis hymn (Phil. 2: 5–11) or at Johannine Christology—attempts written by people unprepared to accept those christologies—to grasp my point. Some scholars do indeed point to the influence that other religions or religious movements had on early Christians in order to solve this mystery, do they not?[6]

---

[6] A remarkable example of this sort of effort, but not by any means the only one, is Michael Goulder's second essay in John Hick (ed.), *The Myth of God Incarnate* (Philadelphia: Westminster Press, 1977), pp. 64–86.

The stronger point, however, is that nowhere in the New Testament or in any of the sources or layers of tradition that supposedly antedate and influence it has any scholar discovered a purely human Jesus. Scholars such as C. F. D. Moule, Martin Hengel, N. T. Wright, and others have convincingly argued that even the most elevated christological notions are very old indeed. Hengel, for example, argued that the title 'Son of God', understood in a theologically robust way (and not just as a term applied to Israel's kings and other exalted men), was applied to Jesus between AD 30 and 50.[7] Moule argued that some of the 'highest' christology in the New Testament is present, either explicitly or by implication, in the Pauline epistles, the earliest datable documents in the New Testament.[8]

5. A fifth reason for my disquiet concerns the frequently made claim that the early Christians were quite blasé about the facts of Jesus' life; what they were interested in was not history but proclaiming the kerygma; the only facts about Jesus that were preserved were those that furthered the evangelistic, liturgical, or apologetic ends of the church. But this assumption seems to me both a priori improbable and irreconcilable with the evidence. It is a priori improbable because the people who believed in Jesus, or were being encouraged to believe in Jesus, would naturally have been quite curious about what he said and did. It is irreconcilable with the obvious and intense interest the early church had in writing gospels, especially in writing detailed Passion narratives. The four Gospels record all manner of items about Jesus that seem, as far as I can tell, unrelated to the needs and language of the church in the second half of the first century. Jesus, for instance, regularly spoke of himself as the 'Son of Man'. But early Christians found that title too puzzling to be of much use in communicating their message about him across the Mediterranean world. They proclaimed him rather as the Christ, Lord, and only Son of God.

For these five reasons (and others), I do not share the scepticism that some New Testament scholars today exhibit towards the Gospels. I accept as accurate the basic New Testament picture of Jesus; the documents are faith statements, to be sure, but reliable nonetheless. My method, then, both in this chapter and elsewhere, is to trust the Gospels as reliable witnesses to Jesus except in instances in which there is compelling reason not to do so.

---

[7] Martin Hengel, *The Son of God: The Origin of Christology and the History of Jewish–Hellenistic Religion* (Philadelphia: Fortress Press, 1976), pp. 2, 10. See also Martin Hengel, *Between Jesus and Paul: Studies in the Earliest History of Christianity* (Philadelphia: Fortress Press, 1983), p. 31.

[8] Charles Moule, 'Three Points of Conflict in the Christological Debate', in *Incarnation and Myth* (n. 2 above) p. 137. See also C. F. D. Moule, *The Origin of Christology* (Cambridge: Cambridge University Press, 1977), p. 207.

V

Why would God choose to become incarnate in human flesh? What was the purpose of the incarnation? My own view is that there were three main purposes. First, the incarnation was designed definitively to show us what God is like, especially that God is loving and works for our redemption. Secondly, the incarnation was designed to make it possible for us to come to know God; apart from Jesus Christ, I would claim, people can have only a hazy knowledge of God. Thirdly, the incarnation was designed to defeat all the forces in the world that are God's enemies—forces such as sin, death, suffering, and despair. (I do not claim it would have been impossible for God to have accomplished these ends in any other way than through incarnation. I do claim that incarnation is the route that God chose in order to accomplish them.)

'God became man'—that is the doctrine. If so, the incarnation means first that Jesus Christ is a person—a real, living, human person. Jesus Christ is not an idea, an ideal, an emanation from God, a divine influence, a principle, a lifestyle, or an ethical system. These notions are ruled out because what God became was a human being ('and the word became flesh and dwelt among us' (John 1: 14)).

If God became a *human being*, then we have here the decisive ruling out of all forms of Docetism. Jesus Christ was a man. He had a human body; he got hungry and thirsty and tired (John 4: 6); he was tempted (Matt. 4: 1–11; Heb. 4: 15); he wept when a friend died (John 11: 35); he was not omniscient, expressing at one time ignorance of who had touched his garment (Mark 5: 30) and at another time of the date of the Parousia (Mark 13: 32); lastly, he died (Mark 15: 36).

But if it is *God* who became a human being, then we also have here the decisive ruling out of all Arianism. Jesus was a man, but not a mere man, not a man *simpliciter*, not even an exalted man. He was a man who was also God. (Arius himself would have denied that Jesus was merely human; nevertheless, I will use the term 'Arianism' to mean views that deny the full divinity of Christ.) But why would anybody want to claim such a bizarre thing as this? Why would anybody want to say Jesus was God incarnate? As a general answer to these questions, Moule said: 'the impact made by Jesus on his own and the next generation was such as precludes an estimate of him as no more than a man.'[9] I agree with this sentiment and wish now to explore what characteristics of Jesus might have led his contemporaries and near contemporaries to such an assessment.

---

[9] Charles Moule, 'A Comment', in *Incarnation and Myth* (n. 2 above), p. 149.

Although I will discuss the matter more thoroughly in Chapter 9, here I will briefly cite four reasons that I believe convinced many such people that Jesus was the divine Son of God.[10] Accepting the Gospel accounts, as I nearly always do, I also find them convincing. Doubtless, none is a strict proof, but all seem to me strong indications.

First, Jesus assumed for himself the divine prerogative of forgiving sins (see Mark 2: 5, 10; Luke 7: 48). All of us as moral agents own the prerogative to forgive sins that have been committed *against us*, but only God (or God incarnate) can forgive sins *tout court*.[11]

Secondly, the intimate, almost blasphemous way Jesus addressed God (often translated 'Abba! Father!'—something perhaps analogous to the English expression 'Papa') indicates at least a uniquely close relationship to God. I suspect the amazement caused by this novel form of address was the reason the church remembered and recorded it.

Thirdly, Jesus spoke 'with authority,' not citing sources or precedents or famous sages. He spoke, not as if he were speaking on behalf of God (he did not say 'Thus says the Lord'), but as if he were God, delivering the truth to human beings. I think it highly significant that Jesus assumed for himself the authority to reinterpret and even overrule the Old Testament law (see Matt. 5: 21–48; Mark 2: 23–8), again something no mere human being could have done.

Fourthly, Jesus claimed to be divine, and his earliest interpreters accepted that claim. I recognize that it is a commonplace of much contemporary New Testament scholarship that the historical Jesus (as opposed to the Jesus of the Gospels) said remarkably little about himself—what he spoke about (so it is said) was not himself, but about God. Apart from an a priori assumption that Jesus simply could not have said such things, I see no rational way of ruling out as inauthentic Jesus' claim to be 'the Christ, the Son of the Blessed' (Mark 14: 61–2), which the high priest took to be blasphemy. I will explore this point more thoroughly in Chapter 9. But apart from an ideology that says that no such strong statements can be authentic, I see no good reason to deny the authenticity of these sorts of statements. Notice also such typical Pauline affirmations of Jesus' robust divine sonship and incarnation as Romans 1: 3–4; 8: 3; Galatians 4: 4; 1 Thessalonians 1: 10.

---

[10] I will not cite as reasons the facts (so I consider them) that Jesus performed miracles, predicted the future, and was raised from the dead. These are important considerations, but the other reasons I will cite are more compelling.

[11] The situation is slightly more nuanced than this. Christians believe, for example, that God granted the church the right to forgive sins (John 20: 22–3), although I understand this as the right confidently to declare that *God has forgiven* a sin that has sincerely been confessed and repented of.

Does the New Testament actually teach that Jesus was God incarnate? Frances Young (in an early essay) and Don Cupitt have said no.[12] They admit that it teaches Jesus' divine sonship, pre-existence, nearness to God, mission from God, and eschatological return as judge; Jesus is God's chosen agent, a transcendent human being—but not God incarnate. Surely these two scholars are being contentious. Where in the New Testament do we find the claim that Jesus is (merely) 'a transcendent human being'? Although few people want to claim that Jesus went about saying 'I am God' (and I surely do not claim he did so), there are places in the New Testament where Jesus' status as God incarnate is evidently being affirmed, for example, John 1: 1, 18; 20: 28, 31; Philippians 2: 6–7; Colossians 1: 15–19; 2: 9; 1 John 5: 20.[13] (Depending on how one solves the textual problem, Heb. 1: 8 might be included; and depending on how one solves the grammatical problem, Titus 2: 13 might be included.)

Furthermore, I argue that the best way for God's aims in the incarnation (already discussed) to be achieved would be for Jesus to be 'fully divine and fully human'. First, why should Jesus have been 'fully human'? For the following reasons: (1) Pure God in our midst would only dazzle and frighten us; we would not understand what God wanted to show us or say to us unless God were at least partially veiled, incognito (Exodus 33: 20). (2) God wanted to declare as fully as possible his love for us and solidarity with us; the incarnation means that our fate is intimately (rather than remotely) tied to God; because he was fully involved and immersed in human weakness, Jesus Christ can empathize with us and be our redeemer (Heb. 2: 17–18; 5: 2; 4: 15). (3) God cannot die. Accordingly, Docetism in any form is unacceptable.

Secondly, why should Jesus have to be 'fully divine'? There are three reasons which, when taken together as a kind of cumulative case, answer this question. (1) We human beings are incapable of saving ourselves. If we are to be reconciled to God, God must do the reconciling. (2) We human beings cannot defeat death. If death is to be overcome (along with God's other enemies), God must do the overcoming. (3) If Jesus were a mere human being, he would in the end amount to nothing more than a great religious hero or genius

---

[12] Don Cupitt, 'Professor Stanton on Incarnational Language in the New Testament', in *Incarnation and Myth* (n. 2 above), pp. 167–8; and Frances Young, 'The Finality of Christ', in *Incarnation and Myth* (n. 2 above), p. 179.

[13] Since the title 'Son of God' appears in some of the texts I have just cited, I should point out that there are many places, especially in the Old Testament, where this term is a title for a king of Israel or some other exalted personage and has nothing to do with any notion of incarnation. When the title is applied to Jesus in the New Testament, however, it is often perfectly clear that something much more theologically robust is intended. This is in part revealed by the use of the terms 'only Son of God' or 'only begotten Son of God' (John 1: 18; 3: 18).

among all the others. Like all prophets, he would be fallible. There is in my opinion no compelling reason to believe or follow one guru rather than another apart from purely subjective ones ('My guru speaks to me; your guru leaves me cold'). Some gurus of course speak the truth, but even they teach truth that is not intimately connected to their person or personal authority. Even the opponents of incarnation recognize that if Jesus is God incarnate there is a non-gainsayable finality about him and his path to God. Accordingly, denial of the incarnation of Jesus is unacceptable.

VI

Let me now consider briefly three implications of the christology I hold (and will develop more fully and defend in Chapters 9 and 10).

1. I promised earlier to mention the deepest reservation I have about all forms of minimal christology. Minimal christology would be a perfectly acceptable theological option, in my opinion, if Christianity were at heart an ethical system and if the Pelagian notion that we can save ourselves by hard spiritual effort were true. But Christianity is not primarily an ethical system. It involves an ethic, to be sure. But at heart it is a set of beliefs and deeds that form our feeble response to a surprising and quite undeserved act of infinite love that God has performed on our behalf.

We are not able to save ourselves, no matter how hard we try. The Protestant Reformers were quite correct on that point. We are in bondage, and the Jesus of minimal christology is anything but the (or even a) redeemer from bondage. Of course we do desperately need spiritual teachers these days, and we do desperately need supreme examples of openness to God; minimal christology provides both. Yet in truth we need far more than this: we do not need a guru, but we need a saviour. The classical doctrine of the incarnation, recognizing as it does that Christianity is a religion of grace, provides this. That is to me the deepest reason why it should be preferred to all versions of minimal christology.

2. John Hick said: 'If Christ was (literally rather than metaphorically) God incarnate, it would seem clear that the religion which he founded must be intended to supersede all other religions.'[14] Here Hick is surely correct. If the classical doctrine is correct, then doubtless Jesus is, after all, 'the way, and the truth, and the life' (John 14: 6), and doubtless it is true that 'there is

---

14 John Hick, 'A Response to Hebblethwaite', in *Incarnation and Myth* (n. 2 above), p. 194.

salvation in no one else' (Acts 4: 12). The incarnation is of cosmic rather than local significance, in my view; any human being who is reconciled to God is reconciled through Christ. One of the main objections global theologians have to absolutistic interpretations of Christianity is that these interpretations imply that non-Christians are 'outside the sphere of salvation'. That of course does not follow. The view that no non-Christian can be saved is not taught in the Bible (people like Abraham, Hagar, and Jeremiah were hardly Christians); few Christians of even a conservative persuasion hold it; nor do I hold it.[15]

Christianity is a metaphysical and theological system, not a set of discrete gems of heavy spiritual wisdom from which we can pick and choose. (The same can be said, I suspect, about most of the other religions of the world.) So the emerging discipline known as global theology is, in my opinion, untoward. To attempt a syncretistic amalgamation of the 'best insights' of various equally valid and valuable religious systems is ill-advised.

3. In the New Testament a strong connection is made between Jesus' status as Son of God and his resurrection from the dead (see Rom. 1: 3–4.). We live in a world in which messiahs, gurus, and holy people proliferate. In such a world, how can we know whom to believe? Which messiah is the true Messiah? Paul's answer (through Luke) to the Athenian philosophers was that Jesus is the man whom God has appointed and 'of this he has given assurance to all men by raising him from the dead' (Acts 17: 31). Many messiahs have commanding personalities. Many gurus are full of spiritual wisdom. Many holy people recommend noble lifestyles. But none of them has been resurrected from the dead.[16]

Of course Jesus is not the only person ever to have been raised from the dead. Others (Lazarus, the daughter of Jairus) are mentioned in the Bible. Such stories appear in other religions too, and perhaps some of them are true. I am willing to believe that God performs miracles in other contexts than the Christian context. But these raisings were of an entirely different character from Jesus'. These people were restored to their former earthly life; they were resuscitated. Jesus was transformed into what Paul calls a glorified body. He was raised never to die again. He lives today. He was resurrected. In my opinion, Jesus is the only person in the history of the world ever to have been resurrected from the dead.

---

[15] My own views on this subject are more fully developed in Stephen T. Davis, 'Evangelicals and the Religions of the World', *The Reformed Journal*, 31 (June, 1981), pp. 9–13.

[16] The resurrection is not a rigorous proof of the incarnation. God could cause a mere human to be not merely resuscitated but resurrected. But Christians have always taken the resurrection as a kind of vindication of Jesus, a sign rather than a proof of the truth of Christian claims about him.

If Jesus had not been raised, Christianity would not exist today. He would have ended up a fine teacher of religion and ethic—like Socrates or Gandhi, perhaps—but not the Saviour of the world. I believe the resurrection was God's way of pointing at Jesus and saying: He is the one you are to believe. He is the Saviour. He is Lord.[17] The resurrection of Jesus from the dead was a graphic way for God to repeat what the villagers of Sychar had said about him: 'This is indeed the Savior of the world.'[18]

---

[17] My own views on the resurrection are more fully developed in Stephen T. Davis, *Risen Indeed: Making Sense of the Resurrection* (Grand Rapids, MI: Eerdmans, 1993).

[18] I would like to thank Thomas V. Morris and John Schneider for their helpful comments on an earlier draft of this chapter.

7

Was Jesus Raised Bodily?

I

We must explore one crucial fact about the Christian Church's view of Jesus, and that is its conviction that God raised him from the dead. No christology that omits that point makes any sense. I will not argue in this book in favour of the claim that God raised Jesus from the dead, although I have done so elsewhere.[1] I want to explore the nature and meaning of the resurrection. I will begin with the traditional claim that Jesus' resurrection was a bodily resurrection.

The claim that Jesus was raised bodily seems firmly embedded in Christian tradition. For example, the Creed of Epiphanius (c. 374) says, 'The same Christ also suffered in his flesh; and he arose and ascended into heaven in that very body.' The Second Council of Lyon (1274) declares, 'The third day he rose from the dead by a true resurrection of the body. With the body of his resurrection and with his soul, he ascended into heaven on the fortieth day after the resurrection.' The Second Helvetic Confession (1561) says, 'We believe and teach that the same Jesus Christ our Lord, in his true flesh in which he was crucified and died, rose again from the dead, and that not another flesh was raised other than the one buried, or, that a spirit was taken up instead of the flesh, but that he retained his true body.' Finally, the Westminster Confession of Faith (1646) states, 'On the third day he rose from the dead, with the same body in which he suffered; with which also he ascended into heaven, and there sitteth on the right hand of his Father.'

But we live in an age when many theologians, biblical scholars, and clergy are expressing doubts about the notion that Jesus was bodily raised. Such doubts usually revolve around apparent inconsistencies in the New Testament accounts of Jesus' resurrection, around views about the dating of those accounts, or around claims that the concept of bodily resurrection is

---

[1] Stephen T. Davis, *Risen Indeed: Making Sense of the Resurrection* (Grand Rapids, MI: Eerdmans, 1993) (hereinafter *Risen Indeed*). See also N. T. Wright, *The Resurrection of the Son of God* (Minneapolis, MN: Fortress Press, 2003) and Richard Swinburne, *The Resurrection of God Incarnate* (Oxford: Oxford University Press, 2003).

outmoded, old-fashioned, incredible, or the like. Some denials of bodily resurrection seem motivated by a desire to lessen or at least de-emphasize the miraculous aspect of the Easter story or by a desire to render it immune to the criticisms of historical-critical scholarship. In this chapter, I will explore such claims. Again, I will not ask here whether it is rational to believe that Jesus rose from the dead (in some form or other); I will simply assume that Jesus rose from the dead and ask whether it is rational to believe that he rose *bodily*. I will argue that it is rational to believe that Jesus bodily rose and that Christians ought to continue to affirm it.

But first I will explain briefly what I take to be the various possible views that are or might be held by contemporary Christians on the question of Jesus' resurrection. All four of the following theories have their contemporary defenders among Christians (although the first, to my knowledge, is not advocated by any scholar or theologically sophisticated Christian).

1. *Bodily resuscitation*. This theory affirms that Jesus was indeed genuinely dead and later genuinely alive, that the tomb of Jesus was empty, that Jesus' physiologically identical body was restored in the resurrection to the same sort or condition of life that it experienced before the crucifixion, and that Jesus' resurrection body had the same properties as it did before his death. The resurrection, in effect, prolonged his once-interrupted life.

2. *Bodily transformation*. This theory also affirms that Jesus was genuinely dead and later genuinely alive and that the tomb was empty, but it denies that Jesus was restored to the kind of life he experienced earlier. In the resurrection, his earthly body was transformed into a new 'glorified body' that was indeed physical, but possessed strange new properties. There was continuity between the old body and the new body, but the new body was no longer as bound by certain of the laws of nature as was the old. (Whenever I use the term 'bodily theories of the resurrection', I am referring to theories 1 and 2.)

3. *Spiritual resurrection*. This theory also affirms that Jesus was genuinely dead and later genuinely alive, but it does not necessarily affirm that the tomb was empty. The idea is that what was raised was Jesus' spirit or soul or self, quite apart from his body. His bones might still be decomposing in Palestine, but nevertheless he lives. Now, there are many ways in which the concept of spiritual resurrection can be interpreted; perhaps the most natural is to view it in terms of a sort of Platonic body–soul dualism.[2] Subsequently I will explore this point further, but here I would simply note that there are several theories

---

[2] As William L. Craig says, 'With all the best will in the world, it is extremely difficult to see what is the difference between an immaterial, unextended, spiritual "body" and the immortality of the soul.' See his 'The Bodily Resurrection of Jesus', in R. T. France and D. Wenham (eds.), *Gospel Perspectives*, vol. i (Sheffield: JSOT Press, 1980), p. 64.

that fall between bodily transformation and spiritual resurrection. One theory says that the tomb was empty and had to be so, that no corpse of Jesus was to be found there or elsewhere, that what was raised was Jesus' *person* but not his body. Another theory says that the tomb was empty and that Jesus' resurrection body was physical but that this body had no physical continuity with Jesus' pre-mortem body.

4. *Reductive Resurrection Theories*. These theories in effect deny that Jesus was genuinely dead and later genuinely alive; accordingly, no claim need be made about the tomb being empty. The resurrection appearances of Jesus are explained psychologically, in terms of the disciples' inner states of mind. The appearances are called visions, subjective visions, or even hallucinations. What 'Jesus is risen' really means, advocates of such theories say, is something like, 'The cross of Jesus has saving efficacy today' or 'Jesus' work goes on' or 'The source of my faith is Jesus.' I call such views *reductive* because they deny, or at least do not necessarily involve, the claim that a dead man lived again.

Except for a few concluding comments, I will largely ignore reductive theories here. What I want to do is argue that those Christians who affirm a genuine resurrection ought to affirm the second theory, bodily transformation. That is, I will argue against bodily resuscitation and spiritual resurrection in favour of bodily transformation.

II

It is fascinating that the bodily resuscitation theory is so frequently and vehemently attacked. It is hard to understand exactly who is being criticized; perhaps some unlettered believers accept this view, but, as noted earlier, I am aware of no scholar who defends it (for reasons that I will mention momentarily). Perhaps the reason for the frequent attacks on this theory is that some who advocate either spiritual resurrection or reductive theories believe they have refuted *both* bodily theories of the resurrection once they have refuted bodily resuscitation.

At any rate, bodily resuscitation is an unacceptable theory of the resurrection because (as I will argue) the New Testament does not support it. The proper biblical inference is not that Jesus was restored to his old mode or condition of life (as the Gospels indicate that Lazarus, the daughter of Jairus, and the son of the widow of Nain were), only to die a second time at some later point. Rather, the New Testament suggests that Jesus was raised to a new and exalted condition of life, never to die again. He defeated death once and for all; he was transformed to a glorified condition of life.

Since I have now rejected the first and fourth theories of the resurrection, the main issue of the chapter is to argue on behalf of bodily transformation over spiritual resurrection. So it must be asked at this point exactly what the concept of spiritual resurrection amounts to. This is not an easy question to answer. Theology doubtless has many vague areas, but this is an area where vagueness and imprecision seem commonplace. Theologians who affirm that Jesus was raised, but deny that he was raised bodily, almost never explain exactly what they mean.

As I suggested earlier, the most natural way to interpret spiritual resurrection is in terms of Platonic dualism. The survival-of-death doctrine associated with this theory is usually called 'immortality of the soul'. The basic ideas of this form of dualism (to be discussed further in Chapter 14) are:

- Human beings consist of material bodies and immaterial souls.
- The soul is the essence of the person (i.e. the locus of thought, feeling, personality, etc.).
- During ordinary life the soul is incarnate in or (to use the Platonic metaphor) imprisoned in the body.
- At death the body permanently decays, but the soul escapes to live on because souls are immortal.

It can be doubted that this notion is what Christian advocates of spiritual resurrection have in mind. There are two reasons for this doubt. First, it can easily be shown that biblical notions of human nature are quite unlike Plato's (despite the Bible's frequent use of the word 'soul'). The Bible seems rather to envision human beings as normally in a state of psychosomatic unity; souls are perhaps seen as separable from bodies in some sense (see Matt. 10: 28; 2 Cor. 5: 6–9; Rev. 6: 9; 20: 4), but certainly not in the sense postulated by Platonic dualism. The 'soul' in the Bible is the principle of life; an ensouled person is a whole, living person, existing bodily (Mark 8: 35; Luke 12: 19–20). Secondly, the Bible makes it clear that resurrection is a surprising and unexpected gift of God, not a natural event we should all expect on the grounds that our souls are essentially immortal. Christians affirm that life is a gift from God, as is human nature itself, so it is un-Christian to affirm that once life has been granted by God, one naturally (i.e. without further divine intervention) survives death. In other words, Platonic dualism is not the Bible's view. But if this doctrine is not what advocates of spiritual resurrection have in mind, it is not usually clear what notion of human nature they are suggesting.

To pick one theologian as an example, Hans Küng argues in *On Being a Christian* that the identical *person* rises from the dead, but denies that there is any physiological continuity:

Corporeal resurrection? Yes and no, if I may recall a personal conversation with Rudolf Bultmann. No, if 'body' simply means the physiologically identical body. Yes, if 'body' means in the sense of the New Testament *soma* the identical personal reality, the same self with its whole history. In other words, no continuity of the body: questions of natural science, like that of the persistence of molecules, do not arise. But an identity of the person: the question does arise of the lasting significance of the person's whole life and fate.[3]

This discussion cries out for a precise explanation of what a 'self' or 'person' (quite apart from a 'body') *is*: we need some proposals in the areas of the problems that philosophers call the mind–body problem and the problem of personal identity. And that, I say, is the sort of thing that advocates of spiritual resurrection almost never provide.

Such people are usually quite clear, however, in their rejection of bodily theories of the resurrection. It is often suggested that such theories were plausible in the first century but not today. The implied reason for this suggestion (to put it more bluntly than it would usually be put) is that the people who lived in those days were more credulous, superstitious, or just plain primitive than we are. The idea apparently is that 'modern people' will find some notion of spiritual resurrection far more epistemically palatable than bodily resurrection.

Let me simply ask four questions about this sort of argument:

- If bodily resurrections were so commonly accepted in ignorant times like the first century, why was Jesus' purported bodily resurrection taken to be so significant?

- If bodily resurrections were so commonly accepted, why is it that such ancient folk as the apostle Thomas, the Stoic and Epicurean philosophers whom St. Paul encountered in Athens, and others such as Celsus, Porphyry and Valentinus reacted so negatively to the claim that Jesus was bodily raised?

- Why is it that there are so many otherwise quite rational 'modern people' who have no difficulty in affirming that Jesus bodily rose—people such as Karl Barth, C. S. Lewis, and A. M. Ramsey? Aren't they representative of 'modern people'?

- Does the term 'modern people' then just mean contemporary naturalists or deists—people who don't believe in any God at all, or at least not in an interventionist God?

If the answer to the fourth question is yes, then the claim that 'modern people' can't believe in bodily resurrections is true but not significant. It is true only

---

[3] Hans Küng, *On Being a Christian* (trans. Edward Quinn) (New York: Pocket Books, 1976), p. 351.

because of the way the term 'modern people' is defined—a way that I simply do not accept. Thus the claim is question-begging. But perhaps what the claim amounts to is something like this: some people accept theistic or supernaturalist assumptions (e.g. God exists, God occasionally intervenes in human affairs, etc.) while others do not, and, out of the total population, the percentage of people who do not is higher in the twenty-first century than it was in the first century. Thus *most* modern people, or at least *more people today than in pre-modern times*, find it impossible to believe in bodily resurrection. Is this claim true? I do not know. It *may* be. But surely what must be said here is that Christian theologians ought not to base their formulations on the beliefs of those who reject Christian assumptions. Raymond Brown well reminds us that

the fact that creedal terminology involving bodily resurrection has been found satisfactory for a long time should make us very cautious about change, but even long usage does not render terminology irreplaceable. On the other hand, if a critical modern investigation shows that as far back as we can trace the NT evidence, resurrection from the dead was an intrinsic part of Jesus' victory over death, then the observation that modern man does not find bodily resurrection appealing or meaningful cannot be determinative. Nor...can we allow Christian theology to be shaped by contemporary distrust of the miraculous.[4]

But perhaps critics can raise a more plausible argument than the one that I have been considering about what is palatable to modern people. Perhaps critics of bodily resurrection can more sensibly be construed as trying to explain early Christian talk of Jesus' bodily resurrection in some such way as this: 'Some of the Jews of Jesus' day were expecting a bodily resurrection in the last days; enter Jesus, proclaiming the eschaton; put these two together and you naturally get a strong expectation on the part of Jesus' followers that he had bodily risen.' But it need only be said in response to this that (1) the resurrection accounts in the New Testament make it quite clear that Jesus' disciples were not expecting him to be raised, and (2) Jewish expectation of a *general* resurrection in the eschaton differs greatly from the resurrection of just one person before the eschaton. This notion was not part of Jewish eschatological expectation.

Quite apart from the justifications that some theologians give it, my own view of spiritual resurrection theories is this: it might be possible to arrive at a theory of spiritual resurrection that avoids the theological problems associated with traditional dualism—that is, a theory that (1) is based on a solidly

---

[4] Raymond Brown, *The Virginal Conception and Bodily Resurrection of Jesus* (New York: Paulist Press, 1973) (hereinafter *Virginal Conception*), p. 72.

biblical view of human nature, and (2) entails resurrection as a gift of God rather than a natural event. Moreover, as I will argue in Chapter 14, the philosophical objections that have been raised against immortality in recent years (e.g. by Antony Flew and Terence Penelhum) do not in fact refute it.[5] Some form of spiritual resurrection (assuming it is clearly spelled out and not just vaguely suggested) seems to me a *possible* view of the resurrection. But I nevertheless have biblical reasons for denying that it is the proper Christian interpretation of Jesus' resurrection, to which point I will turn shortly.

III

Let us now look in more detail at bodily transformation. One aspect of this theory is that it must emphasize both continuity and change between Jesus' pre-resurrection and post-resurrection bodies. It must emphasize *continuity*, naturally enough, to ensure that it was Jesus who was resurrected and not someone else (i.e. to ensure that the person who rose was the same person as the person who died). It must emphasize *change* to distinguish itself from bodily resuscitation theories.

Two aspects of the theory provide continuity. First, the person remains the same. Jesus identified himself as Jesus ('It is I myself'—Luke 24: 39); he was recognized by the disciples (albeit at times with difficulty); his memory, character, and personality remained the same, as did many of his bodily characteristics (e.g. the pre-resurrection wounds). Secondly, there is material continuity between the two bodies: the one changes *into* the other (see Rom. 8: 11; 1 Cor. 15: 53; Phil. 3: 20–1). Paul uses the simile of a seed growing into a plant: 'You foolish man! What you sow does not come to life unless it dies. And what you sow is not the body which is to be, but a bare kernel, perhaps of wheat or of some other grain. But God gives it a body as he has chosen, and to each kind of seed its own body' (1 Cor. 15: 36–8). In other words, the relationship of material continuity that obtains between Jesus' earthly body and his resurrection body is like the relationship that obtains between a grain of wheat and the plant that grows from it. Thus Paul's view, both here and elsewhere in his writings, is not, as some critics suggest, the *exchange* of one

---

[5] For the objections, see A. Flew, 'Can a Man Witness His Own Funeral?', *Hibbert Journal*, 54 (1956), pp. 242–50; and T. Penelhum, *Survival and Disembodied Existence* (New York: Humanities Press, 1970). For a reply, see chapter 5 of my *Risen Indeed* (n. 1 above).

sort of body for another; it is that the one body *becomes* or is transformed into the other.[6]

In one way, of course, this is an imperfect analogy: presumably the seed does not in the proper sense of the word *die* (though it does cease existing as a *seed*). If it died, the plant would not emerge. The point, then, is that the seed has within it, so to speak, the power to be radically changed into a new plant-like, rather than seed-like, mode of existence. Still, I take it that the main point of the simile holds—that continuity is preserved because the one changes, through materially contiguous stages, into the other.

Still, change must also be emphasized. Just as the seed of wheat looks, and is, radically different from the plant it becomes, so the ordinary earthly body is radically different from the resurrection body. Again following Paul's argument in 1 Corinthians 15, the old body is subject to decay and death, while the new body is immune to decay and death; the old body is dishonourable, while the new body is honourable; the old body is weak while the new body is powerful; the old body is natural while the new body is spiritual (1 Cor. 15: 42–4).

The apostle goes on to say that 'flesh and blood cannot inherit the kingdom of God, nor does the perishable inherit the imperishable' (1 Cor. 15: 50). This statement is frequently cited by defenders of spiritual or reductive theories of the resurrection against the bodily theories, but I believe they misuse it in doing so. Advocates of bodily transformation can quite sensibly interpret Paul's statement as implying simply that what inherits the kingdom of God is not the old natural body (with its frailty and corruptibility), but rather the transformed resurrection body. Understood this way, Paul's statement is quite consistent with, and indeed tends to confirm, the bodily transformation theory. Furthermore, this interpretation seems entailed by the synonymous parallelism that Paul is clearly using here. The 'cannot inherit' clause is defined by the 'nor does the' clause: Paul is not denying that resurrection bodies are physical, but rather that they are perishable. Indeed, Paul insists that a body (*soma*) is raised, even if it is a 'new' or 'spiritual' body. And the claim that what is perishable (i.e. the old natural body) does not inherit the kingdom is consistent with the bodily transformation theory. Thus, what Paul speaks of here is not a movement from bodily existence to incorporeal existence, but rather a transformation of one sort of body (a frail, corruptible one) into another, superior sort of body.

---

[6] See, e.g., Gerald F. Hawthorne, *Philippians* (Waco, TX: Word Books, 1983), pp. 172–3.

IV

But at this point we encounter a serious difficulty, one that critics of the two bodily theories often use as an argument against them—the apparently quite different and perhaps even inconsistent understandings of the resurrection found in the New Testament. It is often claimed, for example, that Paul, the earliest (and therefore according to many scholars most reliable) of the New Testament writers who deal with the resurrection, presupposes some sort of spiritual theory of the resurrection, whereas the evangelists, and especially Luke and John, presuppose some crudely physicalist theory of the resurrection, invented later for apologetic purposes. It is further claimed that the two sorts of accounts are quite inconsistent.

For example, Gerald O'Collins says,

Paul's notion of transformation through resurrection challenges and criticizes the picture of physical reanimation that the third and fourth gospels seem to offer. In a debate with some Sadducees Jesus likewise denies that resurrection means a return to the existence and activities of this world (Mk. 12:24–7). He indicates that risen life will be a glorified, 'angelic' state (Mt. 13:43). By insisting on the strict accuracy of the physical details in the Gospel narratives of Luke and John, we will flatly contradict the understanding of resurrection proposed by Jesus and Paul.[7]

Raymond E. Brown says,

Paul does not conceive of the risen 'body' in a merely physical way. His comments make us wonder whether he would be in agreement with Luke (who was not an eyewitness of the risen Jesus) about the properties of the risen body. Certainly, from Paul's description one would never suspect that a risen body could eat, as Luke reports. Moreover, Paul distinguishes between the risen body that can enter heaven and 'flesh and blood' that cannot enter heaven—a distinction that does not agree with the emphasis in Luke 24:39 on the 'flesh and bones' of the risen Jesus.[8]

Reginald Fuller speaks pointedly about Luke's story of the encounter of the risen Jesus in Luke 24: 36–49. This account, he says,

Has received a highly apologetic coloring not merely absent from I Cor. 15:5 but quite contrary to it. The motif of doubt . . . has been redirected to provide the occasion for a massively physical demonstration. The Risen One invites his disciples to touch him so that they can see for themselves that he is not a 'spirit' or 'ghost' but a figure of flesh and blood. This new interpretation of the mode of the resurrection (resuscitation of

---

[7] Gerald O'Collins, *What Are They Saying About the Resurrection?* (New York: Paulist Press, 1978), p. 49.

[8] Brown, *Virginal Conception* (n. 4 above), p. 87.

the earthly body) is quite contrary to the apocalyptic framework of the earliest kerygma of I Corinthians 15:5, to Paul's concept of the *pneumatikon soma* (see esp. I Cor. 15:35ff.) and to the presentation in Mark 16:1–8 and in Matthew 28:16–20.[9]

And Willi Marxsen goes so far as to suggest that the inconsistencies in New Testament accounts of the resurrection show that the early Christians just were not interested in the facts about Jesus' resurrection body:

All this forces one ultimately to ask whether the question which interests us today (the resurrection body of Jesus) was simply of no interest at the time? For this is what the picture's lack of unity would suggest. . . . When the evangelists were writing their Gospels, there was no longer a unified view in the primitive church about the mode of the Easter happening. This does not seem to have played the decisive part then which is often ascribed to it today. For if people had been really interested in the mode of the resurrection, this would surely have been depicted in uniform terms.[10]

Do we then have here evidence of two contradictory traditions about the resurrection of Jesus, an earlier spiritual tradition and a later corporeal and heavily apologetic tradition? I do not believe so. Let me say first that there are some apparent inconsistencies in the accounts of Jesus' resurrection appearances that seem exceedingly difficult to harmonize sensibly. But I believe critics are far too hasty to claim that we have such a case here. Let us take a look at the various accounts of the discovery of the empty tomb and of encounters with the risen Jesus, categorize them as 'physical' or 'spiritual', and see what we can say about the problem at hand.

I will call any resurrection appearance 'physical' that either presupposes the empty tomb or implies in some way that Jesus' resurrection body was corporeal (e.g. he walked, he ate, the disciples were encouraged to touch his body, the same wounds were there). And I will call any resurrection appearance 'spiritual' that implies that Jesus' resurrection body had strange new abilities that natural bodies do not have. (We must remember, of course, that the evangelists report Jesus as having some such properties—e.g. the ability to heal diseases—during his earthly ministry.)

If we set out to classify the accounts on this basis, the following texts must clearly count as 'physical', because they claim that the tomb was empty: Matthew 28: 1–8; Mark 16: 1–8; Luke 24: 1–10; and John 20: 1–10. Equally, the following texts must be classified as 'physical': Matthew 28: 9–10, because the disciples 'took hold of his feet'; Luke 24: 13–35, because the two disciples

[9] R. Fuller, *The Formation of the Resurrection Narratives* (Philadelphia: Fortress Press, 1980), p. 115.

[10] W. Marxsen, *The Resurrection of Jesus of Nazareth* (trans. Margaret Kohl) (Philadelphia: Fortress Press, 1979), pp. 68, 75–6.

walked with Jesus on the road to Emmaus, and Jesus broke bread and gave it to them; Luke 24: 36–43, because Jesus encouraged the disciples to see and handle him, and he ate a piece of boiled fish; John 20: 11–18, because Jesus' words to Mary Magdalene—'Do not keep holding me'—seem to imply she could have held him; John 20: 19–25, because Jesus showed the disciples (minus Thomas) his hands and side; John 20: 26–9, because Jesus encouraged Thomas to feel his wounds; and John 21: 1–25, because Jesus gave the disciples bread and fish.

The following texts may be classified as 'spiritual': Luke 24: 13–35 (the road to Emmaus story again), because of the strange way Jesus is said to have 'vanished out of their sight'; John 20: 19–25 and 26–9 (again), because of the emphasis on Jesus appearing in the room despite 'the doors being shut'; and Acts 1: 6–11 (one of Luke's two apparent accounts of the ascension), because of the curious way Jesus is said to have been lifted up into a cloud. Though not an account of an appearance per se, 1 Corinthians 15: 35–7 might be taken to belong in the 'spiritual' camp, because of Paul's already noted emphasis on the differences between earthly bodies and glorified bodies.

There are also three resurrection texts that seem neutral or unclassifiable on the physical–spiritual scheme: Matthew 28: 16–20 (an appearance to the eleven in Galilee); Luke 24: 50–3 (Luke's other apparent account of the ascension, which might be classified as 'spiritual' if we interpret it in terms of the apparently parallel Acts 1: 6–11); and 1 Corinthians 15: 3–11, Paul's list of the resurrection appearances of Jesus.

One of the things that we notice immediately is that 'physical' and 'spiritual' motifs are combined in the third and fourth Gospels, even in the same stories. The two Gospels that are most often criticized by defenders of spiritual resurrection for their 'gross physicalism' are the very Gospels in which 'spiritual' motifs are found.[11] This fact at least constitutes prima facie evidence that no inconsistency exists here. One could, of course, claim that 'physical' and 'spiritual' motifs come from quite different pre-Gospel traditions and were rather clumsily combined by the third and fourth evangelists. But this claim seems entirely improbable. An author does not usually offer as true explicitly inconsistent accounts of events. Unless Luke and John were rather dense people, it seems plausible to suppose that they had in mind an

---

[11] Thus Peter Carnley is wide of the mark when he claims that 'in Luke and John the raised Christ, who is said to have been not only seen but handled, seems hardly different from the historical Jesus of the days before the crucifixion.' See his *The Structure of Resurrection Belief* (Oxford: Oxford University Press, 1987), p. 235. In this regard, see Luke 24: 31 and John 20, 19, 26. In his *What Are They Saying About the Resurrection?* (New York: Paulist Press, 1978), Gerald O'Collins calls attention to the spiritual motifs in Luke and John. See pp. 50–1.

understanding of Jesus' resurrection body that unifies what we are calling the 'physical' and 'spiritual' motifs. (I am not here rejecting redaction criticism or the notion that there are layers of tradition or that there was editing; what I am rejecting is the claim that a purely 'redactional' explanation is adequate in this case.)

My point, then, is that some critics argue that the earliest understanding was that Jesus experienced a non-bodily resurrection, something usually called glorification or exaltation, and that physical views of the resurrection (e.g. those reflected in the third and fourth Gospels) came later. But since Luke and John quite obviously consider the two theories (if they are two separate theories) quite compatible, we can ask (1) whether we have any good reason to believe that one is more primitive than the other, and (2) whether it is possible to arrive at an understanding of Jesus' resurrection body that unifies the 'physical' and 'spiritual' motifs that are present in the texts.

Let me propose a possibility. I suggest we admit that the Gospels are puzzling and attempt to interpret what they say about Jesus' resurrection body in terms of what Paul says in 1 Corinthians 15, which, despite being earlier, does more explicit theologizing about the meaning of the resurrection than do the Gospels. It is well known that Paul's first epistle to the Corinthians was written in response to quite specific problems that the church in Corinth faced. When Paul turned to the resurrection in chapter 15, he was probably speaking to those Corinthian Christians who were influenced by some sort of proto-gnostic tradition and who thought that their resurrection had already taken place at their baptism and who therefore concluded that there was no need for a general, eschatological resurrection.[12] (See 2 Tim. 2: 17–18: 'Among them are Hymenaeus and Philetus, who have swerved from the truth by holding that the resurrection is past already.')

Paul's understanding of the resurrection, which we have already partially discussed, avoids the extremes of both bodily resuscitation and dualistic spiritual resurrection. The resuscitation theory—that resurrected persons are restored to their former condition of life—was present in contemporary Jewish thinking. (See 2 Baruch 50: 2: 'For the earth shall then assuredly restore the dead.... It shall make no change in their form, but as it has received them, so it shall restore them.') Spiritualistic theories were also in the air at Paul's time—Platonic and proto-gnostic body–soul dualisms that held that the soul is imprisoned in the body and at death escapes to live on eternally.

---

[12] See Fuller, *Formation* (n. 9 above), p. 19.

In opposition to both extremes, Paul argues for what I am calling bodily transformation, whereby the natural body is changed into a new 'spiritual body' in such a way that material continuity and personality are preserved. Though Paul nowhere speaks of the resurrection of the *flesh* (he usually, though not quite always, used the term *sarx* to indicate something inherently perishable, weak, and even sinful), it is interesting that Luke seems to do so (see Luke 24: 39: 'See my hands and feet, that it is I myself, handle me, and see; for a spirit has not flesh and bones as you see that I have'). James Moffet argues that Paul's theory constituted

a startling challenge to those who saw no alternative to the 'flesh and blood' resurrection of popular Judaism (which meant the reunion of body and soul), except in some adaptation of the purely immaterial Greek idea. At the heart of Paul's thought is the affirmation that the life of Christians after death must continue to possess the capacities for action and affection, insight and understanding (xiii.12) which in the present body have a real though limited range. The spiritual, in other words, is not the immaterial.[13]

Thus we should not be misled by Paul's use of the term 'spiritual body': he is not using this term to signify a body 'formed out of spirit' or made of 'spiritual matter', whatever that might mean, but rather a *body* that has been glorified or transformed by God and is now fully dominated by the power of the Holy Spirit.[14] The word *soma* itself carries heavy connotations of physicality in Paul, but, more importantly, the word *pneumatikon* does not mean 'non-bodily'. A 'spiritual body' is a person taught, led, and animated by the Holy Spirit (see 1 Cor. 2: 15; 14: 37; Gal. 6: 1).

It is clear that Paul holds a physical view of the resurrection. And the crucial conclusion that can then be drawn is that physical understandings of resurrection are not (as is often charged) late additions to New Testament tradition. The physicalism of Luke and John cannot seriously be dismissed as late, legendary, or apologetic. New Testament resurrection traditions were bodily traditions *at least* as early as Paul.

---

[13] J. Moffet, *The First Epistle of Paul to the Corinthians*, Moffet New Testament Commentary (New York: Harper, 1938), p. 260.

[14] On this point, see Gerald O'Collins, *The Resurrection of Jesus Christ* (Valley Forge, PA: Judson Press, 1973), p. 113; A. M. Ramsey, *The Resurrection of Christ* (London: Fontana Books, 1961), pp. 108–9; and George E. Ladd, *I Believe in The Resurrection of Jesus* (Grand Rapids, MI: Eerdmans, 1975), p. 116. William L. Craig argues that the terms Paul uses here ought to be rendered into English not as 'physical body' and 'spiritual body' but as 'natural body' and 'supernatural body'. See his 'The Bodily Resurrection of Jesus', in R. T. France and D. Wenham (eds.), *Gospel Perspectives*, vol. i (Sheffield: JSOT Press, 1980), p. 59.

V

We are now in a position to see that the New Testament accounts of Jesus' resurrection can best be understood on a bodily transformation model. The following points are crucial: (1) Jesus' resurrection was a bodily resurrection: the tomb was empty; the resurrection body could be touched; it was a genuine physical thing—not an apparition or a figment of the disciples' imagination (see Luke 24: 37). (2) Jesus was one and the same person before and after the resurrection: he claimed to be Jesus; he recalled events that had happened before the crucifixion; he was recognized as Jesus by the disciples (albeit at times with difficulty); his wounds were still there. (3) There were also differences in the form that Jesus took after the resurrection: his body was transformed, not merely resuscitated. (Not even the third and fourth Gospels in their most corporeal passages suggest that Jesus' body was merely resuscitated.) Jesus lived in a new mode of existence, liberated from many of the limitations of ordinary life. This difference accounts for the strange new properties the evangelists report him as having—an apparent change in his physical appearance (Mark 16: 12 (from the Markan appendix: 'He appeared in another form')) that rendered him somewhat more difficult to recognize (Luke 24: 31; John 20: 14–15; 21: 4–5), a luminous aspect in some of his post-ascension appearances (Acts 9: 3; 22: 6ff; 26: 12ff.; Rev. 1: 16), and an apparent ability to 'come and go' at will (Luke 24: 31, 36; Acts 1: 21) even despite closed doors (John 20: 19, 26).

Thus, there is no necessary inconsistency between Paul and the evangelists or, more precisely, between 'spiritual' and 'physical' motifs in the relevant New Testament texts. The evangelists themselves, I believe, could well concur with Paul's statement that 'flesh and blood cannot inherit the kingdom of God' (1 Cor. 15: 50), for they nowhere imply that Jesus' earthly body was raised in the sense of restoring it to its old condition of life.[15] They too suggest that it was transformed to a new condition of life. Furthermore, the corporeal motifs of Luke and John (Jesus eating, being touched, etc.) do not deny bodily transformation but were clearly designed to convince the incredulous disciples that it was really Jesus who was raised, that it was not a ghost or a figment of their imagination. Nor do the unusual properties of the risen Jesus in some of the appearance accounts (e.g. the ability to appear or disappear,

---

[15] Craig argues convincingly that the Gospels steer the same middle course as Paul does between immortality of the soul and resuscitation. See his 'The Bodily Resurrection of Jesus' (n. 14 above), p. 68.

luminosity) entail incorporeality. Only a physical object can be located somewhere, can travel from point A to point B, or can glow luminously.

Surely there are some difficult questions we are entitled to ask here. For example, was the resurrected Jesus genuinely hungry, or was he just accommodating himself to the disciples' level of understanding? Was this the only way for him to prove that he was not an apparition? Can 'spiritual bodies' get hungry and eat? Isn't eating an aspect of earthly decay? Can ordinary food be digested by glorified bodies? For that matter, how were the atoms and molecules of Jesus' earthly body related to the atoms and molecules of his glorified body? These are good questions, to which I have no complete answer.

Indeed, it must be emphasized that there is a great deal of mystery involved in the resurrection of Jesus. As to the nature of Jesus' resurrection body, I believe that this much can be affirmed and confidently taught within the Christian community: it was numerically identical with his pre-resurrection body (i.e. it was one and the same body), but not qualitatively identical with it (some of the old properties were still there, but it possessed new ones as well). We already accept the principle that two qualitatively non-identical things can be numerically identical: my body today is qualitatively different from my body of a week ago, but the one is still numerically identical to the other. The change that Jesus' body underwent in resurrection was no doubt far more radical than normal changes bodies undergo in a week's time; still the principle holds. As I have emphasized, Jesus was not resuscitated but resurrected; his body was transformed. Much more than this is unknown; the opinions of scholars about the exact nature of Jesus' body during the forty days that marked the span from the first to the last of his resurrection appearances is little more than educated hypothesizing or guesswork.

Notice, for example, the following three theories of the nature of Jesus' resurrection body (which I do not mean to suggest are at all exhaustive of the possibilities): (1) The essential nature of Jesus' resurrection body did not change for the forty days. It was physical (i.e. it took up space, could be located, could be seen under the right conditions, etc.) but also in some sense supernatural (which accounts for the 'spiritual' motifs in Paul and some of the appearance stories in the Gospels). (2) Jesus' resurrection body was primarily and normally physical in the same sense in which his pre-resurrection body was physical, but miraculous acts of God occasionally gave it strange 'spiritual' properties, such as invisibility and 'agility' (a word used by medieval theologians to denote the ability to come and go unimpeded). (3) Jesus' resurrection body was primarily and normally spiritual and thus invisible, but miraculous acts of God occasionally gave it physicality so that it could be seen, touched, located, and the like.

It should be clear by now that I am inclined towards the first theory and would be prepared if pressed to argue against the other two. The first appears to be the simplest way to handle the complexity of the biblical texts. But I regard all three as acceptable theories in that they violate nothing found in either scripture or essential Christian teachings. In plain fact, scripture does not clearly answer the question of which of these three theories is best. Neither the second nor the third theory constitutes a denial of the classical Christian claim that Jesus was bodily raised from the dead.

VI

I will add two final matters before concluding. First, a word about the empty tomb. My own view is that the New Testament tradition of the empty tomb is one of the strongest reasons for holding that Jesus was bodily raised. The empty tomb is not only compatible with the bodily transformation theory that I have been arguing for, but is also required by it. (Naturally, you could have an empty tomb and a spiritual resurrection, but spiritual resurrection theories do not *require* an empty tomb, and defenders of spiritual theories in fact often argue against the empty tomb.)[16]

Secondly, a word about how resurrection was viewed in the first century. The point is often made that some first-century Jews envisioned a bodily resurrection. Conservative scholars use this claim in support of interpreting the New Testament texts in terms of bodily resurrection. If the New Testament writers affirmed bodily resurrection, they say, so should we. But critics of bodily resurrection can grant that the New Testament writers had bodily resurrection in mind and still insist that the theory is wrong. They might argue that the New Testament writers were not able or at least not inclined to comprehend or entertain other more plausible conceptions of life after death, that they simply misinterpreted the limited facts at their disposal and char-acterized a purely spiritual resurrection as the sort of physical resurrection they were expecting.

But it is interesting that even the most radical Christian interpreters of the resurrection texts tend to claim that their own theories capture what the New Testament writers were trying to say or *really* had in mind, that the proper interpretation of the texts is along the lines of their own theory. This sort of exegetical legerdemain has always struck me as the most grotesque aspect of reductive theories of the resurrection.

---

[16] For my own defence of the empty tomb, see chapter 4 of my *Risen Indeed* (n. 1 above).

For example, theologian Gordon Kaufman holds that the resurrection of Jesus means something like 'God's act begun in Jesus still continues.' He explicitly points out that 'the question whether Jesus was alive again or not does not bear directly on this issue.'[17] He goes on to comment on the New Testament resurrection texts as follows:

Although the earliest Christians certainly thought the man Jesus, who had died on the cross, had again come alive, a historical reconstruction of the evidence in the Bible hardly supports that interpretation.... The extraordinary hypothesis accepted by the early church...is not intrinsically connected with the central claim the church wished to make in proclaiming Jesus' resurrection, namely, that the God who had been acting through Jesus' ministry and especially in his death was still actively at work in the community of believers.[18]

Despite the reductive theories of such individuals as Kaufman (and others) who interpret the New Testament along these lines, I maintain that there is still significance to the argument that, in concert with contemporary Jewish thinking, the New Testament writers most probably had bodily resurrection in mind. Unfortunately, this argument is sometimes oversimplified. For example, it is occasionally suggested that the Jewish mind simply had no other way of understanding the concept of life after death than bodily resurrection, that the New Testament writers would not have comprehended, for example, what a spiritual resurrection was, and that therefore bodily resurrection was a well-intentioned but wrong-headed interpretation of the meaning of Jesus' resurrection. This is not a convincing argument, however. Dualistic theories seem to have been very much alive in the first century, and even the Old Testament contains stories of entry into everlasting life (e.g. Elijah being taken into heaven) that are not strictly speaking bodily resurrection stories.[19]

It does seem sensible, however, to say that the disciples could not have believed, or convinced others to believe, that Jesus was alive had there been no empty tomb or appearances interpreted as bodily appearances. Resurrection from the grave is what Jews of Jesus' day would naturally have meant by the term 'raised from the dead'. And in the absence of compelling evidence for the claim that they had some other theory in mind (which evidence, as I have

---

[17] Gordon Kaufman, *Systematic Theology: A Historicist Perspective* (New York: Scribner's, 1958), p. 430.

[18] Ibid., pp. 467–8.

[19] On this point, see Brown, *Virginal Conception* (n. 4 above), p. 76. Jewish apocalyptic literature contains references to immortality (e.g. Wisdom 3: 1–8), and there are references to disembodied existence as well (see 1 Enoch 9: 3, 10; 22: 3; 2 Esdras 7: 75–101; Apocalypse of Moses 32: 4).

argued, is not forthcoming), the proper conclusion is that the New Testament writers had bodily resurrection in mind.

But to return to the main theme of this chapter, once we understand the implications of bodily transformation, we have a way of interpreting and unifying the quite disparate New Testament accounts of the resurrection.[20] Properly interpreted, all the New Testament accounts of the resurrection of Jesus present it as a case of bodily transformation rather than of resuscitation or spiritual resurrection, despite the different ways they describe it. By far the most sensible conclusion, then, is that Christians ought to continue to affirm the traditional doctrine that Jesus was bodily raised.

---

[20] William L. Craig makes this point carefully in his *Assessing the New Testament Evidence for the Historicity of the Resurrection of Jesus* (Lewiston, NY: The Edwin Mellen Press, 1989); see especially pp. 147, 158, 328–30, 359, 395.

8

'Seeing' the Risen Jesus

I

As we saw in Chapter 7, one crucial aspect of Christian belief in the resurrection of Jesus is the notion that it was a bodily resurrection. A second crucial aspect is the claim that certain people encountered the risen Jesus. That is, he appeared—in his risen body—to certain people. They saw him. It is that claim that I will consider in the present chapter.

So the New Testament claims that certain people—Mary Magdalene, Peter, Thomas, Paul, and others—saw the risen Jesus. 'Have I not seen Jesus our Lord?', Paul asks (1 Cor. 9: 1). Through the three women at the tomb, the disciples receive the promise: 'he is going ahead of you to Galilee; there you will see him' (Mark 16: 7). And the other disciples say to Thomas (John 20: 25), 'We have seen the Lord.'[1]

Suppose we assume with the Christian tradition that Jesus really was raised from the dead and really did appear to certain people—that is, that the whole story of his post-resurrection appearances to individuals and to groups was not simply a legend or a case of fraud or a mistake of some sort. Suppose, that is, that the witnesses to the resurrection did, as claimed, see the risen Jesus.

What kind of 'seeing' was this? Was it normal or abnormal seeing? Was the thing that they saw—that is, Jesus' risen body—a material object like a tree or a house or another human body? Were the perceptual processes that were at work in seeing Jesus normal; that is, were they working in the same way as they worked when Mary Magdalene saw a tree or a house or another human body? This is what I aim to discuss in the present chapter: what *kind* of seeing was involved in those experiences described by such words as 'We have seen the Lord'?

Let me distinguish among three different ways of seeing or visualizing something. The first is *normal vision*. In such cases, something like this happens: photons of light are disturbed—that is, are either scattered,

---

[1] Note the fact that the claim to have seen Jesus alive after his death runs from the earliest NT witness (Paul) through Mark to one of the later books (John).

deflected, or absorbed by interacting with an external object—and some of those disturbed photons are absorbed by the retina of the eye. They contain information; that is, the specific wavelength of the light, as well as its intensity and distribution on the retina, determine our interpretation of what we see. From the eye, electrical-chemical messages are sent to the brain, which interprets those signals and recognizes the shape, location, colour, and so on of the external object. I shall assume that normal vision entails both (1) that the perceptual processes work as they regularly do, and (2) that the object seen is a material object.

At the other extreme is what I will call *subjective vision*. This is a situation where someone sincerely claims to see something; no one else can see it; and the reason that no one else can see it is precisely because the item purportedly seen is not real, is not objectively there to be seen. (I will say little about this category—usually called a hallucination—in the present chapter.)

The third category fits between the first two and is important for present purposes. Let us call an *objective vision* a situation where someone sincerely claims to see something; no one else can see it; and the reason that no one else can see it is because it is not the sort of thing that can be seen by normal vision. That is, God has enabled the person who has the objective vision to see the real and objective presence of the thing; the seer has an ability to see it that others lack.[2]

Thus the issue that I will discuss—what sort of seeing was involved in seeing the risen Jesus—is, so to speak, an intramural debate among people who believe that Jesus really was raised from the dead and really was seen. People who hold that Jesus was *bodily* raised from the dead can also engage in the debate, because it is still open to question what sort of body we are talking about.

Given the assumption that Jesus really was raised and, accordingly, that the appearances were not subjective visions, the two possibilities with which we must concern ourselves are normal vision and objective visions. The first possibility is, as noted, that the seeing of Jesus by the witnesses to the resurrection was fully normal in every or virtually every sense. Mary Magdalene's seeing Jesus was like my seeing a colleague walking down the

---

[2] I choose to refer to this category as 'objective vision' because that term is already in use in the theological literature on resurrection. (See, e.g., W. Pannenberg, *Jesus—God and Man* (Philadelphia: Westminster Press, 1977), pp. 93–9.) 'Grace-assisted seeing' or even 'graced seeing' might otherwise have been better terms. It should be noted that the distinction between objective and subjective vision is sometimes understood in a different way; an objective vision is a situation where God intentionally and perhaps telepathically grants Jones a vision of some-thing despite the fact that the thing visualized is not objectively there in external reality, and a subjective vision is a situation where Smith's vision of something is in some sense self-induced.

corridor in Pitzer Hall. Mary's eyes and brain were working normally, and what she saw was a material object—that is, a body that took up space, occupied a certain location, deflected photons, and so forth. (This first possibility does not entail, incidentally, that Jesus' resurrection was a mere resuscitation; as I argued in Chapter 7, his raised body might well have been both a transformed, 'glorified' body and a material object.) Anybody who had been there beside Mary Magdalene could also have seen the risen Jesus. A camera could have taken a snapshot of the risen Jesus.

The second possibility, as also noted, is that what Mary saw (Jesus' raised body) was so abnormal (a 'spiritual body' from heaven) that it could only have been seen by her with special assistance from God. It was not the sort of object that human eyes, working normally and unaided by God, can see. Her 'seeing' of Jesus was enhanced, graced seeing, seeing illuminated by the Holy Spirit, an objective vision. No one else who was there, unaided by God, would have perceived or recognized Jesus. A camera would have detected nothing, or at least nothing recognizable.

Let us call these two perceptual experiences 'seeing' and 'visualizing', respectively. (These are technical definitions; I do not claim that they reflect ordinary usage.) Seeing is the first possibility, where Mary's perception of Jesus was entirely or basically like normal sight, and visualizing is the second possibility, where Mary's perception of Jesus was assisted by God, an objective vision. I will use the words 'perceive' and 'encounter' as neutral between seeing and visualizing; that is, when I say that someone perceived or encountered the risen Jesus, I am leaving the question open whether it was normal sight or an objective vision.

I will argue here that seeing is much preferable to visualizing.[3] That is, contrary to the tendency of many recent and contemporary theologians who hold that Jesus truly was resurrected from the dead (and of course some theologians do not allow as much), the witnesses who encountered Jesus in the resurrection appearances *saw* him.[4]

[3] In my *Risen Indeed: Making Sense of the Resurrection* (Grand Rapids, MI: Eerdmans, 1993), I expressed the opinion that the witnesses to the resurrection saw the risen Jesus in a normal sense of the word 'see', but I did not argue for that point. In the present chapter I try to do so.

[4] There is an important question that is related to the one that I am discussing: whether the resurrection appearances recorded in the NT were of a unique and limited sort, in principle unavailable to later Christians. Despite the arguments of Wilhelm Michaelis and others (see his article 'Horao', in *Theological Dictionary of the New Testament*, ed. Gerhard Kittel and Gerhard Friedrich, vol. 5 (Grand Rapids, MI: Eerdmans, 1976), pp. 315–82), I will assume that the answer is yes. The point has been conclusively made by Daniel Kendall, S.J. and Gerald O'Collins, S.J. in their article, 'The Uniqueness of the Easter Appearances', *CBQ* 54/2 (April, 1992), pp. 287–307. Seeing Jesus, they say, 'was an experience restricted to the first generation of disciples, above all to the apostolic eye-witnesses of that generation. Other and later Christians relate personally to Jesus (through faith and love), but they do not see him' (p. 299).

II

There is no denying that a quick and pre-critical reading of the appearance stories in the New Testament (together with some brief references to encounters with the risen Jesus—e.g. Luke 24: 34; 1 Cor. 9: 1; 15: 8) would naturally lead one to hold that the witnesses to the resurrection saw, rather than visualized, him. The natural impression that we get from these stories—their plain sense—is that normal vision was involved.[5]

Perhaps the history of Christian art depicting the resurrection has had an unconscious effect on the way we read the stories—countless paintings, drawings, and frescos depict the resurrected Jesus as being just as solid and perceivable and made of flesh and bone as the others in the pictures.[6] With the possible exception of a halo, his body looks like everybody else's.

But how might a more critical and theologically sophisticated reader of the New Testament argue that the witnesses saw (rather than visualized) the risen Jesus? Primarily by attending to the biblical descriptions of the appearances, as summarized by Luke: 'After his suffering he presented himself alive to them by many convincing proofs, appearing to them during forty days and speaking about the kingdom of God' (Acts 1: 3). From a synoptic view of all the stories and brief claims, Jesus is said *to have been seen* (or to have appeared or to have shown himself) (Matt. 28: 17; Luke 24: 34, 39–46 ('Look at my hands and feet'); John 20: 14, 18 ('I have seen the Lord'), 21; 1 Cor. 15: 5–8), *to have spoken* (Matt. 28: 9, 18–20; Luke 24: 17–30, 36–49; John 20: 15–17, 19–23, 26–9; 21: 5–23; Acts 1: 4–8), *to have walked* (Luke 24: 13–28), *to have distributed food* (Luke 24: 30; John 21: 13), *to have eaten* (Luke 24: 41–3; Acts 1: 4; 10: 41), *to have performed 'signs'* (John 20: 30), *to have given a blessing with his hands* (Luke 24: 50), *to have shown his hands and side* (John 20: 20), and *to have been touched* (Matt. 28: 9; Luke 24: 39; John 20: 17, 27 (only the first of these three texts specifically states that Jesus' body was touched; the other two may imply it)).

My point is not that all this physical detail in the appearance stories settles the question of seeing versus visualizing. Thus far I am only claiming that the natural way to read these stories—prior, that is, to approaching them critically

---

[5] I do not oppose the attempt of scripture scholars to arrive at sensible conclusions about the dating and early forms of existing biblical texts (in this case, the resurrection accounts). But my view is that Christian theology ought to be done on the basis of those texts that the church has taken as canonical, not on the basis of their hypothesized literary ancestors.

[6] This plausible suggestion has been made by Gerald O'Collins, S.J., in his *What Are They Saying About the Resurrection?* (New York: Paulist Press, 1978), pp. 47–8.

or with certain theological convictions in place—is in terms of seeing. In the absence of convincing reasons to the contrary (and we will momentarily explore some such purported reasons), it seems sensible to understand the perception of the risen Jesus in the appearance stories in terms of normal sight. (I will return to this point in Section VI of this chapter.)

III

Nevertheless, many contemporary exegetes and theologians opt for visualizing as opposed to seeing, and we need to consider the reasons for this. As Gerald O'Collins points out, 'Most New Testament scholars would be reluctant to assert that the risen Christ became present in such a way that neutral (or even hostile) spectators could have observed him in an ordinary "physical" fashion.'[7] Unfortunately, arguments for this position are rarely given, so I have endeavoured to supply a few. There seem to be six arguments that can be given in favour of the resurrection appearances being instances of enhanced perception. Let me discuss them in turn.

1. *The risen Jesus appeared only to believers.* If this claim were true, it might constitute a powerful argument for the conclusion that perceptual abilities enhanced by God were necessary to perceive the risen Jesus, for it might make sense to hold that only those who believed were blessed by God with the requisite enhanced perceptual abilities.

However, the main claim being made here is false, and it is altogether surprising that so many scholars make it. I will mention three people who were unbelievers at the time of their encounter with the risen Jesus: (1) Thomas was hardly represented as a believer in Jesus as the risen Lord when he encountered Jesus in the house with the doors shut (although immediately on perceiving Jesus he became a believer in him as 'My Lord and my God' (John 20: 28)). (2) It seems quite possible that James the brother of Jesus was not a believer when the risen Jesus appeared to him (1 Cor. 15: 7). James was apparently a non-believer during Jesus' earthly ministry (Mark 3: 21, 31–5; 6: 3; John 7: 5), and it can plausibly be argued that he came to believe *because* the risen Jesus appeared to him. Note that James is listed among the 120 disciples who were together in Jerusalem after Jesus' ascension (Acts 1: 13–15; cf. also

---

[7] See Gerald O'Collins, *The Resurrection of Jesus Christ* (Valley Forge, PA: Judson Press, 1973), p. 59.

15: 3; Gal. 2: 1–10).[8] (3) The apostle Paul is another obvious example, but I will postpone until later a discussion of the issues surrounding his conversion and the appearance of the risen Jesus to him.

The only claim of which we can be sure, in this general neighbourhood, is that the risen Jesus made no great and grandiose appearances to the general public—that is, to friend and foe alike. There is no record of any appearance to Pontius Pilate or to Caiaphas or to the crowd that had so recently called for his execution. As Luke has Peter openly admit, Jesus appeared not to 'all the people but to us who were chosen by God as witnesses' (Acts 10: 39–40). The testimony in favour of the resurrection of Jesus in the New Testament all comes from insiders in the Christian movement, not from neutral or antagonistic observers.

But it is obvious that this rather thin fact is a frail reed with which to buttress a claim that the resurrection appearances were episodes of visualizing rather than seeing. As noted, some who were not yet believers (and thus were probably not ideal candidates for graced perception) encountered the risen Jesus.

2. *The resurrection of Jesus was not a resuscitation.* As I noted in Chapter 7, this claim has long puzzled me. Let me explain why. Suppose we define the term 'resuscitation' as the restoration of clinically dead or nearly clinically dead human beings to their previous lives. Resuscitations occasionally occur in hospitals these days, and there were several apparent resuscitations in the Bible, too—for example, Jesus' raising of Lazarus. One key criterion for a raising from the dead being a resuscitation (as opposed to a resurrection) is that the resuscitant must inevitably die a second time at some later point, and at that time death would presumably be permanent.

What puzzles me is not the claim itself that Jesus' resurrection was not a resuscitation—it is obviously and unremarkably true. The New Testament's witness holds that Jesus was not merely restored to his previous life, but rather was transformed to a new and glorious life fit for the kingdom of God. What I find odd is the vehemence with which it is argued. Especially those scholars who set out to argue that the resurrection of Jesus did not genuinely occur, or occurred only in some 'spiritual' sense, invariably begin with a robust attack

---

[8] The difficulty here is that of identifying which James, among the three or so mentioned in the NT, Paul was referring to in 1 Cor. 15: 7. It seems probable that he had in mind James the Lord's brother, the one who became a 'pillar' of the early church (Gal. 2: 9). Note that Cephas and James are mentioned by name in both 1 Cor. 15: 5–8 and Paul's own account of his first post-conversion visit to Jerusalem (Gal. 1: 18–19). Indeed, Reginald Fuller says, 'If there were no record of an appearance to James the Lord's brother in the New Testament we would have to invent one in order to account for his post-resurrection conversion and rapid advance.' *The Formation of the Resurrection Narratives* (Philadelphia: Fortress Press, 1980), p. 37.

on resuscitation. One almost gets the impression that there are defenders of resuscitation hiding behind every tree and that everything depends on their being refuted.

Indeed, *I* got this impression about fifteen years ago when, as an interloper from another discipline (i.e. from philosophy), I started reading the theological literature on resurrection. I kept waiting to encounter the books or articles of those (obviously slightly obtuse) resuscitation theorists. It took me a while to realize that there are no such people. Perhaps some unlettered Christian folk, if asked what they believe about resurrection, would come up with an inchoate version of resuscitation, but I am aware of no scholars who defend such a view.

Nevertheless, as noted, the New Testament certainly teaches that Jesus was resurrected rather than resuscitated, and some scholars take this fact to be an argument for visualizing as opposed to seeing. But there appears to be confusion here. It is true that the resurrected body of Jesus possessed strange new properties. With an apparent ability to appear and disappear at will, it seemed to be free of certain of the natural laws that we must obey. Note the way John depicts Jesus as appearing in a room despite its locked door (John 20: 19, 26), the way he suddenly disappeared from the sight of the Emmaus disciples (Luke 24: 31), and the way he ascended out of the disciples' sight (Luke 24: 51 and Acts 1: 9). Some hold these strange properties of the body of the risen Jesus to mean that the appearances were not encounters with a resuscitated Jesus, but rather were 'eschatological disclosures "from heaven" of an already exalted One.'[9] I agree with that point.

However, it does not follow from any of this that Jesus' raised body was not a material object (although it certainly was an unusual one), something that took up space, occupied a certain location, *and could be seen*. Perhaps the following fallacious argument has had a certain influence here:

(1) A resuscitated body can be seen.
(2) Jesus' body was not a resuscitated body.
(3) Therefore, Jesus' body could not be seen.

Here is a related point: nobody takes the sudden transportation of Philip from the desert road near Gaza (where he had been speaking with the Ethiopian eunuch) to Azotus (Acts 8: 39–40) as evidence that he had no physical body.[10]

---

[9] O'Collins, *What Are They Saying About the Resurrection?* (n. 6 above), p. 11.

[10] I owe this point to Robert Gundry, 'The Essential Physicality of Jesus' Resurrection According to the New Testament', in Joel B. Green and Max Turner (eds.), *Jesus of Nazareth, Lord and Christ: Essays on the Historical Jesus and New Testament Christology* (Grand Rapids, MI: Eerdmans, 1994), p. 214.

Paul Badham has argued[11] that there is a contradiction involved in Jesus' resurrection body being both sufficiently spiritual to pass through walls and sufficiently physical to be seen and touched. But not only is there no logical contradiction here—there is not even much in the way of a difficulty. The only sort of thing that logically *can* appear and take up space in a room, locked doors or not, is a physical object. Immaterial objects like, say, the number six, failing as they do to possess physical location, never take up space in a room (or anywhere else). If the risen Jesus appeared in a room, the risen Jesus' body was a material object, and so presumably could be seen and touched.

But perhaps Badham's deepest concern is to understand how a physical body can, as he says, pass through walls. But where does the New Testament say that Jesus 'passed through the walls' of the room? I would have thought the idea was that Jesus simply appeared or materialized in the room. It is, of course, not part of our normal experience that physical objects simply appear in a given place—that is, without having traversed the intervening places between the place where they were and the place where they are. Still, I see no logical or conceptual difficulty here. There is no doubt that a violation of natural law, a miracle of some sort, must be involved here. That this event was an act of God was surely what the Evangelist had in mind. It seems that an omnipotent being would have it well within its power to make a human body materialize in a room.

3. *The meaning of* ophthe. *Ophthe* is the aorist passive form of the Greek verb *horao* (I see). The word is used nine times in the New Testament in relation to the raised Jesus (Luke 24: 34; Acts 9: 17; 13: 31; 26: 16a; 1 Cor. 15: 5–8 (four times); and 1 Tim. 3: 16). When used with the dative, it is usually translated 'He appeared', and as such emphasizes the revelatory initiative of the one who appears. The sense is almost, 'He let himself be seen' (as opposed to something like 'he was seen').

Some scholars who favour objective visions rather than ordinary seeing argue that the New Testament's use of *ophthe* entails this conclusion. Thus Badham says: 'most New Testament scholars believe that the word *ophthe...* refers to spiritual vision rather than to ocular sighting.'[12] The argument is that the religious use of *ophthe* is technical, marks a clear difference from ordinary visual perception of physical objects, and entails some sort of spiritual appearance, vision-like experience, or apprehension of a divine revelation.

---

[11] Paul Badham, 'The Meaning of the Resurrection of Jesus', in P. Avis (ed.), *The Resurrection of Jesus Christ* (London: Darton, Longman and Todd, 1993), pp. 28–9.

[12] Ibid., p. 31. Michaelis (in his article cited in n. 4 above) is probably the most influential recent scholar who holds that the appearances were revelatory encounters with Jesus that primarily involved hearing rather than sight.

But other scholars have pointed out that *ophthe* can also be used (and is so used in both the New Testament and the Septuagint) for ordinary visual apprehension of a human being or a material object (e.g. Acts 7: 26). That is, it can be used both for ordinary seeing of material objects and for the visualizing of supernatural beings. Indeed, there are other Greek words (*horama* and *optasia*) that are normally used for what we would call visions, especially of things that are normally invisible, like God or angels (see Matt. 17: 9; Acts 9: 10; 16: 19).

It is true that the use of *ophthe* does not *require* that the sense be that of normal vision, but neither is normal vision ruled out. Indeed, the word covers a whole range of visual phenomena. When Paul says that the risen Jesus 'appeared to me', the notion of normal vision of a material object is neither required nor ruled out. However, for non-linguistic reasons, the appearance to 'more than five hundred' that Paul mentions (1 Cor. 15: 6) must surely refer to seeing rather than visualizing. Raymond Brown rightly ridicules the very idea of more than five hundred people having the same objective vision as 'synchronized ecstasy'.[13]

Simply stated, *ophthe* does not require the sense of visualizing as opposed to seeing, and in view of examples like Acts 7: 26 the argument that it does collapses. We must decide what is meant in each instance of its use by analysis of the context (among other things), not simply by lexical fiat. It is not possible to decide the nature of Jesus' resurrection appearances on the basis of a linguistic analysis of one verb.[14]

4. *Doubt and failure of recognition.* An argument in favour of visualizing as opposed to seeing concerns the common motifs in the appearance stories of (1) failure at first to recognize Jesus (Luke 24: 16, 31, 37; John 20: 14–15; 21:4; cf. also the appendix to Mark: 'He appeared in another form to two of them' (16: 21)), and (2) doubt that it is Jesus (Matt. 28: 17; Luke 24: 11; John 20: 24–5). The argument would be that those who were not blessed with enhanced perception—that is, who were not recipients of the objective vision of the risen Jesus—either did not recognize Jesus (until with God's help they were able to visualize him) or else doubted.

This is certainly a possible interpretation of the appearance stories. But one item that might be taken in support of it seems to me actually to argue against it: the explicit statements in the Emmaus story (Luke 24: 13–35) that Cleopas

---

[13] Raymond E. Brown, *The Virginal Conception and Bodily Resurrection of Jesus* (New York: Paulist Press, 1973) (hereinafter *Virginal Conception*), p. 91. No doubt an omnipotent being could achieve such a thing as a vision shared by over five hundred people, but in the light of all the evidence it strains credulity to think that God actually did so in this case.

[14] See Hans Grass, *Ostergeschehen und Osterberichte*, 4th rev. edn (Göttingen: Vandenhoeck and Ruprecht, 1970), pp. 186–9.

and his unnamed companion failed to recognize Jesus because 'their eyes were kept from recognizing him' (24: 16) and that later they did recognize him because 'their eyes were opened' (24: 31). This point seems to me to cut the other way: it suggests that the two Emmaus disciples *would quite normally have recognized Jesus* had their eyes not been supernaturally kept from recognizing him. The literal sense seems to be that their eyes were restrained or held back, and that later their eyes were opened by God.[15] In other words, it sounds in this case as if a special act of God was necessary to *prevent* recognition until the appropriate moment.[16] Perhaps, then, *anybody* who had been there on the road to Emmaus could have seen and recognized Jesus (apart from such a special divine act). Perhaps a camera could have taken a picture of him.

Are there other, more sensible ways of explaining the twin motifs of doubt and failure to recognize than to posit objective visions? Yes, I believe there are. For one thing, we need to remind ourselves that the disciples were convinced that Jesus had truly died. And contrary to the claims of some recent theologians (who make it sound as if first-century folk were almost pantingly eager to believe in resurrection and other miracles, and would do so at the drop of a hat), they were as convinced as we are that dead people stay dead. They were definitely not expecting to encounter Jesus.

Accordingly, it ought not to be surprising that initial encounters with the raised Jesus might have produced lack of recognition and even doubt. It should not surprise us that in some cases Jesus was recognized only after he spoke, or after he blessed and broke bread, or after he encouraged observation of the pre-mortem wounds, or after he suggested fishing on the right side of the boat. The disciples first had to deal with their own incredulity before they could accept the resurrection. Later they surely recognized what the church came to call their own 'slowness of heart to believe' (Luke 24: 25).

Secondly, there may be several layers of explanation for the two motifs. As noted, on at least one occasion failure to recognize was said (as I interpret the text) to be due to divine initiative (Luke 24: 13–33). In other cases, there were perhaps more natural explanations, like distance (John 21: 4), a combination of confusion and lack of light (John 20: 14–15), or the suddenness of Jesus' appearing (Luke 24.: 36–7). It also seems possible that, as in the transfiguration accounts (e.g. Mark 9: 2–8), Jesus' countenance was altered somewhat

---

[15] See Joseph A. Fitzmyer, S.J., *The Gospel According to Luke (X–XXIV)* (Garden City, NY: Doubleday, 1985), pp. 1563, 1568. Fitzmyer calls the usage in v. 31 ('their eyes were opened') the theological passive, which suggests that it was an act of God.

[16] Some interpret the blindness of Cleopas and his companion in entirely natural terms, simply as continuing Luke's theme of spiritual blindness (Luke 9: 45; 18: 34; 19: 42). See, e.g., Grant Osborne, *The Resurrection Narratives: A Redactional Study* (Grand Rapids, MI: Baker, 1984), p. 238. I do not read the Emmaus pericope this way, however.

(thus the comment in the Markan appendix, 'He appeared in another form' (Mark 16: 12)). But the key point here is that in every case of doubt and/or failure of recognition, the overriding factors were (1) the fact that the disciples were in shock, dealing with their own anguish over losing Jesus and their fears for their own safety, and (2) the fact that seeing Jesus alive again was the last thing they expected.[17]

5. *Paul's conversion.* The story of Paul's conversion on the road to Damascus, told three times in the book of Acts (9: 1–22; 22: 6–16; 25: 12–18), seems to have influenced the way some scholars read the accounts of Jesus' resurrection appearances. That story does seem to describe something like an objective vision, since the experience was intelligible to Paul (as an encounter with Jesus), but not to his companions. In the first account, the others who were with Paul 'heard the voice but saw no one' (Acts 9: 7); and in the second account, they 'saw the light but did not hear the voice of the one who was speaking' (Acts 22: 9).

I am not interested here in trying to harmonize these two apparently discrepant accounts. My point is that some people may think that all the resurrection appearances of Jesus were like Paul's Damascus Road experience in being unseeable by, or unintelligible to, other people; that is, they were objective visions—this especially since in his own writings Paul insists that he has seen the risen Jesus (1 Cor. 9: 1; 15: 8; Gal. 1: 12, 16), which most scholars read as references to his Damascus Road conversion experience.

Interestingly, Luke seems to limit resurrection appearances of Jesus to the period between his crucifixion and some forty days later (see Acts 1: 3). This limitation must mean that he holds that subsequent encounters with Jesus that involve any sort of visualization should be classified either as visions or as resurrection appearances of a different sort from the earlier ones. Indeed, here we encounter the Church's traditional interpretation of Luke's words: after the ascension, there were no more resurrection appearances of the paradigmatic sort.[18] If this interpretation is correct, it must entail that, according to Luke's scheme, Paul's encounters with Jesus, however many there were, of whatever sort they were, were appearances that were in at least some important sense different from the earlier ones to Mary Magdalene and the others. (This would also apparently include the appearances to Stephen (Acts 7: 53–6) and to John of Patmos (Rev. 1: 12–18).)

[17] See Murray Harris, *Raised Immortal* (Grand Rapids, MI: Eerdmans, 1983), p. 56.
[18] Theologically this seems a wise decision. Otherwise, the church throughout its history would have had to contend with, and reach judgements about, all sorts of purported resurrection appearances with all sorts of purportedly authoritative new revelations from the Risen One. (I do not claim that this pragmatic consideration was the reason that the church placed a moratorium on post-forty-days-after-Pentecost appearances of the Risen Jesus. Their central reasons were historical, not pragmatic.)

Paul himself may have recognized something like this distinction when he introduced a reference to his own encounter with Jesus with the words, 'last of all, as to one untimely born, he appeared also to me' (1 Cor. 15: 8).[19] Luke also represents Paul as referring to his conversion experience as 'a heavenly vision (*optasia*)' (Acts 26: 19). Note also that in 2 Corinthians 12: 1–7 (where Paul was almost certainly not referring to his conversion experience),[20] he seems to be distinguishing between two sorts of ecstatic or revelatory experiences, those 'in the body' and those 'out of the body'. Perhaps the first sort includes real experiences and the second sort includes visions.

If this conclusion is correct, then Paul's Damascus Road experience (at least as it is described by Luke) is not a proper model for interpreting the resurrection appearances of Jesus, for deciding whether the witnesses saw or visualized Jesus. The point is this: there is no good reason to interpret the resurrection appearances recounted in the Gospels and listed in 1 Corinthians 15: 5–7 as experiences that were like Paul's conversion experience. Indeed, there is every reason to deny this 'Damascus Road' interpretation of them because it requires complete rejection (perhaps as legendary accretions) of all the physical detail of the appearance stories. And even if Paul's conversion experience does (contrary to what it seems that Luke is saying) count as a resurrection appearance in the fullest sense, this does not mean that it can be used as a grid to be imposed on the other appearance accounts. As I have been arguing, they simply do not fit it very well.

6. *The Pauline notion of 'spiritual body'.* Some theologians argue that in 1 Corinthians 15 Paul is talking about a resurrection body that is normally invisible to humans on earth and that therefore all perceptions of the risen Jesus are objective visions. In responding to this line of argument, I will skim lightly over certain points that were made in Chapter 7 and others that will be made in more detail in Chapter 14. In summary, they are (1) that Paul's notion of a spiritual body involves corporeality—that is, that Paul was talking about a material object; (2) that Paul's notion of a spiritual body reconciles what otherwise might look like discrepancies between the heavily physical motifs in the appearance stories in the Gospels (eating, being touched, etc.) and the more ethereal or numinous motifs in those same stories (appearing in

---

[19] Here I disagree with Brown, *Virginal Conception* (n. 13 above), p. 53n., who says: '[Paul] regards the appearance to himself on the same level as the appearance to the others, even if it is the last.' At one level, of course, Brown is correct—Paul surely considered his encounter an important part of what validated his status as an apostle, and he held that he was second to none of the other apostles in this regard. My question is whether Paul considered his encounter with the risen Jesus as being on an epistemic par with the earlier appearances to the others. The evidence cited in the present paragraph makes me doubt it.

[20] The phrase 'fourteen years ago' points to a date in the early 40s rather than to the conversion experience in the 30s.

a room despite locked doors, etc.); (3) that the New Testament accordingly offers a unified view of the resurrection of Jesus; (4) that all redactional attempts to argue that the physical motifs are late and unreliable and that they emerged through a long and quasi-evolutionary process from earlier 'spiritual' appearance traditions have failed;[21] and (5) accordingly, that the notion of bodily resurrection (but not resuscitation) is the best way for Christians to understand and preach the Easter message.

Although he does not specifically mention seeing, Willi Marxsen perhaps implies that a spiritual body cannot be seen, but only visualized. He says, 'And of course a spiritual body in the Pauline sense cannot eat or be touched.'[22] Even my friend Gerald O'Collins (normally highly reliable on all matters resurrectional) seems to me to lose his way at this point by referring to 'glorious (normally invisible?) matter'.[23] (But perhaps he redeems himself with the inserted question mark.)

My question is: Where did Marxsen learn that a Pauline spiritual body cannot eat or be touched? What made O'Collins even questioningly suggest that a Pauline glorified body cannot be seen? It seems perfectly possible to accept everything that Paul says in 1 Corinthians 15 about resurrection bodies and still hold that they are material objects that can be seen. Paul does insist that 'flesh and blood cannot inherit the kingdom of God' (1 Cor. 15: 50). But this verse means that the old, earthly body cannot enter the kingdom of God as it is (this is one of the powerful theological arguments against resuscitation), that it must first be transformed into a glorified body (Phil. 3: 32). But a glorified body (*soma*) is still a body—that is, still a material object that can be seen.[24]

IV

We have been discussing six arguments that might be given in favour of the claim that the appearances of the resurrected Jesus to Mary Magdalene and the others were objective visions rather than instances of ordinary seeing.

[21] In my opinion, no one has convincingly argued that there was ever a period in the history of the church, let alone a document, in which the resurrection of Jesus was understood in non-physical terms. Note that 1 Cor. 15: 3–7, probably the oldest datable Easter tradition in the NT, speaks of resurrection rather than exaltation.

[22] Willi Marxsen, *The Resurrection of Jesus of Nazareth* (trans. Margaret Kohl) (Philadelphia: Fortress Press, 1970), p. 70.

[23] O'Collins, *What Are They Saying About the Resurrection?* (n. 6 above), p. 46.

[24] This point is compellingly argued by Robert Gundry, *Soma in Biblical Theology: With Emphasis on Pauline Anthropology* (Cambridge: Cambridge University Press, 1976), pp. 159ff. See also William L. Craig, *Assessing the New Testament Evidence for the Historicity of the Resurrection of Jesus* (Lewiston, NY: The Edwin Mellen Press, 1989), pp. 120–6, 133–7, 158.

Some of the arguments are stronger than others, but, as we have seen, serious objections can be raised against all six of them.

The central claim of the first argument—that the risen Jesus appeared only to believers—is simply false, no matter how many times it is repeated. The second argument—the one that concerns resuscitation—is irrelevant to the matter at hand once it is granted (as I argue it must be) that a glorified (and not just resuscitated) raised body can be a material object. The third argument—about *ophthe*—is a serious one, but, as we saw, the frequent use of this word in connection with Jesus' resurrection appearances does not by itself settle the question of seeing versus visualizing. The fourth argument—which concerns the motifs of doubt and failure to recognize Jesus in the appearance stories—is also an important consideration, but I argued that these motifs can be adequately explained even if the raised Jesus was seen rather than visualized. About the fifth argument—which concerns the influence of Paul's conversion story in Acts on the 'objective vision' interpretation of the appearance stories—I argued that there should be no such influence. In response to the sixth argument—about Paul's notion of a 'spiritual body'— I argued that there is no good reason to think of it as something that is normally invisible or unobservable.[25]

The strongest argument in the opposite direction—that is, in favour of seeing (as opposed to visualizing)—is the massive physical detail of the appearance stories. Suppose the risen Jesus really did (as the stories claim) appear (in various settings, at various times of day, for various lengths of time, to various people and groups of people), walk, talk, distribute food, perform signs, and allow himself to be touched. If so, it seems sensible to interpret the stories in the way that the church and Christian artists have traditionally understood them: that the risen Jesus was physically present in a way that could, in a perfectly normal sense, be observed.[26]

It is sometimes said that the physical detail of the appearance stories in Luke and John was to convince the disciples not that Jesus was physical, but that he was real. But those who make this claim never seem to go on to answer

---

[25] Note that Paul does *not* say in 1 Corinthians 15: 42–51, 'What was sown visible was raised invisible.'

[26] Here again I disagree with O'Collins, who argues that the physical detail of the stories is designed to highlight '(a) the reality of the resurrection, (b) the continuity between the risen Lord and the earthly Jesus, and (c) the disciples' status as witnesses'. He adds: 'The graphic, physical touches of the Easter stories in Luke and John serve to express these points and no more' (*What Are They Saying About the Resurrection?* (n. 6 above), pp. 49–50). I can affirm everything here except the crucial last three words.

the question: a real *what*?[27] Perhaps this omission is so prevalent because those who fail to answer the question recognize that any answer to it that did not involve a physical body would inevitably lead to a thoroughly non-biblical view of survival of death—for example, to the Platonic notion of the immortality of the soul. I have no problem with the claim that the physical detail of the stories was designed to prove the physical and thus personal continuity of the risen Lord with the Jesus who had been crucified. But I am arguing that the primary reason for the physical detail is that, in its canonical writings, the early Church was correctly remembering the actual nature of the appearances themselves.

Given the status of the evidence at our disposal (so it seems to me), it is much preferable to hold that the risen Jesus was seen rather than visualized. But why is this view so commonly rejected? One sometimes gets the impression from the friends of objective visions that the notion of a physically present resurrected Jesus is somehow uncouth or *outré*.[28] I do not share such feelings; I feel no sense of embarrassment whatsoever in holding that a camera could have taken a snapshot of the risen Jesus, say, feeding the seven disciples beside the Sea of Tiberius (John 21: 1–14).

V

I have been arguing that the biblical stories of the resurrection appearances of Jesus should be understood in terms of ordinary vision. Thus far my argument has been based entirely on historical-critical grounds, and I want to rest the case that this chapter makes primarily on those grounds. However, it seems to me possible to argue for the same conclusion in two other ways. I will now briefly do so.

1. *The early Church interpreted the resurrection appearances in terms of ordinary vision.* I will not try to establish this point in detail, especially since the modern concept of an objective vision was obviously not used by early

[27] See Robert H. Gundry, 'The Essential Physicality of Jesus' Resurrection According to the New Testament', in Joel B. Green and Max Turner (eds.), *Jesus of Nazareth, Lord and Christ: Essays on the Historical Jesus and New Testament Christology* (Grand Rapids, MI: Eerdmans, 1994), p. 210.
[28] Brown echoes the feeling of many theologians and scripture scholars when he says, 'The partial ambiguity of our sources about the nature of "seeing" makes incredible some of the modern speculation as to whether the risen Jesus could have been photographed or televised, and whether he could have been seen by non-believers. This type of question does not show any appreciation for the transformation involved in the Resurrection' (*Virginal Conception* (n. 13 above), p. 91n.).

Christian thinkers. Still, it is clear that orthodox treatments of the resurrection in the second century all took it for granted that Jesus was seen by the witnesses in an ordinary sense of the word 'see.'

One extreme example, where it was made explicit that non-believers saw the risen Jesus, is the remarkable resurrection scene in the Gospel of Peter. In that account, the guards at the tomb actually observed the risen Jesus leaving the tomb supported by two angels. 'The heads of the two reached to heaven', it says, 'but the one whom they bore with their hands reached beyond the heavens.' Explaining the events at the tomb to Pontius Pilate, the guards declared, 'Truly he was a son of God.'[29]

To turn to the Church Fathers, Ignatius of Antioch (*c.* 30–107) is a good place to begin. He cited and stressed the biblical accounts of Jesus' encouraging the disciples to touch his resurrection body and to examine the pre-mortem wounds. Jesus rose from the dead, Ignatius said, not just 'in appearance' but 'in the body'. 'He both ate and drank with [the disciples] during forty entire days.' Ignatius concluded, 'And I know he was possessed of a body not only in his being born and crucified, but I also know that He was so after His resurrection, and believe that He is so now.'[30]

Like Ignatius, Justin Martyr (*fl. c.* 150) was critical of those who maintained that 'Jesus himself appeared only as spiritual, and not in flesh, but presented merely the appearance of flesh.'[31] Against Docetic tendencies in the church, Justin emphasized the resurrection of the body. He argued that it was to confirm his bodily resurrection that Jesus appeared in physical form, allowed the disciples to examine the pre-mortem wounds, and ate with them. Justin went on to say, 'And when he had thus shown them that there is truly a resurrection of the flesh [and] that it is not impossible for flesh to ascend into heaven . . . , "He was taken up into heaven while they beheld," as he was in the flesh.'[32]

Doubtless with some of the same heresies in mind, Irenaeus (d. *c.* 200) also stressed the 'fleshiness' of the resurrection and the biblical accounts that underscore that notion. He said, 'In the same manner, therefore, as Christ did rise in the substance of the flesh, and pointed out to his disciples the mark of the nails and the opening in his side (now these are the tokens of that flesh which rose from the dead), so "shall he also", it is said, "raise us up by His own power".'[33]

---

[29] See David R. Cartlidge and David L. Dungan (eds.), *Documents for the Study of the Gospels* (Philadelphia: Fortress Press, 1980), p. 85. The quotations are from vv. 40 and 45.

[30] Alexander Roberts and James Donaldson (eds.), *Ante Nicene Fathers*, vol. i (Grand Rapids, MI: Eerdmans, 1989), p. 85 (*The Epistle of St. Ignatius to the Smyrnaeans*, vol. iii).

[31] Ibid., 295 (*Fragments of the Lost Work of Justin on the Resurrection*, vol. ii).

[32] Ibid., 298 (*Fragments*, vol. ix).

[33] Roberts and Donaldson, p. 532 (*Irenaeus Against Heresies*, vols. v, vii, i).

There are, of course, limitations on how far this first argument can take us. For one thing, some people do not particularly care what the Fathers had to say. For another, some might argue that the opinions of the Fathers on this topic are suspect because they wrote before the advent of the historical-critical method in scriptural studies. For a third, some might try to relativize the views of the second-century Fathers by arguing that their emphasis on the physicality of the resurrection merely reflects their theological context, one in which orthodoxy was endangered by Docetic and Gnostic tendencies.

But there are people who want to take Christian tradition seriously and who think (as I do) that any theological opinion which all or virtually all the Fathers held is at least prima facie probable. For them, it is certainly worth noting that the second-century Fathers all appeared to hold that the resurrected Jesus was seen in an ordinary sense.

2. *The theological significance of appearances amenable to ordinary vision.* As noted, my primary argument in this chapter is the historical one that Jesus' resurrection appearances were seen rather than visualized. But this does not preclude theological or even apologetic significance. I reject the notion, implicit in some New Testament scholarship, that finding a theological purpose behind a certain scriptural account is inconsistent with that account being a true account of what actually occurred.

Well then, what theological difference does it make (if I am correct) that the risen Jesus was seen rather than visualized, that anybody (believer or not) who had been in the right place at the right time could have seen him, that no special or extraordinary divine assistance was needed? There are several points that could be made, but I will focus on two, the first a brief point about Christian doctrine, the second a more detailed apologetic point.

The doctrinal item is this: the claim that the witnesses saw, rather than visualized, Jesus underscores the Christian notion of incarnation, the claim that God became a human being in Jesus Christ.[34] As Aquinas says in a slightly different context (he was discussing the question of why the angel of annunciation was seen by the Virgin Mary via normal sight), the angel was seen by Mary because 'he came to announce the Incarnation of the invisible God. Wherefore it is becoming that, in order to make this known, an invisible creature should assume a form in which to appear visibly.'[35] In other words, incarnation rules out all Gnostic-like denigration of bodily existence and the

---

[34] I owe this point to Janet Martin Soskice. See her essay, 'Sight and Vision in Medieval Christian Thought', in Martin Jay and Teresa Brennan (eds.), *Vision in Context: Historical and Contemporary Perspectives on Sight* (London: Routledge, 1996), pp. 29–43.

[35] *Summa Theologica* (trans. Fathers of the English Dominican Province) (New York: Benzinger Brothers, Inc., 1947), 3a. 30. 3.

bodily senses. The claim that God became flesh means that sight and the other senses are not to be belittled or abhorred. Of course I am not saying that the friends of graced seeing deny or even consistently should deny incarnation. But the claim that the risen Jesus was seen rather than visualized strongly underscores the notion that God took on a human body, and that the human body cannot, accordingly, be all bad. The body was not only created by God and is thus good; the body is also the vehicle through which we come to know God. Those like Mary Magdalene who saw Jesus saw God made visible.

Let me now turn to the apologetic point. As everyone recognizes, the claim that Jesus was raised from the dead was at the centre of the message that the earliest Christians preached. They were very much interested in trying to convince people to believe as they did. Now imagine the following situation. One of the witnesses to the resurrection (say, Mary Magdalene) is speaking to a non-believing friend. She says: 'Yes, I saw him; that's why I believe he was raised from the dead; that's why I'm so sure. Sorry, but you wouldn't have seen him even if you had been there beside me. Only those who were especially blessed by God with enhanced vision could have seen him. The most you would have seen was possibly a bright light. But I was one of the lucky ones; I saw him.'

One suspects—to put it mildly—that such an argument would lead the non-believing friend to be suspicious. Even if it were obvious that Mary was sincere—that is, was not lying or perpetrating a fraud—the thought would strongly occur to the friend that Mary had been deluded. There would be every reason to hold that her purported 'especially blessed vision' was not veridical. Of course, this same suspicion could be raised—and doubtless was raised—even if Mary had claimed to see rather than visualize the risen Jesus. Still, it is clear that there is far more room for doubt on the 'visualization' account than on the 'ordinary sight' account. On the second account, Mary's claims at least *could have been* empirically verified in a respectable public sense. On the first account, they could not have been. Accordingly, the apologetic task faced by the witnesses to the resurrection was slightly easier because they could say (if I am right in my central claim here), 'I saw Jesus.'

That Jesus was seen rather than visualized by the witnesses to the resurrection accordingly has this theological implication: what they saw was Jesus, not an impostor or a hallucination or a mass of ectoplasm or a sort of interactive hologram. And the fact that it was Jesus could have been verified in a quite ordinary sense—in a similar way to how I might verify a claim that a colleague of mine is walking down the hall—that is, simply by looking. In other words, convincing evidence for the resurrection of Jesus was present for anyone to have seen. It was not held in reserve for the benefit of a few initiates. The evidence for the resurrection of Jesus was not arcane and psychological, but public and empirical.

VI

Let me explain what I take to be the logic of my overall argument in this chapter. As I argued earlier, any sensible attempt to arrive at the plain sense of the scriptural accounts of the resurrection appearances of Jesus—whether that reading is done in the second century or the twenty-first—would entail that the risen Jesus was seen rather than visualized. That is, the risen Jesus was a physical body that was objectively present to the witnesses in space and time, and he was accordingly seen in a normal sense of that word. Now, that reading of the stories, like any reading of any text, can be overturned in favour of another reading by convincing reasons. We have examined six arguments that can be used to overturn the traditional reading. We have found them all unconvincing and, in some cases, rather easy to defeat. In my view, then, we are left with the church's traditional reading of the resurrection texts. Jesus was seen.[36]

Suppose I am right in my main claim: that it was seeing rather than visualizing. That is, anybody who had been there with Mary Magdalene could similarly have seen Jesus; a camera could have taken a picture of him. Does anything of interest follow about the nature of resurrection faith?

Here it would be helpful to distinguish (as Brown does[37]) between sight and insight. Anybody who had been there (I hold) could have seen Jesus. It would even have been possible (I suggest) for an unbeliever—one, let us say, who happened to have known Jesus—to have recognized him. 'This is Jesus of Nazareth,' such a person could have said. But apart from the illumination of the Holy Spirit, such a person would lack insight. 'What on earth happened? I thought he had died,' such a person might have reflected. Or: 'I have no idea why he seems to be here, but there must be some rational explanation.'

Were enhanced powers of perception—powers that were granted to some and denied to others—necessary to have seen the risen Christ? I am arguing that the answer to that question is no. But was a special grace necessary to see the risen Christ in such a way as to recognize him as Lord and to grasp what he was calling one to be and do? Of course.

---

[36] Or, as Sherlock Holmes says (near the end of 'The Beryl Coronet'), 'It is an old maxim of mine that when you have excluded the impossible, whatever remains, however improbable, must be the truth.'

[37] *Virginal Conception* (n. 13 above), pp. 112–13.

In other words, only the person to whom God has given the gift of faith will have the insight to be able to say, 'He is here alive because God raised him from the dead.' Or even, 'He is Lord.'[38] A person who makes such a confession, whether that person was a member of the first generation of Christians or lives today, is a witness to the resurrection.[39]

---

[38] Indeed, 'We have seen the Lord' seems to be the normal testimony of the witnesses to the resurrection (1 Cor. 9: 1; Luke 24: 34; John 28: 18, 25; 21: 7), rather than 'We have seen Jesus.' (The one exception is Matthew—see 28: 5, 9, 10, 16, 18.)

[39] I would like to thank Gerald O'Collins, S.J., William L. Craig, Carey Newman, and Pheme Perkins for their helpful comments on earlier drafts of this chapter.

9

Was Jesus Mad, Bad or God?

I

In Chapter 5 I pointed out that Christian tradition holds that Christ was not just raised by God from the dead but was (and is) the incarnate Son of God. That he was, in the words of the Nicene Creed, 'truly human', few people doubt. That he was nonetheless 'truly divine' is the controversial point. In the present chapter we will see whether that point can be not just *claimed* (on the basis of revelation) *but argued* for.

The argument that Jesus was either 'mad, bad, or God' (let's call it the MBG argument) is sometimes used by popular Christian apologists as a way of defending the incarnation. Since Jesus claimed to be the divine Son of God—so the argument goes—then if he was not in fact divine he must have been either a lunatic or a moral monster. No sane and righteous person can wrongly claim to be divine. But since Jesus was evidently neither a lunatic nor a moral monster—so the argument concludes—he must indeed have been divine.

Occasionally one encounters this argument in serious Christian literature as well. For example, C. S. Lewis wrote:

Then comes the real shock. Among these Jews there suddenly turns up a man who goes about talking as if he was God. He claims to forgive sins. He says He has always existed. He says he is coming to judge the world at the end of time.... I am trying here to prevent anyone saying the really foolish thing that people often say about Him: 'I'm ready to accept Jesus as a great moral teacher, but I don't accept his claim to be God.' That is the one thing we must not say. A man who was merely a man and said the sort of things Jesus said would not be a great moral teacher. He would be either a lunatic—on a level with the man who says he is a poached egg—or else he would be the Devil in Hell. You must make your choice. Either this man was, and is, the Son of God: or else a madman or something worse.[1]

---

[1] C. S. Lewis, *Mere Christianity* (New York: Macmillan, 1960), pp. 40–1. I have been unable to locate any published uses of the argument prior to the twentieth century. G. K. Chesterton does not state the argument as clearly or succinctly as does Lewis, but its premisses can be found in *The Everlasting Man* (Garden City, NY: Doubleday, 1955 [1925]), pp. 185–212.

And even J. A. T. Robinson, in the midst of a discussion of the Fourth Gospel in which he argues for the early dating of the book and the general historical reliability of its picture of Jesus, can say: 'No sane person goes about saying "Before Abraham was I am" or "Whoever eats my flesh and drinks my blood shall live forever." These are theological interpretations, not literal utterances. Yet at the deepest level of faith they may indeed be the truth about the eternal Word of life, made flesh in this supremely individual and uniquely moral man of history.'[2]

On the other hand, the MBG argument is often severely criticized, both by people who do and by people who do not believe in the divinity of Jesus. For example, Donald MacKinnon criticized the argument on the grounds that it presupposes that we know what it is like to be God.[3] And John Hick makes critical reference to the MBG argument in *The Myth of God Incarnate*. He recalls that he was taught the argument in his childhood confirmation class and comments that it reflects a pre-critical attitude towards the Christian faith, one in which the idea of supernatural divine interventions in human history are acceptable and in which the Gospels are read as straightforward historical accounts of the life of Jesus.[4] Others object to the MBG argument on the grounds that the statements made by Jesus about himself in the Gospels that form the basis of the argument are being misinterpreted; properly understood, they do not constitute 'claims to divinity'. Finally, and doubtless most importantly, some argue that the statements about himself that are attributed to Jesus in the Gospels were not really said by him; they express the views not of Jesus, but of the Christian church forty to sixty years later.

It is odd that the MBG argument is subject to such differing evaluations— all the way from people who endorse and use it, presumably because they consider it a good argument,[5] to people who dismiss it as unworthy of serious

---

[2] J. A. T. Robinson, *Can We Trust the New Testament?* (Grand Rapids, MI: Eerdmans, 1977), p. 91. See also Reginald H. Fuller and Pheme Perkins, *Who Is This Christ? Gospel Christology and Contemporary Faith* (Philadelphia: Fortress Press, 1983), p. 24: 'Therefore, the question of Jesus' identity, role, or relationship to the divine forced itself on those who came in contact with him. Either he was blasphemous, a fool, or he spoke with divine authority.'

[3] MacKinnon made this remark in a lecture attended by me at the Divinity School, Cambridge, in the Lent Term of 1978.

[4] John Hick (ed.), *The Myth of God Incarnate* (Philadelphia: Westminster Press, 1977), p. 4.

[5] Two contemporary apologists who make use of the argument are William L. Craig and Peter Kreeft. See William L. Craig, *Reasonable Faith: Christian Truth and Apologetics* (Wheaton, IL: Crossway Books, 1984), pp. 233–54, and Peter Kreeft and Ronald K. Tacelli, *Handbook of Christian Apologetics* (Downers Grove, IL: Inter-Varsity Press, 1994), pp. 150–74. For a more extended discussion of the argument, see Peter Kreeft, *Between Heaven and Hell: A Dialog Somewhere Beyond Death with John F. Kennedy, C. S. Lewis, and Aldous Huxley* (Downers Grove, IL: Inter-Varsity Press, 1982). See also James M. Boice, *Foundations of Christian Faith* (Downers Grove, IL: Inter-Varsity Press, 1986), pp. 275–7.

consideration.[6] Is it a good argument, or not?[7] Probably no central issue of Christian belief depends on the argument. Orthodox Christians could go on believing in the divinity of Jesus even if the argument fails. (On the other hand, if the argument succeeds, those who deny the incarnation at the very least have some explaining to do.) But the frequency with which the argument appears in popular defences of the divinity of Jesus, and its almost total absence from discussions about the status of Jesus by professional theologians and biblical scholars, makes one curious what to make of the argument.

This chapter constitutes a defence of one version of the argument. I will claim that the MBG argument, properly understood, can establish the rationality of belief in the incarnation of Jesus. But a caveat is called for: I do not want to be interpreted as implying that any validation of Jesus' divinity must rest solely on what Jesus himself (explicitly or implicitly) claimed to be. Along with the memory of Jesus' sayings and doings, the post-Easter response to his death and resurrection (as well as the coming of the Holy Spirit) also played a crucial role in forming the early Christian confession of Jesus as divine Lord and Son of God. Even if it concentrates on what we know of Jesus' pre-Easter activity, the MBG argument should not be taken to belittle or ignore the post-Easter developments. I am definitely not suggesting that the MBG argument is the only, or even the best, argument that Christians can give for the divinity of Jesus.

II

It will facilitate matters if I lay out the argument in what I take to be its logical form:

---

[6] One such person is John Beversluis, who strongly criticizes C. S. Lewis' version of the MBG argument on pp. 54–7 of his *C. S. Lewis and the Search for Rational Religion* (Grand Rapids, MI: Eerdmans, 1985). He calls the argument 'emotionally inflammatory' and claims it is based on a 'fallacious strategy', i.e. a 'false dilemma'. It is 'not a philosophical argument but a psychological spell'. Beversluis is correct that the truth and value of Jesus' moral teachings need not be affected by a judgement that he was mistaken in claiming to be divine; even if he were a lunatic, his moral teachings may still stand. But the major problem with Beversluis' critique is that he does not succeed in explaining how a sane person can be sincerely mistaken in claiming to be God. When Beversluis sets out to explain this point, he inexplicably switches from Jesus' claim to be divine to his claim to be the Messiah. These are two quite different things. Of course there were sane people in ancient Judaism who mistakenly claimed to be the Messiah; indeed, that was almost commonplace. But how can a sane person—especially a first-century Jew—mistakenly claim to be *divine*?

[7] In the present chapter I am presupposing the discussion of the nature of argument, proof, validity, soundness, and success for an argument in my *God, Reason, and Theistic Proofs* (Edinburgh: Edinburgh University Press, 1997), pp. 1–14, 188–93.

(1) Jesus claimed, either explicitly or implicitly, to be divine.
(2) Jesus was either right or wrong in claiming to be divine.
(3) If Jesus was wrong in claiming to be divine, Jesus was either mad or bad.
(4) Jesus was not bad.
(5) Jesus was not mad.
(6) Therefore, Jesus was not wrong in claiming to be divine.
(7) Therefore Jesus was right in claiming to be divine.
(8) Therefore, Jesus was divine.

Let me now comment on each premiss. Some will require more extended discussion than others.

Premiss (1) will turn out to be crucial—indeed, it is probably the crux of the argument—so let us postpone comment on it till later. Premiss (2) is a substitution-instance of a well-recognized law of logic, namely the law of excluded middle. Some philosophers have raised questions about this law (which says that every proposition is either true or, if not true, then false), but it nevertheless seems about as secure as any premiss of any argument can be. The vast majority of philosophers will agree that (2) is not just true, but necessarily true. The claim, 'Jesus was correct in claiming to be divine,' is either true or, if not true, then false. The MBG argument cannot be successfully challenged here.

But premiss (3) *can* be questioned. Let us say that the statement, 'Jesus was mad,' means that he was insane or mentally deluded, just like those confused and frequently institutionalized people today who sincerely believe themselves to be the Virgin Mary or Napoleon. Let us say that the statement, 'Jesus was bad,' means that he was a liar, or was at least lying about who he was, just like someone today who intentionally deceives people by claiming to be someone else.

Perhaps Jesus claimed to be divine, was neither mad nor bad, but was merely *sincerely mistaken* about the matter, just as it is possible for a person to be sincerely mistaken about who her true parents are. Now the defender of the MBG argument will surely not want to claim that it is logically or even causally impossible[8] that Jesus was sincerely mistaken in claiming to be divine. But such a person will ask whether it is *probable* that he was sincerely mistaken. Is it probable that

---

[8] Let us say that 'Jesus was sincerely mistaken in claiming to be divine' is logically impossible if the statement amounts to or entails a contradiction. Let us say that 'Jesus was sincerely mistaken in claiming to be divine' is causally impossible if its truth entails a violation of one or more of the laws of nature—gravity, thermodynamics, the speed of light, etc.

(9) Any good person who mistakenly claims to be divine is mad

is false? Or is it probable that

(10) Any sane person who mistakenly claims to be divine is bad[9]

is false? These are difficult questions. I am inclined to accept both (9) and (10) (and thus (3) as well), but I do not know how to prove them. Certainly a sane and good person could be sincerely mistaken about who her true parents are. Doubtless this very thing has occurred. But it is hard to see how a sane and good person could be sincerely mistaken in holding the extremely bizarre belief that she is divine (assuming she uses the word 'divine' as Christians normally do in this context, i.e. as indicating a robust identity with the omnipotent, omniscient, loving creator of the world). There *is* something extremely odd about the notion of a sincere, good, and sane person mistakenly claiming to be God. Accordingly, (9) and (10) (and thus (3)), seem to have a high degree of plausibility. I conclude, then, that while (3) may be false, it is most probably true and can stand as a premiss in a successful argument.

One suspects that few will want to dispute (4) and (5). It is possible, however, that someone might want to use them against each other, so to speak, and argue either that

(11) If Jesus mistakenly claimed to be divine and wasn't mad, then, improbable as it seems, he must have been bad

or else

(12) If Jesus mistakenly claimed to be divine and wasn't bad, then, improbable as it seems, he must have been mad.

But, again, I believe there is good reason to accept both (4) and (5). Unless the most radical of Gospel critics are correct—those who claim we can know virtually nothing about the historical Jesus[10]—there is precious little in the Gospels to suggest that Jesus was either a lunatic or a liar, and much to suggest strongly that he was neither.

Virtually everyone who reads the Gospels—whether committed to Christianity or not—comes away with the conviction that Jesus was a wise and good man. He was loving, compassionate, and caring, hardly the sort who tells lies for reasons of self-interest. During his lifetime Jesus was apparently accused by his enemies of being demon-possessed and 'out of his mind'

---

[9] The Reverend Jim Jones, whose cult followers committed mass suicide in Guyana in 1978, is reported to have said to them: 'I'm the closest thing to God you'll ever see.'

[10] 'I do indeed think that we can now know almost nothing concerning the life and personality of Jesus.' Rudolf Bultmann, *Jesus and the Word* (trans. Louise Pettibone Smith and Ermine Huntress Lantera) (New York: Scribner's, 1958 [1934]), p. 8.

(cf. John 10: 20), but Peter Kreeft argues convincingly that Jesus shows none of the character traits usually associated with those who have delusions of grandeur or 'divinity complexes'. Such people are easily recognizably by their egotism, narcissism, inflexibility, predictable behaviour, and inability to relate understandingly and lovingly to others.[11] Other seriously disturbed people show signs of extreme irritability, debilitating anxiety, or inappropriate beliefs and behaviour. This is not the sort of picture of Jesus that we form by reading the Gospels.

We live in an age when scholars confidently make all sorts of bizarre claims about the historical Jesus. But few scripture scholars of any theological stripe seriously entertain the possibility that Jesus was either a lunatic or a liar. When we return below to premiss (1), we will have to enter more deeply into the question of the reliability of the New Testament picture of Jesus. Suffice it to say here that there seems to be every good reason to accept both (4) and (5).[12]

Premiss (6) is entailed by premisses (2), (3), (4), and (5). It is impossible for them to be true and (6) false. Premiss (7) is entailed by premisses (2) and (6). If they are true, it is true. Finally, step (8), the conclusion of the MBG argument, is entailed by premiss (7). If (7) is true, then (8) must be true as well. What we have in the MBG argument, then, is a *valid* argument. That is, there are no mistakes in logic in the argument; it is logically impossible for its premisses (i.e. (1)–(7)) to be true and its conclusion (i.e. step (8)) false.

But is the argument also *sound*? Let us say that a sound argument is a valid argument whose premisses are all true. It appears thus far that while premisses (3), (4), and (5) can be criticized, a plausible case can be made for their truth. Clearly the premiss that will seem most vulnerable to criticism is premiss (1).

Is it true that Jesus claimed, either explicitly or implicitly, to be divine? Before addressing this question directly, it will be helpful to consider the notion of an 'implicit claim', since my argument in the present chapter is that Jesus *implicitly* claimed to be divine. First, what is a 'claim'? Let us say that a claim is an assertion or statement, the kind of linguistic utterance that has a truth value. That is, according to the law of excluded middle, it is true or, if not true, then false. Now an *explicit* claim that a proposition p is true would be a statement like 'p is true' or 'Not-p is false' or 'It is true that p is true' or even simply 'p'.

---

[11] *Handbook of Christian Apologetics* (n. 5 above), p. 159.

[12] For a fascinating argument against any claim that Jesus was mad, written by a practising clinical psychiatrist, see O. Quentin Hyder, 'On the Mental Health of Jesus Christ', *Journal of Psychology and Theology*, 5/1 (Winter, 1977), pp. 3–12. Hyder's argument falters at one or two places, but he skilfully shows that we find no convincing evidence in the biblical materials that Jesus was delusional, paranoid, schizoid, or manic depressive, and lots of convincing evidence that he was an emotionally sound and healthy person.

What then is an *implicit* claim that p is true? Well, there appear to be several ways of implicitly claiming that p is true. (1) One might implicitly claim that p is true by explicitly asserting that x, y, and z are true, where x, y, and z logically entail p. If one were explicitly to assert 'R. E. Lee was a Confederate general' and 'R. E. Lee was a famous general' and 'R. E. Lee was a great general,' that could be taken as an implicit claim to the effect that 'R. E. Lee was a great and famous Confederate general.' (2) Or one might implicitly claim that p is true by explicitly asserting x, y, and z, where only people who hold that p is true can reasonably hold that x, y, and z are true. If one were explicitly to assert that 'R. E. Lee was a Confederate general' and 'R. E. Lee was a famous general' and 'R. E. Lee was a great general,' that could be taken as an implicit claim to the effect that 'R. E. Lee was a human being.'[13] (3) Most importantly, one might implicitly claim that p is true by *doing* action A, where the only people, or the only sensible people, who do A are people who believe p. Suppose that Jones, tired and perspiring at the end of a long run, bends over and drinks from a drinking fountain. This action might be taken as an implicit claim on Jones' part to the effect that 'The liquid emanating from this drinking fountain is water (and not, say, vodka or battery acid).'

We are now able to return to the question of whether Jesus implicitly claimed to be divine. This is a good question, to say the least. Much ink has been spilled over it, especially in the past two centuries. (Before that it would have been taken as virtually axiomatic that the answer is yes—indeed, that he *explicitly* claimed as much.) What is clear, and I think is quite beyond dispute, is that a literal and ahistorical reading of the Gospels, and especially the fourth Gospel, strongly supports premiss (1). Notice, for example, the following statements that are attributed to Jesus there (as well as, in some cases, the reactions of those who heard him):

But Jesus answered them, 'My Father is still working, and I also am working.' For this reason the Jews were seeking all the more to kill him, because he was not only breaking the sabbath, but was also calling God his own Father, thereby making himself equal to God. (John 5: 17–18)

The Father judges no one but has given all judgment to the Son, so that all may honor the Son just as they honor the Father. (John 5: 22)

'Very truly, I tell you, before Abraham was, I am.' So they picked up stones to throw at him, but Jesus hid himself and went out of the temple. (John 8: 58–9)

---

[13] The difference between (1) and (2) is perhaps not very great. In the case of (2), it is quite possible that the one who is making the implicit claim has never consciously formulated the belief, 'R. E. Lee was a human being', while that seems less probable for the one who is making the implicit claim that 'R. E. Lee was a great and famous Confederate general' in (1).

'The Father and I are one.' The Jews took up stones again to stone him. (John 10: 30–1)

'The Father is in me and I am in the Father.' Then they tried to arrest him again, but he escaped from their hands. (John 10: 38–9)

'Have I been with you all this time, Philip, and you still do not know me? Whoever has seen me has seen the Father.' (John 14: 9)

Now there appear to be four main attitudes that might be taken towards claims such as these. First, perhaps Jesus explicitly taught his own divinity, that is, perhaps words such as these constitute the *ipsissima verba* of Jesus. Secondly, perhaps Jesus only implicitly taught his own divinity. Thirdly, perhaps Jesus said the things, or some of them, that have been taken to imply his own divinity in John's Gospel and elsewhere, but this is not the proper interpretation of those sayings. Those who defend this option (which corresponds to the third objection to the MBG argument mentioned in Section I) might argue as follows: the words from Jesus like those just cited should be interpreted as indicating something less than robust identity with God; perhaps Jesus was only indicating unity of purpose or will with the Father, or something of that sort. What Jesus *really meant*—so it might be said—is that he had a very special place in God's redemptive plan, or he had an extraordinarily strong desire to do God's bidding, or he felt such an intimate closeness to God that it was almost as if God were his own father.[14] Fourthly, perhaps Jesus said nothing about the matter, and the relevant statements attributed to him in the Gospels are inauthentic; they amount to representations of the beliefs not of Jesus, but of the Christian church at the time that the Gospels were being written.

In the present chapter, I do not intend to defend the first option, but rather the second; thus I must argue against options three and four.

III

As noted in Section I, there appear to be four main criticisms that can be raised against the MBG argument. First, it presupposes that we know what it is like to be God. Secondly, it presupposes a naive world-view, one that allows for special divine acts in history. Thirdly (the same point as the third option

[14] This is certainly the route that must be taken by all those who, like Jehovah's Witnesses, claim to accept the full theological authority of the Bible but reject the idea that Jesus was God incarnate.

just discussed), it misinterprets what Jesus meant by the statements about himself that we find in the Gospels. Fourthly, it presupposes a pre-critical view of the Gospels (and especially John), one that views them as straight-forward history. Let us consider these objections in turn. (When we get to the fourth objection, we will also be replying to the fourth option noted at the end of Section II—that the high christological statements attributed to Jesus in the Gospels are inauthentic.)

As to the first criticism, it is not easy to understand precisely what MacKinnon had in mind. What he said was that the MBG argument presup-poses that we know what it is like to be God. And of course it is true that we do not know what it is like to be God. But it is hard to grasp exactly why the MBG arguer must presuppose that we have that knowledge. Let us make a distinction between *knowing what it is like to be God* and *knowing what God is like*. It is surely true that it would border on blasphemy for those who use the MBG argument—or anybody else, for that matter—to presuppose that they know what it is like to be God. In the fullest sense, we do not even know what it is like to be another human being, or what it is like to be a bat.[15]

But is it possible for human beings to know what God is like? The answer to this, at least from a Christian perspective, is surely yes. One of the defining ideas of the Christian faith (as well as other versions of theism) is that God has been revealed. God has chosen to show us and tell us what God is like. God is self-revealed. We learn in the scriptures, for example, that God is the creator, that God is all-powerful, that God is all-knowing, that God is to be wor-shipped and obeyed, that God is loving, that God works for the salvation of humankind, that God forgives our sins, and so on.

It is true that the MBG argument presupposes that we know something of what God is like. If a person is morally despicable, that person is not God. If a person makes insane claims, that person is not God. But, as noted, Christians hold that we *do* know what God is like (to the extent that it has been revealed to us by God),[16] and there seems to be nothing blasphemous or otherwise theologically untoward here. For the MBG argument to work, our knowledge of God need not be comprehensive; we need to know only a little about God. So the limited nature of our knowledge of God need not constitute a problem for the MBG argument. But does the MBG argument presuppose that we

---

[15] See Thomas Nagel's article, 'What is it Like to Be a Bat?', in Douglas Hofstadter and Daniel Dennett (eds.), *The Mind's I* (Toronto: Bantam Books, 1981), pp. 391–403.

[16] To avoid any hint of circularity (since Christians claim that the fullest revelation of God's nature is Christ), we could even limit our knowledge of God to what can be known about God apart from Christ. We could limit ourselves to what has been revealed about God in the natural order, or in the Old Testament law, or in the words of the prophets.

know what it is like to be God? Certainly not. Or at least, it is not easy to see how it does so. I conclude that MacKinnon's criticism does not damage the MBG argument.

As to the second criticism, Hick argues that the MBG argument presupposes 'a pre-critical worldview', one in which special divine acts in human history are allowable. But there is something slightly off-target about this criticism: Hick's objection appears to be directed more against the idea of incarnation as such, than against the MBG argument in favour of the incarnation. Hick is right that the very idea of incarnation—of God becoming a human being—presupposes divine interventions in human history. This is why Deists must deny not only all miracles, epiphanies, visions from God, and prophetic messages from God, but all incarnations as well.

And it is true that if the very idea of incarnation is discredited, then the MBG argument can hardly constitute a successful argument in favour of incarnation. Still, since Hick's criticism is not directed against the MBG argument per se, and especially since many contemporary Christian philosophers have defended the adequacy of theism versus Deism (i.e. of the possibility of special divine acts),[17] I will discuss this matter no further here. (An atheist could similarly argue that belief in incarnation is irrational because belief in *God* is outmoded, but again that would not count as an objection to the MBG argument itself.)

As to the third objection, the violent reactions of Jesus' enemies in the texts cited (and in many other texts where Jesus speaks about himself, some from the Synoptic Gospels) seem to preclude any such minimalist interpretation as, 'Jesus just meant that he felt extraordinarily close to God.' As well as the reactions mentioned in the above citations, note the argument of the chief priests at John's trial account: 'We have a law, and according to that law he ought to die because he has claimed to be the Son of God' (John 19: 7). These sorts of strong reactions to Jesus by the religious leaders are so pervasive throughout the Gospels that it would be odd to rule that, since John's Gospel was late (which is true), this statement that he attributes to the chief priests cannot be authentic. It seems very much in line with what we find in the Synoptics. And it would hardly have constituted an offence worthy of arrest and execution had Jesus simply been declaring his own unity of purpose or will with the Father, or claiming to have a special place in God's plan. Odd, maybe; egotistical, maybe; but hardly blasphemous.

As noted earlier, the fourth criticism—that the MBG argument presupposes a pre-critical view of the Gospels and especially John as straightforward

---

[17] Including myself in chapter I of Stephen T. Davis, *Risen Indeed: Making Sense of the Resurrection* (Grand Rapids, MI: Eerdmans, 1993).

history—is the really important one. This criticism amounts to a denial of premiss (1) of the MBG argument. Is premiss (1) true?

As was noted in Chapter 5, it is a commonplace of much contemporary New Testament scholarship that words such as those cited above from the fourth Gospel do not constitute the *ipsissima verba* of Jesus. These statements, it is said, and the many other statements in the New Testament that imply or seem to imply the divinity of Jesus, tell us more about the faith of the early church at the time the Gospels were being written or were receiving final form than they do about the actual teachings of Jesus. Later Christians wrongly attributed these words to Jesus as part of their theological programme. Thus—so a critic of the MBG argument will argue—the MBG argument for the incarnation cannot even get going. Its first premiss is false; Jesus never claimed—explicitly or implicitly—to be divine.

IV

Is this a good objection? Well, there is much in the neighbourhood that is beyond reproach. As noted, it is true that the Gospels are statements of faith with definite theological agendas rather than 'facts-only' biographies of Jesus. It is also almost certainly true that John's Gospel was the last canonical Gospel written, and thus the furthest removed from the events it records. But it is a long way from these sensible admissions about the Gospels to the claim that none of the sayings of Jesus that imply his own divinity can be authentic. Let us see what can be said on behalf of the historical reliability of some of the statements that Jesus makes about himself in the Gospels, especially in the Synoptics. I will *not* presuppose the view that the evangelists were offering straightforward, theologically neutral history. Moreover, I take it as given that the church translated, edited, rearranged, recontextualized, paraphrased, abbreviated, and expanded the sayings of Jesus. Furthermore, since the New Testament was written in Greek, then assuming that Jesus spoke and taught in Aramaic, precisely *none* of the sayings attributed to Jesus in the Gospels constitute his *ipsissima verba*.

Again, premiss (1) of the MBG argument says:

(1) Jesus claimed, either explicitly or implicitly, to be divine.

Is this premiss true? I am going to argue that it is. But I should first note three things that I am not claiming. First, I am not claiming that Jesus went about saying 'I am God' or making any sort of *explicit* claim to status as deity. The radical monotheism to which first-century Judaism was committed, in all its various forms, made anything like that impossible. Secondly, I am not claiming that Jesus expressed his consciousness of his divinity in the language of later creedal orthodoxy, for example, 'truly divine and truly human', 'of one substance with the Father', 'Second Person of the Blessed Trinity', and so on. Thirdly, I am not claiming to be able to psychoanalyse Jesus. As N. T. Wright points out, historians are frequently concerned with the motivation and self-understanding of the figures they write about, especially as they find expression in what these figures can sensibly be concluded to have said and done. These same sorts of concerns motivate what I am trying to do here.[18]

My claim is that, given his words and deeds, it is highly probable that Jesus implicitly saw or experienced himself as divine, as having a unique relationship of divine sonship to God. This claim does not necessarily mean that Jesus, throughout his life or even throughout his ministry, ever formulated or expressed the idea precisely in language, although I hold that at some point he was able to do so. I suspect his sense of mission and identity was shaped and confirmed by various crucial events during his ministry, for example, the baptism, temptation, transfiguration, and passion. It is possible to have a vague and inchoate awareness of something that one only later is able to capture in words. So the question, 'Did Jesus know that he was God?' is ill-formed. Jesus surely did not confuse himself with God the Father to whom he prayed. But did he implicitly claim to be divine or to have divine prerogatives? Did he implicitly claim to have a unique relationship to the Father which in effect placed him on a par with God? I believe the answer to these questions is very probably yes. (Again, my argument will not presuppose a naive and ahistorical reading of the Gospels.)

How do we go about deciding what someone believes or implicitly claims? Well, the most obvious way to find out whether Jones believes p is to ask her or wait till she expresses some sort of epistemic attitude towards p (assertion, denial, certainty, doubt, uncertainty, etc.). And in cases where there is no good reason to doubt Jones' word, this will normally be convincing evidence. In other cases, we might have to listen to other things that Jones says or watch things that she does to see if any of them constitute convincing evidence that Jones implicitly claims that p (or not-p) is true. It is possible, as noted above, for a person to believe that p is true without ever having formulated 'p' as a conscious belief. There are probably people who walk to work every day who believe, without ever having consciously formulated the belief, that 'the pavement will hold me up'.

I will present my argument in two stages. The first will presuppose the basic correctness of the methods and conclusions of some of the most radical of

---

[18] N. T. Wright, 'Jesus and the Identity of God', *Ex Auditu*, 14 (1998), p. 51.

biblical critics.[19] Its aim is to open the door to the *possibility* of showing, even on the methods of people like Bultmann, Perrin, and the members of the Jesus Seminar, that Jesus implicitly taught his own divinity. The second stage (which contains five sub-arguments) will try to confirm the point that Jesus *actually did* this very thing. At this second stage, I will continue to eschew any naive or ahistorical view of the Gospels, but I will no longer consider myself limited by the views of the radical critics.

In this first stage of my argument, I want simply (1) to point out a fact about early Christian history that is becoming clearer and clearer, even if radical methods of criticism are employed, namely, that *worship of Jesus* was a very ancient phenomenon in the Christian community; and (2) to ask why this fact is so. As to the fact that worship of Jesus was primitive in the Christian community, Richard Bauckham says, 'The prevalence and centrality of the worship of Jesus in early Christianity from an early date has frequently been underestimated.... In the earliest Christian community Jesus was already understood to be risen and exalted to God's right hand in heaven, active in the community by his Spirit, and coming in the future as ruler and judge of the world.'[20]

Notice that prayers *addressed* to Jesus can be found from the earliest times. It is significant that Greek-speaking churches preserved in Aramaic the cry *Maranatha* ('Our Lord, come!') (1 Cor. 16: 22; *Didache* 10: 6); this fact shows its primitive origin. Personal prayers to Jesus seem to have been commonplace (2 Cor. 12: 8; 1 Thess. 3: 11–13; 2 Thess. 2: 16–17; 3: 5, 16; Acts 1: 24; 7: 59–60). There were also doxologies addressed to Christ, or to Christ and the Father together, although most appear in relatively late New Testament texts (2 Tim. 4: 18; 2 Pet. 3: 18; Rev. 1: 5–6, 13; cf. 7: 10). In earlier texts, doxologies with the phrase 'through Jesus Christ' appear (Rom. 16: 27; cf. 2 Cor. 1: 20). Hymns of praise to Christ were also common (Phil. 2: 6–11; 1 Tim. 3: 16; cf. Eph. 5: 19; Col. 3: 16).[21]

---

[19] Here I indicate my indebtedness to Royce Gordon Gruenler, who follows a similar methodology in his *New Approaches to Jesus and the Gospels: A Phenomenological and Exegetical Study of Synoptic Christology* (Grand Rapids, MI: Baker Book House, 1982), especially pp. 19–108.

[20] Richard Bauckham, 'Jesus, Worship of', *The Anchor Bible Dictionary*, vol. iii (New York: Doubleday, 1992), p. 812. See also L. W. Hurtado, 'Pre-70 C.E. Jewish Opposition to Christ Devotion', *Journal of Theological Studies*, 50/1 (April, 1999), pp. 35–58.

[21] The hymn from Philippians 2, in particular, witnesses to the way in which early Christians viewed the crucified and exalted Jesus as meriting the adoration of the universe. In *The Changing Faces of Jesus* (London: Penguin, 2000), Geza Vermes has recently suggested that a later, anonymous copyist inserted this hymn into the text of the letter (pp. 78–9)—a proposal which enjoys no support whatsoever from the manuscript evidence.

In a recent paper, L. W. Hurtado argues that a careful reading of Matthew and Mark reveals that there was vigorous Jewish opposition in the pre-70 period to Jewish-Christian worship of Jesus.[22] Bauckham claims that the transition from prayers to Jesus, thanksgiving to Jesus, and reverence for Jesus to actual *worship* of Jesus (cf. Acts 13: 2) was a smooth and perhaps not even conscious process; there is no evidence, he says, of anybody in the earliest Christian community contesting it. He concludes that 'the role which Jesus played in the Christian religion from the beginning was such as to cause him to be treated as God in worship.'[23]

All this came about despite the fact that the earliest Christians were Jews, people whose rigid monotheism and antipathy to worship of any other gods besides the Lord was perhaps their defining religious characteristic. Indeed, the New Testament church did not see itself as backing away from mono-theism; in 1 Corinthians 8: 4–6 Paul accepts the classic *Shema* of Judaism (Deut. 6: 4), but interprets the monotheism of the Christian community as including the lordship of Jesus. And in the Book of Revelation, Jesus is considered worthy of divine worship because worship of Jesus can be included in worship of the one God (Rev. 5: 8–12). Worship of Jesus *was* worship of (not a competitor to God but) God.

Next, a question. If Bauckham is correct that worship of Jesus was primitive in the Christian community, *why* is this the case? There appear to be two main possibilities. First, perhaps the early church worshipped Jesus because social, economic, liturgical, polemical, or other sorts of needs and pressures that the early Christians faced pushed them in that direction. That is, the early church made up the idea that Jesus was divine. Secondly, perhaps they worshipped Jesus because Jesus himself implicitly encouraged, instructed, or allowed them to do so. That is, perhaps Jesus himself was conscious of being divine and implicitly communicated that fact, by his words and deeds, to his followers.

Interestingly, the Synoptic Gospels, and especially Matthew, opt for the second alternative. That does not settle the case, because for now we are accepting the methodology and conclusions of some of the radical critics, and many of them regard Matthew's Gospel as an unreliable guide to the life of Jesus. Still, Matthew commonly uses one or another form of the word *proskynesis* (obeisance, prostration before someone in worship) in relation to Jesus. Jesus is worshipped by the wise men from the East (2: 2, 11), by the disciples in the boat (14: 33), by Mary Magdalene and the other Mary after the resurrection (28: 9), and by the eleven disciples on the mountain (28: 17).

---

[22] L. W. Hurtado, 'Pre-70 C.E. Jewish Opposition to Christ-Devotion', *Journal of Theological Studies*, 50/1 (April, 1999), pp. 5–6, 10.
[23] 'Jesus, Worship of' (n. 20 above), p. 815.

Bauckham argues that 'Matthew's consistent use of the word *proskynein* and his emphasis on the point show that he intends a kind of reverence which, paid to any other human, he would have regarded as idolatrous.'[24]

As a strict logical point, the mere fact that worship and prayers were addressed to Jesus does not entail that Jesus himself accepted the idea that he was divine. It is highly significant, however, that despite being a religious Jew who upheld the authority of the Hebrew Bible, he allowed worship of him to take place. There is no record of his interfering with the practice on the grounds that the disciples were coming dangerously close to idolatry or blasphemy.

Let us now look at a few Synoptics texts that are accepted as authentic by people like Bultmann, Perrin, and the members of the Jesus Seminar. Even in limiting ourselves in that way, I believe a probable case can be made that Jesus implicitly taught his own divinity.

But if it is by the finger of God that I cast out the demons, then the kingdom of God has come to you. (Luke 11: 20; par. Matt. 12: 28)

Bultmann enthusiastically accepted the authenticity of this statement from Jesus.[25] In it, Jesus is clearly claiming to be exhibiting in his exorcisms the eschatological power of the finger of God. Note the parallel to Exodus 8: 19, where the Egyptian magicians confess their inability to duplicate the plague of gnats and declare, 'This is the finger of God.' Jesus is claiming to be acting as the agent through whom the reign of God, with all God's power, enters history.

On a different vein, notice:

Listen to me, all of you, and understand; there is nothing outside a person that by going in can defile, but the things that come out are what defile. (Mark 7: 14–15; par. Matt. 15: 10–11; Thomas 14: 5)

This text, which Perrin accepts as authentic[26] and which the Jesus Seminar rates pink (i.e. places in the category of 'Jesus probably said something like this'),[27] is remarkable in the authority that Jesus is taking upon himself to relativize and de-emphasize Jewish dietary law. Jesus is in effect abolishing the divinely given food laws, that is, is dismantling one of the major barriers between Jews and Gentiles that God was understood to have erected. Jesus is

---

[24] 'Jesus, Worship of' (n. 20 above), p. 813.

[25] Rudolf Bultmann, *History of the Synoptic Tradition* (trans. John Marsh) (New York: Harper and Row, 1976), p. 162.

[26] Norman Perrin, *Rediscovering the Teaching of Jesus* (London: SCM Press, 1967), pp. 149–50.

[27] Robert Funk et al. (eds.), *The Five Gospels: The Search for the Authentic Words of Jesus* (New York: Macmillan, 1993), pp. 36, 69.

saying that, in the light of his own presence in the world, a radically new attitude towards religion is required. Along the same lines, notice this statement (again coloured pink by the Jesus Seminar):

The sabbath was made for humankind, and not humankind for the sabbath; so the Son of Man is Lord even of the sabbath. (Mark 2: 27–8; par. Matt. 12: 8; Luke 6: 5)

Here again Jesus is taking upon himself the authority to reinterpret the teachings of Moses in a radically new way. Even more dramatically, notice this text (accepted as authentic by Perrin and coloured pink by the Jesus Seminar):

Follow me, and let the dead bury their own dead. (Matt. 8: 22; par. Luke 9: 59),

where Jesus is clearly opposing and correcting the Mosaic law. Proper burial, especially of one's relatives, was one of the most sacred duties in Palestinian Judaism (cf. Gen. 50: 5–6; Lev. 21: 2–3; Tobit 4: 3); this duty took precedence over study of the Torah, Temple service, circumcision rites, and even reciting the *Shema* (Megillah, 3b; Berakath 3: 1). Jesus was declaring that the need for people immediately and unconditionally to become his disciples took precedence even over the solemn responsibility to bury one's own father.

It would be helpful to ask at this point what sort of first-century Jew would take upon himself the authority to set aside requirements of the Mosaic law and replace them with his own teachings. It seems that Jesus' view of his own authority was such that he took the duty to follow him as a far more urgent task than burying one's father. Gruenler pointedly asks, 'Who could possibly make such an offensive and insensitive statement except one who is absolutely convinced that following him is worth more than anything else in the world?'[28] In other words, in all probability, Jesus considered himself to be divinely authoritative.

Notice also the new attitude towards enemies, sins, and the forgiveness of sins that Jesus introduced. (I am not here speaking of Jesus' taking upon himself the authority to forgive sins; we will discuss that point later.) Most famously, note:

You have heard that it was said, 'you shall love your neighbor and hate your enemy.' But I say to you, 'Love your enemies and pray for those who persecute you.' (Matt. 5: 43–4; par. Luke 6: 27, 35)

The 'love your enemies' piece of this text of coloured red by the Jesus Seminar; they are suspicious of the rest of it (it is either black or grey); but Perrin accepts the whole antithesis as authentic. The point is that those who were once considered unforgivable enemies (Gentiles, outcasts, sinners, etc.) are

---

[28] *New Approaches to Jesus and the Gospels* (n. 19 above), p. 61.

now, in the light of the inbreaking of the kingdom of God in Jesus, seen as recipients of God's love and forgiveness, and as worthy participants in table-fellowship in the kingdom of God. Jesus is again apparently taking upon himself the authority to reorder religious life, in this case around the principles of love and forgiveness. We see this same point more fully and dramatically in the parable of the prodigal son (Luke 15: 11–32; coloured pink by the Jesus Seminar). Gruenler comments, 'Only one who is conscious of exercising divine privileges (or is mad) could assume the right to proclaim the eschatological presence of the forgiveness of sins with such authority.... [Jesus] is consciously speaking as the voice of God on matters that belong only to God, and accordingly is creating a new and decisive Christology which far exceeds in claim to authority the messianic models of Judaism.'[29] Jesus' idea seems to have been that salvation has arrived in his own person and ministry, that salvation for humans is to be understood in terms of his own person and mission, and that he can speak with divine authority. Apparently, Jesus had an extraordinarily high opinion of his own status and mission.

Notice finally the parable of the wicked tenants in Mark 12: 1–9 (coloured grey by the Jesus Seminar but pink in the Thomas version (65: 1–7)).[30] The owner of the vineyard unsuccessfully sends two employees to collect the harvest and then finally sends his son, whom the tenants recognize as the son and heir, and then murder him. Clearly, the son in the parable allegorically stands for Jesus himself, who is different from and superior to God's previous emissaries (the prophets), and who is indeed God's son and heir.

Now I am not claiming that Bultmann, Perrin, Funk, Crossan, et al. accept my interpretations of these texts. Doubtless they do not. My claim is simply that they consider these statements from Jesus to be authentic or probably authentic, and that from these texts alone a very high christology can be inferred.[31] That is, a probable case can be made that Jesus implicitly taught his own

---

[29] *New Approaches to Jesus and the Gospels* (n. 19 above), p. 46.

[30] As they themselves admit in their commentary on this text, the members of the Seminar were bothered by the allegorical aspect of the parable in its synoptic versions, with its obvious application to Jesus (= the son) himself. *The Five Gospels* (n. 27 above), p. 101.

[31] Without question, the interpretation of all these texts, especially those that bear on the Jewish law, is controversial. Vermes for example interprets the sayings about the Sabbath, the dietary laws, and the antitheses ('but I say unto you...') as entailing no high claims for Jesus' personal identity. They are, he says, the kinds of statements that could have been made by Jewish teachers of Jesus' time (*Changing Faces of Jesus* (n. 21 above), pp. 196–7). Yet some of the evidence to which Vermes points comes from rabbis who lived one or two centuries later. Besides, the more one portrays Jesus as religiously 'normal' and not scandalously offensive, the more puzzling becomes the opposition that led to his crucifixion. The present chapter attempts to sketch out the various steps in the MBG argument. For a full discussion of the key texts about Jesus and the Jewish law, see the work of such scholars as J. D. G. Dunn, E. P. Sanders, and the earlier Vermes, as well as the data supplied by commentaries on Matthew, Mark, and Luke from such writers as J. A. Fitzmyer, R. A. Guelich, D. Hagner, and J. Nolland.

divinity. Perhaps, then, one reason for the existence of worship of Jesus in the primitive Christian community is that Jesus himself expected and accepted it.

V

I will now proceed to the second stage of my argument that premiss (1) is true, that Jesus implicitly taught his own divinity. By the use of five sub-arguments, I will try to prove not just the possibility that Jesus implicitly taught his own divinity, but its actuality. Again, I will strive to avoid ahistorical use of the Gospel texts, but I will no longer limit myself to texts accepted as authentic by radical critics. This slightly more relaxed methodology will allow some new points to be introduced.

Let me then discuss five reasons why Jesus can be said to have implicitly claimed to be divine. (I briefly noted several of these considerations in Chapter 8; here I will explore them in more detail.) No one reason constitutes, in and of itself, a convincing argument. There is no 'smoking gun' on this issue. What we do find are various considerations which together, and together with points already made, constitute a powerful cumulative case argument in favour of premiss (1). The best interpretation of the five considerations that I am about to discuss—so I am arguing—is that Jesus did indeed implicitly view himself as divine.

First, Jesus assumed for himself the divine prerogative to forgive sins (see Mark 2: 5, 10; Luke 7: 48). Now, all human beings as moral agents have the prerogative to forgive sins *that have been committed against them*, but only God (or God incarnate) can *forgive sins*. Now, some have objected to this point. John Hick, for example, argues that Jesus did not usurp God's prerogatives, but only 'pronounced forgiveness, which is not the prerogative of God, but the priesthood'.[32] But this is hardly a convincing argument. For one thing, it concedes part of the point at issue, namely, that Jesus was usurping prerogatives that were not his. He was a layman, not of the priestly tribe, and was forgiving sins outside what were understood to be the divinely established means of obtaining forgiveness. More importantly, there are several texts that cannot be reconciled with Hick's argument. Note the story of the healing of the paralytic in Mark 2: 1–12. There is no evidence here on the part of the paralytic of any of the religious acts normally requisite to forgiveness—no

---

[32] John Hick, *The Metaphor of God Incarnate: Christology in a Pluralistic Age* (Louisville, KY: Westminster John Knox Press, 1993), p. 32. Here Hick is quoting E. P. Sanders, *Jesus and Judaism* (Philadelphia: Fortress Press, 1985), p. 240.

sorrow for his sins, confession, repentance, sacrificial acts at the temple, or the like. This is surely the reason the scribes were so incensed when Jesus said to the paralytic, 'Your sins are forgiven.' They said: 'Why does this fellow speak in this way? Who can forgive sins but God alone?' In other words, the violent reaction of the scribes belies Hick's interpretation of such texts.

Secondly, the intimate, almost blasphemous way Jesus addressed God (usually translated '*Abba*, Father!'—something perhaps analogous to our English expression 'Papa' or even 'Daddy')—indicates at least a uniquely close relationship to God. I suspect that the amazement caused by this novel way of speaking to God—whose name was sacred to first-century Jews—was the reason that the church remembered and imitated it (Rom. 8: 15; Gal. 4: 6). Hick also objects to this point. '*Abba*' was fairly commonly used of God in first-century Judaism, he claims, and simply meant 'father'; while Jesus certainly sensed that God was his Heavenly Father, this had nothing to do with incarnation.[33] But other scholars deny that there are any Jewish parallels to referring to God in prayer the way Jesus does; nobody has ever produced a convincing example of *Abba* being used of God in pre-Christian first-century Judaism.[34] The argument that Jesus' use of *Abba* shows a consciousness on his part of a unique position in relation to God stands. In all probability, then, Jesus thought of himself as God's special son.[35]

Thirdly, Jesus spoke 'with authority', not citing sources or precedents of famous rabbis. He was no mere prophet or religious teacher (as is so often asserted about him today); no such person would have acted and spoken with such independence of the Mosaic law as Jesus did. Note the way he quotes, and then corrects, the Mosaic teaching about divorce in the Sermon of the Mount (Matt. 5: 31–2; cf. Mark 10: 2–12). Jesus spoke, not as if he were speaking *on behalf of God* (he did not say, as the prophets had done, 'Thus says the Lord'), but *as if he were divine*, delivering the truth to human beings.

---

[33] *The Metaphor of God Incarnate* (n. 32 above), p. 31. Hick is following the lead of James Barr at this point. See Barr's 'Abba Isn't "Daddy" ', *JTS* 39 (1988), and 'Abba, Father', *Theology*, 91/741 (1988). For a response to Barr, see Gordon D. Fee, *God's Empowering Presence: The Holy Spirit in the Letters of Paul* (Peabody, MA: Hendrickson Publishers, 1995), pp. 408–12.

[34] Thus Joachim Jeremias: 'Nowhere in the literature of the prayers of ancient Judaism . . . is this invocation of God as *Abba* to be found, neither in the liturgical nor in the informal prayers.' Joachim Jeremias, *The Central Message of the New Testament* (London: SCM Press, 1965), p. 19, cited in Craig, p. 245. See also Gerald O'Collins S.J., *Christology: A Biblical, Historical, and Systematic Study of Jesus* (Oxford: Oxford University Press, 1995), p. 123, and John P. Meier, *A Marginal Jew: Rethinking the Historical Jesus*, vol. ii (New York: Doubleday, 1994), pp. 358–9, both of whom support Jeremias' conclusion.

[35] Ben Witherington sensibly discusses all the arguments and evidence and supports the notion that Jesus' use of *Abba* in prayer was unique and indicative of a relationship of intimacy with the Father. See his *The Christology of Jesus* (Minneapolis, MN: Fortress Press, 1990), pp. 215–21.

As J. A. T. Robinson said, 'This is epitomized in his characteristic and distinctive form of address, "Amen, I say to you"...While a pious Jew concluded his prayer with an "Amen", ...Jesus prefaces his words with an "Amen", thus identifying God with what he would say.'[36] As Raymond Brown points out, nowhere in the Gospels does it say anything like, 'The word of God came to Jesus.' The idea instead seems to have been that he already had or even (in John's terminology) *was* the word.[37] His words are true and binding because of his own personal position and authority; he is in a position to give the law's true meaning, to reveal God's will.

Ernst Kasemann argues that Jesus' 'but I say to you' sayings 'embody a claim to an authority which rivals and challenges that of Moses.'[38] The fact that Jesus claimed Moses-like authority, an authority to supervene all other authorities, has been noticed, and reacted to negatively, by contemporary Jewish scholars who write about Jesus. For example, Schalom Ben-Chorin says, 'The sense of the unique, absolute authority that is evident from [Jesus'] way of acting remains deeply problematic for the Jewish view of Jesus.'[39] And Jacob Neusner, in an interview about his book *A Rabbi Talks With Jesus: An Intermillenial, Interfaith Exchange*,[40] states that Jesus' attitude towards the Torah makes him want to ask: 'Who do you think you are? God?'[41] It is highly significant that Jesus assumed for himself the authority to reinterpret and even overrule the Old Testament law (see Matt. 5: 21–48; Mark 2: 23–8), again something no mere human being could do. Jesus considered his words as permanent and indestructible (Mark 13: 31). In short, in all probability, Jesus did not think of himself as just another prophetic spokesperson for God; he spoke as if he were divine.

Fourthly, even in the Synoptic Gospels, Jesus said things that can sensibly be interpreted as implicit claims to divinity. I see no way of ruling out as inauthentic Jesus' claim to be 'The Christ, the Son of the Blessed' (Mark 14: 61–2), which the high priest took to be blasphemy. Notice again this claim, the so-called 'Johannine thunderbolt', which seems a kind of bridge from the christology of the Synoptics to the christology of the fourth Gospel: 'All things have been delivered to me by my Father; and no one knows the Son except the

[36] J. A. T. Robinson, *Can We Trust the New Testament?* (Grand Rapids, MI: Eerdmans, 1977), p. 104.

[37] Raymond Brown, 'Did Jesus Know He Was God?', *Biblical Theology Bulletin*, XV/2 (April, 1988), p. 77.

[38] Ernst Kasemann, 'The Problem of the Historical Jesus', in Ernst Kasemann (ed.), *Essays on New Testament Themes* (Naperville, IL: Allenson, 1964), p. 37.

[39] Schalom Ben-Chorin, *Jesus in Judenthum* (Wuppertal: R. Brockhaus, 1970), p. 41, cited in Craig, *Reasonable Faith* (n. 5 above), p. 241.

[40] New York: Doubleday, 1993.

[41] Cited in Wright, 'Jesus and the Identity of God' (n. 18 above), p. 22.

Father, and no one knows the Father except the Son and anyone to whom the Son chooses to reveal him' (Matt. 11: 27).[42] Here Jesus seems to be claiming to be the Son of God in a unique and exclusive sense, the only true and authoritative revelation of the Father.

Fifthly, Jesus, the coming 'Son of man', implicitly made two dramatic claims: first, that our relationship to him would determine our final status before God (Mark 14: 21; Luke 9: 25–7; 12: 7–9); secondly, that he himself would be the judge of all human beings at the end of history (Matt. 16: 27; 19: 28).[43] Both seem to be claims to stand in a divine role.[44]

So Jesus probably saw himself as having the right to act as God and do what God appropriately does. The argument in favour of this point does not depend on ahistorical readings of the Gospels, nor on the claim that the sayings cited from the fourth Gospel above come directly from Jesus (though I believe that in substance they do).[45] Jesus implicitly claimed divine status. That is the best interpretation of the five considerations I have been citing. Accordingly, a strong case can be made that premiss (1) of the MBG argument is true.

VI

Where then do we stand? Is the MBG argument a successful argument, or not? Can it be used as a convincing piece of Christian apologetics (as Lewis clearly thought it could), or not? The conclusion we reached earlier is that the argument, as outlined in steps (1) to (8), is valid. But of course that does not show much. The argument

(13) Everybody in Tibet believes in Jesus;
(14) Bertrand Russell lives in Tibet;
(15) Therefore Bertrand Russell believes in Jesus

[42] Witherington argues convincingly that these words are authentic. See *The Christology of Jesus* (n. 35 above), pp. 221–8.

[43] See Gerald O'Collins S. J., *Christology: A Biblical, Historical, and Systematic Study of Jesus* (Oxford: Oxford University Press, 1995), pp. 60–2.

[44] There is a curious tribute to this argument from an unexpected source in George W. E. Nickelsburg's essay, 'Son of Man', in *The Anchor Bible Dictionary*, vol. vi (New York: Doubleday, 1992), p. 149. As I read the conclusion of Nickelsburg's essay, he is saying that Jesus could not have implied that he was the 'Son of man', because that would mean (what Nickelsburg cannot accept) that he went around claiming to be the eschatological judge of all.

[45] A brief note about the christology of the Fourth Gospel: it is often pointed out that alongside the texts such as those cited above that seem to indicate Jesus' oneness with God and equality with the Father, there are texts that point towards Jesus' dependence on the Father, who is greater than he (see 7: 16; 5: 19, 30–1; 14: 28). My only comment is that the best way to keep both sorts of texts theologically in view is the classic doctrine of the incarnation, where Jesus is both 'fully divine' and 'fully human'.

is also a valid argument, but is obviously a rhetorically useless device for providing rational support for its conclusion.

So is the argument *sound* (i.e. valid plus true premisses)? Well, as we have seen, premiss (2) is virtually beyond reproach; and while premisses (3), (4), and (5) can be disputed, an excellent case can also be made for their truth. But premiss (1), which I take to be the crux of the argument, not only can be but frequently is disputed, even by some who believe in the incarnation. I take it that the perceived weakness of premiss (1) is the most important reason why the MBG argument has not often been used or defended by Christian theologians and exegetes (as opposed to a few apologists) since Lewis. But, as we have also seen, a strong (and, in my view, convincing) case can also be made in favour of premiss (1), a case that does not depend on viewing the Gospels ahistorically. The MBG argument also seems immune to such informal fallacies as equivocation, question-begging, arguing in a circle, and the like.

Whether the MBG argument is a successful argument accordingly depends on what 'success' for an argument amounts to. That is, it depends on what is taken to be the goal, purpose, or aim of the argument. And as we saw in Chapter 2, there are many quite different ways of envisioning the goal or purpose of a deductive argument. Suppose the goal of the MBG argument were *to convince all non-believers in the incarnation of Jesus to believe in it* or *to constitute an argument that rationally* should *convince all non-believers in the incarnation of Jesus to believe in it.* Then one must doubt that the MBG argument can count as successful. Few non-believers will be converted by it; no matter how hard we argue for the truth of premiss (1) (or even premisses (3), (4), or (5)), the non-believer can go on disputing it (or them). Indeed, it seems a non-believer in the incarnation can always say something like this: 'I do not know whether Jesus was mad, bad, honestly mistaken, or never said or implied that he was divine—after all, that was twenty centuries ago, and by now it's hard to tell—but one thing I do know is that he was not divine.' This is why I do not hold that the MBG argument establishes the irrationality of unbelief in the incarnation of Jesus.

But suppose the aim of the MBG argument is *to demonstrate the truth of the incarnation of Jesus* or (see the very end of Section I, above) *to demonstrate the rationality of belief in the incarnation of Jesus.* If one of these constitutes the true aim or goal of the MBG argument, then it will not matter whether non-believers in the incarnation can rationally reject one or another of the argument's premisses.

My own view is that the last goal mentioned—to demonstrate the rationality of belief in the incarnation of Jesus—is the proper goal or aim of the MBG argument. And given what we have concluded in this chapter, I believe it succeeds in doing that very thing.[46] Accordingly, the MBG argument can constitute a powerful piece of Christian apologetics.[47]

[46] I relegate to a footnote a possible objection to the idea of Christ's divinity. Maybe there is evidence in the Gospels that he was *not* divine. After all, he admitted he was not omniscient (Mark 13: 32), was wrong about the kingdom of God arriving before his own generation had passed away (Mark 13: 30), and 'could do no deed of power' in Nazareth (Mark 6: 5). The first and the third of these points do not refute the divinity of Christ once the notion of incarnation is understood properly (see Chapters 6 and 10). As to the second, Christians affirm that the kingdom of God both has come (in the advent, crucifixion, and resurrection of Christ, and Pentecost) and is still coming (in the sense of its final apocalyptic manifestation). Jesus' statement was not wrong.

[47] I would like to thank C. Stephen Evans, Daniel Howard-Snyder, Carey Newman, Gerald O'Collins, S.J., and Alan Padgett for their helpful comments on an earlier version of this chapter. I should add that debate about the MBG has continued. Daniel Howard-Snyder has criticized it in his 'Was Jesus Mad, Bad, or God . . . *or Just Plain Mistaken?*', in *Faith and Philosophy*, 21/4 (October, 2004). My reply is: 'The Mad/Bad/God Trilemma: A Reply to Daniel Howard-Snyder', *Faith and Philosophy*, 21/4 (October, 2004).

10

Is Kenotic Christology Orthodox?

Suppose it is true, as I argued in Chapters 6 and 9, that Jesus Christ was indeed the incarnate Son of God. That still leaves open the question, so to speak, of how the incarnation worked. How is it possible for one person to be 'truly God and truly divine'? As noted, we will never be able to answer that question fully, but surely something about the manner of the incarnation must be said.

This chapter primarily addresses the question whether kenotic christological theories are orthodox. Naturally, this will require discussion of what makes a christological theory count as kenotic. It will also require discussion of what makes a christological theory orthodox as opposed to, say, unorthodox or even heretical. Roughly, I will use the word *orthodox* in such as way as to imply that 't is orthodox' (where 't' is some theological theory or claim) means roughly 't is acceptable for belief by the people of God.' It does not mean 't is *required* for belief by the people of God.'

It should be noted that in this chapter I am presupposing the truth of a 'high' christology like those developed in the chapters just mentioned, that is, a christology that is consistent with the decrees of Nicaea I and Chalcedon. My intended audience here consists primarily of those who also hold to a high christology, but are suspicious of kenosis. I make this point because many biblical and theological scholars today reject the 'truly human and truly divine in one person' formula, argue instead for a minimal christology, and would doubtless reject the kenotic theory as *too* orthodox.

What, then, is a *kenotic* christological theory? Roughly, let us say that such a theory is one that interprets the incarnation in terms of the Logos 'giving up' or 'laying aside' or 'divesting itself of' or 'emptying itself of' certain properties that normally belong to divinity. Some kenotic theorists take this divestment to be temporal and temporary, with the period of divestment corresponding to the time-span of the earthly life of Jesus. After Jesus' earthly life, that is, in the exaltation, the Logos resumes possession of all divine properties. Kenotic theories always emphasize, however, the voluntary and redemptive aspect of kenosis: it was out of love for us and for the sake of our redemption that the Logos 'emptied himself'.

It should go without saying that kenotic theories have no necessary connection whatsoever with (1) denying that Jesus really performed the miracles attributed to him in the Gospels or attempting to explain them naturalistically; (2) arguing that Jesus Christ was a mere man, not really and essentially God;[1] (3) making Jesus Christ a sort of demigod by enlarging his humanity with a few divine properties;[2] (4) implying that the Logos, shorn of many of its divine attributes in the incarnation, is temporarily excluded from the Trinity;[3] (5) affirming pantheistically that God and human beings are different forms of the same thing or are at least not very different; (6) claiming that we too, like Jesus, can be incarnations of God; or (7) insisting that women should be subordinate to men.[4] I do not hold, assert, or argue for any of these items.

A kenotic theory of the incarnation should be understood as contrasting with what I will call a *classical* theory of the incarnation, which makes no reference to the Logos giving up any properties. Classicists argue that, in the incarnation, the Logos simply took on a new, that is, human, condition. Some classical theorists add that the human nature was amplified or enhanced in order to make it fit for unity with the divine nature.

There are two basic issues that divine kenoticists and classicists. The first, which I will discuss a bit later in this chapter, is whether the incarnation of the Jesus depicted in the Gospels is best understood along kenotic or classical lines. The second is a philosophical issue: kenoticists hold (and classicists deny) that Jesus cannot be *truly human* (as orthodoxy requires) unless his divine properties (which he had in virtue of also being *truly God*) were to some extent limited. A basic intuition of kenoticists is that someone who is omnipotent (in a straightforward sense), for example, is hardly 'fully human'.

Kenotic theories of the incarnation differ on whether the incarnation of the Logos should be distinguished from the kenosis, and on (so to speak) how long each lasts. I am defending the view that the kenosis is indeed distinct from the incarnation, with the kenosis lasting only for the thirty years or so of

---

[1] Donald Baillie wrongly describes the kenotic theory as follows: 'He who formerly was God changed Himself temporarily into man, or exchanged his divinity for humanity.' See his *God Was in Christ: An Essay on Incarnation and Atonement* (New York: Scribner's, 1948), p. 96.

[2] As is charged by Dietrich Bonhoeffer in *Christ the Center* (trans. John Bowden) (New York: Harper and Row, 1966), p. 97.

[3] As is charged by Wolfhart Pannenberg in his *Jesus—God and Man*, 2nd edn. (trans. Lewis L. Wilkins and Duane A. Priebe) (Philadelphia: Westminster Press, 1977), p. 311.

[4] See the critique of kenosis in Daphne Hampson, 'On Autonomy and Heteronomy', in Daphne Hampson (ed.), *Swallowing a Fishbone? Feminist Theologians Debate Christianity* (London: SPCK, 1996), pp. 1–17.

Jesus' lifetime, and the incarnation lasting from the moment of Jesus' conception into eternity. In other words, after (say) 4 BC, the statement, 'The second person of the Trinity is God incarnate' is always true, while the statement, 'The second person of the Trinity is kenotically incarnate' was true only from about 4 BC until about AD 30, and indeed is now (i.e. as I write this sentence in the twenty-first century) no longer true. The incarnation accordingly begins in time and, unlike the kenosis, does not ever cease.[5]

Kenotic christological theories were first proposed in the early nineteenth century, although 'kenotic' notions can be found much earlier in Christian tradition, and of course in scripture itself, as kenoticists always insist. The first explicit kenotic theologians were the Germans, Gottfried Thomasius (1802–75) and W. F. Gess (1819–91).[6] Next, the theory was defended by a series of able British theologians, including P. T. Forsyth (1848–1921), Charles Gore (1853–1932), H. R. MacKintosh (1870–1936), and Frank Weston (1871–1924).[7] Interestingly, one of the themes emphasized by the early kenoticists, namely, that Jesus' temptations and sufferings were real, is now considered commonplace. Within the last thirty years, kenosis has enjoyed a renaissance among a small group of theologians and philosophers of religion, including Hans Urs von Baltasar,[8] Brian Hebblethwaite,[9] and Ronald J. Feenstra.[10]

Some kenotic theories were doubtless intended by their authors as substitutes for, rather than interpretations of, Chalcedon. But, as noted, the version that I am defending presupposes the full humanity and divinity of the one Person of Christ. Accordingly, I am suggesting a kenotic theory as a way of interpreting Chalcedon.

The name and essence of the theory derive from the great christological hymn of Philippians 2: 6–11, where Paul says of Christ (in the NRSV): 'who, though he was in the form of God, did not count equality with God a thing to

---

[5] See C. Stephen Evans, 'The Self-Emptying of Love: Some Thoughts on Kenotic Christology', in Stephen T. Davis, Daniel Kendall, S.J., and Gerald O'Collins, S.J. (eds.), *The Incarnation: An Interdisciplinary Symposium on the Incarnation of the Son of God* (Oxford: Oxford University Press, 2002), pp. 246–72.

[6] See Claude Welsh (ed. and trans.), *God and Incarnation in Mid-nineteenth Century German Theology* (New York: Oxford University Press, 1965).

[7] See, for example, Frank Weston, *The One Christ: An Enquiry into the Manner of the Incarnation* (London: Longmans Green, 1907).

[8] In such works as *Mysterium Paschale: The Mystery of Easter* (trans. Aidan Nichols, O.P.) (Edinburgh: T. and T. Clark, 1990), *Theo-Drama III: The Dramatis Personae: The Person in Christ*, (trans. Graham Harrison) (San Francisco: San Francisco Press, 1992), and *Theo-Drama IV: The Action* (trans. Graham Harrison) (San Francisco: Ignatius Press, 1994).

[9] See Brian Hebblethwaite, *The Incarnation: Collected Essays in Christology* (Cambridge: Cambridge University Press, 1987), especially pp. 27–44.

[10] See his 'Reconsidering Kenotic Christology', in Ronald J. Feenstra and Cornelius Plantinga (eds.), *Trinity, Incarnation, and Atonement: Philosophical and Theological Essays* (Notre Dame, IN: Notre Dame University Press, 1989), pp. 128–52.

be grasped, but emptied himself [the Greek term Paul uses here, *ekenosin*, is a derivative of the word *kenosis*], taking the form of a servant, being born in the likeness of men'.

II

I will now sketch out a possible kenotic theory of the incarnation.[11] The basic idea is that Christ was indeed simultaneously truly divine and truly human, possessing as he did all properties essential to divinity and humanity, and that this status was made possible by the Logos emptying itself, during the period of Jesus' earthly life, of those properties that normally characterize divinity but are inconsistent with humanity.

All things or substances have properties. Some properties are essential to them and some are accidental to them. An *essential property* of x is an attribute that x has and cannot lose without ceasing to exist or to be x. Three-sidedness is an essential property of any triangle; if a given triangle were to lose its three-sidedness, it would no longer be a triangle. An *accidental property* of x is an attribute that x has but can fail to have and still be x. Being a philosophy professor is presumably an accidental property of mine; it seems that I could both exist and still be the very individual that I am if I stopped being a philosophy professor. A *common property of a kind k* is an attribute that all members of k have (e.g. for the natural kind 'human being', *having been born on earth* is a common property).

Let us list some properties of God and human beings:

God	Human beings
1 Existing necessarily.	1′ Existing contingently.
2 Living for ever.	2′ Living only for a finite time.
3 Being omnipotent.	3′ Being non-omnipotent.
4 Being omniscient.	4′ Being non-omniscient.
5 Being incorporeal.	5′ Being corporeal.

Now here is a problem for all orthodox views of the incarnation: if properties 1–5 are essential to God; and if properties 1′–5′ are essential to all human beings; and if the orthodox doctrine of the incarnation (which includes the 'truly human and truly divine' clause) affirms that Jesus Christ must

---

[11] An earlier version is explained in more detail in *Encountering Jesus* (Atlanta: John Knox Press, 1988) and in Chapter 8 of Stephen T. Davis, *Logic and the Nature of God* (London: Macmillan, 1983).

simultaneously possess all the members of both sets of properties; and if (as it surely seems) it is logically impossible for any being simultaneously to have all the members of both sets of properties; then the orthodox doctrine of the incarnation spelled out at Nicaea and Chalcedon is contradictory.[12]

But how do we go about deciding which properties of human beings are essential to them? And how do we go about deciding which divine properties are essential to God? 1′–5′ certainly seem to be properties of human beings (although 2′ can be debated); and 1–5 certainly seem to be properties of God, at least as Christians conceive of God. But must we affirm that 1′–5′ are *essential* properties of human beings? And must we affirm that 1–5 are *essential* properties of God?

Again, how do we know which of a being's properties are essential to it and which are accidental to it? With abstract or mathematical objects (e.g. circles, sets, etc.) the decision is usually easy. For concrete things such as human beings, it is seldom easy. People who accept the orthodox doctrine of the incarnation will be much inclined to *deny* that all the properties listed in the table above are essential properties of God and human beings, respectively. Indeed, Christian theology has always insisted that Jesus Christ is both the pre-eminent revealer of God and the model human being. Looking at the incarnation of Christ, then, is one fruitful way (maybe the best way) of finding out about divinity and humanity, of discovering which properties of God and human beings are essential and which are accidental. If Jesus Christ is 'truly human and truly divine', then perhaps the properties listed above are either not essential properties or else are consistent with all the others.

Thomas Morris, who is not a defender of kenosis, has nevertheless made a helpful suggestion that kenoticists can use: perhaps the 1′–5′ properties are essential properties not of *being human* but of *being merely human*.[13] And of course orthodox Christians do not want to affirm that Jesus Christ was 'merely human'. Perhaps, then, the 1–5 properties are essential properties not of *being divine* but of *being divine simpliciter* (i.e. being divine without also being human). And of course orthodox Christians do not want to affirm that God is 'God *simpliciter*'. Indeed, Christians hold that there never has existed any 'God *simpliciter*'; the one and only God who exists is a God who becomes incarnate in a human being. Accordingly, what Christians want to say about Jesus Christ is that he was *truly human* but not *merely human, truly divine* but not *divine simpliciter*.

---

[12] Orthodox christologists have always been aware of the problem of apparent incoherence. Thus the many complex discussions in the tradition of communicable and incommunicable properties and of communion of attributes.

[13] Thomas V. Morris, 'Divinity, Humanity, and Death', *Religious Studies*, 19 (1983), p. 457.

Here is where kenosis comes in. The core idea is that Jesus Christ was 'in the form of God' as the Logos, or the Second Person of the Trinity, and that at a certain point in human history he voluntarily and obediently 'emptied himself' both of the divine glory and of certain other divine properties; he then took on 'human form', that is, became a human being. That is, in the incarnation, Jesus Christ 'emptied himself' by temporarily giving up those divine properties that are inconsistent with being truly human, while retaining those divine properties that are essential to remaining truly divine; and he did not assume those common human properties that are inconsistent with being truly divine, but assumed those human properties that are essential to being truly human. In the incarnation, then, Jesus Christ was not *a mere human*, but truly human; he was not God *simpliciter*, but rather truly divine. Perhaps one cannot simultaneously be a mere human and truly divine; and perhaps one cannot simultaneously be God *simpliciter* and truly human. But Christians hold that it is possible to be 'truly divine and truly human'.

The whole kenotic scheme depends on there not being any essential divine properties that no human being can have and on there not being any essential human properties that no divine being can have. And following another acute suggestion from Morris,[14] a coherent kenotic theory will accordingly hold that what is essential to God is not, for example, omniscience, but rather the more complex property of being *omniscient-unless-freely-and-temporarily-choosing-to-be-otherwise*. The same point will then be made with other divine properties such as omnipotence, omnipresence, and so on.

What does it mean for God to 'give up' a property? Well, as long as the property in question is accidental, there is no big problem. We certainly give up properties constantly, for example, the property of having long hair whenever we cut it short, or the property of being seated whenever we stand. 'God gives up property p' would roughly mean, then, that at a given point God has property p, but at a later point, of God's own free choice, God does not have property p. Suppose, for example, that God is in fact omniscient, but that God could still exist and still be divine if God were slightly less than omniscient (if there were, say, some few things that God does not know). That is, suppose that omniscience is a property of God, but an accidental one. Then 'God gives up the property of omniscience' means that at one point God is omniscient and that at later point God voluntarily becomes non-omniscient, while still existing and remaining God.

But a problem remains. While some properties can surely be given up (e.g. having long hair, being seated), others, whether essential or accidental, seem to be (so to speak) 'ungiveupable'. These are time-indexed properties or

---

[14] Thomas V. Morris, *The Logic of God Incarnate* (Ithaca, NY: Cornell University Press, 1986), p. 75.

properties one has because of events that occurred in the past, for example, properties such as *not having been created, having existed in the sixteenth century,* and *being the creator of the heavens and the earth*. Without arguing that these properties are essential to any being who has them (they may or may not be essential properties), the point is that they cannot be given up. Any being who has them at one temporal point has them at all temporal points. Thus kenosis is in trouble, because it makes no sense to say, for example, that the Logos gave up the property of *not having been created* in order to be truly human or that Jesus Christ gave up the property of *having been created* in order to be truly divine.

In response to this problem, defenders of kenosis can use a traditional way of making christological affirmations, namely, that Jesus Christ has some properties *as* God and some *as* a human being. The Chalcedonian Definition itself seems to imply as much: 'of one substance with the Father *as regards his Godhead.* and at the same time of one substance with us *as regards his manhood*' (emphasis added). This way of making christological affirmations has been explored in a preliminary way by P. T. Geach,[15] who calls them 'reduplicative propositions'. He distinguishes what we ought to say that God *as God* can do from what we can say that God *as a human being* can do. In sentences such as 'A as P is Q,' Geach says, we are not to think of Q as a predicate attached to the complex subject 'A as P'—rather, we ought to read the sentence as 'A is, as P, Q.' Thus we can sensibly say such things as 'Jesus Christ is, as God, unable to die' and 'Jesus Christ is, as a human being, able to die' without nonsense.

There are dangers here: if the notion is pushed too far, Christ might seem divided into two persons, one of which was, and the other of which was not, able to die. To divide Christ like that would be to fall dangerously close to the Nestorian heresy, condemned at the Synod of Ephesus in AD 431. And if the unity of Christ's person is emphasized, the following objection might arise: 'Well then, is the one person Jesus Christ able to die or not? Surely it must be one or the other: which is it? If he is able to die, he is not divine; if he is not able to die, he is not human.'

How can a single person simultaneously possess and lack a given property? This seems to be what orthodoxy requires: Jesus Christ is both uncreated (in virtue of being divine) and created (in virtue of being human), both unable to die (in virtue of being divine) and able to die (in virtue of being human). Analogies do not seem to be helpful in allowing us to grasp how this is possible, because we are unaware of other cases where a thing, while retaining its old nature, takes on a new nature.

---

[15] P. T. Geach, *Providence and Evil* (Cambridge: Cambridge University Press, 1977), pp. 25–8.

It is accepted by all Christians that Christ died on the cross. This was not an apparent death, but a real one. Now I suspect that few Christians want to say that Christ's divine nature, in the incarnation, took on or assumed the ability to die, and accordingly died (along with his human nature). This possibility raises the unacceptable spectre that the Godhead was—for parts of three days—a binity. Accordingly, the other possibility looks more attractive: since God by definition cannot die, only Christ's human nature died on the cross (which was sufficient for the death of the one person Jesus Christ).

So we are already committed to saying that in some sense Christ had certain properties *as divine* (e.g. inability to die) and certain other properties *as human* (e.g. ability to die). So it looks as if some properties of Christ were properties of the human nature alone (e.g. ability to die—otherwise only the Father and the Spirit existed between Good Friday and Easter), some were properties of his divine nature alone (e.g. inability to die—otherwise the man Jesus was a necessary being), and some were properties of both natures (e.g. having memories, being sinless). To see things otherwise is to 'confuse the properties', which Chalcedon forbids.[16]

'Well, then'—so the critic will ask—'did the *one person* Jesus Christ have the property of *being able to die*'? The answer to that question is yes. 'But then'— so the critic will continue—'why do you deny that the whole person with his two natures died?' The answer to that question is that the whole person (Jesus Christ the God-man) did die, but only in his human nature; it is also true that the whole person was unable to die, but only in its divine nature. 'So then aren't you saying'—so the critic will conclude—'that Jesus Christ was simultaneously both able to die and not able to die?' The answer to that question is: Exactly. And we express the point by saying: he was, as human, able to die; he was not, as divine, able to die.

But then the critic will surely respond as follows:

Wait a minute. This whole proposal is bogus. I can prove as much by showing that the same sorts of games can be played with concepts that everyone, including Christians, will admit are incoherent. Take the concept of a *married bachelor*, an unmarried adult male who is married. Let me now prove that Jones can be a married bachelor: he has a wife in his married nature but has no wife in his bachelor nature. We might even say: He is, as married, the possessor of a wife; he is, as bachelor, in possession of no wife. But this is surely nonsense. Is the one person Jones in possession of a wife, or not?

---

[16] This conclusion is not in conflict with the theological tradition of the *communicatio idiomatum* (communication of properties), in which both divine and human attributes can sensibly be predicated of the same one person Jesus Christ.

And in response to the critic I would say: Yes, that argument *is* nonsense. This is because nothing can simultaneously and in the same sense both possess and not possess a wife.

But, as we see in Christ, if you are the Son of God you *can* simultaneously and in the same sense both be able to die and unable to die. It is metaphysically impossible to be a married bachelor. It is not metaphysically impossible—not if you are the Son of God, anyway—to be both able and unable to die. To put the point in another way, a 'bachelor nature' cannot coherently be combined with a 'married nature'. But—as we see with Jesus Christ—a divine nature (when limited in certain ways) *can* be combined with a human nature. As a human being (i.e. in his human nature), Jesus Christ was able to die; as God (i.e. in his divine nature), he was not able to die.

'But then'—so the critic will reply—'if because of his two natures Jesus Christ was both able to die and unable to die, does not that result show that the whole idea is incoherent, that there can be no such thing as one person with both a divine and a human nature?' Not so. This is because the expressions, 'able to die' and 'unable to die', are being used here in different senses, or as having different referents. What is able to die is his human nature (indeed, it *did* die); what is unable to die is his divine nature.

There is no escaping the fact that the notion of incarnation is paradoxical. We will not be able to use kenosis, or any other theory, to remove all mystery from the doctrine. But kenosis does help us towards a coherent way of understanding incarnation. It helps provide a sense in which we can legitimately (although admittedly somewhat paradoxically) say, 'Jesus Christ is truly divine.' It helps provide a sense in which we can legitimately (although admittedly somewhat paradoxically) say, 'Jesus Christ is truly human.'

It is important to note that the kenotic theory defended here has nothing whatever to do with a human being becoming or turning into God (or the reverse), or with human properties changing into divine ones (or the reverse). Nor does it end up with the kenotically incarnate Logos as a lessened or reduced God. If the theory could be shown to deny the *homousious* principle of Chalcedon, it would not be worth defending. But it does not do so. The kenotically incarnate Logos is indeed 'of one substance with the Father', because the Father's nature or substance just *is* the set of his essential properties, which the theory insists Christ had. And since we do not accordingly have a minimized deity who dies on the cross, the theory has no untoward salvific implications either.

Let me make three last points before concluding my explanation of the kenotic theory that I am defending. First, kenosis is based on the idea that the human essence or nature has a natural receptivity to the divine nature. In this way, it is quite unlike a coyote nature or an amoeba nature. It is possible for a divine nature (with some limitations) and a human nature to be united in one person because human beings, unlike coyotes and amoebas, were created 'in the image of God' (Gen. 1: 27).

Secondly, many kenotic theorists are disinclined to claim that incarnation can *only* be explained via kenosis. Accordingly, they should not be seen as enemies of classical theories of the incarnation. Indeed, my own view is that kenoticists should be friends of classical theories. This especially for those kenoticists who hold (1) the incarnation of the Logos is everlasting after Jesus' conception (i.e. it is still—in the twenty-first century—true that 'The Logos is God incarnate'); and (2) the kenosis lasted only for the period of Jesus' earthly life. Thus such kenoticists face the question of how incarnation without kenosis is possible. Accordingly, they will have to appeal to non-kenotic theories to understand how it is true in the twenty-first century that 'The Logos is God incarnate.'

Thirdly, every orthodox christologist is a kenoticist in some sense. Even those who criticize and reject kenosis either explicitly or implicitly allow that in the incarnation the Logos divested itself of at least *some* divine properties. Almost everybody admits that, in the incarnation, the Logos gave up certain divine prerogatives like the divine glory (this point seems a clear implication of the kenosis hymn). And even determined rejecters of kenosis seem, on close analysis, to be implying (whether openly or not) that the Logos gave up certain other divine properties. Even Thomas V. Morris, defender of his own decidedly non-kenotic 'two-minds' theory, seems to me to be an unwitting kenoticist, for the 'two-minds' theory entails that in the incarnation the Logos 'gave up' or 'emptied itself of' invulnerability to human pains and sufferings.[17]

I have been arguing that kenosis is logically possible. But a stronger point is equally true. If incarnation is to occur, some sort of kenosis is *necessary*. We can see this point most easily with the embodiment of the Logos. For God to take on a human body is necessarily for God to divest himself of or give up or empty himself of (at the very least) the traditional divine property of ubiquity or omnipresence. The earthly Jesus was clearly not ubiquitous. That property must be 'given up'.

---

[17] This seems a clear implication of the argument of pp. 88–107 of Morris, *The Logic of God Incarnate* (n. 14 above).

III

How do we go about discovering whether kenosis—or any theological theory—is orthodox? Let me briefly summarize in this section of the chapter
certain conclusions that will be reached in Chapter 15.

On this question, Catholics and Protestants differ. Catholics classically
recognize two sources of theological authority, scripture and tradition.
Accordingly, in order to show that a given theological claim is orthodox,
Catholics will typically try to show that it is to be found in, or agrees with, or
is entailed by what is found in either scripture or tradition or both. Protestants classically recognize but one source of theological authority, namely,
scripture. Accordingly, in order to show that a given theological claim is
orthodox, a Protestant will typically try to show that it is scriptural. That is,
the claim is either explicitly taught or else is entailed by one or more properly
interpreted texts of scripture.

So in the area of theological authority, Roman Catholics speak of 'scripture
and tradition'. The word 'tradition' can mean several things, but here we will
use it primarily to refer to decisions of church councils and *ex cathedra*
pronouncements of popes. There appear to be two Catholic theories on the
relationship of scripture and tradition, what I will call the 'older theory' and
the 'revisionist theory'. The older theory (which I will explain in more detail in
Chapter 15) claims that revelation is to be found in two separate sources,
scripture and tradition; that some revelation is found in tradition but not in
scripture; and that in some senses scripture is inferior to tradition.

However, since Vatican II, a revisionist theory has replaced the older theory
among most Catholics. Revisionists still hold (1) that scripture and tradition
constitute two sources of religious truth; (2) that since it was the church that
canonized the texts that we now call 'the Bible', scripture is the creation of the
church; and (3) that scripture needs authoritative interpretation by the
church. But revisionists—instead of subordinating scripture to tradition and
affirming the material insufficiency of scripture—insist on the unity of
scripture and tradition. It is the function of the magisterium, or church
teaching office, authoritatively to interpret scripture and tradition and to
decide what Catholic teaching is, that is, to explain, apply, and sometimes
develop Catholic teaching.

In contrast, the Protestant motto in the area of theological authority is
'Scripture alone (also to be explained further in Chapter 15)'. 'Scripture
alone' connotes a whole constellation of related claims. (1) There is no
source of religious truth that rivals scripture in its authority, accuracy, and
power to convince; tradition is only a secondary authority, and is a norm

only to the degree that it agrees with scripture. (2) Scripture is the final criterion of all religious claims; scripture does not receive its authority from the church but rather from its author or inspirer (God); accordingly, every theological, moral, or liturgical development in the church should be tested by scripture. (3) Scripture is intrinsically clear and needs no infallible church or tradition to interpret it; individual believers are capable of reading and understanding it; and scripture is the judge of tradition and sometimes stands over against tradition as a critique of beliefs and practices in the church. (4) Nothing can be added to scripture; the Bible tells us all that is necessary for our salvation.

As a Protestant myself, I naturally tend to accept at least some version of 'Scripture alone'. But I also want to retain an important place for tradition in determining which theological theories or claims are orthodox. In Chapter 15, I will explore in detail various things that 'Scripture alone' might be said to mean. For present purposes, let me suggest it means something like: *Scripture is our source of religious truth above all other sources, our norm or guide to religious truth above all other norms or guides.* In other words, all other sources of theological truth are subordinate to scripture and are to be tested by scripture. Scripture has the last word, the final say. There may be other criteria of religious truth—for example, tradition, reason, experience—but scripture is the final test, the sure norm, the infallible rule of what we are to believe.

But tradition remains indispensable in interpreting scripture. All who do serious exegesis or theology must be knowledgeable about the history of Christian thought and practice. Such knowledge creates a barrier against private or eccentric interpretations of scripture. The church must have criteria for rejecting off-beat interpretations. Tradition is the church's best protection against the misuse of the Bible. Tradition shows us that certain texts of scripture take hermeneutical priority over others, and shows us how to interpret them. Tradition also helps us grasp that a doctrine can be deemed normative for Christians, despite the absence of any clear proof texts specifically teaching it.

Fortunately, many of the differences between Catholics and Protestants on the issue of theological authority have narrowed in recent years. Most Christians rejoice in that fact. What remains is not the question whether scripture needs to be interpreted. All can agree that it does. But Catholics and Protestants disagree about whether scripture must be *authoritatively* interpreted. Protestants hold, contrary to Catholics, that scripture needs no binding interpreter other than the Holy Spirit. All who interpret scripture, including those in church teaching offices, stand under scripture.

My own view, then, is twofold: (1) tradition is necessary for interpreting scripture; and (2) scripture, our highest source and norm of religious truth, takes priority over tradition. Ideally scripture and tradition always agree. But in fact, the two probably never completely coincide, and that is why part of scripture's role, whenever necessary, is to correct tradition. Tradition guides the interpretation of scripture, but never controls it. Protestants can affirm the Roman Catholic notion of the Holy Spirit's gracious guidance of the church in doctrinal (as well as other) matters. But the fact of human depravity, as well as a glance at the history of doctrine, convinces most Protestants that no human institution has been kept free from error. So all institutions, including the church, must stand under the authority of scripture.

IV

Our central concern in this chapter is whether kenotic christological theories are orthodox. It now seems that in order to answer that question we must ask three other questions. (1) Is kenosis as a christological theory scriptural? (2) Does kenosis agree with the christological tradition? And (3) can defenders of kenosis successfully reply to criticisms of the doctrine, especially those criticisms that explicitly or in effect impugn its orthodoxy? These questions will be taken up in this and the following two sections.

So far as question (1) is concerned, I will not say much. Let me begin my discussion of this point with an autobiographical note. Although raised in a nominally Christian home, I was a teenage convert to Christianity. I believe it was several years before I learned that the doctrine of the incarnation meant that Jesus was 'truly God and truly human'. But I had read the Gospels by then, and as a child had of course heard many of the stories about Jesus. I found myself naturally thinking of the incarnation along (what I later found were called) kenotic lines.

Indeed, to this day the fit of kenosis with the New Testament picture of Jesus is its greatest attraction for me. This attraction corresponds to the point I made in Section I about the way that kenosis matches the New Testament picture of Jesus. To insist, as classicists do, that in the incarnation the Second Person of the Trinity simply took on an additional (human) nature, does not seem to kenoticists to square well with that picture.

I have in mind points like the fact that Christ grew in wisdom as a child (Luke 2: 52), was tempted (Matt. 4: 1–11; Heb. 4: 15), did not know who had touched his cloak (Mark 5: 29–31), did not know the date of the Parousia (Mark 13: 32), on one occasion could do no mighty works in his hometown (except a few healings) (Mark 6: 5), learned by his suffering (Heb. 5: 8–9), and uttered the cry of dereliction (Mark 15: 34).

Nevertheless, so far as a christological theory is concerned, we would not expect to find it explicitly taught in scripture. The biblical writers were not concerned with the question whether in the incarnation the Logos emptied itself of certain properties normally characteristic of divinity or else simply assumed a human nature (perhaps an enhanced human nature) to its already existing divine nature. What we would be looking for, then, would be (so to speak) scriptural *permission* for the theory. And that is precisely what defenders of kenosis claim that we do have, both in Philippians 2 and elsewhere.

Despite disagreement on each of the points listed below, there is, I believe, at least some degree of consensus among Pauline scholars that Philippians 2: 6–11 is a unified text that contains a 'high' christology. And although not much rides on these next points for present purposes, there is also significant opinion that this text is in the form of a hymn,[18] and with the possible exception of a few words (e.g. 'death on a cross'), is pre-Pauline. That is, Paul is citing words that he did not compose; accordingly, the hymn reflects beliefs of the very young church. So the text has the authority both of Paul and the pre-Pauline community. But unfortunately the text is also an exegetical and especially lexical minefield, and there has been controversy about it from the early church until today.[19]

Here would be my own rough summary of the text. It is important to note that Paul starts off with the intention of expressing an ethical imperative: (1) that the Philippians should behave in the same sort of self-giving and even self-sacrificial way that Christ Jesus did, in his incarnation. (2) Exploring that last point further through the use of the pre-Pauline hymn, Paul says that Christ Jesus was at one time, that is, before his appearance in the form of a servant, in the form of God (*en morphe theou*). (3) But he did not count the status of equality with God (*to einai isa theo*) something to be grasped or held on to or exploited (*harpagmos*—a 'thing to be seized'). (4) Rather, he obediently emptied himself (*heauton ekenosen*), taking the form of a servant, being born in human likeness, and being obedient to God even to the point of death by crucifixion. (5) Accordingly, God has highly exalted him (*auton huperuphosen*) and has given him the name that is above every name (*to onoma to huper pan onoma*); that at the name of Jesus every knee should bow and every tongue should confess that Jesus Christ is Lord (*kurios Iesous Christos*), to the Glory of God the Father. That is to say, within the context of Jewish monotheism, Jesus Christ is made God's equal as worthy of praise and worship.

---

[18] Some would dispute this point. For assessments of the evidence, see Stephen E. Fowl, 'What Is A Hymn?', *JSNT*, Supp. 36 (Sheffield, 1990) and Marcus Bockmuehl, ' "The Form of God" (Phil. 2: 6): Variations on a Theme of Jewish Mysticism', *Journal of Theological Studies*, 48/1 (1997), p. 123.

[19] See the essays in Ralph P. Martin and Brian Dodd (eds.), *Where Christology Began: Essays on Philippians 2* (Louisville, KY: Westminster John Knox Press, 1998), especially the essays by Larry J. Kreitzer and Richard Bauckham.

Language that the Old Testament would apply only to God is here applied to Jesus.

So far as our purposes in the present chapter are concerned, we can rejoice along with all who affirm the full divinity of Christ, whether their christology is classical or kenotic, in the high christology of the kenosis hymn. A plausible exegetical case can be made here that part of what Christ Jesus emptied himself of in the incarnation was the divine glory and majesty. This was at least part of what was involved in taking on human likeness. But the specific issue we are interested in—whether in the incarnation the Logos 'emptied' himself of some of the properties God normally has—does not appear to be answered by exegetical considerations alone.

He 'emptied himself, taking on the form of a servant', the text says. Some who oppose the kenotic interpretation insist that since the text does not precisely say what Christ Jesus emptied himself of (which is true), it follows that he did not empty himself *of* anything, and thus certainly not of any divine attributes. But surely that is not an impressive argument. Both in English and in Greek, some verbs, when used, immediately cry out for a direct or indirect object. If I say, 'I repeat', you can sensibly wonder what I am about to repeat. If I say, 'I listen', you can sensibly wonder what I am listening to. (This is not true of all verbs, of course, e.g. 'I stand'.) Now any vessel that is 'emptied', whether that vessel be a bottle, a room, a human life, or even a divine life, must be emptied of something. It seems clear that Paul holds that the 'emptying' that Christ underwent had something to do with *his prior status*, in which he was not 'in the likeness of man' or 'in the form of a servant'. Beyond that point, however, the question of what the hymn implies or presupposes that Christ Jesus 'emptied himself' of is still an open question.

Some who resist kenotic theories of the incarnation insist that what Christ Jesus emptied himself of was not any of the divine *attributes*, but rather certain divine *prerogatives*, like the divine glory. Yet that solution will work (i.e. this is a possible reading of the text) only if one can formulate a coherent distinction between the divine attributes and the divine prerogatives. But I doubt that it can. It seems to me that 'having the divine glory' is just as much an attribute or property as 'being omnipotent' or 'being omniscient'. I do not know of any prerogatives that do not entail properties. So if that distinction cannot be coherently formulated, and if the text implies that he at least emptied himself of the divine glory, we are already halfway there to a kenotic interpretation of the incarnation.

Others who resist kenoticism argue that the 'emptying' spoken of in Phillipians had nothing to do with the incarnate Logos temporarily *no longer possessing* certain attributes (like, say, omnipotence or omniscience). It had to do instead with the incarnate Logos *voluntarily not exercising* those attributes for the duration of Jesus' earthly life. Again: maybe so. Here the crucial issue is not exegetical but philosophical: is a person who at any time has the ability to be omnipotent, but voluntarily and temporarily decides not to call on that ability, 'truly human' (as the creed insists)?

Further, it would be a mistake to believe that the only biblical basis for the kenotic theory is Philippians 2. Note also John 17: 4–5, where Jesus prays, 'I glorified you on earth by finishing the work that you gave me to do. So now, Father, glorify me in your own presence with the glory that I had in your presence before the world existed.' What exactly is being said here? Possibly several things: first, that Jesus Christ once had divine glory and complete oneness with the Father (cf. John 17: 11, 20–6); secondly, that at the time of his prayer (i.e. during his earthly ministry) he did not possess the fullness of divine glory; and thirdly, he looked forward to regaining it. (See also 2 Cor. 8: 9; 12: 9; Heb. 2: 9, 17.)

I conclude that exegetical considerations do not explicitly confirm the kenotic theory. But neither do they rule out the idea that the Logos temporarily gave up certain properties that God normally possesses. Scripture seems to allow the theory.

V

Let us then turn to our second question: Are kenotic interpretations of the incarnation consistent with church tradition? In this case, the texts we must look to, by almost universal consent, are the Creeds of Nicaea I (AD 325) and Chalcedon (AD 451). These are the creeds that the church has always taken as spelling out the limits of orthodoxy in christology. The relevant part of the Nicene Creed reads:

And in one Lord Jesus Christ, the only-begotten Son of God, begotten of the Father before all worlds, God of God, Light of Light, Very God of Very God, begotten, not made, being of one substance with the Father by whom all things were made.[20]

And the relevant part of the Creed of Chalcedon declares that Jesus Christ is

At once complete in Godhead and complete in manhood, truly God and truly man, consisting of a reasonable soul and body; of one substance with the Father as regards his Godhead, and at the same time of one substance with us as regards his manhood; like us in all respects, apart from sin; one and the same Christ, Son, Lord, Only-begotten, recognized in two natures, without confusion, without change, without

---

[20] *The Book of Confessions* (New York: Office of the General Assembly of the Presbyterian Church [USA], 1983), 1.1–3.

division, without separation; the distinction of the two natures being in no way annulled by the union, but rather characteristics of each nature being preserved and coming together to form one person and subsistence.[21]

The core ideas here appear to be that (1) Jesus Christ is one unified person (2) in whom two natures coexist, a divine nature and a human nature; (3) these natures are neither confused with each other nor separated from each other in him; and (4) he is accordingly at once truly divine and truly human. What the Church Fathers produced, in my opinion, is not an explanation of the incarnation (that was wisely left for individual theologians), but rather a guideline or boundary. It was a way of letting the church know what is acceptable and what is not acceptable in christology. At heart, it says: any christology is acceptable that affirms the divinity, the humanity, and the unity of the person of Christ.

Sarah Coakley points out that some of the crucial terms in the Chalcedonian definition (terms like *physis* ('nature') and *hypostasis* ('person')) are left undefined, which leaves the statement somewhat open-ended. No attempt is made to explain precisely how two natures can cohere in one person, let alone a divine nature and a human nature. She argues that Chalcedon should be viewed as a theologically regulatory and binding text, as a grid through which reflections on christology must pass. The statement, she says, intends to rule out aberrant christologies (e.g. Apollinarianism (in which the two natures are mixed because the human nature is 'taken up' into the divine nature), Eutychianism (in which after the union there is but one nature, the divine nature), and extreme Nestorianism (in which there are two different persons in Christ, two separate subjects, linked only by a union of love)); it does not 'intend to provide a full systematic account of Christology, and even less a complete and precise metaphysics of Christ's make-up. Rather, it sets a "boundary" on what can, and cannot be said.'[22]

There are, then, many important christological issues that Chalcedon cannot solve. As Coakley says, Chalcedon does not tell us in what the divine and human 'natures' consist, what *hypostasis* and *physis* mean and how the two are related to each other in Christ, how many wills Christ has, whether the *hypostasis* is identical to the pre-existent Logos, or what happens to the human *physis* at Christ's death and in his resurrection.[23] I would only add that since kenotic theories of the incarnation have nothing whatever to do with Apollinarianism,

---

[21] Henry Bettenson (ed.), *Documents of the Christian Church*, 2nd edn. (London: Oxford University Press, 1960), pp. 72–3.

[22] Sarah Coakley, 'What Does Chalcedon Solve and What Does it Not? Some Reflections on the Status and Meaning of the Chalcedonian "Definition"', in Stephen T. Davis, Daniel Kendall, S.J., and Gerald O'Collins, S.J., *The Incarnation: An Interdisciplinary Symposium on the Incarnation of the Son of God* (Oxford: Oxford University Press, 2001), p. 161.

[23] Ibid., pp. 162–3.

Eutychianism, or extreme Nestorianism, and affirm the two unmixed natures and the one person, the Chalcedonic definition does not rule out kenosis. Kenosis may be mistaken as a christological theory; there may be better christological theories in the neighbourhood; but kenosis is orthodox.

VI

But perhaps kenosis is unorthodox at some deeper level. The best way to test for that possibility is to consider those criticisms of the theory that intentionally or in effect impugn its orthodoxy. I will now turn to that task. I will discuss three such criticisms.

1. *In the kenotic theory, the earthly Jesus is not really divine.* This is a standard criticism of kenosis, and impugns the orthodoxy of the theory because orthodoxy requires that the earthly Jesus Christ is indeed 'truly divine'. The objection revolves around an insistence on the part of the critic that such divine properties as omnipotence and omniscience are essential properties of God. Since on kenosis the kenotically incarnate Logos 'emptied himself' of such properties, it follows that Jesus Christ was not, as orthodoxy insists, 'truly divine'.

Surely, this is too quick. It is true that the one and only God is omnipotent and omniscient. The statement, 'All Gods in existence are omnipotent and omniscient' is true. But it does not follow that these are essential properties, that is, that a being who was nearly but not quite, say, omnipotent cannot go on existing or cannot be God. Returning to a point made earlier, perhaps these are *common* divine properties, but not *essential* divine properties. (Similarly, the property of *having been born on earth* is a common human property but not an essential human property.) Again, perhaps what is essential to God is having the property of being *omnipotent-unless-freely-and-temporarily-choosing-not-to-be-otherwise*. If this property is essential to God, kenosis remains untouched by the present criticism.

And to repeat a point made earlier, Christians believe that Jesus was 'truly divine and truly human'. So if the claim that omnipotence *simpliciter* is an essential property of God is inconsistent with Jesus Christ being 'truly divine and truly human', Christians will be inclined to say, 'So much the worse for the doctrine that omnipotence *simpliciter* is an essential property of God.'

2. *In the kenotic theory, the glorified Logos is not truly human.* This criticism also impugns the orthodoxy of kenosis for those who accept the permanent embodiment and humanity of the Logos. There is (so it is said) a kind of necessary reverse 'emptying' in kenosis, where the glorified Logos, on returning to heaven, emptied itself of humanity.

But since I affirm (1) that incarnation without kenosis is possible, and (2) that the exalted Christ continues eternally as the incarnate Son of God, there is no real problem here. Kenoticists can consistently affirm the true humanity of the exalted Logos.

To be more specific, here are two ways in which kenoticists can answer this objection.[24] The first, which is defended by Evans, claims that the kenosis of Christ continues in his glorification; Christ receives some properties in his glorified state because, as a human, he has, so to speak, earned them precisely by being human. This would not include properties like ignorance (surely in the glorification he will reassume omniscience), but enough human properties to remain fully human. So there are kenotic theories that fully accept the idea of everlasting kenosis; they are accordingly not vulnerable to the present criticism.

The second reply, which has been defended by Feenstra,[25] claims that kenosis is not necessary to *being incarnate*, although it might be necessary to *becoming incarnate*, or at least to becoming incarnate for the purposes of redemption. So it is at least possible that the kenosis cease while the incarnation continues. Jesus Christ remains fully human but the kenosis ends. The incarnation and the kenosis are conceptually distinct. The incarnation is the Second Person of the Trinity everlastingly becoming human at the point of his human birth, and the kenosis is that same Person temporarily sharing our lot. And since I stated earlier my own view that the incarnation is distinct from the kenosis, I find this second reply to the criticism attractive. It should be noted that adopting this reply requires defenders of kenosis to accept the idea that incarnation apart from kenosis (or at least *after* kenosis) is possible—indeed, actual. As also noted earlier, I fully accept that implication; accordingly, I have never seen myself as an enemy of non-kenotic theories of the incarnation.

3. *In the kenotic theory, divine immutability must be given up.* This criticism is raised by John Hick, who earlier in his career had argued that all orthodox christologies are logically incoherent.[26] His point now is that the kenotic theory 'clashes with any traditionally orthodox understanding of God' by requiring rejection of divine immutability.[27] Perhaps Hick's point

---

[24] They are skilfully explored by Evans. See 'The Self-Emptying of Love' (n. 5 above), pp. 263–7.

[25] See Feenstra, 'Reconsidering Kenotic Christology' (n. 9 above) pp. 148–9.

[26] John Hick (ed.), *The Myth of God Incarnate* (Philadelphia: Westminster Press, 1977), p. 178.

[27] John Hick, *The Metaphor of God Incarnate: Christology in a Pluralistic Age* (Louisville, KY: Westminster John Knox Press, 1993), p. 75. Hick also mentions divine aseity, which for lack of space I will not discuss. I will note briefly an admittedly *ad hominem* point: it is odd that Hick, of all people, raises this criticism, since throughout his career he has rejected traditional Christian doctrines fairly readily.

is that kenoticists want to be orthodox, but cannot be, since their own doctrine requires them to jettison divine immutability, which they themselves take to be orthodox.

It is true that in the tradition we can find notions of divine immutability that seem inconsistent with kenosis. Suppose we say that 'strong immutability' is the notion that no statement about God's possessing a certain property can have different truth values at different times. It certainly seems true that anybody who holds *that* doctrine will be singularly unattracted to the kenotic theory of the incarnation (in which the statement, 'The Logos is kenotically incarnate in a man,' was once true but is now false). But what if we accept 'soft immutability', that is, the doctrine that God is not fickle, capricious, mercurial, or moody; God's holy and benevolent nature remains ever and eternally the same; God is faithful in keeping God's promises; God's aims and intentions for human beings do not change? Now I have no idea whether Hick would find soft immutability attractive, but I do. And it is perfectly consistent with kenosis.

It seems, then, that all three objections can be answered. Accordingly, we are within our rights in concluding that the kenotic theory of the incarnation is orthodox.

VII

In this chapter I have presented a version of the kenotic theory of the incarnation. I have argued that it is within the bounds of Christian orthodoxy. My argument for that point has consisted of three parts: (1) kenosis is allowed by scripture; (2) kenosis is consistent with the great christological creeds; and (3) kenosis can be defended against three criticisms that charge it with being non-orthodox.

Despite being a Protestant, I believe, as Catholics do, that there exists, and must exist, a magisterium. This is an authoritative church teaching office, an office that normatively decides which teachings are orthodox and which are not. But I do not believe that the magisterium is anything remotely like a committee that holds meetings in a room somewhere. Indeed, I believe the real Christian magisterium consists of the voice of the entirety of the people of God, past, present, and future. They together constitute the authoritative interpreters of the Christian tradition.

Of course the church can err. It has doubtless done so at many times in the past. But for those Christians who earnestly desire to be faithful to the apostolic traditions and ecumenical creeds, past Christian teaching is always important. I believe God preserves the church at crucial points from dangerous theological error. So in the final analysis, whether the kenotic theory is orthodox depends on whether the people of God accept it as orthodox.[28]

[28] 1 would like to thank Sarah Coakley, Stephen Evans, Gordon Fee, Bruce Fisk, Ron Feenstra, Edward Oakes, Gerald O'Collins, S.J., and Susan Peppers-Bates for their helpful comments on earlier drafts of the present chapter.

Part III

How Are We Saved? Redemption

11

Karma or Grace?

Those whose conduct here has been good will quickly attain a good birth (literally womb), the birth of a Brahmin, the birth of a Ksatriya or the birth of a Vaisya. But those whose conduct here has been evil, will quickly attain an evil birth, the birth of a dog, the birth of a hog or the birth of a Candala [outcast].[1]

The predominating sense of grace in the New Testament is that which the word bears in the writings of Saint Paul, who thinks of the Divine salvation primarily as a 'boon' flowing from the generous, unmerited graciousness of God to sinful, lost humanity, as expressed supremely on the cross of Christ. For Saint Paul the free outgoing and self-imparting of the redeeming love of God to man in Christ is constitutive of the whole of salvation. God deals with men in Christ purely on the basis of infinite, undeserved mercy.[2]

I

Thus far we have discussed, among other things, the rationality of belief in God, the nature of God, and the revelation of God to human beings in the person of Jesus Christ. We turn now to the topic of redemption. Precisely how are human beings saved? How does God achieve his purpose of reconciling sinful human beings to himself, as well as to other human beings? The quotations just cited are meant to exemplify two great and contrasting methods of redemption. I will call them 'Karma' and 'Grace'.

All religions contain both a description and a diagnosis of the human predicament. People are unhappy because they are avaricious and striving. The gods are angry with us. The world is a terrible place because people care about themselves more than they do about others. People suffer because they have sinned against God.

---

[1] Cited in Bruce R. Reichenbach, *The Law of Karma: A Philosophical Study* (Honolulu: University of Hawaii Press, 1990) (hereinafter *The Law of Karma*), p. 194 (*Chandogya Upanishad*, v, 10, 7).

[2] William Manson, 'Grace in the New Testament', in William T. Whitley (ed.), *The Doctrine of Grace* (New York: Macmillan, 1932), p. 59.

Each religion also typically offers a solution to the problem. The gods must be placated by proper ritual. People can escape ignorance and achieve liberation. People should engage in proper practices of meditation, and so achieve self-realization. People need to obey God's laws. People must accept God's mercy and be forgiven.

Let us say that human beings at the diagnostic stage of the problem are at 'Stage 1'. And let us say that saved, transformed, redeemed, liberated, enlightened (or whatever term is preferred) human beings are at 'Stage 2'. The point is that every religion has a proposed way of moving people from Stage 1 to Stage 2. They offer both a diagnosis and a cure of the human condition. Let us call any religious method of achieving this a *system of salvation*.[3]

In this chapter I will contrast two quite different systems of salvation. As noted, I will call them *Karma* and *Grace*.[4] I want to stress that my intent is to talk about these two concepts theoretically or in the abstract. Although I do think that these terms, as I will define them, broadly fit some of the religions of the world (and Grace does fit the Christian religion, as I understand it), I will make little reference to actual religions or religious teachings. There are two reasons for this. First, I am not a historian of religion, and my knowledge of religious traditions apart from my own is limited. Secondly, I want to treat Karma and Grace as if they were entirely opposed or irreconcilable systems of salvation, whereas in fact the notions of karma and grace are mixed in some (but by no means all) karmic religious traditions in complex and fascinating ways.[5]

Indeed, it might be more historically accurate to distinguish among *three* systems of salvation: (a) grace-oriented systems that involve one lifetime only and no karma (e.g. Judaism and Christianity); (b) grace-oriented religious systems that include reincarnation and karma (e.g. the Ramajuna and Madhva schools of Hinduism or Pure Land Buddhism); and (c) reincarnational and karmic religious traditions in which one reaches Stage 2 not via the grace of a higher being but by one's own efforts—through meditation, for example, or ethical action (e.g. Advaita Vedanta Hinduism or Zen Buddhism).[6] But in the interest of simplicity, I will instead simply posit two abstract systems of salvation, Karma and Grace, and will compare them. In other words, I will

---

[3] The very word 'salvation' has connotations that make it more appropriate to grace-oriented than to karma-oriented religious systems. Still, I will try to use the term as a neutral reference to what I am calling 'Stage 2'.

[4] I will capitalize these two terms only when referring to them as systems of salvation.

[5] Some Western scholars even try to synthesize them. See, for example, three works by Geddes MacGregor: *Reincarnation in Christianity* (Wheaton, IL: Theosophical Publishing House, 1978); *Reincarnation as a Christian Hope* (London: Macmillan, 1982); and *The Christening of Karma* (Wheaton, IL: Theosophical Publishing House, 1984).

[6] There are also schemes in Western philosophy (e.g. those of Spinoza or Hegel or McTaggart) in which reality is intelligible, pervaded by thought, and even purposive, but not personal. I will not consider these fascinating options in the present chapter.

ignore systems of salvation like those falling in category (b) and concentrate on two abstract ones that are like (a) and (c). Although in the end I will not be able to give a definitive answer, my aim in this chapter is to ask, on philosophical grounds, which system of salvation shows more promise of moving people from Stage 1 to Stage 2.[7]

I do not pretend to write from a neutral, detached perspective. I am of course a believer in a religion of grace, and so it is not surprising that I will end up defending that system of salvation. Indeed, I will argue that it is subject to fewer serious difficulties than is karma. But I also hope to be fair to the concept of karma.

Before contrasting the two systems of salvation, I will also note that there are crucial points of agreement between Karma and Grace. First, both systems of salvation agree that the deepest human problems are spiritual in nature. This point is important, because some people suppose that the deepest human problems are economic in nature, or perhaps political, or perhaps medical. Karma and Grace agree that what is wrong in human life is, at its deepest level, spiritual in nature.

Secondly, Karma and Grace agree that moral right and wrong are 'object-ive'—they are facts about the nature of reality itself.[8] Moral relativism is false; what is right and wrong does not depend on who you are or what you happen to believe. This is a controversial point in our day. Many people hold that right and wrong have nothing to do with the way things are. There are brute facts and there are evaluative opinions, and the two are in totally different realms. Both Karma and Grace, in contrast, reject any rigid distinction between facts and values. Followers of both Karma and Grace hold that certain things are morally right and certain other things are morally wrong. Intentions and actions can be objectively judged to be right or wrong.

Thirdly, Karma and Grace agree that justice lies behind the real or apparent injustices and inequities that we see in the world. The traditional problem of

---

[7] It is technically incorrect to consider karma a system of salvation. Karma simply means action, and the law of karma (an extension of karma as action) states that what happens to us in a later life or in later lives results from our own actions in this life and previous lives. So the law in karma may in some sense explain why things happen to us, but it does not, by itself, recommend any spiritual or moral conduct. Those recommendations—the Eightfold Path, renunciation, etc.—come from particular karmic religious traditions. So it is important to note that in the present chapter I am offering a technical definition of the word 'Karma'. I mean it to include both (1) the law of karma and (2) particular religious or moral ways of achieving Stage 2 as found, say, in typical karmic religious traditions.

[8] This point needs to be nuanced in relation to some Asian karmic systems. In some such systems, evil appears to have no logical place or seems a muddled category. It is either illusory (as in Sankara); or the good–evil opposition is ultimately transcended and ethical levels are merely transitional (as in Aurobindo Ghose); or the world is considered a kind of 'body' for God (as in Ramajuna), in which case evil is essential to this ultimate reality.

evil may be a more serious intellectual difficulty for the advocate of Grace than for the advocate of Karma, but both theories suggest that evil will be punished and virtue rewarded in some future life. Both hold that the universe is essentially moral. It is not true that the world operates with complete indifference to morality, like the movements of a planet or the operation of a machine. Morality is at the heart of reality.

II

It is time for me to describe the two systems of salvation. There are of course many different karmic theories and many different theologies of grace. So let me again note that in creating these categories I am abstracting from the teachings of any particular religion. However, as noted, my own view is that the system of salvation that I call Grace does fit Christianity, and the system of salvation that I call Karma does broadly fit some—but not all—karmic systems of salvation in certain Asian religions.

Karma. Karma denies that any personal God exists; it posits instead an impersonal absolute that might be called Reality Itself.[9] People are born, and then die, and then are reborn in another body. Their new stations in life are karmic consequences ('fruits') of the sorts of moral lives that they lived in previous lives.[10] Not everything that happens to a person is due to karma: some things that occur are consequences of one's genetic inheritance, some of one's own choices, some of the choices of others or of natural events. Nor does Karma hold that everything karmic is ineluctably determined or fated. Those who are hungry should try to find food; those who are sick should try to be cured. Karma is an impersonal law, like gravity or thermodynamics, which says that all actions for which one can be held morally responsible have consequences, good or bad, in this and subsequent incarnations.

The Karmic theory stresses cause and effect: you get just what you deserve, no more and no less. Nothing happens that is unjust. Actions that are due to

---

[9] The law of karma, by itself, neither affirms nor denies that a personal God exists. And there are religious traditions that are both theistic and karmic. But since the law of karma is usually associated with non-theistic religious systems, I simply posit that my technically defined system of salvation called 'Karma' is non-theistic.

[10] I recognize that certain Buddhists, Hindus, and other advocates of karmic religions interpret karma symbolically or non-realistically. They do not literally believe that after death they will be reborn elsewhere with karmic consequences intact; they rather interpret the karma doctrines of their religions as emphasizing certain ethical imperatives. In the present chapter, however, I will interpret the system of salvation that I am calling 'Karma' as entailing a realist understanding of the doctrine.

craving, greed, hatred, or ignorance will produce bad karma. Moral acts will produce good karma. This aspect of karma is not a matter of retribution. Good karma is conducive to spiritual growth; bad karma is less conducive. One important thing that karma can do is move us along the path of spiritual growth. By hard spiritual and moral effort it is possible to grow spiritually and eventually to escape from the cycle of reincarnation. A liberated, enlightened state is possible for human beings. Achieving it means reaching the ultimate spiritual goal, which is oneness with Reality Itself.

Grace. Human beings were created by a holy and personal creator. We are required to obey the creator's laws. When we fail to do so, we sin and accordingly separate ourselves from God. Sin must be punished. The punishment for sin is permanent separation from God. Human beings—who live but one life on this earth—are in bondage to self-centredness, violence, pride, greed, and lust. They are quite unable, on their own strength, to overcome the pervasive effects of sin in their lives. They can do nothing to save themselves; no matter how hard they try, they fail. So, although they do not morally deserve it, God reveals himself to them and offers to forgive them of their sins and reconcile them to him. This offer is a free gift of grace. People do not deserve it—indeed, they deserve to be separated from God. Grace means that God treats us better than we morally deserve to be treated. Still, there is something that humans must do in order to be recipients of grace, namely, sincerely ask for it and sincerely receive it. But the main effort in achieving salvation, so to speak, is God's not ours. Those who accept the gift of grace live eternally with God in heaven. Accordingly, whereas Karma presents salvation as ultimately within human control, in Grace salvation depends on the grace of God.[11]

There are many differences between these two systems of salvation. Probably the most important is the presence of higher personal agency—the agency of God—in Grace. (As noted, there are theistic karmic religions, but the abstract theory called 'Karma' that we are considering in this chapter is non-theistic.) A second is that Karma affirms and Grace denies that one gets only what one deserves in this life, that perfect justice rules here and now. Grace affirms that many things that happen to people are undeserved, including the gift of grace itself. A third difference, to which I will return later, is that Karma attributes the human predicament primarily to what we might call false consciousness or spiritual blindness, while Grace attributes it to guilt.

---

[11] On the Christian theology of grace, see Henri Rondet, *The Grace of Christ* (Philadelphia: Westminster Press, 1966), and Piet Fransen, *The New Life of Grace* (New York: Seabury, 1969).

III

At this point, I want to raise several criticisms of each system of salvation, objections that advocates of one system would or might raise against the other. Let me begin with five criticisms of Grace.

1. *Who gets the grace?* Why is it that some people receive the grace of God and are forgiven while others do not receive it and are condemned? Is this not unfair? Some advocates of Grace respond to this charge by arguing that we all deserve condemnation, and so those who do not receive grace (and stay condemned at Stage 1) have no right to object.

But this reply, while it does accomplish something, does not entirely solve the problem. What it accomplishes is that it shows that no one can rightly complain that he or she is receiving an undeserved punishment. And that is an important point. God must punish sin, but is not obligated to bestow grace on everyone, or even on anyone. If grace is a free gift, God can bestow it on anyone God wants to. But I can illustrate the limitation of the point by telling a story. Suppose a certain parent has two children, John and Jane, who are both equally guilty of some fault. Let us say they both intentionally trample on some prized geraniums in the flowerbed, and so both equally deserve punishment. Then suppose the parent says to them, 'You are both equally guilty and both deserve to be grounded for a week. John, you are grounded to your room for a week. But as a free gift of grace, Jane, you are forgiven. You will not be punished in any way.' Is it not obvious that this scenario is radically unfair?

2. *Why doesn't God intervene more often?* The problem of evil is a pervasive intellectual problem for all theistic systems of salvation that presuppose the ability of God graciously to intervene in human affairs from time to time. Why doesn't God do so more often? Why didn't God intervene to prevent the Holocaust, for example? The fact that God allows so much human suffering entails either that God is not strong enough to prevent it, or that God is not morally good enough to want to prevent it, or that God does not exist. Whichever is true—so the criticism runs—the system of salvation called Grace collapses.

3. *Grace can be morally corrupting.* Some argue that followers of religions of grace can easily lapse into moral listlessness or even moral turpitude because of their conviction that 'grace covers everything'. In other words, it is easy for grace to become cheap and morally worthless if it leads people to evade their moral responsibilities out of the belief that no matter how much moral wrong they do, God's grace will overcome it and they will be forgiven.

4. *Not enough time.* One aspect of the system of salvation called Grace is that human beings live only one life on this earth and then are judged on the basis of that life. But surely one lifetime is not enough to achieve salvation. This claim is substantiated by the simple observation that most people die in far less than an optimal or perfect spiritual state. Obviously, for the vast majority of people, many more lives than one are needed to reach the spiritual end-state. A loving God will make that possible; a God who does not is a moral monster.[12]

5. *Grace is immoral.* Even if the first criticism (about the unfairness of grace for some people and not others) is waived, it can still be argued that the very idea of grace is inherently unjust and unfair. Morality requires that people should be treated exactly as they deserve. Just as it is unfair to treat people *worse* than they deserve (e.g. by sentencing someone to twenty years in prison for failing to put a stamp on an envelope), so it is unfair to treat people *better* than they deserve. Justice must be upheld at all times, and it is radically unjust to forgive people who do not merit forgiveness. Moving from Stage 1 to Stage 2 must be achieved by the moral agents themselves. If it comes as a free and undeserved gift from someone else, it will not be appreciated. Human beings must work hard spiritually and morally, and if they do they can move themselves to Stage 2. That is the far better way.

IV

How might advocates of Grace criticize Karma? I will now consider five objections that can be raised. The first, in my opinion, is a serious point but can be answered; the cogency of the second depends on theological considerations that are beyond the scope of the present chapter; but the final three, in my opinion, create serious difficulties for karmic systems of salvation.

1. *Karmic explanations are unfalsifiable.* Karma is said to be an impersonal law that prevents injustice in the world. Whatever happens to a person, whether it is good or bad, is an entirely just consequence of that person's actions in the present or in previous incarnations. It follows from this claim that there is no such thing as undeserved human suffering. But one conceptual difficulty with this system of salvation is that karmic explanations—for example, 'Sally is suffering from arthritis as a consequence of her unforgiving,

---

[12] See MacGregor, *Reincarnation as a Christian Hope* (n. 5 above), p. 11. John Hick has also used this argument. See, for example, his *Death and Eternal Life* (New York: Harper and Row, 1976), p. 408.

condemning spirit in previous incarnations'—are completely unfalsifiable. As Paul Edwards argues, no matter what happens to a person, some plausible sounding karmic explanation or other can be generated. There is no way that any karmic explanation could be tested against alternative karmic explanations.[13]

One way of understanding this criticism is to point out that even if the basic claims of Karma as a system of salvation were true, there would be no way that the law of karma could accurately predict future events. Karma is empty and unfalsifiable because it is compatible with anything that could possibly occur. Accordingly, karma cannot be convincingly used to show that everything is just, that there is no undeserved suffering.

But it seems that Karma can be defended at this point. Even if karmic explanations of events are strictly unfalsifiable, what follows is that the law of karma cannot be used to show *empirically* that everything that happens is just. However, there may be other, non-empirical, grounds for accepting the law of karma, and thus other grounds for holding that nothing unjust occurs. Edwards may believe that it is always wrong to accept religious doctrines that are not empirically falsifiable, but few religious people, including advocates of Grace, will agree with him.

Moreover, it may be that predictability is too narrow a criterion to use for the purpose of judging the acceptability of religious or non-religious claims. As Bruce Reichenbach has argued,[14] the law of karma may be like the theory of evolution in this way: neither can be used to make predictions and hence are strictly unfalsifiable; both are instead postdictive (that is, they have to do with explaining past events rather than predicting future ones), so that criteria relevant to postdiction can be brought to bear. Both theories claim to provide (Darwinian or karmic) histories of events leading up to the present—histories that are said to be helpful and powerful in explaining the present situation, more so than alternative theories. In other words, non-predictive theories, whether scientific or religious, can in principle be justified on the basis of how well they explain existing facts.

Finally, while karma certainly implies that nothing morally significant happens 'accidentally', it may be that the present objection misrepresents karma. Perhaps karma does not produce predictable consequences in future lives, but rather sets contexts for and limitations on future events. Presumably, what actually will occur in a future life will be a function of many factors, not just karma, with karmic laws acting as setters of conditions or contexts,

---

[13] See Paul Edwards, 'Karmic Tribulations', in Paul Edwards (ed.), *Immortality* (New York: Macmillan, 1992), pp. 200–12.

[14] Bruce Reichenbach, 'Justifying In-Principle Nonpredictive Theories: The Case of Evolution', *Christian Scholars Review*, 24/4 (May, 1995).

much as a card player is dealt a certain hand and then can make free choices how to play the hand.[15]

2. *Can we save ourselves?* An important criticism that defenders of Grace will make of karmic religious systems is that human beings are quite unable to save themselves and need the help of God's grace if they are to progress from Stage 1 to Stage 2. This, indeed, is perhaps the deepest issue that divides the two systems of salvation: Are human beings able to save themselves, or not?

Obviously, some facts about myself are such that I have it within my power to change them. I can make a decision to change the fact that I am now sitting at my computer; I can change the fact that I have not yet replied to a certain letter; maybe I can even change the fact that I have never been to Thailand. Some people have even changed more embedded facts about themselves—cured themselves of the need to smoke cigarettes, for example. Equally obviously, there are some facts about myself that I cannot change, no matter what I do. I cannot change the fact that I was born in Nebraska, for example, or the fact that I am not a horse. So the crucial question is this: Is it or is it not within my power to bring it about that I achieve the spiritual state of salvation or liberation?

That will depend in part on what exactly is meant by salvation or liberation (which of course can only be answered in the context of specific religious traditions) and in part on one's view as to the spiritual powers and abilities of human beings. Some religions stress the inability of human beings by themselves to bring about the necessary spiritual changes (and most of the religions of grace fit here). Others hold that human beings can actually effect the required changes, difficult as it might be to do so (and most of the karmic religions fit here). We will return to this point below.

3. *Can karma be impersonal?* As already noted, Karma posits no godlike personal judge or administrator who decides, say, that the past lives of some person cause her to suffer terribly in this life. The idea is rather that karma works impersonally, just like gravity. No person or agent decides that unsupported things that are heavier than air tend to fall towards the centre of the earth—this is just how things always behave. Now perhaps some karmic consequences can be explained impersonally, especially those that operate within a given lifespan. Suppose for years I live a life of hostility and selfishness, and thus do moral harm to myself later in the same lifetime—say, make myself into a bitter and hateful person. That scenario seems quite plausible. But what about a situation where Karma says that a given individual who suffers for years from a terrible and painful disease does so because of that

---

[15] I will not discuss the often-repeated criticism that karmic theories are sometimes used to rationalize suffering and injustice (on the grounds that the suffering people are justly being punished for actions in past lives), and thus to discourage efforts to alleviate suffering or correct injustice. This is because the criticism does not speak to the *truth* of Karma.

person's misdeeds in previous lives? Here the connection is much more difficult to discern, and it is not easy to see how the system is supposed to work.[16] What exactly is the impersonal causal connection between this person's misdeeds in past lives and the pain of this life? How is it 'decided' that the just karmic consequence in this case is suffering from the painful disease rather than, say, living as a poor beggar? If the pain is indeed due to misdeeds in past lives, then, without some sort of personal administrator or supervisor of karma, it is not easy to see how karmic 'decisions' as to what are the just and proper consequences are to be made.[17] The upshot is that karma needs a personal judge or administrator who makes karmic decisions.

4. *Does karma really solve the problem of unjust suffering?* Believers in karmic religious systems typically aver that the strongest argument in favour of their theory is that it solves the problem of why there is so much undeserved suffering and inequality of human birth and circumstance. As already noted, the argument is that there is no injustice; those who suffer are actually paying the price of bad karma accumulated in previous lives. But suppose the question is put in this way: How did suffering begin? That is, how did it become part of the world that we experience?

If the defender of Karma believes that there was a first incarnation, that is, a beginning of human or sentient life before there was any karma or reincarnation, then the question is whether suffering and inequality existed then. If they did, then karma obviously cannot explain why there is suffering. But the opposite claim—the claim that at some time in the past history of human or sentient life perfect justice and equality existed—seems implausible and, at the very least, requires some kind of story about how suffering and inequity entered the world.

Such a story is rarely told in karmic religions because most of them deny that there was ever a first life; reincarnation and karma—so it is usually said— have always existed. There was no beginning. But if that is the case, then of course no explanation of unjust suffering is given. Every event of suffering is explained in terms of things that occurred in previous lives. Accordingly, the explanation of apparently unjust suffering is never in fact given, but is only indefinitely postponed.[18] There would be an explanation for any particular evil event, but not for why there is any evil at all.

---

[16] This point is discussed skilfully in Reichenbach, *The Law of Karma* (n. 1 above), pp. 96–100, 121–2, 159, 189–90.

[17] Perhaps the self—if it continues as a conscious agent between incarnations—can make decisions about which station in the next life will best serve its own karmic interests. But I am unaware of any karmic systems of salvation that affirm that this in fact occurs.

[18] This point has been argued by John Hick. See his *Death and Eternal Life* (n. 12 above), pp. 308–9.

5. *Me and my karmic heir.* The system of salvation that we are calling Karma presupposes that every human being will have karmic heirs—that is, future persons who are the reincarnations of those human beings and who inherit their karma. Suppose that a person, Bill, dies, and then has a karmic heir, Tom, who is born soon after Bill's death. Notice that Karma only seems just—and that this system of salvation is entirely just is one of the most important claims made by its defenders—if Tom *is* (the reincarnation of) Bill. That is, Tom must be a continuation of the life of Bill. Otherwise it will hardly be fair that Tom experience the karmic consequences of Bill's deeds. But the conceptual difficulty here is that on philosophical grounds it seems that Tom cannot be Bill.

Notice first that Tom will share nothing of Bill's body. Reincarnational theories insist on this much; Tom's body will be totally different from Bill's.[19] Furthermore, apart from the possibility of a few yoga memories (which only a tiny minority of human beings claim to experience), Tom will share precisely none of Bill's memories and need not share any of his personality, likes, dislikes, or opinions. What is there, then, that, so to speak, holds Bill and Tom together? What makes it the case that they are two different temporal episodes of one and the same person?

In some reincarnational theories the only connecting thread is the putative fact that Bill and Tom possess the same soul or jiva (or some sort of immaterial essence), together with its karmic imprints and latent memories. Of course defenders of Karma might just insist that sameness of immaterial essence entails sameness of the person. And if they are right, that solves the metaphysical problem. (In Chapter 14, I will analogously argue that the soul can be the locus and carrier of personal identity during the interim period in the usual Christian way of understanding the general resurrection.)

But an epistemological issue remains: in the absence of other bodily or memory similarities, there seems to be no good reason to accept such a strong claim. Suppose it is true that some immaterial aspect of the person passes from one incarnation to the next. This would perhaps be enough to make us consider that there are similarities and maybe even causal connections between Bill and Tom. However, it would hardly seem sufficient to establish a claim of identity between them. So it is a serious problem for defenders of Karma to explain—even if it is true that all human beings have karmic heirs—why I should believe that my karmic heir is me. (In resurrection this precise

---

[19] Grace-oriented religions that stress resurrection rather than reincarnation also wrestle with the problem of identity in the next life. See Stephen T. Davis, *Risen Indeed: Making Sense of the Resurrection* (Grand Rapids, MI: Eerdmans, 1993), pp. 85–146. But their emphasis on bodily continuity makes the problem much easier to solve.

problem does not emerge because of the similarities between the pre-resurrection and post-resurrection bodies and memories.)

Some karmic systems explain the connection this way: it is in principle possible for Tom to recover all or many of Bill's memories; and it is similarly in principle possible for Bill to have many of Tom's character traits—temperament, taste, outlook, and so on. But I would argue that the second point is not nearly enough to establish identity—presumably there will be many people of Tom's generation who will roughly possess Bill's character traits. And as for memory, the mere *possibility* of Tom recovering Bill's memories is not enough. What will go a long way towards establishing identity is Tom *actually having* Bill's memories. And that kind of thing rarely happens in actual fact, as even defenders of Karma admit. Yoga memory claims are rare, and exceedingly difficult to verify when they do occur.

I do not claim that this and other difficulties make Karma logically impossible or incoherent. I do claim that they create serious problems for the theory.

V

My own view is that each of the five criticisms of Grace mentioned above can be answered. Let me now set out to do so.

1. Who gets the grace? The moral problem that supposedly exists is greatly mitigated by the claim of many grace-oriented systems of salvation that divine grace is offered freely to all people (in one way or another, God lovingly reaches out to all people), and that those who freely choose to receive it benefit from grace. Moral problems remain—I do not say they cannot be solved—for predestinarian theological systems that stress election, reprobation, and other such notions that entail that the choice of who receives grace and who does not is God's and God's alone. But it seems that grace-oriented theologies in which human beings freely choose whether to receive the grace of God can answer the present criticism fairly readily.

Of course the critic of Grace might reply in this way: clearly, not everyone has an equal access to grace, or an equal grasp of it, and that is surely unfair. Given their historical and religious backgrounds, most of the people who have ever lived or will live will find it difficult to accept a grace-oriented religious system; that is simply not a realistic option for them. And this much certainly seems to be true. But while this point does constitute a difficulty for Grace, it does not seem to constitute a reason to prefer Karma to Grace, for karmic systems of salvation are doubtless hidden from most people as well. Presumably the law of karma, if it is true, operates equally for all people, whether or not they have ever heard of it. Moreover, the specific moral or religious actions that typical karmic systems of salvation recommend are also known to but a few. Most people have never heard of the Eightfold Path, for example.

But then what must a Reformed Christian say about this issue? First, all wrongdoing must be punished. There are two ways in which punishment can be paid. The punishment is paid either by Christ's death on the cross (and that applies to all those who receive God's mercy), or by sinners themselves in hell (and that applies to all the rest). No sin is simply ignored by God. Secondly, God is the sovereign creator of the heavens and the earth and of human beings. Throughout history God makes sovereign choices that include some and exclude others—God's choice of Israel as God's own people, for example. In the end, we have no right to complain about where he bestows his mercy and where he does not.

2. Why doesn't God graciously intervene more often? This question is of course an aspect of the traditional problem of evil, which is by nearly universal consent the most serious intellectual difficulty that theists face. I will not try to solve the problem here.[20] Let me simply suggest that theists hold (1) that God has good moral reasons for graciously intervening in human history on some occasions and not others; (2) that we do not always know those reasons and are asked to trust in God's goodness nonetheless; (3) that God will triumph in the end over all evil, pain, and injustice, and will bring about a supremely good eschaton; and (4) that the optimal way for God to achieve this conclusion is to create a world like this one, with its natural laws and regularities (including human moral freedom).

Moreover, if it is God's desire that human beings be morally free, this fact places stringent limits on the frequency of divine interventions. Suppose we say that God is morally obligated to remove the most bothersome evils (which seems to be the main concern of many who use the problem of evil to criticize theism). But virtually all evils can be considered horrendous by those who are aware of no worse ones. Accordingly, consistent application of that principle would eliminate virtually all evils. This in turn would also eliminate human moral freedom, that is, freedom to do either the good or the evil. The conclusion seems to be that God has no such moral obligation.

3. Can grace be morally corrupting? Yes, grace can indeed be morally corrupting in the indicated ways. The sense that one will be forgiven by God no matter what, that forgiveness depends not on one's own performance

---

[20] I have addressed the problem on other occasions. See my essay, 'Free Will and Evil', in Stephen T. Davis (ed.), *Encountering Evil: Live Options in Theodicy*, 2nd edn. (Louisville, KY: Westminster John Knox, 2001), pp. 73–107.

or dispositions but on the free and undeserved grace of God—such convictions may well lead certain persons to succumb to temptation. If that happens, however, it is taken by grace-oriented systems of salvation as a moral failure and as a mistaken interpretation of grace.[21]

The proper way to understand grace is to see it as costly and as requiring effort and risk. Grace involves, on our part, genuine contrition, confession, repentance, renunciation, obligation, and discipline. It involves a sense of gratitude to God so strong that it entails a sincere desire to follow God's path. Our wanting to follow God is not what saves us—that is one of the basic implications of Grace; only God's work achieves that. But those who use grace as an excuse for moral laxity or moral turpitude are not genuine recipients of grace.

4. What about the 'not enough time' criticism? The defender of Grace can happily grant that the vast majority of people die without having achieved spiritual or moral sainthood, and that this would be a better world if many more people *did* achieve such a state before dying. But since the core idea is that by God's grace one has been forgiven and cleansed of sin, the problem is not fatal to the theory. The point is not that we all achieve sainthood, but that we are graciously forgiven—in this, the one and only, life—for *not* achieving it. Moreover, it is simply an unanswerable question whether more people would accept God's grace if human lives were longer than they are, or if human beings lived more than one life.[22]

5. Is grace immoral? What about the claim of defenders of karma that grace is wrong, that people ought to be treated only as they deserve? It is certainly morally wrong to treat people *worse* than they deserve. Again, it would be wrong to sentence someone to prison for failing to put a stamp on an envelope. Let us then take it as an established moral principle that *people ought not be treated worse than they deserve*. Determining precisely which punishments 'fit' which crimes is not always easy, of course, but in extreme cases—like sentencing someone to twenty years in prison for failing to put a stamp on an envelope—every morally sensitive person can see that we are talking about something that is morally wrong.

Defenders of Karma also seem to be on firm moral ground when they extend the principle that people should not be treated worse than they deserve and insist on the wider principle that *normally people ought to be treated precisely as they deserve*. For moral as well as pedagogical reasons, this principle seems acceptable. I mention pedagogy because clearly excessive leniency and

---

[21] Certain Christian theologians have noticed this problem. See, *inter alia*, Dietrich Bonhoeffer, *The Cost of Discipleship* (New York: Macmillan, 1958), pp. 37–49.

[22] Grace-oriented religious systems have other options for dealing with the 'not enough time' problem, e.g. the Roman Catholic notion of purgatory, or the notion of degrees of reward in heaven.

giftgiving is no way to train someone morally. It is often said that children who are allowed to do anything at all with impunity and who are spoiled with excessive gifts often grow up to become the kinds of people whom we do not morally admire.

But the defender of grace will respond to this argument as follows: yes, normally we should treat people just as they deserve, but for two important reasons this admission does not rule out Grace as a system of salvation. First, although it is never *required*, at times it is morally *allowable* to treat someone better than he or she deserves. There are, in morality, recognized acts of supererogation, where people do more than what is strictly morally required. We would not accuse of immorality the soldier who sacrifices his life for his buddies by jumping on a hand grenade. This certainly constitutes a case where certain people—the surviving soldiers—are treated better than they deserve or have any right to expect. Now, defenders of Karma could rightly point out that this act in itself does no moral harm to his buddies, while excessively lenient acts of grace might well harm the people at whom they are directed. But the defender of Grace will argue that we are not talking about 'excessively lenient' acts of grace, but rather gracious divine acts that make our salvation possible.

This leads directly to the second point. The defender of Grace will explain that the rightness or wrongness of grace cannot be settled by pointing to examples of moral behaviour in the natural or human realm. What we are talking about is the rightness of *God's* graciously forgiving our sins in situations where, apart from that grace, no one at all would be saved. If it is morally desirable that human beings be saved, and if no one can be saved apart from through God's grace, then it is not only morally allowable, but also morally praiseworthy, that God act graciously towards us.

Again we see that the deepest issue in relation to the Karma–Grace dispute centres on whether we have it within our power to save ourselves. If we *can* move ourselves by our own efforts from Stage 1 to Stage 2, grace seems superfluous and excessively lenient. If we *cannot* do so, and if God wants us to be saved, then God's treating us graciously is not only morally allowable, but also morally praiseworthy.

VI

It is time to conclude. I will repeat a caveat that has been implicit throughout the discussion. It is possible that my argument has little real-world application because the category I have created called 'Karma' fits few actual religious traditions. But I think my argument does apply to real religious systems. As noted, I hold that Grace does fit Christianity. I also think Karma does in a rough and broad way fit certain extant religious traditions—Advaita Vedanta Hinduism, for instance.

I have tried to answer the criticisms of Grace that were introduced earlier. I will also express the opinion that defenders of Karma have serious work to do in defending their theory against some of the criticisms of that theory that I also introduced, especially the third, fourth, and fifth.[23]

It would be desirable to reach a definitive decision as to which system of salvation is preferable or even true (if indeed one is true). For three reasons it is probably not possible to do so. First, the issue cannot be decided apart from metaphysical considerations that are outside the purview of this chapter. The central questions would be: What sort of world do we live in? Do we live in a world that was created by a personal God who cares about us and works for our salvation, or not? And, is the putative natural law that we call karma true, or not?

Secondly, perhaps the notions of salvation, of Stage 2, in the two systems of salvation are so different as to be incommensurate. That is, what religions of grace mean by 'salvation' differs markedly from what religions of karma mean by such terms as 'liberation', 'emptiness', 'enlightenment', and so on. If so, this incommensurability will make it impossible to answer, at least on the basis of philosophical considerations alone, what appears to be the crucial question that has emerged from our discussion. That question is, is it possible for human beings to save themselves, to progress from Stage 1 to Stage 2 on their own initiative and by their own effort?

The third point relates closely to the second. Is the central spiritual problem for human beings false consciousness or guilt? Most religions of Karma seem to teach that the central human problem grows out of our clinging to a false view of reality and that what we most deeply need is enlightenment. Most religions of grace teach that the human predicament develops out of our guilt for wrongdoing and that what we most deeply need is forgiveness or redemption. It may be difficult to decide whether human sinfulness is due to false consciousness or whether false consciousness is due to human sinfulness.

As we have seen, defenders of Grace insist that we cannot reach Stage 2 by our own efforts. They hold that only a full revelation of the gracious love of God can break down and overcome hardened human hearts. Indeed—so they

---

[23] It should be noted that defenders of certain karmic religious traditions have tried to address some of the objections to Karma raised above. I leave open the possibility that some of the problems that I have pointed out are answerable from the perspective of actual religious traditions, even if they are not answerable from the perspective of the abstract system of salvation that I am calling Karma.

claim—since suffering and injustice fall in this life on the innocent as well as the guilty, grace is necessary to bring about the ultimate justice of the kingdom of God.

Let me conclude with two thoughts. First, I have made a case, based entirely on philosophical considerations (i.e. not on any particular revealed theology), that grace should be preferred to karma. This conclusion follows because, as I have argued, karma is subject to telling objections, while grace is not. In the very nature of the case, this is admittedly a weak sort of argument. (Perhaps Karma can be defended after all; perhaps the objections to Grace are stronger than I have recognized.) Still, the argument of the present chapter does constitute at least a prima facie case for preferring Grace to Karma.

Secondly, suppose it is true (as defenders of Grace claim) that human beings are *not* able to save themselves. Then if the law of karma holds (you get precisely what you deserve), that would seem to lead to nothing but pessimism and despair. Indeed, it might be taken to lead to the spiritual ruin of the human race. If, on the other hand, Grace is true (despite our inabilities, we can still be saved by God's grace), that would seem to lead to an attitude of profound religious gratitude. Grace could then correctly be seen as offering relief and even escape from karma.[24]

[24] I would like to thank Robin Collins, Paul Copan, Douglas Geivett, William Hasker, Gerald O'Collins, S.J., Bruce Reichenbach, Charles Taliaferro, William Wainwright, and Ellen Zhang for their helpful comments on earlier drafts of this chapter.

12

The Wrath of God and the Blood of Chirst

I

If we are saved by grace, as Christianity affirms, there still remains the question of precisely how our salvation is accomplished. 'Atonement' is a word in Christian theology that refers to the mechanism of our redemption. That is, a theory of atonement attempts to explain how the Christ-event (that is, the incarnation, life, teachings, and especially death and resurrection of Christ) accomplished or made possible the forgiveness of our sins and our 'at-one-ment' with God. Since scripture does not provide Christians with a full-blown theory of atonement, it is not surprising that many such theories have been suggested in the history of theology, all of them based on various biblical texts or themes. Debates about the proper way to understand atonement continue to this day.

My aim in this chapter is limited. I do not propose to develop and argue for a theory of atonement, although I suspect that some species of an 'objective' or roughly Anselmian[1] sort of theory is implicit in much of what I will say. My aim instead is to argue for the preliminary point that atonement (of some robust sort) is necessary. There seem to be many Christians today who, in their understanding of the faith, have no need or room for any notion of atonement (except perhaps for something like Abelard's 'moral influence' theory). Such folk seem to me to place more emphasis on the teachings of Jesus and the example of his life than on his death and resurrection. Let us call these people 'exemplarists'. In this chapter, I want to argue, against the exemplarists, that some strong notion of atonement is an essential part of Christian theology. In this chapter I will also discuss hell; I will argue that its existence is compatible with the love of God.

The idea that God is angry with sinners is affirmed virtually throughout the Bible. Despite that fact, almost no topic in biblical theology is less popular

---

[1] For the classic statement of Anselm's theory, see *Why God Became Man* (*Cur Deus Homo*), (ed. and trans. Jasper Hopkins and Herbert Richardson) (Lewiston, NY: The Edwin Mellen Press, n.d.).

these days than the topic of God's wrath. Another equally unpopular topic is the blood of Christ. From professional theologians to pulpit preachers, almost everybody who is in the business of interpreting the Bible or doing Christian teaching these days ignores these two topics. Indeed, they are topics that many Christians today find embarrassing.

Now I do not recommend that we return to the 'fire and brimstone' preaching that characterized Christian preaching in earlier eras. The attempt to move people towards Christian commitment by fear of future divine judgement does not strike me as the optimal methodology for evangelism in our day. Nor am I an admirer of the tradition of Christian preaching that paints lurid pictures of the sufferings of Jesus. Still, I hold that we are wrong to ignore these two biblical themes. Indeed, I will argue that God's wrath is our only hope as human beings. I will also argue that we are wrong to ignore or de-emphasize the topic of atonement, within which the concept of the blood of Christ is usually imbedded.

II

Let me begin with some thoughts about Psalm 90, which crucially showcases the concept of God's wrath. One of the greatest passages in the Bible and indeed in the whole of literature, this text is a stately, sublime, and majestic meditation on the differences between God and human beings. It stresses the fact that God and human beings differ in two important ways. First, God is everlasting and human life is ephemeral. Secondly, God is righteous and human beings are sinful.

The psalm begins with the thought that God is everlasting:

> Lord, you have been our dwelling place in all generations.
> Before the mountains were brought forth, or ever you had formed
>   the earth and the world, from everlasting to everlasting,
>   you are God.
> You turn us back to dust and say, 'Turn back, you mortals,'
> For a thousand years in your sight are like yesterday when it is
>   passed, or like a watch in the night.
> You sweep them away; they are like a dream, like grass that is
>   renewed in the morning; in the morning it flourishes and is
>   renewed; in the evening it fades and withers.

The psalmist affirms that God has always existed and has always been God. For such a being, a thousand years pass as quickly as an instant or a few moments do for us.

In contrast, all created things, including human beings, have finite life-spans. Some of us live longer than others. Some die as infants; some live to be a hundred. There is one man in the Bible, Methuselah, who is recorded as living for 969 years (Gen. 5: 27). But for all human beings, their time eventually runs out, and they die. Human beings are dust (Gen. 3: 19). As the psalm says, their life is fleeting like grass, ephemeral like a dream.

The psalmist continues with the second great difference: God is righteous and we are sinners.

> For we are consumed by your anger;
>   by your wrath we are overwhelmed.
> You have set our iniquities before you,
>   our secret sins in the light of your countenance.

Unlike God, who is holy and morally perfect, human beings are disobedient, rebellious, and prone to lust and violence. God's face is like a miner's hat that illuminates our sins, even the secret ones. Our deepest thoughts, attitudes, and motives betray our pride and self-centredness, and God is aware of them all.

The natural and correct response of a perfectly moral creator to the degree of sin and suffering that exists in this world is wrath. God is angry at sin, and at sinners. Thus Paul declares: 'The wrath of God is revealed from heaven against all ungodliness and wickedness of those who by their wickedness suppress the truth' (Rom. 1: 18). The psalmist feels this wrath so forcefully that he feels consumed and overwhelmed by it. As the writer to the Hebrews put it: 'Our God is a consuming fire' (Heb. 12: 29).

Sin is essentially a state of being. It is a state of separation from God. This alienation is caused by our refusal and inability to obey God's commands. Our pride and self-centredness creates a barrier between God and us. And God's response is wrath. Unlike God, we will all die; but even when we are alive, we experience 'toil and trouble'.

> For all our days pass away under your wrath;
>   our years come to an end like a sigh.
> The days of our life are seventy years,
>   or perhaps eighty if we are strong;
>   even then their span is only toil and trouble;
>   they are soon gone, and we fly away.
> Who considers the power of your anger?
>   Your wrath is as great as the fear that is due you.
> So teach us to count our days,
>   that we may gain a wise heart.

The Bible elsewhere stresses that point that these two important facts about human beings—that we are sinful and that we die—are related. As God said to Adam and Eve in the Garden, 'You may eat freely of every tree of the garden; but of the tree of the knowledge of good and evil you shall not eat, for in the day that you eat of it you shall die' (Gen. 3: 16–17). And later God cursed Adam and Eve with the words, 'By the sweat of your face you shall eat bread until you return to the ground; you are dust, and to dust you shall return' (Gen. 3: 19). And Paul adds: 'Sin came into the world through one man, and death came through sin' (Rom. 5: 12).

Both these facts about human beings—that we are sinful and that we will die—are painful to us. Most people do not want to die; they would prefer to live for ever. And most human beings would prefer to consider themselves (and be considered by others) as morally upright persons. Thus the somewhat melancholy tone of Psalm 90.

But the Psalm provides a solution:

> Turn, O Lord! How long?
> > Have compassion on your servants!
> Satisfy us in the morning with your steadfast love,
> > so that we may rejoice and be glad all our days.
> Make us glad as many days as you have afflicted us,
> > and as many years as we have seen evil.
> Let your work be manifest to your servants,
> > and your glorious power to their children.
> Let the favor of the Lord our God be upon us,
> > and prosper for us the work of our hands—
> O prosper the work of our hands.

The solution to both human dilemmas—our wretched sinfulness and our unwanted mortality—is the steadfast love of the Lord. God is radically different from human beings, yet the eternal God is not detached from us. Indeed, God is involved lovingly in our lives. The psalmist affirms that God is at work in the world, showing God's glorious power, favouring us and prospering our work. Given the reality of God's grace in our lives, we can, despite our 'toil and trouble', 'rejoice and be glad all our days'.

III

However, the psalmist also pointedly asks: 'Who considers the power of your anger?' He then affirms that 'your wrath is as great as the fear that is due you.' What exactly is God's wrath? And how is it related to God's love and grace?

God's wrath is simply God's opposition to, and anger at, sin and evil. What God wants from us is obedience to his commands. As God said:

'I am the Lord your God: sanctify yourselves therefore, and be holy, for I am holy' (Lev. 11: 44). God's wrath is only analogically related to the anger that we experience. Human wrath normally involves imperfections like ill-advised words and deeds. But God's wrath does not. It is closer to what we mean by 'righteous indignation', although that term sometimes has connotations of unattractive self-righteousness. I take acceptable righteous indignation to be morally acceptable opposition to and even resentment at an evil action or event. The wrath of God normally leads to some sort of punishment of sinners, which is designed to chasten them and move them to repentance.

I do not believe that the biblical concept of the wrath of God is anthropomorphic or merely symbolic. I believe it is literally true—in a straightforward sense—to say that God loves us and works for our salvation. Similarly, I believe it is literally true to say that God hates sin and punishes sinners.[2] The term 'God's wrath' can refer either to God's attitude towards or mental state regarding sin or to God's acting on the basis of the divine attitude towards sin (e.g. striking Ananias and Sapphira dead).

Loving the good is an essential property of any moral being. (If there exists a moral being, goodness exists.) Hating the evil is in effect an accidental property of a moral being, since it depends on the existence of evil. Still, in the presence of evil, a moral being like God will hate and oppose it. And that is the meaning of God's wrath. Some Christian theologians have argued that God's wrath is impersonal, like a physical force (e.g. gravity or thermodynamics) and that it is directed at evil, but not at sinners. However, this hardly seems a biblical notion. God's reaction to evil in scripture seems like the reaction of a personal being, not a mere mechanical force, and it is not easy to see how God can be angry at evil without being angry at evil's perpetrators.

Earlier I opined that God's wrath is our only hope as human beings. God's anger at sin allows us to see that there are many wrong ways, and one right way, of living life. The right way is the way of honouring, obeying, and loving God (although, of course, there are different ways of doing that). We live in an age when it is grossly counter-cultural to claim that there is but one way to live. All roads lead to the top of the mountain—so it is said—and as long as you are sincere, any way of living one's life is okay.

Unfortunately, this contemporary viewpoint is not the biblical picture. Thus Ephesians 5: 6: 'The wrath of God comes on those who are disobedient.' Note also Colossians 3: 5–6, which says,

---

[2] Here I agree with Robert Oakes, 'The Wrath of God', in David Shatz (ed.), *Philosophy and Faith: A Philosophy of Religion Reader* (Boston: McGraw-Hill, 2002), pp. 9–15.

Put to death, therefore, whatever in you is earthly: fornication, impurity, passion, evil desire, and greed (which is idolatry). On account of these the wrath of God is coming on those who are disobedient.

And 2 Thessalonians 1: 7–9 speaks of the time

when the Lord Jesus is revealed from heaven with his mighty angels in flaming fire, inflicting vengeance on those who do not know God and on those who do not obey the gospel of our Lord Jesus Christ. These will suffer the punishment of eternal destruction, separated from the presence of the Lord and the glory of his might.

Finally, Revelation 19: 15 says:

From his mouth comes a sharp sword with which to strike down the nations, and he will rule them with a rod of iron; he will tread the winepress of the fury of the wrath of God the almighty.

So if it were not for God's wrath, we might all sink into the pit of moral and religious relativism, which is one of the many roads to hell.

The wrath of God is both a facet and an expression of God's just and righteous nature. Justice is not a temporary whim of God, but an eternal necessity. God's justice is the moral equilibrium of the world. Of course Christians know that in many ways the world is not in moral equilibrium. Like human beings, the world is corrupted by evil and needs to be redeemed (Rom. 8: 18–23). But it is important to note that most people, most of the time, know what is right and what is wrong. People know that normally there are consequences for wrong-doing; people reap what they sow. People know that when one person harms another, some sort of apology or reparation must be made. People also know that it is normally costly to rectify a terribly wrong situation. Most people react negatively—with righteous indignation—to terrible wrongdoing.

It is possible, of course, to imagine worlds in which these facts do not hold, where there is no moral equilibrium. Perhaps something like Hobbes' 'state of nature' is close to such a picture. This would be a world in which people do whatever they want, unencumbered by communal or moral considerations, a world where only self-interest and power determine actions. And what keeps us from such a world—so I am arguing—is the wrath of God. It reminds us that there is right and wrong, and that there are consequences for going wrong.

IV

But what about the blood of Christ? I will introduce a consideration of that question by relating a conversation about religion that I had several years ago with a friend who is a rabbi. He was bothered by the Christian notion of atonement, by the idea that the forgiveness of our sins is only possible because of the death of Jesus on a cross. 'Why was all that necessary?' he asked. 'Why do Christians think atonement was needed at all? Why didn't God just forgive us without anybody dying on any cross?'

He wanted to know whether the Christian notion of atonement made moral sense. At heart his question was, Why did Jesus have to die? But perhaps the question needs disambiguation. Was he asking, (1) *Why do Christians think that atonement (of some sort) was necessary at all?* Or was he asking, (2) *Why do Christians think that divine forgiveness was impossible without, or only occurred because of, Christ's atoning sacrifice on the cross?* Or was he asking, (3) *Why do Christians think it was proper or best for Christ's sacrifice on the cross to occur?*

I will attempt here mainly to answer question (1). This is because my friend's question, 'Why didn't God *just forgive* us?' seems to me to be a question about the need for atonement at all. I did point out to him that it seemed odd to me for a rabbi to ask this question; surely he had read the book of Leviticus and knew all about *Yom Kippur* in chapter 16 and the need for atonement. But the main point I tried to make and want now to establish is one that I just noted: *it is always costly to rectify a terribly wrong situation.* Let me illustrate this principle in two ways.

My first illustration concerns war. I am old enough to have been a young child during the Second World War, and I grew up thinking a great deal about warfare. I knew that my stepfather, as well as two of my uncles, were overseas in the military, and I knew that the others in my family were worried that they might be killed or wounded. I remember pondering a childhood fantasy of mine: why didn't the nations fight each other not with flesh and blood human beings, but just with machines, with robots? I could not understand why that was not a much better idea. After all, that way no one's fathers or uncles would have to be killed or wounded.

Nobody would take my idea seriously, and it was not until years later that I understood why. It has to do with this principle that *it is always costly to rectify a terribly wrong situation.* A nation at war stops fighting when its leaders and citizens realize that continuing to fight would be too costly: too much territory lost to the enemy, too much damage done to the homeland, and especially too many lives lost. And that was precisely the problem with my five-year-old's fantasy. If a nation is only losing robots, that realization—that continuing to fight would be too costly—would never be reached. Conflict between nations is always horrible, and restoring peace is costly. It is terrible to have to say it, but first people have to die.

My second illustration concerns the theatre. Since almost everyone knows this play, I will discuss *Romeo and Juliet.* The drama centres on a problem. There are two prominent families in the town of Verona, the Capulets and the

Montagues. They have been feuding for years. Two young people, Romeo, son of Lord Montague, and Juliet, daughter of Lord Capulet, fall in love. With the help of a sympathetic priest, Friar Laurence, who hopes to end the feud between the families, they secretly marry, and plan to elope to Mantua. But things go wrong. Onrushing events overtake their plans and ruin them. Tybalt, a Capulet, kills one of Romeo's best friends, and an enraged Romeo then kills Tybalt. A crucial message to Romeo is not delivered. And in the end, with a kind of fatal inevitability, six people die, five of them before our very eyes on stage, including the young lovers themselves. Only then can the heads of the two clans, in their inconsolable sorrow, make up and end the feud.

Now I want to imagine a different ending to *Romeo and Juliet* than the canonical one that Shakespeare gave it. I ask, how would we react to the play if the story ended like this:

In the closing scene all the principal characters are on stage. There is anger and shouting. Swords are drawn. A battle is about to break out between the two families.

But then a stranger enters the stage. He shouts: 'Wait. Let me speak. Don't you people realize that this feud is a bad idea? Think of all the people who have died, and the people who could die today. Wouldn't it be better for the two families just to forgive and make up?'

And then, simultaneously, the Lords of the two houses realize that this stranger is correct. 'Yes,' they say, each hitting himself in the head, 'that's right. Why didn't we think of that? It *would* be better just to make up. Let's end the feud right here and now.'

And at that, there is a group hug of all the actors on stage; everybody goes home happy; and the curtain falls.

Now I am sure everyone will agree with me that that ending would make the play ridiculous, a farce. Nobody would accept *that* as a realistic ending, certainly not of a great play.

And why not? I think it is because something deep in the human heart recognizes the truth of the principle that I mentioned earlier: *it is always costly to rectify a terribly wrong situation.* The Lords of the two households could not have just said, 'Ah well, let's just let bygones be bygones.' The truth is that there first had to be something like atonement. Somebody had to die.

In my opinion, the deepest problem with exemplarism is that its view of sin is not serious enough. It would be nice if all that we needed was to try our best to follow Jesus' teachings. The Christian gospel could then be reduced to the simple injunction, 'Let's all try to be good people' or even, 'Please be nice.' Sadly, that is not enough. The truth is that sin has an iron grip on us. We are unable to save ourselves, no matter how hard we try to live Christ-like lives. As I said in Chapter 6, we need more than Christ as a guru; we need him as a saviour.

It might seem that the right way for atonement to occur would be the way it usually occurs in human life. That is, the offending party apologizes and makes amends. And the amends in this case—so it might seem—would be for each person to die on a cross in payment for his or her sins. But the trouble with that idea is that it would accomplish nothing. It would be a meaningless death. Recall Leviticus 16. Yom Kippur was the annual day when the High Priest would enter the Holy of Holies and the sins of Israel would be forgiven. Atonement required sacrifice and substitution. It required that something spotless—a bull or ram or goat without blemish—die in the place of the sinner. Doubtless that is why the writer to the Hebrews, many centuries later, wrote, 'Without the shedding of blood, there is no forgiveness of sins' (Heb. 9: 22).

If we tried to die for our own sins, it would be meaningless because we are not spotless. Trapped by sin and self-centredness as we are, we are stained, soiled, marred. Not even the death of a prophet or martyr or saint would have sufficed. We human beings cannot save ourselves. Only God can do that. It had to be the Son of God who died.

V

Let us return to the questions of my friend. Why did Jesus have to die? Why was atonement necessary? Why didn't God 'just forgive'?

Suppose it is true that *it is always costly to rectify a terribly wrong situation.* The very worst of all terrible situations is the estrangement of human beings from God. In creating human beings, what God wanted, of course, was loving fellowship with them. That fellowship was to be intimate and sweet and permanent. It was based on a covenant. As was noted in Chapter 1, a covenant is simply a two-party agreement that says: I will do this if you will do that. The prophet Jeremiah sublimely sums up the essence of this covenant for us, where he says (speaking in God's voice), 'I will be your God, and you will be my people' (Jer. 7: 23).

But how were we to go about fulfilling our end of the bargain? How were we to go about being God's people? It was by obeying God's commands. Again notice Leviticus 11: 44: 'I am the Lord your God: sanctify yourselves therefore, and be holy, for I am holy.' But, sadly, none of us is obedient. We all go our own way. We all want to run our own lives. We are mired in pride and self-centredness and lust and violence. We neither love God nor obey God. With the psalmist, we can say to God, 'Against you, you alone, have I sinned, and done that which is evil in your sight' (Pss. 51: 4). Our disobedience has erected a huge barrier, like an immense iron wall, between God and us. There is nothing we can do to knock down or climb over that wall. We are helpless, and our plight is hopeless. There is nothing we can do to save ourselves.

This, then, is the very worst of all terribly wrong situations. In order to rectify it an enormous cost first had to be paid. God could not 'just forgive'. That would have been as pointless as fighting wars with robots or ending *Romeo and Juliet* with a group hug. A terribly wrong situation had to be set right. Somebody had to die. And the one who died was Christ. His blood paid the penalty for our sins. His death made possible the forgiveness of our sins. That was the price that had to be paid. Christ's death on the cross made possible our redemption. When our sins are forgiven, the iron wall is knocked down. The estrangement is over. We can have fellowship with God.

God is a God of love and grace, but also a God of justice. Justice is not a temporary whim of God's, but an eternal necessity. Justice is not the same thing as vengeance or even punishment. Justice is the character of God, and it creates the moral equilibrium of the world. When sins are committed, there are consequences. God's righteous nature rules out forgiveness without atonement. God requires that the proper punishment for sins be paid. As Paul says, 'The wages of sin is death' (Rom. 6: 23). The death of Jesus on a cross shows the lengths to which God had to go in order for God's righteousness to be satisfied, and for us human beings to grasp the costliness of God's mercy.

I believe we can understand something of how expensive it is because we accept the principle that *fixing what is wrong is costly.* That is why we understand that you cannot fight real wars with robots or end great plays with cheap solutions.[3] This would be my answer to the rabbi's question, interpreted as question (1). As to questions (2) and (3), there is not a great deal that I can say. Christ's death on the cross was the vehicle for redemption that God, in his sovereign freedom, chose. We do not now fully understand, and may never fully understand, God's reasons for so choosing.

But perhaps a bit more can be said. It is not good or appropriate for forgiveness to be granted lightly. Doing so trivializes sin, the sinner, and the offended party. At least in the case of serious sin, sinners ought to offer a costly penance, both as a reparation and as a sign of their sincere sorrow and repentance. The offended party usually has the right to determine what the penance will be. She is sometimes free to forgive without any apology or penance at all. But much more than that is normally required. Accordingly, in the Old Testament, penitents must kill a healthy, beautiful, and thriving

---

[3] Since this principle can be misunderstood, I should point out that it does not entail an endorsement of violence as the solution to any and all problems.

animal. It must be a thing of value, and its loss is a real loss. Christians hold that the death of Christ on the cross was the costliest of all sacrifices, because it 'takes away the sin of the world' (John 1: 29). He was without sin, and offered himself freely.[4]

VI

Bernard of Clairvaux once incisively asked why God chose to accomplish our salvation through the death of his Son:

'We are reconciled to God through the death of his Son' [Rom. 5: 10]. Where is this reconciliation, this remission of sin? . . . In this chalice, [Christ] says, 'of the blood of the New Testament, which is poured out for you' [Matt. 26: 28; Luke 22: 20]. . . . We obtain it by the interceding death of the only Begotten and are justified by grace in the same blood. . . . Why, you ask me, by blood when he could have done it by word. I ask the same question. It is given to me only to know that it is so, not why it is so.[5]

Despite my arguments in the first five sections of this chapter, I wish to express my willingness to join the queue that consists of Bernard, his imagined interlocutor, and all others who wonder about this question. Although there are helpful things that can be said, the question remains puzzling.

It certainly seems, given the freedom of God, that God could have accomplished our salvation in some other way than through the crucifixion of his only begotten Son. As Bernard suggested, it seems that God could have accomplished this merely by saying the word. After all, God brought the creation into existence merely by the words, 'Let there be light' (Gen. 1: 3). Why didn't God accomplish redemption by just saying to human beings, 'You are forgiven'?

The deepest question in this neighbourhood is whether redemption via the blood of Christ was God's chosen method (1) for our sakes, so to speak; that is, we would not comprehend the gravity of the situation or the depths of God's love had God chosen another method; or (2) for the sake of something in the nature and character of God. My own view is that it is both. Part of the 'image of God' in us is the ability to recognize the gravity of sin and the

---

[4] I should point out that much of my argument in this chapter presupposes some of the pioneering work done by Richard Swinburne on atonement. See his *Responsibility and Atonement* (Oxford: Oxford University Press, 1989).

[5] Cited in Caroline Walker Bynum, 'The Power in the Blood: Sacrifice, Satisfaction and Substitution in Late Medieval Soteriology', in Stephen T. Davis, Daniel Kendall, S.J., and Gerald O'Collins, S.J., *Redemption* (Oxford: Oxford University Press, 2004). (J-P. Migne (ed.), *Patrologia cursus completes: series latina*, 221 vols. (Paris, 1841–64), vol. 182, col. 1069.)

seriousness of rebellion against God. But—although I have suggested some reasons in this chapter in answer to Bernard's question, and I do think they carry some weight—in the end it must be admitted that Bernard of Clairvaux was right. Redemption was brought about by the death of Christ: we know that it is so but not why it is so.

VII

Can a loving God condemn people to hell? I hold that the answer to this important question is yes. Let me explain why.

An important point must be made first: we know little about hell. Much of what the New Testament says about it is metaphorical or symbolic. For example, the New Testament uses the metaphor of fire to portray the suffering of people in hell. But this fact need not mean that the damned actually suffer the pain of burns. Indeed, I do not believe that they suffer fiery agony. Note that Mark 9: 48 describes hell as a place where 'the worm never dies, and the fire is never quenched.' Why take the second literally and not the first? I would say that both are metaphors of the eternality of hell.

The parable of the rich man and Lazarus (Luke 16: 19–31) is taken by some interpreters as a picture of the afterlife, but this interpretation does not seem to me correct. It is a parable, that is, a made-up story designed to teach a religious message. It is difficult to believe that heaven and hell are separated by a 'great chasm' which cannot be crossed but across which communication can take place. In fact, there are many biblical metaphors for hell, for example, eternal fire (Matt. 25: 41), bottomless pit (Rev. 9: 2), outer darkness (Matt. 8: 12), place of weeping and gnashing of teeth (Matt. 8: 12), place of no rest (Rev. 14: 11), place where the last penny must be paid (Matt. 5: 26). None, I believe, is a literal description.

In some sense, it is true that hell can be spoken of as a place of punishment. But I do not hold that it is primarily a place of retribution, where God gets even with those who hate God. The central fact about hell is that it is a place of separation from God. Not total separation, of course—that would mean that hell would not exist. Moreover, the biblical tradition denies that anyone can ever be totally separated from God (Pss. 139: 7–12). But hell is separation from God as the source of love, joy, peace, and light. It is not a place of agony, torment, or torture. (I oppose the lurid and even sadistic pictures of hell envisioned by some Christian thinkers.) But there is no deep or ultimate joy in hell and I believe its citizens are miserable. To be apart from the source of love, joy, peace, and light is to live miserably.

Why are the damned in hell? I have already ruled out retribution or any notion of God's 'getting even' with them (although there are biblical texts that might be taken to suggest such an idea). To put the point radically, I believe they are in hell because they choose to be there; no one is sent to hell kicking and screaming, against his or her will. Sadly, some people choose to live their lives apart from God, harden their hearts, and will continue to do so after death; some will doubtless do so for ever. For such people, living in the presence of God will seem worse than living in the absence of God. Allowing them to live for ever in hell is simply God's continuing to grant them the freedom that they enjoyed in this life to say yes or no to God. Yet I suspect that the people in hell are deeply remorseful. Can people both freely choose hell over heaven, knowing that they would be unable to endure heaven, but still rue the fact that they cannot happily choose heaven? Yes, this is quite possible.

Is the existence of hell consistent with the love of God? Yes, I believe it is. Some Christians try to justify the existence of hell by speaking of it as the 'natural consequence' of a life of sin. I accept the notion that hell is the natural consequence of a life of rebellion against God (and it is in this sense that hell is a punishment). But this consideration in itself does not justify God in sending people to hell, because it does not justify the divinely ordained laws of natural necessity that make hell sin's natural consequence. I claim, then, that the people who are in hell are there because they freely choose to be there. That is, they freely choose not to live in God's presence. If so, then hell is an expression not only of divine justice but of divine love.

The point is that such folk have hardened their hearts and would be unable to endure heaven. Unless one submits to God and makes the divine will one's own, heaven is too much to bear and one chooses hell. That is why it is not only just but loving that God allows them to live for ever apart from his presence. Indeed, life in hell may well strengthen their resolve never to repent; sin will voluntarily continue, and so will the need for just punishment for sin.

It is important to recall that salvation is a matter of grace alone. We deserve to be condemned, but out of love God forgives us and reconciles us to God. The point to notice is that if hell is inconsistent with God's love, that is, if a loving God cannot condemn anyone to hell, then our salvation (i.e. our rescue from hell) is no longer a matter of grace. It becomes a matter of our justly being freed from a penalty we do not really deserve. In the end, the argument that hell is inconsistent with God's love overturns the Christian notion of grace.[6]

---

[6] Although he would not agree with everything I've said in this section, I happily note my indebtedness to Jonathan L. Kvanvig's work, *The Problem of Hell* (Oxford: Oxford University Press, 1993). I have also been influenced by C. S. Lewis', *The Problem of Pain* (New York: Macmillan, 1973). See also my 'Universalism, Hell, and the Fate of the Ignorant', *Modern Theology*, 6/2 (January, 1990), pp. 173–86.

How then are God's justice (wrath) and God's mercy (love, grace) related? The answer is that both are essential aspects of God's nature. But they are not—as is often implicitly presupposed—opposed or conflicting character traits. There is no question of God having a split personality, of (for example) paying off with the loving side of his character a debt incurred against the just side. As noted above, God's love and kindness are intrinsic and essential properties of God, while God's wrath is a result of human sinfulness. Since grace amounts to treating sinners better than they deserve, grace, too, is a reaction to human sinfulness.

Paul argues that God patiently withholds his wrath against us in order to make room for mercy. He asks, 'What if God, desiring to show his wrath and to make known his power, has endured with much patience the objects of wrath that are made for destruction; and what if he has done so in order to make known the riches of his glory for the objects of mercy?' (Rom. 9: 22–3). He also argues that it is Jesus' blood that rescues us from God's wrath (Rom. 5: 9–10; 1 Thess. 1: 9–10). Indeed, it is precisely because of God's mercy and love for human beings that our sinfulness, and the suffering that it produces, can provoke God's wrath.[7]

Paul also asks: 'Do you not realize that God's kindness is meant to lead you to repentance?' (Rom. 2: 4). The odd point being made here is that we naturally think that it is God's *wrath* that is meant to produce human repentance. But the fact that Paul insists that it is God's *mercy* that is designed to do so shows that the divine wrath and the divine love are not opposed to each other after all. Indeed, a totally moral person will react positively to right-doing and negatively to wrongdoing. Indeed, a totally moral person who is also full of grace will react negatively to wrongdoing, but give wrong-doers a chance to receive mercy.

Accordingly, God's wrath and God's mercy are simply two aspects of God's character. I said earlier that God's justice is the moral equilibrium of the world. It now appears that God's grace can equally be said to constitute the moral equilibrium of the world.

The wrath of God and the blood of Christ are related in this way: only if we take God's righteous judgement and wrath seriously do we understand the depth of meaning of Christ's death on the cross and what it accomplished for us.

---

[7] As Oakes argues. See 'The Wrath of God' (n. 2 above), p. 10.

13

Bodily Redemption

I

In Part III of this book, we have been discussing the question, How are we saved? In Chapter 11 we saw that our redemption is through the grace of God. And in Chapter 12, we saw that our redemption is possible because of the atoning work of Christ. But more needs to be said in answer to the question we are considering. We need to discuss faith and the concept of justification by faith. And we need to consider the implications of the fact that we are to be redeemed as embodied persons. We will consider those issues in the present chapter.

Let me begin with a fact about our common life as human beings. We face (among others, of course) two overarching problems: the problem of guilt and the problem of death.

Most human beings experience at least some degree of guilt. Indeed we refer to those who experience no feelings of guilt at all or are not influenced by the few that they do experience as 'sociopaths'. We want to be admired and respected by others, and indeed by ourselves. But most of us are acutely aware of our own moral failings. We do not excel at obeying even the precepts of our own (usually flawed and self-serving) moral standards. And when we compare our behaviour with the ethical standards expressed, say, in the Ten Commandments or the teachings of Jesus, we see clearly how far we are from measuring up. Thus we feel guilty and, according to Christianity, *are* guilty. So the first great human problem is, what to do about our guilt.

Most human beings want to live for ever. Death ends our lives, careers, and projects, and brings our hopes for future accomplishments to nothing. We do not know for sure what, if anything, awaits us after death, and many human beings are frightened at the prospect. We do not want to deprive our loved ones of our presence and support, nor do we want to be deprived of their love and companionship. The thought of no longer existing, of literally *not being*, frightens most people. Thus the second great human problem is, what to do about death and our fear of it.

Christianity insists that these two problems, guilt and death, are connected. It also claims to offer to human beings, through Jesus Christ, the solution to both problems. This chapter is about that solution.

Since I will be touching on several different topics in this chapter, I should provide a brief roadmap of where we will be going. After dealing with introductory issues in this opening section, I will turn in Section II to some of the theological and salvific implications of our existence as embodied beings. In Section III I will say more about the Christian notion of God, since it undergirds everything that is said in soteriology. In Section IV the topic will be the work of Jesus Christ, and its relation to redemption. In Section V I will turn to the questions of how, why, and to whom redemption occurs; I will specifically discuss the notion of justification by faith, and especially traditional Catholic–Protestant differences on that issue. In Section VI I will return to the notion of human embodiment and will consider two possible bodily resurrection scenarios. Finally, in Section VII I will consider briefly what the medieval theologians called the beatific vision.

II

Almost from the beginning of recorded philosophy, thinkers have recognized that human beings have both an inner and an outer aspect. The outer aspect is of course our lives as embodied beings. Information about our outer aspect is public in the sense that anybody—myself or anybody else—in principle can look and see, for example, that I have grey hair, or even (if I were, say, scowling and shouting) that I seem to be angry. But there are also things about human beings that are private in the sense that they are inner; they can only be known directly by the person to whom they are inner. For example, you can infer (by observing my behaviour) that I am angry, but I am the only one who knows that fact directly. I do not have to infer that I am angry (or that I am in another mental state like thinking, remembering, intending, or feeling): I simply *know* these things. I am directly aware of them.

Also quite early in philosophy, some thinkers emphasized the inner (i.e. mental, spiritual) aspects of human beings and de-emphasized the bodily aspects. Indeed, both Plato and Descartes share (with some differences) a doctrine that illustrates what I am talking about. It is called metaphysical dualism (and will be discussed in more detail in Chapter 14). This doctrine claims that (1) human beings have two parts, physical bodies and incorporeal souls; (2) the soul is the essence of the person (that is, the real Stephen Davis is Stephen Davis' soul, not his body); (3) the soul, although united with a body in this life, can exist quite apart from the body; and (4) after bodily death, the soul and thus the person quite naturally go right on existing. Some have even combined these sorts of notions with the further idea that (5) the body is essentially evil, while the soul or spirit is essentially good. So our task as human beings, on this view, is to escape from the body into the realm of pure spirit or pure intellect.

The point that I wish to make is that the picture I have just painted is not a Christian picture. (This despite the fact that (1), (2), and (3) are consistent with Christianity, and are accepted by many Christians.) Christianity says that (1) human beings are, in their most complete and perfect form, embodied persons; accordingly, while disembodied human existence is in some sense possible, it is a radically reduced and attenuated form of life, not at all what God intended for us; (2) matter and thus bodies were created by God as parts of a world that was originally 'very good' (Gen. 1: 31); accordingly, matter is not inherently evil; (3) embodied human beings fall into sin and corrupt both themselves and the whole of creation; accordingly, the material universe, including embodied human beings, needs redemption (Rom. 8: 19–22); and (4) God is effectively at work in the world; accordingly, one day all of creation will be redeemed (Rev. 21 and 22).

III

Also from the beginning of recorded philosophy, thinkers have asked, 'What is ultimately real?' Christianity denies many of the answers that have been given. As I argued in Chapter 1, reality does not ultimately consist of water, as Thales thought. Nor does it ultimately consist of atoms in motion, with physical matter being eternal and uncreated, as most contemporary philosophers think. Nor does it ultimately consist of a karmic cycle or the law of karma, as many Hindus believe. Christianity says that ultimate reality is God. Having discussed the nature of God in Chapter 3, I will merely repeat here that human beings are important to God. We were created for the sake of an intimate, loving relationship with God. Our supreme goal in life is to glorify God (Isa. 43: 7; 1 Cor. 10: 31) and to enjoy fellowship with God for ever.

From a cosmic perspective, the relationship between God and human beings was shattered by the entrance of evil into the world. From a personal perspective, it is severed whenever we separate ourselves from God by sin. All of God's actions in history are expressions of God's love and providential care for us (including God's acts of judgement). God is working to redeem us.

But what exactly is the nature of the relationship between God and human beings? It is a covenant. As noted in Chapter 1, a covenant is simply a two-way agreement. I will add here that the classical biblical covenants are between two persons who are not peers. A covenant is initiated by the superior party and involves obligations and mutual responsibilities: 'I will do this if you will do that.' God is the initiator of this covenant, not human beings. As also noted, the essence of this particular covenant that God offers to human beings is beautifully summarized by the prophet Jeremiah: 'I will be your God, and you shall be my people' (Jer. 7: 23).

Christians believe that God not only initiates but also, through God's actions in the world, fully restores the covenantal relationship between God and human beings. These actions are of many sorts (Heb. 1: 1), but as argued in Chapter 12, the restoration occurs pre-eminently through the life, death, and resurrection of Jesus Christ, the incarnation of God (Heb. 1: 2). Thus, at the centre of reality is a God who acts to reconcile us to Himself.

IV

So redemption occurs, according to Christians, through Jesus Christ. Salvation is not our own doing. We are forgiven and reconciled to God through the work of God, not through anything we do or deserve. Indeed, we do not deserve redemption. That God loves us and works for our salvation is a sheer fact of grace. Grace (unmerited favour) means that God loves us even though we are unlovable, accepts us even though we are unacceptable, forgives us despite our being unforgivable. God did not have to redeem us. Grace means that God freely chose to redeem us despite our inability to merit redemption.

So redemption occurs through the life, death, and resurrection of Jesus Christ. Following Calvin, most Reformed Christians would place great emphasis on the cross. Although I do not explore the topic of incarnation in this chapter, I would add that, in the cross and in the resurrection, we see most fully who Jesus is: the Son of God, condescending to the point of death on our behalf.

1. The *life and teachings of Jesus* are redemptive in that they show us what God is like and how we are to live in such a way as to honour God. In Jesus, we see that God loves us unconditionally, loves us enough to send his son to live with us in the midst of the fears, contingencies, and perils of human life. Jesus Christ is the supreme example of how human life should be lived. In his perfect obedience, Jesus fulfilled all the requirements of the law; accordingly, in his death he became a perfect sacrifice for our sins.

In Chapter 12 I criticized exemplarism, the theory which holds that what is central in the Christian faith and in our redemption are the teachings of Jesus and the example of his life. I still hold, in the light of the seriousness of sin, that exemplarism is an inadequate theory. Still, there is truth in the theory, and it would be wrong to miss it. Jesus' life and teachings do indeed provide for us a supreme example of a morally good life. And that example can indeed motivate people to try to live in more Christ-like ways. Moreover, many people's hearts are broken and they become open to the Christian good news when they consider seriously the life and especially death of Jesus.

2. The *death of Jesus* on the cross is redemptive, as Anselm of Canterbury argued, because in that event Jesus, 'the Lamb of God who takes away the sin of the world' (John 1: 29), paid the full penalty for our sins and thus set right a disturbed moral order. The penalty for sin is death. In the Genesis account of the fall, God said to Adam and Eve, 'of the tree of the knowledge of good and evil you shall not eat, for in the day that you eat of it you shall die' (Gen. 2: 17). And the penalty had to be paid. Jesus died on our behalf, paying with his blood (Rom. 5: 9; Heb. 9: 21–3) the penalty for our sins. Thus we can be forgiven and a right relationship with God restored.

3. The *resurrection of Jesus* is redemptive because in that event God defeated death and promised us eternal life. Since death—along with all God's other enemies—has been defeated, we too can be raised from the dead. Christians take the resurrection of Jesus from the dead as both the model and the promise of our resurrection (see Rom. 8: 11; 1 Cor. 15: 20, 23; Phil. 3: 20–1; 1 Thess. 4: 14; 1 John 3: 2), which takes place at the time of the general resurrection.[1]

V

For whom does the life, death, and resurrection of Jesus result in redemption? Here virtually all Christians would answer, those who have faith in Christ. Those who are redeemed are redeemed not because of any good deeds that they have ever done, laws they have obeyed, or lifestyle they have lived. It is because they entrust their lives to Jesus Christ. The Protestant Reformers called this notion 'justification by faith'.

Our sinfulness is such that we can do nothing to save ourselves. Theologians in the Reformed tradition speak of 'total depravity'. The idea is not that human beings are incapable of doing anything good or that we are as morally

---

[1] Although it is important for the topic of bodily redemption, I will add little in this chapter to what I said about atonement and theories of atonement in Chapter 12. Christian thinkers, in my opinion, are allowed to try out various theories to see what best fits with the biblical data and church teachings. No one theory is theologically mandatory.

despicable as we can possibly be: of course we can do morally good deeds. People do them frequently. Rather, the point is that evil corrupts and taints everything we do—even our good deeds. We do our good deeds in part for mixed reasons: so that others will think highly of us, for example, or so that we can feel good about ourselves. We can do good, but not any good that contributes to our salvation.

Since we can do nothing to earn God's approval, if salvation were based on the works that we do, we would all be condemned. It would be hopeless. No matter how hard we might try, no matter how many self-sacrificial acts we might perform, no matter how many tears we might shed, it would be impossible. God is holy and demands absolute and perfect obedience from us. We cannot save ourselves.

As noted, the term 'grace' means that God loves us despite the fact that we are unlovable and acts to save us despite our lack of merit. Justification by faith means that God forgives us (1 John 1: 9), justifies us (Rom. 5: 1), adopts us (Rom. 8: 15, 23; Gal. 4: 5), and reconciles us to himself (2 Cor. 5: 18–20), because of our faith in Jesus Christ (Rom. 3: 22–4; Gal. 2: 21). 'Faith' means both believing *that* and believing *in*. The first (which the medieval theologians called *fides*) is cognitive; it entails believing that certain things are true, for example, that Jesus is the messiah and Son of God, and is our saviour. The second (*fiducia*) involves trust, specifically trusting one's life to God in Christ. Faith is a response—a believing and trusting response—to the Gospel. It is the result of hearing the Gospel (Rom 10: 17; Gal. 3: 2, 8) and being drawn by the Holy Spirit (Acts 16: 14; Eph. 1: 17; Phil. 2: 13).

In faith, we are united with Christ; Christ dwells in us; we are incorporated into his risen life. Thus we are transformed. We are born again (John 3: 3). We become new creations (2 Cor. 5: 17). We are sanctified (1 Cor. 6: 11). Because of our faith, we are able to fulfil our responsibilities under the covenant. The person of faith is part of 'God's people'.

It is important to see that faith is not itself a good work. Indeed, Reformed Christianity insists that faith is not our own doing. And virtually all Christians insist that it is not *entirely* our own doing. Faith is a gift of God (2 Cor. 4: 6; Gal. 3: 23–6; Eph. 2: 8).[2]

---

[2] I do not have the space to address in detail the (to some, notorious) Reformed notion of election. I will make just one point: Calvin argued that the doctrine ought to constitute a source of comfort rather than fear for believers. I agree with him. Knowing how fickle, mercurial, and erratic human beings are (and as I know myself to be), I do indeed find it comforting to believe that my salvation is primarily a matter of God's choice, not mine (Eph. 1: 4). If it were just a matter of my personal choice, I might in a moment of weakness one day decide to deny God.

We are not saved by our good works, but Reformed Christians insist that faith is followed by obedience. 'So faith by itself, if it has no works, is dead' (Jas. 2: 17). Good works are a necessary sign that faith is genuine. Motivated by the Holy Spirit, they are a response of gratitude on our part for what God has done for us. Obedience is a natural consequence of our new sanctified life in Christ.

Since the Reformation, important differences on the doctrine of justification have separated Roman Catholics and Protestants. In recent years, there have been efforts to reconcile some of those differences.[3] The issues here are complex; let me try to contribute just a bit to the enterprise.

One point of disagreement between Catholics and Protestants in the area of justification concerns the righteousness of justified human beings.[4] Catholics typically hold that Christians are justified by an infusion of Christ's righteousness and thus that they are *made righteous* by God ('So by the one man's obedience will the many be made righteous' (Rom. 5: 19)). My sin was imputed to Christ on the cross, and his righteousness is infused into me via faith, love, obedience, and the sacraments. Although it is provided by God, justifying righteousness becomes a righteousness that is inherent in me.

Protestants typically hold that in justification God forensically forgives human beings[5] and thus that they are *regarded by God as righteous* (or declared or pronounced righteous) (Rom. 9: 6–8; Gal. 3: 6). Justification is accordingly a kind of legal fiction, since justified human beings clearly remain sinners. Justifying righteousness is imputed to me, but remains external to me.

Both sides agree, of course, that we are not able to save ourselves (Eph. 2: 8–9); that justification is a gift of God, based on the work of Christ, to those who have faith (Rom. 5: 1); that in justification God does not count our sins against us (2 Cor. 5: 19); that in Christ we 'become the righteousness of God' (2 Cor. 5: 21); and that good works are the natural result of genuine faith.[6]

I will make two points about this controversy. First, although there are real differences here, terminological confusion has made the differences appear to be much larger that they in fact are. The two sides have

---

[3] I refer both to the official Catholic–Lutheran discussions on justification and to the 'Evangelicals and Catholics Together' document.

[4] There are other differences that I will not discuss, e.g. the debate between Catholics and Protestants about Luther's notion of '*simil justus et peccator*', and the debate between Catholics and Reformed Protestants about the degree of libertarian or incompatibilist free will that is involved in justification.

[5] Not all Protestants believe in forensic justification. The Anabaptists and John Wesley, among others, struggled with the idea.

[6] I will not speak on this occasion about those practical or ecclesiastical implications of the Catholic view of justification that still divide Catholics and Protestants, e.g. indulgences, purgatory, masses for the dead, prayers to the saints, baptismal regeneration, etc.

understood the term 'justification' differently. Protestants typically sharply distinguish between *justification* (the event that begins the Christian life, namely, God regarding us as righteous) and *sanctification* (the process after justification of the Holy Spirit helping us to grow in living holy lives). Catholics understand the word 'justification' to include what Protestants mean by both terms. So when Protestants insist that justification is by faith alone and Catholics insist that justification is by faith and love, they are not necessarily disagreeing.

When Catholics object to the slogan, 'Justification is by faith alone,' they are (quite understandably) arguing that this motto omits the obedience and acts of love that are supposed to characterize the Christian life. When Protestants object to the Catholic formula, 'Justification is by faith and love,' they are (quite understandably) arguing that we cannot contribute anything to our justification, that we are not saved by any loving deeds that we do. As Alister McGrath points out: 'In fact, there is general agreement between Protestant and Roman Catholic that the Christian life is *begun* through faith and *continued and developed* through obedience and good works.'[7]

My second point concerns the difference between *being righteous* and *being regarded as righteous*. When the person doing the regarding is a fallible human being, the difference between 'being x' and 'being regarded as x' can be a huge difference. Obviously, this is because the perception and judgement of a human person may be mistaken. But when the person doing the regarding is a divine person, the difference collapses. Just as God's word is effective (Heb. 4: 11–13), so too is God's 'regard'. If God regards me as righteous, I *am* righteous. All talk of 'fiction' is misplaced.

On the other hand, the fact remains that justified persons remain sinners, and so the sense in which a justified sinner is *made righteous* by God must allow for that fact. The right sense of 'made righteous', in my view, is simply 'forgiven'. And, hopefully, the person who is forgiven by God will grow in righteousness, and have fewer things in the future that will need forgiveness.

Accordingly, in my opinion, the debate between Catholics and Protestants at this one point is largely about a distinction that does not make much difference. Catholics do not hold that we save ourselves, and Protestants do not hold that justification occurs without sanctification. It turns out, then, that Catholics and Protestants simply use two equally legitimate ways of

---

[7] Alister McGrath, *Studies in Doctrine* (Grand Rapids, MI: Zondervan: 1997), p. 400. I have been assisted in writing this section by several of McGrath's fine essays on justification.

talking about the same reality. Justification can equally be said to be an act of God that *pronounces* sinners righteous and an act of God that transforms sinners by grace so that they *are* righteous.[8]

There is, of course, a genuine difference between justification as a once-and-for-all forensic event and justification as a process in part of which we cooperate. And this fact will lead to two objections from traditionalist Protestants to the reconciling line that I have been following.

First, they will point out that the Council of Trent infallibly declared that good works are a necessary condition of salvation, which of course the Reformers strongly opposed.[9] Despite the fact that Catholics always add that those good works necessary to salvation are prompted by God's grace, it will be insisted that the Catholic notion seems clearly contrary to the 'faith alone' motto of the Reformation.

But both Catholics and Protestants agree that good works are a necessary implication of genuine faith. That is, there is no genuine faith without good works; good works are a necessary criterion of genuine faith. Accordingly, if faith is necessary to salvation (as all sides agree), then so is everything entailed by faith. If the Constitution of the United States requires that you cannot be President without being a native-born citizen of the United States, it also requires anything that is logically entailed by being a native-born citizen. Thus it does no violence whatsoever to the Constitution to say that you have to have been *born* (which is logically entailed by being a native-born citizen) in order to be President.

Secondly, traditionalist Protestants are likely to object that the Catholic theory raises the spectre of our never really being justified, since growth in holiness is never complete in this life. If what God demands and requires is absolute holiness, there will never exist in this life a sufficient basis for our acceptance by God.[10]

But is this an important difference? Perhaps not. Catholics and Protestants can still agree that our acceptance and forgiveness by God depend on the action of God and not on how much progress we make in holiness. They can agree that our salvation depends on what God has once-and-for-all done for us in the life, death, and resurrection of Jesus Christ.

---

[8] As I understand it, this is similar to the solution found in the Lutheran–Roman Catholic Dialogue in the United States in the 1980s. See *Salvation and the Church: An Agreed Statement* (London: Church House Publishing/Catholic Truth Society, 1987), 'Justification by Faith', §158, p. 298.

[9] Thus Norman Geisler and Ralph E. MacKenzie, *Roman Catholics and Evangelicals: Agreements and Differences* (Grand Rapids, MI: Baker Books, 1995), pp. 221–48.

[10] Thus Michael S. Horton, 'What Still Keeps Us Apart?', in *Roman Catholicism: Evangelical Protestants Analyze What Divides and Unites Us* (Chicago: Moody Press, 1994), p. 255.

VI

Let us return to the fact of our embodiment as human beings.[11] (I will discuss this point in much more detail in Chapter 14, but there are a few preliminary points that are best made here.) The basic Christian claim about the general resurrection is this: on some day in the future, all the dead will be bodily raised, both the righteous and the unrighteous, to be judged by God; and the guarantee and model of the 'general resurrection' is the already accomplished resurrection of Jesus Christ. But from here Christian tradition diverges. There seem to be two main ways of understanding the general resurrection, and especially the 'intermediate state' (i.e. the state of the person after death and before the general resurrection in the eschaton). I will call the theories 'temporary non-existence' and 'temporary disembodiment'.

Temporary non-existence (which in its non-dualistic versions is in some ways similar to a theory called 'soul sleep'[12]) is by a wide margin the minority report of Christian theology. On this theory (which is neutral vis-à-vis metaphysical dualism or physicalism), a given person (we'll call him Smith) is born, and then dies. After Smith's death, Smith simply does not exist until the eschaton, when God raises Smith's body from the ground and reconstitutes Smith as a living person.

This theory has some assets. The first is purely philosophical, namely, the fact that it is consistent with both metaphysical physicalism and dualism. That is, you can consistently believe in temporary non-existence no matter which theory of the mind–body problem you ascribe to. The second is that defenders of temporary non-existence often argue that certain scriptural texts (John 11: 11; Acts 13: 36) support this view. Yet there are problems as well: much of the Bible seems not to support this theory (see the texts listed under the next theory). Moreover, some philosophers argue that the temporal gap in the existence of Smith that the theory requires raises grave doubts about whether the resurrected Smith-like person really is Smith. (I will not attempt to adjudicate that dispute here.)

In contrast, the majority of Christian theologians who speak of the intermediate state defend temporary disembodiment. As I will explain in more

---

[11] I have addressed the issues discussed in this section of the chapter in much more detail in *Risen Indeed: Making Sense of the Resurrection* (Grand Rapids, MI: Eerdmans, 1993), especially pp. 85–131.

[12] The main difference is that soul-sleep entails that during the interim period the soul is in an unconscious or semi-conscious state.

detail in Chapter 14, the theory (which is based on metaphysical dualism as defined earlier) says this: a given human being Jones is born, lives as a soul incarnate in a body, and dies; when the body dies, Jones' soul goes on existing in an incomplete, disembodied state with God until the general resurrection in the eschaton; at that point Jones' body is resurrected and permanently reunited with Jones' soul.

This theory, too, has a weakness (in the eyes of some): it essentially depends on at least some version of metaphysical dualism. If that theory turns out to be philosophically indefensible, temporary disembodiment is in trouble. The theory requires that personal identity be retained during a period when a once-embodied person temporarily exists without a body. Nor need it depend on the dualist notion that souls survive death naturally, so to speak. That is, it can retain the Christian notion that we survive death only if and when God miraculously steps in and causes it.

But the theory also has several strong points. First, it does not entail a problematic temporal gap. Since there is no moment in time when Jones does not exist in some form or other, it will surely be Jones and not a replica of Jones who exists in the kingdom of God. Secondly, if the real Jones is Jones' soul (as dualism requires), then Jones' pre-mortem and post-mortem bodies do not have to consist of the same particles, nor do they even have to be similar; Jones' resurrection body can be a whole new 'glorified' body and it will still be Jones. Thirdly, defenders of temporary disembodiment claim to see a close fit between their theory and biblical, and especially Pauline, notions of the afterlife. The apostle seems to hold that human beings consist of both material bodies and immaterial souls, that the body is not merely an adornment or drape for the soul, but that it is indeed good, since it can be the temple of the Holy Spirit (1 Cor. 3: 16–17; 6: 19–20); and that the soul is in some sense separable from the body (2 Cor. 5: 6–8; 12: 2–3; Phil. 1: 23). Fourthly, temporary disembodiment solves an otherwise tricky problem in biblical theology: how it can be true both that the general resurrection will not occur until the eschaton (which seems to be taught in the New Testament—see 1 Thess: 4: 13–18) and that Jesus said to the good thief on the cross: '*Today* you will be with me in paradise' (Luke 23: 43; emphasis added). The solution is this: the thief was and is with Jesus in paradise in the form of a disembodied soul; his body will be raised later.

Temporary disembodiment is the standard theory in the tradition and appears to be the stronger theory in any case. Accordingly, that is the view of the intermediate state that I accept and defend.

VII

The whole of the Christian tradition unites in seeing the end or goal of redemption as our eternal presence with God in paradise. And our redemption is to be understood as bodily redemption. Given that fact, it is not surprising that one concrete way of conceptualizing heaven in the tradition is in terms of the 'beatific vision'. That is, in paradise, redeemed humanity will see God's face.

Is it possible to *see God*? Well, if God is what is ultimately real, and if God desires a loving relationship between God and human beings, and if the incarnation of the Logos is permanent (as the tradition holds), and if resurrected human beings are embodied beings, then it should be possible for us in some sense to see God. This despite the fact that, apart from the incarnation, God is not an embodied being (John 4: 24).

The Bible takes us on a long journey on this issue of seeing God. I will simply make three points about it. First, several texts insist that seeing God, or at least seeing God's face, is forbidden. There is, for example, the curious passage in Exodus 33 where Moses wants to see the glory of God. Eventually God does pass by, while Moses is hidden in the cleft of a rock, and (speaking anthropomorphically) he only gets to see God's back. But the key phrase of the text is clearly Exodus 33: 20: 'You cannot see my face, for no one shall see me and live.'[13]

Secondly, many biblical passages stress that it is because of our sinfulness that we are forbidden to see God's face. This follows from the fact that the scriptures declare that people who are upright, holy, and pure in heart do get to see God. Psalm 11: 7 says that 'the upright shall behold his [the Lord's] face.' The sixth beatitude says, 'Blessed are the pure in heart, for they will see God' (Matt. 5: 8). In Matthew 18: 10, Jesus declares, speaking of children, 'in heaven their angels continually see the face of my father.' And Hebrews 12: 14 says, 'Pursue peace with everyone, and the holiness without which no one will see the Lord.' These are wonderful thoughts, but if our aim is to see God, to achieve the beatific vision, these words sound like bad news. Which of us can truly claim to be upright, pure, or holy?

Still, the hope of seeing God persists. In Psalm 27: 7–8, the poet pleads for the sight of God:

> Hear, O Lord, when I cry aloud,
>   Be gracious to me and answer me!

---

[13] But the Pentateuch also insists that God and Moses spoke face-to-face. See Num. 12: 8; 14: 14, and Deut. 5: 4; 34: 10.

'Come,' my heart says, 'seek his face!'
Your face, O Lord, do I seek,
Do not hide your face from me.

And although there are thorny textual and lexical problems connected with this passage, the NRSV translates Job 19: 25–7 as follows:

For I know that my redeemer lives,
and that at the last he will stand upon the earth;
and after my skin has been thus destroyed,
then in my flesh I shall see God,
whom I shall see on my side,
and my eyes shall behold, and not another.

Thirdly, this hope that we will see God is surely eschatological. In 1 John 3: 2, it says, 'Beloved, we are God's children now; what we will be has not yet been revealed. What we do know is this: when he is revealed, we will be like him, for we will see him as he is.' And a text about the New Jerusalem in Revelation 22 says, 'But the throne of God and of the lamb will be in it [i.e. in the city], and his servants will worship him; they will see his face.'

The expression, 'seeing God', can be used in two different senses. The first is the sense in which believers do and non-believers do not, here and now, see God. This sense is clearly to use the word 'see' in a metaphorical (or at least non-literal) way. It means roughly that believers cannot avoid interpreting their experience, and indeed all of life and reality, in terms of the presence of God; and that non-believers do not do so. The second is the sense in which no one can now see God, at least not God's face, and that one day the redeemed *will* see God. This, I think, is a literal sense of the word 'see'. Believing as I do in both (1) the permanent incarnation of the Son of God, and (2) bodily redemption (i.e. in a general resurrection that is essentially bodily), I have no trouble accepting the idea that the redeemed will one day literally see God.[14]

---

[14] I relegate to a footnote a brief thought about 'theosis' (divinization, deification). This concept was used by several of the Church Fathers (e.g. Irenaeus, Athanasius), and is an important part of the soteriology of Eastern Orthodox Christianity to this day. Some contemporary Mormon scholars have made reference to theosis, presumably as a way of deflecting the criticism that the LDS notion of 'eternal progression' is heretical or unorthodox. I briefly make two comments: (1) I believe the Church Fathers (as well as Orthodox theologians today) who speak of theosis would be shocked and horrified at the suggestion that their notion entails that human beings can ontologically become God; and (2) nowhere in the classical Christian tradition is there any hint of the correlative LDS idea that God was once a man and has progressed to Godhood.

VIII

We began with the idea that human beings face two great problems, guilt and death. Christian redemption—salvation through faith in Jesus Christ—is the divine solution to those problems. To those who are troubled by guilt (and we all are), Christianity says that God has freely and graciously provided for our forgiveness. To those who fear death (and nearly everyone does, to some degree or other), Christianity says that God freely and graciously grants us new life after death. Together, forgiveness and resurrection make possible our eternal life in the presence of God.[15]

---

[15] I would like to thank Jack Bonavich, Gerald O'Collins, S.J., Roger Olson, Susan Peppers-Bates, and Marguerite Shuster for their helpful comments on an earlier draft of this chapter.

14

The Resurrection of the Dead

I

Christians believe that resurrection—the last step, so to speak, in our redemption—comes in two stages. The first stage is the resurrection of Christ, which we discussed in Chapters 7 and 8. The second stage is the 'general resurrection'. It will occur at some time in the future, and involves the resurrection of all dead human beings (Acts 24: 15). In Chapter 13 we introduced two theories of the general resurrection. But much more about them needs to be said.

One traditional Christian view of survival of death runs, in outline form, something like this: on some future day all the dead will be bodily raised, both the righteous and the unrighteous alike, to be judged by God; and the guarantee and model of the general resurrection (that is, the raising of the dead in the last days) is the already accomplished resurrection of Jesus Christ from the dead.

My aim in this chapter is to explain and defend this basic view of resurrection. There are many ways it might be understood, of course, and perhaps more than one is coherent and, even from a Christian point of view, plausible. I shall defend one particular interpretation of the theory—an interpretation advocated by very many of the Church Fathers, especially second-century Fathers, as well as by Augustine and Aquinas. But in the end I will argue that a different, more contemporary theory works as well.

It may help to clarify matters if I first provide a brief guide to where we will be going in this chapter. After introducing the topic, I will discuss in turn three important claims made by the version of the theory I wish to defend. Then I will consider one typical aspect of the traditional theory that has important philosophical as well as theological ramifications, namely, the notion that our resurrection bodies will consist of the same matter as do our present earthly bodies. Finally, since the version of the theory that I wish to defend envisions a period of existence in a disembodied state, I will defend the theory against some of the arguments of those contemporary philosophers who find the notion of disembodied existence incoherent.

II

There are several ways in which the basic concept of resurrection sketched in the second paragraph of this chapter can be fleshed out. One option is to understand the nature of the human person, and hence the nature of resurrection, in a basically materialist or physicalist way. Perhaps human beings are essentially material objects, perhaps some vision of identity theory or functionalism is true. Now I was once attracted to this option, but I hold it no longer. I will discuss it no further here.[1]

Another option is to collapse talk of resurrection into talk of the immortality of the soul. A closely related move (and a popular one in recent theology) is to interpret resurrection in a spiritual rather than bodily sense (if this in the end differs significantly from immortality of the soul). Such a view will doubtless be based on some version of mind–body (or soul–body) dualism. Let us define classical dualism as the doctrine which says that (1) human beings consist of both material bodies and immaterial souls; (2) the soul is the essence of the person (the real you is your soul, not your body); and (3) although united with a body in this life, the soul can exist apart from the body. It then can be added that the body is corrupted after death and eventually ceases to exist but the soul is essentially immortal.

It is surprising (to me at least) that so many recent and contemporary Christian thinkers are tempted towards some such notion as this. For it is quite clear, in both scripture and tradition, that classical dualism is *not* the Christian position. For example, the biblical view is not that the soul is the essence of the person and is only temporarily housed or even imprisoned in a body; human beings seem rather to be understood in scripture as psycho-physical entities, that is, as unities of body and soul. And the notion that the body is essentially evil and must be escaped from (an idea often associated with versions of classical dualism) was condemned by virtually every orthodox Christian thinker who discussed death and resurrection in the first two hundred years after the apostolic age. The Christian idea is rather that the body was created by God and is good; the whole person, body and soul alike, is what is to be saved. Finally, the biblical notion is not that we survive death because souls are naturally immortal; if we survive death it is because God miraculously saves us; apart from God's intervention, death would mean annihilation for us. Thus Irenaeus says: 'Our survival forever comes from his greatness, not from our nature.'[2]

---

[1] The last vestige of my former materialist views is found in chapter 6 of my *Risen Indeed: Making Sense of the Resurrection* (Grand Rapids, MI: Eerdmans, 1993).

[2] Cyril Richardson (ed.), *Early Christian Fathers* (Philadelphia: Westminster Press, 1953), p. 389.

It would be interesting to discuss this option further, and especially to ask why so many contemporary Christian theologians are drawn towards it, how they might distinguish 'spiritual resurrection' from immortality of the soul, and how they might defend the theory against criticisms such as those just noted. However, I will not do so here. As noted above, my aim here is rather to explore and defend a third way of understanding the traditional Christian notion of resurrection, a theory virtually all (but not quite all) of the Church Fathers who discussed resurrection held in one form or another.[3] As noted in Chapter 13, I will call this theory 'temporary disembodiment'.

This theory of resurrection is based on a view of human nature which says that human beings are essentially material bodies *and* immaterial souls; the soul is separable from the body, but neither body nor soul alone (that is without the other) constitutes a complete human being. Thus Pseudo-Justin Martyr says:

Is the soul by itself man? No; but the soul of man. Would the body be called man? No, but it is called the body of man. If, then, neither of these is by itself man, but that which is made up of the two together is called man, and God has called *man* to life and resurrection, He has called not a part, but the whole, which is the soul and the body.[4]

What this theory says, then, is that human beings are typically and normally psycho-physical beings, that the soul can exist for a time apart from the body and retain personal identity, but that this disembodied existence is only temporary and constitutes a radically attenuated and incomplete form of human existence.

I call the theory temporary disembodiment because it envisions the following scenario. We human beings are born, live for a time as psycho-physical beings, and then die. After death we exist in an incomplete state as immaterial souls; and some time later in the eschaton God miraculously raises our bodies from the ground, transforms them into 'glorified bodies', and reunites them with our souls, thus making us complete and whole again.

Temporary disembodiment has several theological and philosophical assets. For one thing, many Christian thinkers have seen a comfortable fit between it and the view of human nature expressed in the Bible and in the Pauline writings particularly. The apostle seems to hold that human beings consist both of material bodies and immaterial souls, that the body is not

---

[3] See Harry A. Wolfson, 'Immortality and Resurrection in the Philosophy of the Church Fathers', in Krister Stendahl (ed.), *Immortality and Resurrection* (New York: Macmillan, 1965), pp. 64–72. See also Lynn Boliek, *The Resurrection of the Flesh* (Grand Rapids, MI: Eerdmans, 1962).

[4] Alexander Roberts and James Donaldson (eds.), *The Ante-Nicene Fathers*, vol. i (New York: Charles Scribner's Sons, 1899), pp. 297–8.

merely an adornment or drape for the soul, and is indeed good, since it can be the temple of the Holy Spirit (1 Cor. 3: 16–17; 6: 19–20), and that the soul is in some sense separable from the body (2 Cor. 5: 6–8; 12: 2–3). The body provides the soul with a vehicle for action in the world and expression of intentions and desires; and the soul provides the body with animation and direction.[5]

For another thing, the theory seems a neat way of reconciling the traditional view that the general resurrection does not occur until the eschaton with Jesus' statement to the good thief on the cross, 'Today you will be with me in paradise' (Luke 23: 43). The explanation (which naturally goes far beyond Jesus' simple statement) is as follows: the thief would be with Jesus in paradise that very day in the form of a disembodied soul, only to be bodily raised much later. The theory may also help resolve a similar tension that is sometimes said to exist in Pauline thought, with texts like 1 Corinthians 15 and 1 Thessalonians 4 pointing towards the idea of a future, eschatological, resurrection (with those who die beforehand existing till then in a kind of bodiless sleep) and texts like 2 Corinthians 5: 10 and Philippians 1: 23 suggesting the idea that death for the Christian is an immediate gain since one is immediately at home with the Lord.

Finally, the problem of personal identity after death seems in one sense more manageable on this theory than on at least some others, for this theory posits no temporal gap in the existence of persons (although there is a gap in their existence as complete, human beings). There is no moment subsequent to our births in which you and I simply do not exist—we exist as embodied souls or as mere souls at every moment till eternity.

III

There are three main aspects of temporary disembodiment that require discussion from both a philosophical and a theological perspective. I will now consider them in turn. The first is the notion that after death the soul exists for a time, that is, until the resurrection, in an intermediate state without the body. The second is the notion that at the time of the parousia the body will be raised from the ground and reunited with the soul. And the third is the notion that the body will then be transformed into what is called a 'glorified body'.

[5] Robert H. Gundry, *Soma in Biblical Theology: With Emphasis on Pauline Anthropology* (Cambridge: Cambridge University Press, 1976), p. 159.

The first main claim of temporary disembodiment, then, is that after death the soul temporarily exists without the body. This claim differs from certain physicalist concepts of resurrection on which the person does not exist at all in the period between death and resurrection. Temporary disembodiment need not be based on classical dualism as defined earlier, but it shares one tenet of classical dualism, namely, the claim that human beings consist (or in this case at least normally consist) of both material bodies and immaterial souls. (The soul need not be said to be the essence of the person, however, and is said to survive death not because immortality is one of its natural properties, but because God causes it to survive death.)[6]

Now almost all Christians believe that there is some kind of interim state of the person between death and resurrection. But beyond this point there are very many theological differences. Some, for example, think of the interim state as purgatorial in nature, and others do not. Some hold that spiritual change, for example, repentance, is possible during the interim period, and others do not. Some think that the soul rests or sleeps, that is, is not active or conscious, during the interim period, and others do not. It is not part of my purpose here to express an opinion on either of the first two items of disagreement. However, I will argue on the third that the soul is conscious in the interim state. The biblical metaphor of sleep (cf. Luke 8: 52; 1 Cor. 15: 20) should not be taken as a literal description. This is because it is difficult to make sense of the notion of a disembodied thing being in the presence of God ('Today you will be with me in paradise') if that thing is unconscious and thus unaware of the presence of God.[7] Furthermore, since sleeping is essentially a bodily activity, it seems incoherent to suggest that a disembodied soul could sleep.

The state of being without a body is an abnormal state of the human person. This is one of the clear differences between temporary disembodiment and immortality of the soul, for the second doctrine (at least in versions of it influenced by Plato) entails that disembodiment is the true or proper or best state of the human person. On the theory we are considering, however, the claim is that a disembodied soul lacks many of the properties and abilities that are normal for and proper to human persons. Disembodied existence is a kind of minimal existence.

---

⁶ Wolfson (n. 3 above), pp. 56–60, 63–4.

⁷ It does not seem to make sense to speak of some disembodied thing x being 'in the presence of some other thing y', where 'in the presence of' means 'in the spatial vicinity of'. The notion may be coherently understood, however, as something like 'being acutely aware of and sensitive to'. This is why I am unable to provide a sensible construal of the notion of a disembodied and unconscious person being in the presence of God.

Which properties typical of embodied human persons will disembodied souls have and which will they lack? Clearly they will lack those properties that essentially involve corporeality. They will possess no spatial location, for example, at least not in the space–time manifold with which we are familiar. They will not be able to perceive their surroundings (using the spatial word 'surroundings' in a stretched sense)—not at least in the ways in which we perceive our surroundings (that is, through the eyes, ears, and so on). They will not be able to experience bodily pains and pleasures. They will not be able to engage in bodily activities. Taking a walk, getting dressed, playing catch—these sorts of activities will be impossible.

But if by the word 'soul' we mean to include the constellation of those human activities that would typically be classified as 'mental', then the claim that our souls survive death entails the claim that our mental abilities and properties survive death. Accordingly, human persons in the interim state can be spoken of as having experiences, beliefs, wishes, knowledge, memory, inner (rather than bodily) feelings, thoughts, language (assuming memory of earthly existence)—in short, just about everything that makes up what we call personality. H. H. Price, in his classic article 'Survival and the Idea of "Another World" ', argues convincingly that disembodied souls can also be aware of each other's existence, can communicate with each other telepathically, and can have dreamlike (rather than bodily) perceptions of their worlds.[8]

But Aquinas argues that the disembodied existence of the person in the interim state is so deficient that attainment of ultimate happiness is impossible. No one who lacks some perfection is perfectly happy, for in such a state there will always be unfulfilled desires. It is contrary to the nature of the soul to be without the body, Aquinas says. He takes this to mean both that the disembodied state must only be temporary, and that the true bliss of the human person is only attained after re-embodiment, that is, in the general resurrection. He says: 'Man cannot achieve his ultimate happiness unless the soul be once again united to the body.'[9]

---

[8] H. H. Price, 'Survival and the Idea of "Another World" ', in John Donnelly (ed.), *Language, Metaphysics, and Death* (New York: Fordham University Press, 1978), pp. 176–95. I do not wish to commit myself entirely to Price's theory; John Hick, among others, has detected difficulties in it. See his *Death and Eternal Life* (New York: Harper and Row, 1976), pp. 265–77. But Price's main point—that disembodied survival of death is possible—seems to be correct.

[9] Thomas Aquinas, *Summa Contra Gentiles* (trans. Charles J. O'Neil), book IV (Notre Dame, IN: Notre Dame, 1979), IV, 79.

IV

The second main claim of the theory that I am calling temporary disembodiment is that at the general resurrection the body will be raised from the ground and reunited with the soul. As the second century writer Athenagoras says:

> There must certainly be a resurrection of bodies whether dead or even quite corrupted, and the same men as before must come to be again. The law of nature appoints an end ... for those very same men who lived in a previous existence, and it is impossible for the same men to come together again if the same bodies are not given back to the same souls. Now the same soul cannot recover the same body in any other way than by resurrection.[10]

As Athenagoras stresses, the idea is that each person's selfsame body will be raised; it will not be a different and brand new body, but the old body. Aquinas (echoing the argument of very many of the Fathers) notes the reason for this: 'If the body of the man who rises is not to be composed of the flesh and bones which now compose it, the man who rises will not be numerically the same man.'[11] Furthermore, in the resurrection there will be only one soul per body and only one body per soul. As Augustine says: 'Each single soul shall possess its own body.'[12] Otherwise (for example, if souls split and animate more than one body or if multiple identical copies of one body are animated by different souls) the problem of personal identity is unsolvable, and the Christian hope that we will live after death is incoherent.

The Fathers and scholastics insisted, then, that both body and soul must be present or else the person, the human being, does not exist. 'A man cannot be said to exist as such when the body is dissolved or completely scattered, even though the soul remain by itself'—so says Athenagoras.[13] And Aquinas agrees: 'My soul is not I, and if only souls are saved, I am not saved, nor is any man.'[14] Thus the Christian hope of survival is not the hope that our souls will survive death (though on temporary disembodiment that is one important aspect of it), but rather the hope that one day God will miraculously raise our bodies and reunite them with our souls.

---

[10] Athenagoras, *Embassy for Christians and the Resurrection of the Dead* (trans. Joseph H. Crehan, S.J.) (London: Longmans, Green, 1956), pp. 115–16.

[11] Aquinas, (n. 9 above), IV, 84.

[12] Augustine, *The Enchiridion on Faith, Hope, and Love* (trans. Henry Paolucci) (Chicago: Henry Regnery, 1961), LXXXVII.

[13] Athenagoras, (n. 10 above), p. 115.

[14] Cited in P. T. Geach, *God and the Soul* (London: Routledge and Kegan Paul, 1969), pp. 22, 40.

What is it, then, that guarantees personal identity in the resurrection? What is it that ensures that it will really be us in the kingdom of God and not, say, clever replicas of us? Aquinas argues as follows: since human beings consist of bodies and souls, and since both souls and the matter of which our bodies consist survive death, personal identity is secured when God collects the scattered matter, miraculously reconstitutes it as a human body, and reunites it with the soul.[15] And this surely seems a powerful argument. If God one day succeeds in doing these very things, personal identity will be secure. It will be us and not our replicas who will be the denizens of the kingdom of God.

V

The third main claim of temporary disembodiment is that in the resurrection the old body will be transformed into a 'glorified body' with certain quite new properties. This claim rests primarily on Paul's discussion of the resurrection in 1 Corinthians 15, and secondarily on the unusual properties the risen Jesus is depicted as having in some of the accounts of the resurrection appearances (for example, the apparent ability of the risen Jesus in John 20 to appear in a room despite the doors being locked). In the Pauline text just mentioned the apostle notes that some ask, 'How are the dead raised? With what kind of body do they come?' His answer is an argument to the effect that the new 'glorified' or 'spiritual' body *(soma pneumatikon)* is a transformation of the old body rather than a *de novo* creation (much as a stalk of grain is a transformation of a seed of grain, that is, it exists because of changes that have occurred in the seed and can be considered a new state of the grain). Further, Paul argues, while the old or natural body is physical, perishable, mortal, and sown in weakness and dishonour, the glorified body is spiritual, imperishable, immortal, and sown in strength and honour. The first body is in the image of the man of dust; the second body is in the image of the man of heaven.

The term 'spiritual body' might be misleading; it should not be taken as a denial of corporeality or as a last-minute capitulation to some version of the immortality of the soul as opposed to bodily resurrection. By this term Paul means not a body whose stuff or matter is spiritual (whatever that might mean) or an immaterial existence of some sort; rather he means a body that is fully obedient to and dominated by the Holy Spirit. Paul says: 'Flesh and

---

[15] Aquinas (n. 9 above), IV, 81.

blood cannot inherit the kingdom of God' (1 Cor. 15: 50). What enters the kingdom of heaven, then, is not this present weak and mortal body of flesh and blood, but the new glorified body. This new body is a physical body (Paul's use of the word *soma* implies as much).[16] And if we take seriously Paul's simile of the seed, it is materially related to the old body, at least in the sense of being derived from it. But it is a body transformed in such ways as make it fit to live in God's presence. If by the term 'physical object' we mean an entity that has spatio-temporal location and is capable of being empirically measured, tested, or observed in some sense, then my argument is that the new body of which Paul speaks is a physical object.

Temporary disembodiment, then, entails that human souls can animate both normal earthly bodies and glorified resurrection bodies. Continuity between the two bodies is provided by the presence of both the same soul and the same matter in both bodies. (The new body will of course consist of transformed matter.) Thus Augustine says:

> Nor does the earthly material out of which men's mortal bodies are created ever perish; but though it may crumble into dust and ashes, or be dissolved into vapors and exhalations, though it may be transformed into the substance of other bodies, or dispersed into the elements, though it should become food for beasts or men, and be changed into their flesh, it returns in a moment of time to that human soul which animated it at the first and which caused it to become man, and to live and grow.[17]

The matter of our present bodies may be arranged differently in the resurrection, he says, but the matter will be restored.

Many of the theologians of the early church and of the medieval period stress also the perfection of the glorified body. It will be free of every bodily defect. It will be immune to evil because fully controlled by the spirit of God. It will not suffer. It will not grow old or die. It will have 'agility'—which is presumably an ability like that of the risen Jesus to come and go at will, unimpeded by things like walls and doors. It will exist in a state of fulfilled desire. It will need no material food and drink, having been prepared for eternal life by the elements of the eucharist.[18]

---

[16] See Gundry (n. 5 above), pp. 164ff. For this and other points made in this paragraph, see C. F. D. Moule, 'St. Paul and Dualism: The Pauline Concept of Resurrection', *New Testament Studies*, 12/2 (1966), and Ronald J. Sider, 'The Pauline Conception of the Resurrection Body in I Corinthians XV: 35–54', *New Testament Studies*, 21/3 (1965).

[17] Augustine (n. 12 above), LXXXVIII.

[18] See Irenaeus, in Richardson (n. 2 above), p. 388; Augustine (n. 12 above), XCI; Aquinas (n. 9 above), IV, 83–7.

VI

Is the picture of resurrection just presented coherent? Is it plausible? The main objections that have been raised against it in recent philosophy revolve around the problem of personal identity. Some philosophers argue that so far as disembodied existence is concerned this problem cannot be solved. That is, they argue that if some immaterial aspect of me survives death, then it will not be me that survives death. Since the view of survival of death that I am defending essentially involves a period of disembodied existence, I must try to defend the view against these sorts of objections. But a prior problem must be considered first—whether the Fathers and scholastics were correct in their strong claim (I will call this claim 'the Patristic theory') that if it is to be me in the kingdom of God, then the very matter of my original earthly body must be raised. Having discussed the point, 1 will then turn in Section VII to the arguments of those philosophers who oppose the notion of disembodied existence because of the problem of personal identity.

Why did Aquinas and the Fathers who influenced him insist that the same matter of my old body must be raised? Let us see if we can construct an argument on their behalf. Like many arguments in the area of personal identity, it involves a puzzle case. Suppose that I own a defective personal computer which I rashly decide to try to repair myself. Having taken it apart (there are now, say, sixty separate computer components scattered on my workbench), I find that I am unable to repair it. I call the outlet that sold me the computer, and the manager suggests that I simply bring all sixty components to that office for repair. I do so, but, through a horrible series of misunderstandings and errors, the sixty pieces of the computer are then sent to sixty different addresses around the country. That constitutes the heart of my story, but there are two separate endings to it. *Ending number one:* it takes three years for everything to be sorted out, for the pieces to be located and collected in one place, for the repairs to be made, and for the parts to be reassembled and restored, in full working order, to my desk. *Ending number two:* After three years of trying in vain to locate and collect the scattered pieces, the manager gives up, collects sixty similar parts, assembles them, and the resulting computer ends up on my desk.

Now I do not wish to raise the interesting question whether my computer *existed* during the three-year period. I am interested in the related question whether the computer now located on my desk is *the same* computer as the one that was there three years ago. And so far as ending number one is concerned, it seems most natural to affirm that the computer I now possess is indeed the same computer as the one that I possessed before. The computer may or may not have had a gap in its existence, that is, a period when it did not exist, but it seems clear that identity has been preserved. And so far as ending number two is concerned, it seems most natural to deny that the computer I now possess is the same computer as the one that I possessed before. Furthermore, we would doubtless insist on this denial even if each of the sixty components the manager used to construct the computer I now possess was qualitatively identical to the sixty old components. What I now have is a qualitatively similar, but numerically different, computer.

Now I doubt that the Church Fathers often pondered personal identity test cases involving computers, and it is obvious that personal computers are different from human beings in many striking ways. But it was perhaps *the sort of* insight arrived at above that led them to take the strong stand they took on the resurrection. Only if God reassembles the very particles of which my body once consisted will it be me who is raised. Otherwise, that is, if other particles are used, the result will be what we would call a replica of me rather than me.

But despite the above argument, does it still not seem that Aquinas and the Fathers in their strong stand have made the solution to the problem of personal identity more difficult than it need be? Even granting the point that some of the particles of the matter of which our bodies consist will endure for the requisite number of years, why insist that God must re-collect it, that is, that very matter, in the resurrection? For surely in the interim state it will be us (and not soul-like replicas of us) who will exist without any body at all; surely the Fathers and scholastics insist on this much. Thus the soul alone must guarantee personal identity. What philosophers call the memory criterion (which is typically taken to include not just memory but all one's 'mental' characteristics and properties) must suffice by itself to establish the presence of the same soul, which guarantees the presence of the same human being. Identity of memory, personality, and other 'mental' aspects of the person are sufficient conditions of personal identity. To admit this much is not necessarily to go back on the traditional notion that the soul is not the whole person and that the whole person must be raised. It is merely to insist that the existence of my soul entails my existence. Otherwise talk of my existence in the interim state is meaningless.

Now I do not claim that the Patristic theory is logically inconsistent. It is possible to hold that when I die my soul will be me during the interim period but that it will no longer be me if my soul in the eschaton animates a body consisting of totally new matter, even if the new body is qualitatively identical to the old one. (Perhaps an essential property of my soul is that it can only animate *this* body—where 'this body' means in part a body consisting of *these* particles. So if *per impossibile* my soul were to animate a different body, the result would not be me. Or perhaps every configuration of particles that can possibly constitute a human body has as one of its essential properties that it can be animated by one and only one soul.) But while logically consistent, this view seems to me exceedingly difficult to defend; it is hard to see how the suggested theses could be argued for.

Thus, so far as the problem of personal identity is concerned, it seems that a defender of temporary disembodiment can dispense with all talk of God one day re-collecting the atoms, quarks, or whatever of our bodies. Perhaps human beings in this regard are unlike computers. Why not say God can award us brand new bodies materially quite unrelated to (although qualitatively similar to) the old ones? If the existence of the soul is sufficient for personal identity, and if the human soul never at any moment subsequent to its creation fails to exist, it will be *we* who exist after the resurrection in the kingdom of God whether or not our old bodies are reconstituted.

Furthermore, it needs to be noted here that identity of particles of bodily matter does not seem necessary to preserve the identity of an ordinary human person even during the course of a lifetime. As Frank Dilley says:

> We constantly replace our atoms over time and there is no reason to think that any eighty year old person has even a single atom in common with the newborn babe. If a person maintains personal identity over a process of total atom-by-atom replacement, it is difficult to see why such identity would not be preserved through a sudden replacement of all the atoms at once.[19]

Dilley's argument seems plausible, but we should notice that his conclusion does not necessarily follow. Perhaps gradual replacement of all the individual atoms of a human body is consistent with personal identity while all-at-once replacement of them is not. One of the difficulties encountered by philosophers who discuss personal identity is that different persons' intuitions run in different directions. For example, in a slightly different connection, Peter van Inwagen argues that sameness of person requires both (1) sameness of atoms and (2) regular and natural causal relationships between those atoms. So if God were now to try to raise Napoleon Bonaparte from the dead by omnisciently locating the atoms of which his body once consisted and miraculously reassembling them, the result would not be Napoleon.[20] Now I do not agree with van Inwagen here; I see no reason for his second requirement. I raise his argument merely to show that his intuitions run in

[19] Frank Dilley, 'Resurrection and the "Replica Objection"', *Religious Studies*, 19/4 (1983), p. 462.

[20] Peter van Inwagen, 'The Possibility of Resurrection', *International Journal for Philosophy of Religion*, IX/2 (1978), p. 119.

a different direction from Dilley's. Since Dilley's case of sudden-replacement-of-all-the-atoms-at-once seems to constitute something unnatural and irregular, van Inwagen would doubtless deny that in such cases personal identity would be preserved.

What if there were, so to speak, some natural way of reassembling persons out of totally new matter? Derek Parfit considers in detail a series of test cases involving an imagined teletransporter.[21] This is a machine that is designed to send a person to distant places like Mars by (1) recording the exact state of all the body's cells (including those of the brain); (2) destroying the body and brain; (3) transmitting the information at the speed of light to Mars; where (4) a replicator creates out of new matter a body and brain exactly like the old one. Suppose Parfit enters the machine and is 'teletransported to Mars'. Would the resulting Parfit-like person on Mars be Parfit? Here again our intuitions might differ, even in this relatively simple case (that is, apart from complications like the original Parfit somehow surviving on earth or fifteen Parfit-like persons appearing on Mars). Those (like the Church Fathers and Aquinas) who hold to some strong requirement about bodily continuity will deny that it is Parfit. Those who stress the memory or psychological criterion are free to affirm that Parfit is now on Mars. So are those (for example, John Hick) who believe that identity is exact similarity plus uniqueness. Those who think that identity is exact similarity plus the right kind of causal origin or causal ancestry might go either way, depending on whether they think the operation of a teletransporter constitutes an appropriate sort of causal origin for the Parfit-like person on Mars.

The moral of the story thus far, I think, is that the Fathers and Aquinas may be right in what they say about resurrection, but it is not clear that they are right. Their position may be consistent, but it does seem implausible to hold both (1) that it will be me in the interim period without any body at all (that is, the presence of my soul is sufficient for personal identity), and (2) that it will not be me in the eschaton, despite the presence of my soul, if the body which my soul then animates consists of new matter. There may be other (perhaps theological) reasons why we should hold that it is the very matter of our old bodies that is raised, but so far as the problem of personal identity is concerned, a strong case can be made that it will not matter.

Recent and contemporary Christian theologians who discuss resurrection seem for the most part to have departed from the Patristic theory. The more common thesis is that our glorified bodies will be wholly different bodies, not

---

[21] Derek Parfit, *Reasons and Persons* (Oxford: Oxford University Press, 1986), pp. 199ff. I mention here only the most simple of the test cases involving teletransportation that Parfit discusses. I do not consider here what I take to be the central theses of part III of his book.

necessarily consisting of any of the old matter at all. As John Hick, an articulate spokesperson for this new point of view, says:

What has become a widely accepted view in modern times holds that the resurrection body is a new and different body given by God, but expressing the personality within its new environment as the physical body expressed it in the earthly environment. The physical frame decays or is burned, disintegrating and being dispersed into the ground or the air, but God re-embodies the personality elsewhere.[22]

Frequently connected with this view is an exegetical claim, namely, that by the term 'the body' St. Paul meant not the physical organism, but rather something akin to 'the whole personality'. What will be raised from the dead, then, is not the old body, but rather the *person*, and in being raised the person will be given a brand new body by God.

It is not hard to see why such a view has come to be widely adopted. (1) As noted above, personal identity does not seem to require the resurrection of the old body. (2) The Patristic theory seems to many contemporary Christians to be scientifically outmoded and difficult to believe; the idea that in order to raise me God must one day cast about, locate, and collect the atoms of which my earthly body once consisted seems to many people absurd. (3) Many such theologians want to hold in any case that the kingdom of God is not spatially related to our present world. It exists in a space all its own, and so can contain no material from this spatio-temporal manifold.

I am unable to locate any philosophical or logical difficulties in the 'modern' theory. It seems to me a possible Christian view of resurrection, and can fit smoothly with the other aspects of the traditional notion I am calling temporary disembodiment. Are there any theological reasons, then, for a Christian to retain the old theory, that is, to believe that our old bodies will be raised? Two points should be made here. The first is that the most natural reading of Paul in 1 Corinthians 15 is along the lines of the Patristic theory. That is, Paul seems to be suggesting there that the old body *becomes* or *changes into* the new body, just as a seed becomes or changes into a plant. Thus, just as there is material continuity between the seed and the plant, so there will be material continuity between the old body and the new; the plant is *a new form of* the seed. Note also Paul's use in verses 42 and 43 of the expression: '*It is* sown ... *it is* raised', as if the one thing (a human body) is at one time in a certain state and at a later time in another state (see also verses 52 and 53).[23]

[22] Hick (n. 8 above), p. 186.
[23] Commenting on Paul's argument in 1 Cor. 15: 53, Tertullian says: 'When he says *this* corruptible and *this* mortal, he utters the words while touching the surface of his own body.' Tertullian, 'On the Resurrection of the Flesh', in Alexander Roberts and James Donaldson (eds.), *The Ante-Nicene Fathers*, vol. iii (New York: Charles Scribner's Sons, 1899), L1.

Furthermore, as noted already, Paul's use of the term *soma* reveals that what he had in mind was a body; it is simply a lexical mistake to say that he merely meant 'the whole personality', or some such thing.[24]

The second point has to do with the difficulty of God one day collecting the atoms, quarks, or whatever fundamental particles human bodies consist of. This may well be the oldest philosophical objection ever raised against the Christian notion of resurrection. Virtually every one of the Fathers who discussed resurrection tried to answer it, as did Aquinas. Such scenarios as this were suggested: What if a Christian dies at sea and his body is eaten by various fishes who then scatter to the seven seas? How can God later resurrect that body? Or what if another Christian is eaten by cannibals, so that the material of her body becomes the material of their bodies? And suppose God later wants to raise all of them from the dead, cannibals and Christians alike. Who gets what particles? How does God decide?

The move made by virtually all of the Fathers in response to this objection is to appeal to omnipotence. You and I might not be able to locate and reconstitute the relevant atoms of someone's body, not surely after many years or even centuries have passed, but God can do this very thing. And as long as (1) the basic constituents of matter (for example, atoms) endure through time (as contemporary physical theory says they normally do); and (2) it is merely a matter of God locating and collecting the relevant constituents, I believe the Fathers were right. An omnipotent being could do that.

But with the cannibalism case and other imaginable cases where God must decide which constituent parts shared at different times by two (or even two thousand) separate persons go where, the puzzle is more serious. The problem does not seem insoluble, but much more needs to be said. Perhaps some constituent parts of human bodies are essential to those bodies and some are not. That is, perhaps God will only need to collect the essential parts of our bodies and use them, so to speak, as building blocks around which to reconstruct our new bodies. And perhaps omnipotence must accordingly guarantee that no essential part of one person's earthly body is ever a constituent part, or an essential constituent part, of someone else's body. If a cannibal eats an essential part of my body, God must ensure that that part never becomes an essential part of his body, and in his body can be replaced by another similar part on the day of resurrection. If these stipulations or ones like them are followed (for example, Augustine's idea that atoms will be raised in that human

---

[24] Gundry makes this point convincingly (see n. 5 above, pp. 429–38). See also Bruce Reichenbach, 'On Disembodied Resurrection Persons: A Reply', *Religious Studies*, 18/2 (1982), p. 227.

body in which they first appeared),[25] it still seems that the Fathers were correct—an omnipotent being will be able to raise us from the ground.

VII

Several philosophers have argued in recent years that the concept of disembodied existence is incoherent or at least that no disembodied thing can be identified with some previously existing human person. Antony Flew,[26] Bernard Williams,[27] D. Z. Phillips,[28] Terence Penelhum,[29] and John Perry,[30] among others, have jointly presented what might be called the standard arguments against survival of death in disembodied form. P. T. Geach[31] has similarly argued against the notion of *permanent* disembodied existence, though he supports something like the theory I am calling temporary disembodiment.

I am inclined to hold that the standard arguments have been successfully answered by defenders of disembodied existence;[32] that is, I believe the notion of survival of death (and even permanent survival of death) in disembodied form is intelligible and logically possible. Furthermore, one result of recent discussion of the puzzle cases in the area of personal identity is that many philosophers are now prepared to defend the notion that we can imagine cases where the memory criterion will suffice by itself. But since the arguments of Flew, Williams, Phillips, and Penelhum have been discussed thoroughly in the journals, let me instead focus on the case that John Perry makes in his excellent little book, *A Dialogue on Personal Identity and Immortality.*

[25] Augustine (n. 12 above), LXXXVIII. See also Augustine, *City of God* (trans. Marcus Dods) (Grand Rapids, MI: Eerdmans, 1956), V, XXII, p. 20.

[26] See Flew's article on 'Immortality', in Paul Edwards (ed.), *The Encyclopedia of Philosophy* (New York: Macmillan, 1967), and the articles collected in part III of Flew's *The Presumption of Atheism and Other Essays* (London: Elek/Pemberton, 1976).

[27] See the articles collected in Bernard Williams, *Problems of the Self* (Cambridge: Cambridge University Press, 1973).

[28] D. Z. Phillips, *Death and Immortality* (New York: St. Martin's Press, 1970).

[29] Terence Penelhum, *Survival and Disembodied Existence* (New York: Humanities Press, 1970).

[30] John Perry, *A Dialogue on Personal Identity and Immortality* (Indianapolis, IN: Hackett, 1978).

[31] Geach (n. 14 above), pp. 17–29.

[32] Among others, see Richard L. Purtill, 'The Intelligibility of Disembodied Survival', *Christian Scholars Review*, V/1 (1975) and Paul Helm, 'A Theory of Disembodied Survival and Re-embodied Existence', *Religious Studies*, 14/1 (1978). See also Bruce Reichenbach, *Is Man the Phoenix? A Study of Immortality* (Washington, D.C.: University Press of America, 1983).

Perry seems, in this dialogue, to speak primarily through the character of Gretchen Weirob, a mortally injured but still lucid philosopher who does not believe in life after death. And Weirob seems to present three main arguments against the conceivability or possibility of survival of death. All are versions of arguments we find elsewhere in the literature, but the virtue of Perry's work is that they are presented with great clarity and forcefulness. Perry's first argument has to do with the soul and personal identity; the second concerns memory and personality identity; and the third is an argument about the possibility of duplication of persons.

The first argument says that immaterial and thus unobservable souls can have nothing to do with establishing personal identity. Personal identity does not consist in sameness of soul, for, if it did, we would never know who we are or who others are. Since souls are not observable, no thesis having to do with souls is testable (not even the thesis, 'My soul is me'). So I cannot know whether other human beings have souls, or even whether I have a soul; I have no idea whether I have one soul or several, or whether I have one soul for a time and then later a different soul. Thus there are no criteria for, and hence no way to make informed judgements about, 'the same soul'. It is possible simply on faith to assume criteria like, 'Same body, same soul,' or 'Same mental traits, same soul,' but, since we never independently observe souls, there is no way to test these principles, and thus no reason to think they hold. But since we evidently are able to make correct personal identity judgements about persons, it follows that personal identity has nothing to do with souls. Personal identity must instead be based upon bodily criteria. Thus, concludes Perry, no thesis about my survival of death via the survival of my soul is coherent.

Perry's second argument is that the memory criterion of personal identity, which those who believe in immortality must rely on, is never sufficient to establish personal identity. That is because of the obvious fact that memory is fallible. Without some further criterion, we will never be able to distinguish between apparent memories and genuine memories. In fact, believers in immortality are committed to a kind of circularity—they claim that genuine memory explains personal identity (that is, a purported Jones in the afterlife really is Jones just in case the purported Jones genuinely remembers from Jones' point of view events in Jones' past). But they also claim that identity marks the difference between apparent and genuine memories (the purported Jones can have genuine memories of events in Jones' past just in case the purported Jones is Jones—otherwise the memories are merely apparent memories). Thus again, the thesis that our souls survive death, which must rely on the memory criterion of personal identity, is incoherent.

Finally, Perry argues that the thesis of survival of death through immortality is rendered incoherent by the possibility of multiple qualitatively identical persons in the afterlife. Perry has Weirob say:

So either God, by creating a Heavenly person with a brain modeled after mine, does not really create someone identical with me but merely someone similar to me, or God is somehow limited to making only one such being. I can see no reason why, if there were a God, He should be so limited. So I take the first option. He would create someone similar to me, but not someone who would *be* me. Either your analysis of memory is wrong, and such a being does not, after all, remember what I am doing or saying, or memory is not sufficient for personal identity. Your theory has gone wrong somewhere, for it leads to absurdity.[33]

When told by one of the discussants that God may well refrain from creating multiple qualitatively identical persons in the afterlife and that if God does so refrain, the immortality thesis is coherent, Weirob replies that a new criterion has now been added. What suffices for personal identity (that is, what makes it such that the purported Jones in the afterlife is Jones) is not just memory, but rather memory plus lack of competition. An odd way for someone to be killed in the afterlife, she remarks—all God has to do is create, so to speak, an identical twin to Jones, and then *neither* is Jones; Jones has not survived death. Identity is now made oddly to depend on something entirely extrinsic to the person involved. Thus if memory does not secure personal identity where there are two or more Joneses in the afterlife, it does not secure personal identity at all. Weirob concludes it is best simply to abandon any thought of survival of death—when my body dies, I die.

Perry's first argument in favour of the notion that survival of death is incoherent is based on an element of truth, but is used by him in an erroneous way. Throughout his book he seems illicitly to jump back and forth between talk about *criteria of* personal identity and talk about *evidence for* personal identity. It is surely true that the soul is not observable, and that the presence or absence of a soul or of a certain soul is not something for which we can empirically test. What this shows is that the soul is not *evidence for* personal identity. We cannot, for example, prove that a given person really is our long-lost friend by proving that this person really has our long-lost friend's soul. But it still might be true that the soul is *a criterion of* personal identity. That is, it still might be the case that the person really is our long-lost friend just in case this person and our long-lost friend have the same soul. It might even be true to say that a purported Jones in the afterlife is the same person as the Jones who once lived on earth just in case the purported Jones has Jones' soul.

---

[33] Perry (n. 30 above), p. 3.

How we might test for or come to know this is another matter. Maybe only God knows for sure who has what soul. Maybe the rest of us will never know—not apart from divine revelation anyway—whether the purported Jones has Jones' soul. But it can still be true that if they have the same soul, they are two different temporal episodes of the same one person.

And the claim that personal identity consists in or amounts to the presence of the soul does not rule out the possibility of our making reliable personal identity judgements on other grounds, as Weirob seems to claim it does. Those who believe in the possibility of disembodied existence need not deny that there are other criteria of personal identity (for example, if the person before me has the same body as my long-lost friend, this person is my long-lost friend) and other ways of producing evidence in favour of or against personal identity claims.

Perry's second argument is also based on an element of truth—memory certainly is fallible; we do have to distinguish between apparent memories and genuine memories. So unless I have access to some infallible way of making this distinction, the mere fact that the purported Jones seems to remember events in Jones' life from Jones' point of view will not establish beyond conceivable doubt that the purported Jones is Jones (though it might count as evidence for it). As above, however, this does not rule out the possibility that memory is a criterion of personal identity—if the purported Jones does indeed remember events in Jones' life from Jones' point of view, then the purported Jones is Jones.

It is sometimes claimed that the memory criterion is parasitic on the bodily criterion and that use of the memory criterion never suffices by itself to establish identity. But such claims are surely false. We sometimes do make secure identity claims based on the memory criterion alone—for example, when we receive a typed letter from a friend. We hold that it is our friend who wrote the letter solely on the basis of memories and personality traits apparently had by the letter's author that seem to be memories and personality traits our friend has or ought to have. Of course if doubts were to arise we would try to verify or falsify the claim that our friend wrote the letter by the use of any evidence or criterion that might seem promising. We might check the letter for fingerprints; we might try to see if it was written on our friend's computer; we might even telephone our friend and ask. What this shows is not that we must always rely on the bodily criterion; there are equally cases where we might try to verify an identity claim originally based on the bodily criterion by means of memories. What it shows is that in cases of doubt we will look at both criteria.

But in the cases where the bodily criterion cannot be used—for example, during the interim period postulated in temporary disembodiment—can identity claims rationally be made? We are talking here not about criteria of personal identity but of making personal identity judgements. Can we ever be sure that a disembodied putative Stephen Davis is Stephen Davis? Given the notorious fallibility of memory, how can we, without recourse to the bodily criterion, distinguish between actual memories and purported memories? I would argue that secure identity claims can be made without use of the bodily criterion, and that this can be achieved in cases where there are very many apparent memories from very many different people that cohere together well. The context would make all the difference. If there are, say, one hundred disembodied souls all wondering whether everyone in fact is who he or she claims to be, it would be irrational to deny that their memories are genuine if they all fit together, confirm each other, and form a coherent picture. Doubt would still be conceivable, but not rational. The argument would be something like an inference to the best explanation. And something like this is precisely what defenders of temporary disembodiment claim will occur during the interim period.[34]

Critics of disembodied existence frequently appeal to the third or duplication argument, but one of the advantages of Perry's *Dialogue* is that he grasps the defender's proper reply to it, and then moves to deepen the objection. After the comment from Weirob quoted above, Perry has Dave Cohen, a former student of hers, say: 'But wait. Why can't Sam simply say that if God makes one such creature, she is you, while if he makes more, none of them is you? It's possible that he makes only one. So it's possible that you survive.' This seems to me the correct response. Of course immortality or resurrection would be difficult to believe in if there were, say, fourteen qualitatively identical Weirobs in the afterlife, each with equal apparent sincerity claiming to be Gretchen Weirob. But surely you can't refute a thesis, or the possible truth of a thesis, by imagining possible worlds where the thesis would be exceedingly hard to believe. Survival of death theses might well make good sense if in the afterlife there is never more than one person who claims to be some pre-mortem person. And since it is possible there will be but one Gretchen Weirob in the afterlife, survival of death is possible.

In response to this point Perry deepens the objection with Weirob's points about there now being two criteria of personal identity (memory and lack of competition) and about the oddness of God's ability to prevent someone's surviving death by creating a second qualitatively identical person. Both points seem to me correct but do not render the survival thesis incoherent or even, as Weirob claims, absurd. What exactly is wrong with saying (in the light of God's evident ability to create multiple qualitatively identical persons)

---

[34] I will not try to answer Perry's circularity charge noted above because I believe Parfit has decisively done so via the notion that he calls quasi-memories. See n. 21 above, pp. 220ff.

that memory plus lack of competition are criteria of personal identity? Lack of competition is a criterion that technically applies in this life as well as the next—we never bother to mention it, because it rarely occurs to us that God has the ability to create multiple qualitatively identical persons here as well. And I suppose it is odd that God can prevent someone's survival in the way envisioned, and that personal identity is here made in part to depend on something entirely extrinsic to the person. These facts are odd, but they do not seem to me to impugn the possibility of the survival thesis.

Christians strongly deny that there will be multiple qualitatively identical persons in the eschaton. They would hold, however, that God has the ability to create such persons, so it is perfectly fair for critics to ask: How would it affect your advocacy of resurrection if God were to exercise this power? Now I prefer to hold that the existence of multiple qualitatively identical Joneses in the eschaton would place far too great a strain on our concept of a human person for us to affirm that Jones has survived death. Our concept of a person, I believe, includes a notion of uniqueness—there is and can be only one instance of each 'person'. Uniqueness or 'lack of competition' (as Weirob puts it) is a criterion of personal identity. So I would argue at the very least that we would not know what to say if there were more than one Jones in the afterlife (perhaps our concept of a human person would have to be radically revised to include amoeba-like divisions, or something of the sort). More strongly, I would argue that Jones (the unique person we knew on earth) has not survived death.[35]

Accordingly, I see no serious difficulty for the survival thesis here. Although the view I am defending—temporary disembodiment—does not require the coherence of any notion of permanent disembodiment (like, for example, the doctrine known as immortality of the soul), I nevertheless would hold both to be coherent. As noted above, however, Geach argues strongly that only temporary disembodiment is coherent; what alone makes the problem of personal identity manageable as regards a disembodied person is its capacity or potential eventually to be reunited with a given body. Otherwise, he says, disembodied minds cannot be differentiated.[36] If Geach is right, only temporary disembodiment is coherent—immortality of the soul is not. Or at least, those who believe in the latter doctrine must add an item to their theory—perhaps something about a permanently disembodied soul permanently retaining the (forever unrealized) *capacity* to be reunited with a given body.

---

[35] The duplication objection is discussed further in chapter 7 of my *Risen Indeed* (n.1 above).
[36] Geach (n. 14 above), pp. 23–8.

VIII

As can be seen from the preceding discussion, I do not consider that what I have been calling the Patristic theory is normative for Christians today. The 'modern' theory seems to me an acceptable interpretation of resurrection. God's ability to raise us from the dead in the eschaton does not seem to depend on God's ability to locate and reunite the very particles of which our bodies once consisted. Nevertheless, the Patristic theory also constitutes an acceptable understanding of resurrection for Christians. The standard objections to it are answerable, and the most natural exegesis of 1 Corinthians 15: 35–50 supports it. Furthermore, respect for Christian tradition must (or so I would argue) grant great weight to views held by virtually all the Fathers of the church unless there is serious reason to depart from what they say. It seems to me quite possible that God will one day raise us from the dead in the very way that the Fathers and Aquinas suggest.

My overall conclusion is that the theory of resurrection I have been considering (which can be interpreted in either the Patristic or the 'modern' way) is a viable notion for Christians. Temporary disembodiment seems eminently defensible, both philosophically and theologically. I do not claim it is the only viable option for Christian belief about life after death; I do claim it is an acceptable way for Christians to understand those words from the Apostles' Creed that say, 'I believe in ... the resurrection of the body.'

Much contemporary philosophy tends, in its understanding of human nature, in a functionalist or materialist direction. No believer in temporary disembodiment can embrace philosophical materialism, but such believers can have great sympathy with any view which says that a disembodied person would hardly be a human person, not surely in the full sense of the word. They too embrace the notion that a disembodied person is only a minimal person, a mere shadow of a true human person—not completely unlike a person who is horribly disabled from birth or from some accident, but who continues to live.

Such Christians will accordingly embrace the notion that full and true and complete human life is bodily life. That is why they look forward to 'the resurrection of the body'. As Pseudo-Justin says,[37] 'In the resurrection the flesh shall rise entire. For if on earth He healed the sickness of the flesh, and made the body whole, much more will He do this in the resurrection, so that the flesh shall rise perfect and entire.'[38]

[37] Roberts and Donaldson (n. 4 above), p. 295.
[38] I would like to thank John Hick, Jim Hanink, Jerry Irish, Kai Nielsen, and Linda Zagzebski for their helpful and incisive comments on earlier versions of this chapter.

Part IV

How to Do Theology? Theological Method

15

Scripture, Tradition, and Theological Authority

I

How should Christians decide what they are to believe?[1] What constraints limit a person who wants to think Christianly on some topic? What criteria can Christians use in determining what they should believe? What are the proper sources of religious authority to which they should look?

On these questions Catholics and Protestants typically disagree. Protestants classically recognize but one source of religious authority, namely, Scripture; Catholics classically recognize two sources of religious authority, namely, Scripture and Tradition. Fortunately, most Catholics and Protestants are united on several nearby points. First, they agree that Christianity is a revealed religion, that is, it is not a religion devised by human wisdom or created by human initiative; instead they hold that it is based on the initiative of God, who in an act of sovereign grace reveals God and God's will to human beings. Secondly, they agree that there is a received and authoritative content to Christian belief; both are opposed to any relativism or individualism in which 'anything goes'; you cannot simply think up any idea and call it Christian. Thirdly, they agree—almost but not quite completely—on what constitutes the Bible or sacred Scripture.

In this chapter I will discuss the sources of religious authority for Christians. I hope to arrive at an acceptable position on the questions with which we began. Although a Protestant myself, I confess to having difficulties with the notion of 'Scripture alone', at least as that motto is often interpreted. I also believe in an important normative role for Tradition in determining the beliefs of Christians. But in the end there is a sense in which I do want to affirm 'Scripture alone', To work out that sense, especially in the light of Tradition, is the central aim of this chapter.

---

[1] In this chapter I will limit myself to the problem of determining Christian beliefs rather than behaviour or action.

I should state—what ought to be clear by now—that I am a Christian of a theologically conservative persuasion. My view of biblical authority is fairly robust.[2] In this chapter I will make no proposals that are relevant to people who either in theory or in practice recognize little theological authority in the Bible. Nor will I deal in any systematic way with the role of reason or experience in formulating religious beliefs. It is also worth noting that the problem I am considering is one that is internal to Christian theology; it is, as we might say, an intramural debate between Catholics and Protestants. Thus I will not raise the question of the relationship between Christianity and the other religions of the world.

My method is as follows: in Section II I will state in more detail what the two mottoes 'Scripture alone' and 'Scripture and Tradition' mean to Protestants and Catholics respectively. I shall avoid suggesting anything that purportedly constitutes *the* Protestant or *the* Catholic view; doubtless in these areas no such thing exists. But it is possible to suggest themes or tendencies that characterize the views of Catholics and Protestants, and I shall do so. Then in Section III I will consider in some detail various ways of understanding the phrase 'Scripture alone.' There are many things that it might mean, and I will look at the strengths and weaknesses of several possible definitions. I hope to arrive at an epistemologically and theologically adequate understanding of that phrase. In Section IV I will discuss the notion of 'Scripture alone' that I propose to defend in relation to Tradition. My aim is similarly to arrive at an understanding of Scripture and Tradition that is epistemologically and theologically adequate. Finally, in Section V, I will reply to four objections that might be raised against the theory that I am recommending.

II

For Protestants, the phrase 'Scripture alone' connotes a whole constellation of related propositions. First, it suggests that there is no source of religious truth that rivals Scripture in its authority, accuracy, and power to convince. As Martin Luther argued in the disputation with John Eck in 1519, popes and councils can and do err, so they cannot constitute theology's highest authority.[3] Classical Protestantism holds that Tradition is only a secondary

---

[2] See my *The Debate About the Bible: Inerrancy Versus Infallibility* (Philadelphia: Westminster Press, 1977).

[3] See Roland H. Bainton, *Here I Stand: A Life of Martin Luther* (New York: Mentor Books, 1950). Bainton quotes Luther as follows: 'Unless I am convinced by Scripture and plain reason— I do not accept the authority of Popes and councils, for they have contradicted each other—my conscience is captive to the word of God.'

authority and is a norm only to the degree that it agrees with Scripture. Secondly, Scripture is the final criterion of all religious claims; Scripture does not receive its authority from the Church, but rather from God, its author or inspirer;[4] accordingly, every theological, moral, or liturgical development in the Church must be tested by Scripture. Thirdly, Scripture is intrinsically clear and needs no infallible Church or Tradition to interpret it; every Christian, guided by the Spirit, is his or her own interpreter. Scripture is the judge of Tradition and sometimes stands over against it as a critique of beliefs or practices in the Church. Fourthly, nothing can be added to Scripture; after those reflected or recorded in Scripture, there are no further acts of divine special revelation that are normative for the entire Church; the Bible tells us all that is necessary for our salvation.

Before turning directly to Catholicism, it will be helpful to distinguish among five different meanings of the word 'Tradition' in theology. (1) *Tradition as the Gospel*. Tradition sometimes means the essential Christian message or Gospel itself; in this sense, of course, the Bible is Tradition, or at least an aspect of it or witness to it. (2) *Tradition as 'passing on'*. Tradition can refer to the transmission or 'passing on' process whereby Tradition in the first sense (or perhaps other senses listed below) is communicated to other groups or to later generations of believers. (3) *Tradition as unwritten teachings*. To the extent that Catholics appeal to Tradition apart from Scripture as a source or norm of religious truth, Tradition in Catholic theology is said to have its ground in teachings of Christ that were passed on orally in the Church, rather than being written down in the Bible.[5] (4) *Tradition as diversity*. Tradition sometimes refers to the diversity of creeds, liturgies, theologies, and practices in the various Churches (as in such expressions as 'the Pentecostal tradition' or 'the Lutheran tradition'). (5) *Tradition as authority*. For Catholics, Tradition refers pre-eminently (though not entirely) to decisions of Church councils and *ex cathedra* pronouncements of the pope, with emphasis placed on the Holy Spirit's gracious guidance of the Church as it attends to Scripture and to the first and third senses of tradition.

---

[4] Thus the Scots Confession, XIX: 'Those who say the Scriptures have no other authority save that which they have received from the Kirk are blasphemous against God and injurious to the true Kirk.' And the Westminster Confession of Faith, I: 4: 'The authority of the Holy Scripture, for which it ought to be believed and obeyed, dependeth not on the testimony of any man or church, but wholly upon God (who is truth itself), the author thereof; and therefore it is to be received because it is the word of God.' Both confessions are found in *The Book of Confessions* (New York: Office of the General Assembly of the Presbyterian Church (USA), 1983). See 3.19 and 6.004.

[5] Although there is some overlap between the two, the first and third senses are not identical; Jesus doubtless said many unwritten but orally circulated things that do not necessarily constitute aspects of the essential Christian message.

Catholics also typically distinguish between *traditio passiva*, which is the changeless treasury or deposit of faith that is passed on from generation to generation (and is roughly equivalent to the first definition above), and *traditio activa*, which is the constantly changing beliefs and practices of the Church as new insights from Scripture and from the *traditio passiva* are reached and elaborated (and is roughly equivalent to the fourth).[6]

On the relation between Scripture and Tradition, let me distinguish between two Catholic views, what I shall call the older theory and the revisionist theory. Found in the writings of the Counter-Reformation theologians and in most catechisms and dogmatic textbooks from the Council of Trent (1545–63) until roughly the time of Vatican II, the older theory recognizes two function-ally equal sources of religious truth: Scripture and Tradition. Referring to the teachings of Christ and the Apostles, the Council of Trent declared: 'This truth and teaching are contained in written books and in the unwritten traditions that the apostles received from Christ himself or that were handed on . . . from the apostles under the inspiration of the Holy Spirit, and so have come down to us.'[7]

According to this theory, Scripture is inferior to the Church, and for two reasons: first, Scripture itself is functionally insufficient, that is, it needs authoritative interpretation by the Church's magisterium;[8] secondly, the canonization of Scripture was an act of the Church. Moreover, in practice, 'older' Catholics hold that divine revelation is materially divided—some of it is located in Scripture and some in Tradition. So Scripture is also materially insufficient; at points Tradition must supplement it. Thus Tradition has occasionally been appealed to by Catholics as the authoritative source of dogmas not found in Scripture. For example, in the 1950 promulgation of the dogma of the assumption of the Blessed Virgin Mary no scriptural support for it was cited (although such support was claimed); the promul-gation applied instead to the consensus of the Church.[9]

The older theory is no longer in vogue in Catholic theological circles (except for very conservative ones). The revisionist view (of people like

[6] There is another related use of the word 'Tradition' in theology that will not concern us in this chapter. Certain pieces of historical information not found in Scripture but passed on to us from the early Church—e.g. the claim that the apostle Peter died by upside-down crucifixion—are attributed to 'Tradition'.

[7] See John Clarkson, S.J., et al. (eds.), *The Church Teaches: Documents of the Church in English Translation* (St. Louis: B. Herder Book Co., 1955), p. 45.

[8] Thus Gustave Weigel: 'If there is no objective decisive norm for the understanding of scripture, then every reader in all sincerity will get a different message out of it....The [Protestant] biblical test for belief, then, is not an effective device for the validity of belief.' Gustave Weigel, S.J., and R. M. Brown, *An American Dialogue* (Garden City, NY: Anchor Books, 1960), p. 208.

[9] *The Church Teaches* (n. 7 above), p. 213.

Josef Geiselmann,[10] George Tavard,[11] and Karl Rahner[12]) dominates recent
Catholic thought. Revisionists still hold (1) that Scripture and Tradition
constitute two sources of religious truth; (2) that Scripture is a creation of
the Church; and (3) that Scripture needs authoritative interpretation by the
Church. But revisionists do not subordinate Scripture to Tradition. The
material insufficiency of Scripture is no longer affirmed; rather, what is
stressed is the unity of Scripture and Tradition.

Revisionists also propose a new interpretation of Trent. It is pointed out
that between 8 February and 8 April, 1546, the Council debated whether to
accept the following wording: 'the truths ... are contained partly in Scripture
and partly in the unwritten traditions.' That wording was defeated in favour of
the formulation cited above (where religious truth is found in 'written books
and in the unwritten traditions'). That is, even at Trent (so revisionists claim),
the idea was rejected that revelation is materially divided, that there are two
sources of separate religious truths. Indeed, the Council left dogmatically
undefined the question of how Scripture and Tradition are related; individual
theologians could work on the question in freedom.[13]

What revisionists suggest instead is that either explicitly or by implication
Scripture contains all revealed truth and that, materially, Scripture takes
priority. (Thus Vatican II affirmed the unity of Scripture and Tradition, but
not the material insufficiency of Scripture.)[14] Accordingly, the role of Tradition is not to add new content to revelation, but rather to interpret Scripture.
As Geiselmann says: 'It is out of the question that Holy Scripture should give
us only fragments of the gospel of Jesus Christ, the rest being given to us by
Tradition. On the contrary, there are good reasons for assuming that the
apostolic kerygma recorded in Holy Scripture announces to us the whole

---

[10] Josef R. Geiselmann, 'Scripture, Tradition, and the Church: An Ecumenical Problem', in
D. Callahan, H. Oberman, and D. O'Hanlon, S.J. (eds.), *Christianity Divided* (New York: Sheed
and Ward, 1961).

[11] George H. Tavard, *Holy Writ or Holy Church* (New York: Harper and Brothers, 1959).

[12] For an excellent summary of his views, see Rahner's own article on 'Scripture and
Tradition', in Karl Rahner (ed.), *Encyclopedia of Theology: The Concise Sacramentum Mundi*
(New York: The Seabury Press, 1975). See also his *Foundations of Christian Faith* (New York:
Crossroad Publishing Co., 1984) (hereinafter *Foundations*), pp. 369–88.

[13] This is the argument of Geiselmann (n. 10 above). See pp. 43–8. See also R. C. Sproul, '*Sola
Scriptura*: Crucial to Evangelicalism', in J. M. Boice (ed.), *The Foundation of Biblical Authority*
(Grand Rapids, MI: Zondervans Publishing House, 1978) (hereinafter '*Sola Scriptura*'), p. 108.

[14] Walter M. Abbott, S.J. (ed.), *The Documents of Vatican II* (New York: Guild Press, 1966),
pp. 111–28. See also Rahner, 'Scripture and Tradition' (n. 12 above), pp. 1550–1: 'It may
therefore be held that the only task of post-biblical tradition is to transmit the Scriptures as
such, to interpret them, and to explicate their implications. In other words ... tradition func-
tions at all times by listening to Scripture, subject always to Scripture as the critical norm which
is universally necessary to distinguish "divine" tradition, the transmission of revelation in
Christ, from human traditions.'

mystery of Jesus Christ.'[15] Catholic doctrine is said to develop under the guidance of the Holy Spirit, as the Church works to unfold the implications of Scripture and Tradition. It is the function of the magisterium, or church teaching office, authoritatively to interpret Scripture and Tradition and to decide what Catholic teaching is.

One clear evidence of the strength of revisionism in current Catholic theology is the fact that few Catholic theologians any longer appeal to pure Tradition (i.e. apart from Scripture) to support their propositions. And this is doubtless for good reason, for the older theory faces the serious difficulty of verifying claims about what is actually contained in 'Tradition as unwritten teachings'.[16]

III

Let me now turn in a more detailed way to the 'Scripture alone' motto of Protestantism. I will consider the strengths and weaknesses of four possible definitions, hoping to arrive at an interpretation that can be defended. I begin with what I take to be the strongest interpretation that has been suggested.

1. *Scripture is our only source of religious truth.* In other words, in matters of religion, truth is found only in Scripture; others religious sources contain only falsehoods, or perhaps truths mixed with falsehoods. Moreover, nothing can be added to the religious truths contained in Scripture. Thus the Second Helvetic Confession of 1566 says, 'And in this Holy Scripture, the universal church of Christ has the most complete exposition of all that pertains to a saving faith, and also to the framing of a life acceptable to God; and in this respect it is expressly commanded by God that nothing be either added to or taken from the same.'[17]

---

[15] Geiselmann, 'Scripture, Tradition, and the Church' (n. 10 above), p. 58.

[16] Thus Karl Rahner, 'Scripture and Tradition' (n. 12 above): 'As regards the dogmas which theologians thought had to be derived from pure "tradition," as not being even implicitly in scripture, there is in fact no other early attestation, historically verifiable, which could show that they derive from apostolic tradition.' See also John K. S. Reid (a Protestant), who says, 'The fact is that there is no evidence for the survival of an independent oral unwritten tradition after the Scriptures have appeared and begun to circulate. While the apostles live, oral and written tradition operate side by side. Once the apostles have disappeared from the scene, the sole normative and authoritative tradition is Scripture.' *The Authority of Scripture* (London: Methuen and Co., 1957), p. 141.

[17] Chapter I. See *Book of Confessions* (n. 4 above), 5.002. See also the much more pointed statement of Heinrich Heppe: 'The only source and norm of all Christian knowledge is the Holy Scripture,' cited in Sproul, '*Sola Scriptura*' (n. 13 above), p. 103.

But the claim that Scripture is the only source of religious truth seems too strong. The Protestant Reformers themselves insisted that some knowledge of God could be gained by contemplating God's works apart from Scripture. John Calvin, for example, following Paul's argument in Romans 1 and 2, claimed that knowledge of God is displayed for all to see in nature and the universe: 'Men cannot open their eyes without being compelled to see him. ... Upon his individual works he has engraved unmistakable marks of his glory, so clear and so prominent that even the unlettered and stupid folk cannot plead the excuse of ignorance.'[18]

But quite apart from the Reformers and natural theology, it seems unacceptable for Christians to hold that the Bible is our only source of religious truth. Many people come to believe religious truths through other sources than the Bible. Indeed, I first came to believe that God exists not through the Bible (I am quite sure that I believed in God before I could read or even knew that there was such a thing as the Bible), but doubtless through the influence of my parents. Now it might be argued that *their* belief in the existence of God, or the beliefs of their parents (or *somebody's* beliefs), had Scripture as its ultimate ground, or something of the sort. But that is a different matter from claiming that the only source of religious truth is the Bible. That is too strong a claim. My parents were for me a source of religious truth.

2. *Scripture is our only salvifically sufficient source of religious truth.* In other words, it is not here denied that religious truth is available in extrabiblical sources; the claim is that the Bible alone contains those truths that can save us. The Westminster Confession of Faith of 1643 makes this point explicitly:

Although the light of nature and the works of creation and providence do so far manifest the goodness, wisdom, and power of God as to leave men inexcusable, yet they are not sufficient to give that knowledge of God and of his will which is necessary to salvation; therefore it pleased the Lord, at sundry times, and in diverse manners, to reveal himself ... and afterwards ... to commit the same wholly unto writing.[19]

But the difficulty is that many people have apparently been saved in Christian terms, that is, have been converted and baptized, quite apart from any exposure to the Bible. Several figures in the Bible itself—for example, the good thief on the cross (Luke 23: 43), the Philippian jailer (Acts 16: 25–34)—were

---

[18] John Calvin, *The Institutes of the Christian Religion* (ed. John T. McNeil; trans. Ford Lewis Battles), 2 vols. (Philadelphia: Westminster Press, 1960) (hereinafter *Institutes*) I, V, 1.

[19] *Book of Confessions* (n. 4 above), I: I (6.001). See also I: 6 (6.006): 'The whole counsel of God, concerning all things necessary for his own glory, man's salvation, faith, and life, is either expressly set down in Scripture, or by good and necessary consequences may be deduced from Scripture: unto which nothing at any time is to be added, whether by new revelations of the Spirit or traditions of men.'

said to have been saved without their ever having read the Bible. Obviously, the book that Christians call the Bible did not then exist. So the Bible cannot be our only source of saving truth; presumably the good thief and the Philippian jailer made use of other sources of truth than the Bible in finding their saving faith.

No Christian will deny that the Bible is a source of religious truth. Indeed, most Christians will insist that the Bible is the source of saving religious truth, the source par excellence. But the upshot thus far is that the 'Scripture alone' motto of Protestantism ought not be interpreted as affirming that the Bible is the only source of religious truth, or even as the only salvifically sufficient source of religious truth.

3. *Scripture is our only sure norm or guide to truth in matters of religion.* Here the focus shifts from Scripture as a source to Scripture as a criterion or rule. In other words, truth in religion or even religious knowledge might come from the Bible or from elsewhere; but only the Bible can stand as a sure test for approval or rejection of religious claims. Thus the Geneva Confession of 1536 says, 'We affirm that we desire to follow Scripture alone as a rule of faith and religion, without mixing with it any other things which might be devised by the opinion of men apart from the word of God.'[20]

Again, the vast majority of Christians will surely want to grant a large role to Scripture as a theological criterion. Scripture, properly interpreted, is indeed our primary criterion or test for theological truth. But Scripture cannot be our only norm or guide to truth in matters of religion. There are three reasons for this claim. First (a point where the Catholic critique of 'Scripture alone' hits the mark), if Scripture is our only criterion of religious truth, how do we know what Scripture is? Scripture itself does not establish which writings count as Scripture; establishing the canon of Scripture was an act of the Church (guided—so most Christians believe—by the Holy Spirit). Now Protestants usually claim that the church, through the 'inner witness of the Holy Spirit', *recognized* (rather than established) what books were scriptural. I agree with that claim. But even if it is true, this 'recognition' was still an act of the Church (guided by the Holy Spirit).

Moreover, Scripture itself does not clear up corruptions that have appeared in the text of Scripture; establishing the proper text of Scripture is an act of the scholarly community. There must, then, be religious norms or criteria other than Scripture, namely those that establish what counts as Scripture.

---

[20] Cited in Sproul, '*Sola Scriptura*' (n. 13 above), p. 105. See also the Second Helvetic Confession, II (*Book of Confessions* (n. 4 above), 5.013): 'Therefore we do not admit any other judge than God himself, who proclaims by the Holy Scriptures what is true, what is false, what is to be followed, or what is to be avoided.'

Of course, it may accordingly be argued that interpretation 3 of 'Scripture alone' is to be construed as claiming that once it is canonically and textually established, Scripture is our only rule or criterion of religious truth.

This leads directly to what I see as the second difficulty (also often raised by Catholics) faced by interpretation 3: how do we decide how Scripture is to be interpreted? What we call the Bible is a series of ancient texts, written in ancient languages, arising out of a variety of historical and cultural settings (perhaps covering some 1500 years of history), composed in many literary genres, and containing all sorts of differences and tensions. The Bible does not interpret itself (although there is a role in hermeneutics for the notion that 'Scripture interprets Scripture'). Even if we say—as classical Protestantism does—that all Christians, under the guidance of the Spirit, are free to interpret Scripture as they best can, this concession does not solve the problem of how Scripture alone can be a theological criterion: for Christians notoriously disagree in interpreting Scripture. Whose interpretation is to count as the norm of theological truth? There must, then, be religious norms or criteria other than Scripture, namely those that establish how Scripture is to be interpreted.

It is not my intention to deny the Reformation notion of the perspicuity of Scripture. The basic message of Scripture is indeed clear; even children and uneducated folk can understand it. Christians can be and are guided by the Holy Spirit in interpreting Scripture; one does not have to be a Scripture scholar or theologian to be touched and moved by the message of the Bible. But no matter how clear the Bible is, it is still an ancient and in many places difficult document that needs (as does any document) interpretation. Thus Hendrikus Berkhof pointedly asks why, in doing theology, we should not just hand out Bibles and await the result. He says:

The Bible is, however, a library full of heights, depths, and plains, with central and marginal sections. To gain entrance and to find its central perspective the reader needs help. The community of believers must offer an introduction, a guide, a summary. This is a daring undertaking which nevertheless, in reliance on the guidance of the Spirit, must be undertaken, and which through the centuries has been undertaken. For evidence we can point to the liturgical creeds of the early church, the confessions of the Reformation, the catechisms, and all kinds of other ecclesiastical statements. Tradition has the never-ending task of preparing explanatory summaries and abridgements of Scripture.[21]

Of course, it may accordingly be argued that interpretation 3 is to be construed as claiming that once it is canonically and textually established *and*

---

[21] Hendrikus Berkhof, *Christian Faith: An Introduction to the Study of the Faith* (trans. Sierd Woudstra) (Grand Rapids, MI: Eerdmans, 1979), p. 93.

interpreted correctly, Scripture is our only rule or criterion of religious truth. I do not wish to dispute this claim. My worry is that the idea of arriving at the correct and agreed-upon interpretation of Scripture is at best an eschatological hope. There is little promise of it here and now.

Moreover, a third difficulty for interpretation 3 remains: if Scripture is our only norm of religious truth, that is, if no other criterion of what is true or false is allowed, then it seems we shall be led into irrational beliefs in those cases of discrepant or apparently discrepant accounts of the same events in Scripture. For if the Bible is our only authority for what to believe in religious matters, then in such cases we must believe both accounts. For example, we must believe both that King David numbered the people because God caused him to do so (see 1 Sam. 24: 1–2) and that King David numbered the people because Satan induced him to do so (see 1 Chr. 21: 1–2). Or again, we must believe both that the cock crowed once when Peter betrayed Jesus (as in Matt. 26: 34, 74–5; Luke 22: 34, 60–1; and John 13: 38; 18: 27) and that it crowed twice (as in Mark 14: 72).

Now certainly either God or the devil was the original cause of David's idea of having a census; it is not sensible to say that it was both. (To say that God, by means of Satan, caused David to do it is to say that God caused David to do it.) And the statement, ' The total number of times that the cock crowed is both one and two,' is contradictory. If we then believe one account but not the other, or even if we try somehow to harmonize them, we are appealing to another criterion of religious truth beside Scripture alone, namely (in this case), reason's sense of what is logically possible. There must, then, be religious norms or criteria other than Scripture.

4. *Scripture is our source of religious truth above all other sources, our norm or guide to religious truth above all other norms or guides.* In other words, all other sources of theological truth are subordinate to Scripture and are to be tested by Scripture. Scripture has the last word or final say; when it is correctly interpreted, whatever Scripture says, goes. Thus the Westminster Confession says: 'The Supreme Judge, by whom all controversies of religion are to be determined, and all decrees of councils, opinions of ancient writers, doctrines of men, and private spirits, are to be examined, and in whose sentence we are to rest, can be no other but the Holy Spirit speaking in the Scriptures.'[22]

There may be other criteria of religious truth than Scripture—for example, reason, experience, Tradition—but Scripture is the highest criterion, the final

[22] Chapter I: 10. *Book of Confessions* (n. 4 above), 6.010. See also I: 8 (6.008): 'The Old Testament in Hebrew...and the New Testament in Greek...being immediately inspired by God, and by his singular care and providence kept pure in all ages, are therefore authentical; so as in all controversies of religion the Church is finally to appeal unto them.' See also the Second Helvetic Confession, II.

test, the sure norm, the infallible rule of what we are to believe in religion. I shall not dispute this last interpretation; indeed, I am in substantial agreement with this way of understanding the 'Scripture alone' motto of Protestantism. But what about Tradition? Where does it now stand?

IV

Johann Adam Möhler, one of the founders of the Catholic Tübingen School of theology of the nineteenth century, suggested an interesting argument against the 'Scripture alone' standard of Protestantism. Citing evidence from the history of the Church, he argued that it leads to heresy and schism:

Ages passed by, and with them the ancient sects; new times arose, bringing along with them new schisms in the Church. The formal principles of all these productions of egotism were the same; all asserted that Holy Writ, abstracted from tradition and from the Church, is at once the sole source of religious truth, and the sole standard of its knowledge for the individual. This formal principle, common to all parties separated from the Church—to the Gnostic of the second century, and the Albigensian and Vaudois of the twelfth, to the Sabellian of the third, the Arian of the fourth, and the Nestorian of the fifth century—this principle, we say, led to the most contradictory belief. What indeed can be more opposite to each other than Gnosticism and Pelagianism, than Sabellianism and Arianism? The very circumstance, indeed, that one and the same formal principle can be applied to every possible mode of belief; or rather that this belief, however contradictory it may be in itself, can still make use of that formal principle, should alone convince every one that grievous errors must here lie concealed, and that between the individual and the Bible a mediating principle is wanting.[23]

This mediating principle, of course, is Church Tradition.

Much of what Möhler says here is misleading. But at one point, his argument is convincing. He was wrong that 'Scripture alone' must lead to heresy and schism, but he was right that it has done so. It has done so partly because Scripture needs to be interpreted and so can be misinterpreted. I shall consider how Tradition can help interpret Scripture presently. Let me note, however, that I reject the idea (as do many Catholics) that Tradition alone can justify a belief or doctrine, that Scripture is materially insufficient. There are no

---

[23] This quotation is from his 1832 book *Symbolism*, excerpted in Peter Hodgson and Robert King (eds.), *Readings in Christian Theology* (Philadelphia: Fortress Press, 1985) (hereinafter *Readings*), p. 39.

revealed and normative truths that are found in Tradition but not in Scripture. Furthermore, it is the constant temptation of any Christian community to make its Tradition superior to Scripture, to shackle the Bible. This is a temptation that must be resisted.

How can Tradition help to interpret Scripture? Anyone who reads Scripture does so in the context of a personal and social history, and usually in the context of a religious community and its history. The message of Scripture can only be mediated to us in those contexts. But Christians believe that Scripture is the Church's book, and that the Church has a peculiar responsibility for interpreting Scripture to its people. It even has a kind of ownership over scriptural interpretation. There is no proper interpretation of the Bible apart from the Church and its history and traditions.

All who do serious exegesis or theology must be knowledgeable about the history of Christian thought and practice. Such learning creates a barrier against private or eccentric interpretations of Scripture. Now, perhaps any well-intentioned interpretation should be listened to, but the Church must have criteria for rejecting those that are unacceptable. These criteria constitute its protection against the misuse of the Bible typically found, as Möhler correctly argues, in cults and heresies. We cannot appeal to the Bible alone as a guarantor of religious truth—as if we could leap back to the first century and ignore all intervening history and tradition. Whether acknowledged or not, every Church or denomination has its own tradition of interpreting the Bible. Even the strongest advocates of 'Scripture alone' tend to interpret the Bible through creeds or confessions that form for them a hermeneutical canon. It is absurd to imagine that Christians today, armed with no knowledge of Christian history but only with their Bibles, could arrive at orthodox theories of, say, the Incarnation or the Trinity. Christians need to read their Bibles in the light of the work of Athanasius and Augustine and Aquinas and Luther and Calvin and Newman and Barth and the scores of others who together constitute the theological tradition.

There has been an alarming de-emphasis on theological tradition at both ends of the Protestant theological spectrum in recent years. Some on the right wing pay insufficient attention to the great creeds and thinkers of the past because they believe that the Bible is all that we need. The idea seems to be that Christians today should simply read the Bible, believe what it teaches, and they will end up holding all the orthodox tenets. To pay much attention to Athanasius or Aquinas or Luther is deemed unnecessary. Some on the left wing pay little attention to the great creeds and thinkers of the past because they find them outmoded and irrelevant to a new age. We need a new paradigm for Christian theology, they say, freed from pre-scientific theories or patriarchal attitudes or Western imperialism. To pay much attention to Augustine or Calvin or Newman is not deemed particularly interesting.[24]

The impotence of the 'Bible alone' approach is exposed by Henry Hamann:

The tendency in fundamentalism is to see in all the many assertions many individual truths, all of which are valuable in themselves, all of them important, all of them the revealed Word of God, and (sometimes) all of them of more or less equal importance as the Word of God. The Bible becomes something like a codex of legal paragraphs, each of which must be upheld for fear of losing the whole. From the fundamentalistic point of view, for instance, it is impossible to prove a Seventh Day Adventist missionary wrong who insists on keeping the Sabbath and who refuses to allow his New Guinea converts to eat pork, in spite of the fact that pork is about the only animal protein a New Guinean villager is ever likely to eat.[25]

Tradition, then, provides a way for us to argue against the hermeneutic that Hamann criticizes. It shows us that certain texts in scripture take priority over others, and it helps us interpret them. It also helps us to grasp—as we see pre-eminently with the doctrine of the Trinity—that a doctrine or idea can be deemed normative for Christians despite the absence of any clear proof texts specifically teaching it.

Nevertheless, the importance of Scripture (and the interpretation of 'Scripture alone' that I affirm) is that all theology, including Tradition, must be under the authority of Scripture. The authority of Tradition depends on Scripture, and not vice versa. Tradition itself has often erred and has often been corrected by appeals to Scripture. Nor is the Bible theologically authoritative merely because the Church opts to deem it so.[26] It is authoritative because it is the written Word of God.[27]

It is frequently said that differences between Catholics and Protestants have narrowed considerably in recent years on the issues discussed in this chapter.

---

[24] I am reminded of a conversation I once had with a professor at a mainstream denominational seminary in another state. He was interested in the theology of film, taught courses in the area, and wrote articles about it. (Nothing I say here should be taken as disparaging this fine field.) In fact, it emerged that this was about all that he taught at his institution. When I asked who was the systematic theologian at his institution—innocently thinking that somebody there had to teach students about the great theologians and doctrines of the Christian faith—he said, 'That would be me.'

[25] *The Bible: Between Fundamentalism and Philosophy* (Minneapolis: Augsburgh Publishing Company, 1980), p. 63.

[26] Thus John Calvin: 'Thus, while the church receives and gives its seal of approval to the Scriptures, it does not render authentic what is otherwise doubtful or controversial.' *Institutes* (n. 18 above), I, VII, 2.

[27] I thus oppose the view of Charles Kelsey, who argues that the authority of Scripture lies not in its content, but in the end to which it is used, i.e. used by God in empowering new human identities. This is certainly one of the proper uses of Scripture, but in my opinion Scripture's authority lies elsewhere. See Kelsey's selection, 'The Function of Scripture', in Hodgson and King, *Readings* (n. 23 above), p. 55.

Indeed, Rahner says, 'The "Scripture alone" of the Reformation is no longer a doctrine which distinguishes and separates the churches.'[28] This statement is almost, but not quite, true. Fortunately, many of the differences that existed on these issues in the sixteenth century, or even early in the twentieth century, no longer loom. But one important difference remains. The issue is not whether Scripture needs to be interpreted—despite their insistence on the sufficiency of Scripture, Protestants agree that it does—but whether it needs to be *authoritatively* interpreted. Protestants hold, contrary to Catholics, that Scripture needs no normative or binding interpreter other than the Holy Spirit.[29] All who interpret Scripture, including those in Church teaching offices, stand under Scripture. Their teachings are revisable by appeal to Scripture.

Karl Barth stressed the Church's need for what he called a 'free Bible'. He argued that exegesis must be controlled neither by Church officials nor by historical-critical scholars. Rather, he said, 'Bible exegesis should rather be left open on all sides, not, as this demand was put by Liberalism, for the sake of free thinking, but for the sake of a free Bible.'[30] That is, Scripture must be free to criticize and revise Tradition, as it has often done. Notice, for example, the influence of the Letter to the Romans on various Christian thinkers and movements—of chapters 5–7 on Augustine's theory of original sin; of chapters 3 and 4 on Luther's theory of justification by faith; of chapters 9–11 on Calvin's theory of predestination and of God's sovereignty; of chapters 6 and 8 on Wesley's theory of 'grace abounding'; and of chapters 1 and 2 on Barth's theory of the righteousness of God.[31] Traditional interpretations of Scripture guide Christians as they read the Bible, and in some cases (e.g. doctrinal definitions accepted as normative) they do so authoritatively. But in the end, these interpretations possess only relative authority, standing as they do under the higher authority of Scripture itself. The Church can never impose a certain exegesis of the Bible on future Christians.

The fact that Christians need a higher religious authority than Tradition was recognized early in Church history and is shown by the Church's strenuous efforts to arrive at a canon of Scripture. There is no need for a canon if Tradition is the final authority. The early Church saw itself as drawing a line separating apostolic witness to the faith from all other witnesses; it implicitly

---

[28] *Foundations* (n. 12 above), p. 378.

[29] See Richard Bauckham, 'Tradition in Relation to Scripture', in Richard Bauckham and Benjamin Drewery (eds.), *Scripture, Tradition, and Reason* (Edinburgh: T. and T. Clark, 1988), pp. 123, 126.

[30] Karl Barth, *Church Dogmatics*, vol. I/1 (trans. G. T. Thomson) (Edinburgh: T. and T. Clark, 1960), p. 119.

[31] I attribute these points to Professor J. A. T. Robinson, who made them in his lectures on the Letter to the Romans that I attended in Cambridge in the spring of 1978.

said that all other authorities must be under the control of apostolic authority, made present and available through the inspired Scriptures. No later tradition, whether it originate with a bishop, saint, theologian, or even pope or council, can ever count equally with apostolic teaching. When the Church in its first few centuries amassed the various writings that we now call the New Testament, it was in effect separating those writings from all other writings and declaring them to have unique theological authority.

My view, then, is both that Tradition is necessary for interpreting Scripture and that Scripture takes priority over Tradition, because it is our highest source and norm of religious truth. Christians believe that ideally (i.e. except in those cases where the Church has erred) Scripture and Tradition ('tradition as diversity') agree. But in fact, the two never fully coincide, and that is why Scripture's role, whenever necessary, is to correct Tradition. Tradition guides the interpretation of Scripture but must never control it. Protestants can affirm the Catholic notion of the Spirit's gracious guidance of the Church in doctrinal matters. But the notion of human depravity, as well as a glance at the history of doctrine, convinces most Protestants that no human institution has been kept completely free from error. All such institutions, including the Church, must stand under the corrective authority of Scripture.

There will frequently be tension between Scripture and Tradition. That tension can be difficult, but it can also be healthy. When Christians set out to decide what they are to believe, the past gets a vote; Christian Tradition must be studied and taken seriously. But in the end Scripture must be free to say no to the past whenever necessary.

V

I will now briefly consider four objections that might be raised against the theory of religious authority that I am suggesting.

Objection 1: How do we decide precisely what Tradition teaches? How can the past 'get a vote' if it is not clear what 'the past' says? These are good questions, especially when directed towards Protestants who recognize no formal magisterium that authoritatively decides what Tradition is. It is obvious that there is a Christian Tradition, and it is equally obvious that there are few places where it speaks with one voice. Some Churches will recognize or emphasize some voices (e.g. Aquinas, Calvin, the Nicene Creed, the Westminster Confession, Vatican II, etc.) over others. The only answer to the questions that form Objection 1 is: good theology, performed prayerfully and (one hopes) illumined by the Spirit of God and producing good fruits in the practice of Christian discipleship. We must do historical theology and determine as best we can what the Christian Tradition is, in both its diversity and unity. Clearly not all Tradition is of equal value to us. Those places where Tradition is unified will be of special importance in determining what we are to believe today. For example, the Eastern Orthodox Churches place great weight on a criterion called 'the consensus of the Fathers', that is, the places where the great thinkers of the early Church agree. I too would honour this criterion, for it was the Fathers who set for us the Christian theological agenda and delineated for us the boundaries of orthodoxy.[32]

Objection 2: How can a book so diverse and unreliable as the Bible be taken as a guide? Here I am reflecting the views of those scholars who deny that there is a clear-cut doctrine of anything in the Bible, or who affirm that, even if there is, the Bible cannot plausibly be taken as a binding religious authority for us today. Some scholars hold that the historical-critical approach to the Bible has thoroughly discredited it as a source or norm of religious truth, and has revealed that it contains so many competing 'theologies' as to be either unbelievable as a source or unusable as a norm. Thus it seems impossible to hold to any strong version of 'Scripture alone.'

I shall not argue against such views of Scripture here. I will simply report that I follow a different path. In the book referred to in note 2 (a first and preliminary excursion into the area of biblical authority for me), I argued not that the Bible is inerrant, but rather that it is infallible. If 'inerrant' means completely errorless, I do not affirm that the Bible is inerrant; in the light of what we find on the pages of the Bible, any definition of 'inerrant' that has any hope of being a property of the Bible will be so convoluted and conditioned as to make the claim that the Bible is inerrant virtually unfalsifiable. But I can and do affirm that the Bible is 'infallible', where 'infallible' means 'does not mislead us in matters that are crucially relevant to Christian faith and practice'.

Difficulties accompany this affirmation, as well as my methodological presupposition that Christians affirm everything they take the Bible to be saying on any subject, unless there are compelling reasons not to do so. But I am still inclined to view biblical authority in roughly this way. The most obvious point is the vagueness of terms like 'crucially relevant' and 'compelling reasons'. But I take this imprecision as a strength rather than a flaw. People will obviously

---

[32] I am influenced here by the argument of Robert E. Webber in his helpful article, 'An Evangelical and Catholic Methodology', in Robert K. Johnson (ed.), *The Use of the Bible in Theology: Evangelical Options* (Atlanta: John Knox Press, 1985). I should add, however, the obvious point that 'the consensus of the Fathers' is not a binding criterion. We are not obliged to accept everything the early Fathers agree on, e.g. the Platonistic assumptions many of them make, and especially the sexism and anti-Judaism that we see in many of them. We should not follow the Fathers here because sexism and anti-Judaism can be shown, by convincing theological reasoning, to be contrary to Scripture and to the core of the Christian message.

differ about what matters are relevant to Christian faith and practice, and about what reasons are compelling, and it is up to the Christian community, in reliance on the Spirit, to settle such disputes as best it can.

The Bible contains discrepancies for which I am unable to find sensible or non-foolish harmonizations. It also reflects the cultural and historical limitations of its writers. But it is 'infallible' in that the heart or essence of what the Bible teaches, that is, its teaching that is relevant to Christian faith and practice, is not mistaken or misleading in any important sense. Such teachings are not merely ethical, spiritual, or theological teachings; many historical claims from the Bible are crucially relevant to Christian faith and practice and are, in my view, infallible. This infallibility is not always obvious or evident, especially to the eye of unbelief; but to the eye of faith as illumined by the Spirit of God, the Scriptures are 'the only infallible rule of faith and practice'.

Interestingly, some of the same scholars who devalue the religious authority of the Bible seem also to de-emphasize the normativity of Tradition and want to push in new theological directions. But if the Bible is not a religious authority, and if Tradition is also at best a tenuous norm for current Christian belief, then we are left with a Christian faith in which virtually 'anything goes'. I would find that result unacceptable. Indeed, my challenge to those who want to de-emphasize the theological authority of Scripture is this: How, on your view, do we avoid theological chaos in which 'anything goes'?

Objection 3: How can the Bible judge Tradition if the correct interpretation of Scripture depends on Tradition? In other words, if the Bible must be interpreted in terms of Tradition, how can Scripture be a norm over Tradition? This conundrum, suggested as a criticism of certain Protestant views by Avery Dulles, does indeed present a difficulty, but not an insurmountable one. What is wrong with saying that the Bible is to be interpreted in terms of Tradition (i.e. our current interpretations are to be guided by traditional interpretations), but that the Bible must always be free to overturn traditional interpretations and produce, like a paradigm shift, new ones? There would exist a nearly overwhelming problem if the position being defended were that Tradition always rules biblical interpretation. This, indeed, seems to be something like the position that Dulles himself advocates. He says, 'All exegesis is ultimately subject to the judgment of the magisterium, which can reject or approve a given interpretation in view of its divinely given mandate.'[33] But I instead agree with James Barr, who says: 'Biblical authority

---

[33] See Avery Dulles, 'Scripture: Recent Protestant and Catholic Views', in Donald K. McKim (ed.), *The Authoritative Word* (Grand Rapids, MI: Eerdmans, 1983), p. 248; cf. also pp. 250, 260. It should be pointed out, however, that although magisterium documents often cite Scripture, in practice the magisterium has rarely legislated as binding a particular interpretation of a particular scriptural text.

on Protestant terms...exists only where one is free, on the ground of
Scripture, to question, to adjust, and if necessary to abandon the prevailing
doctrinal traditions. Where this freedom does not exist, however much the
Bible is celebrated, its authority is in fact submitted to the power of a tradition
of doctrine and interpretation.'[34]

I recommend this fairly 'high' view of biblical authority because I believe
Scripture is the central way that the Spirit guides the Church. Reading a 'free'
Bible ought to be for the Church an adventure, a way in which we are allowed
to see God's ways of making all things new.[35] When the Church reads
Scripture with a believing heart, that is the pre-eminent way that God leads
it into the future.

Objection 4: How can we decide which aspects of 'Tradition as diversity' are
true, normative, and (if they originate from 'Tradition as unwritten teachings') revelatory? Surely some items that we inherit from 'Tradition as diversity' are false, perhaps even heretical, and certainly not normative for
Christians today. In other words, how do we distinguish between genuine
Tradition (a teaching that has been 'passed on' to us and that is normative for
us) from false, merely ecclesiastical Tradition?

The general answer is that we do exegesis and theology as best we can and
see where they fit. As I argued above, Scripture is the judge of Tradition. Some
theological issues are not directly discussed in the Bible, but exegesis of
various texts may help us to see whether the relevant theological proposals
are true or false; helpful or unhelpful; normative, allowed, or forbidden. If the
issue cannot be settled from Scripture, the next criterion to be considered is
the belief and practice of the early Christians. They were the first interpreters
of the New Testament, and they were the ones who were obliged, through fire
and controversy, to work out a consensus as to proper Christian teaching and
practice. What the Fathers of the first five centuries say does not have
scriptural authority; and as noted, some of what they say is unhelpful to us;
but the theological consensus that they hammered out nevertheless has a
degree of normativity for us today. Some items from 'Tradition as diversity'
will surely turn out to be normative; we shall decide that such items are
gracious gifts of divine guidance to today's Church.

A question might be asked at this point: Why are norms or standards
needed at all? That is, why is all this talk about criteria for acceptability in
Christian theology necessary? Standards are needed because Christians want

---

[34] James Barr, *Holy Scripture: Canon, Authority, Criticism* (Philadelphia: Westminster Press,
1983), pp. 31–2.

[35] Something very like this point seems to be the dream of chapter VI of Vatican II's
Constitution on Divine Revelation: a Church reading Scripture with a believing heart and
being shaped by it at every level of her life.

to know what to believe. Without some sort of guide or guarantor, there would be no control over what counts as Christian. There would exist a huge number of proposals for Christian belief—proposals checked only by the limitations of human desire and imagination. No one would have any idea what is Christian and what is not. Christian faith would deny nothing and thus affirm nothing.

The theory of religious authority that I have been suggesting in this chapter stands in opposition to other theories that seem to be alive and well these days. First, it is opposed to those theories which recognize no, or virtually no, limitations on what counts as acceptably Christian. Secondly, it is opposed to those whose central theological motivation is to update the Christian faith to bring it into conformity with current philosophical, scientific, or social scientific theory. Thirdly, it is opposed to those who in effect recognize a selective biblical authority—those, that is, who ignore the Bible where they find its teaching outmoded or distasteful, but affirm it and even cite it where it confirms their views. Fourthly, it is opposed to the older Catholic theory, where certain theological proposals that possess little or no biblical warrant can nevertheless be made binding on the faithful because of an appeal to tradition. Fifthly, it is opposed to the views of those Protestants who try to leap over nearly twenty centuries of Christian history and do theology only on the basis of proof texting from the Bible.

We began by discussing differences between Catholics and Protestants on the matter of religious authority. As we have seen, those differences have narrowed in recent years. What lingers is the Catholic insistence on, and the Protestant refusal to accept, the need for a teaching office that authoritatively interprets scripture for the Church. Despite that difference, my hope is that the proposal I am recommending can be affirmed by biblically oriented Catholics and Protestants alike.[36]

---

[36] I would like to thank John Cobb, Clark Pinnock, Alan Scholes, and Keith Ward for their helpful comments on an earlier draft of this chapter.

16

The Bible Is True

I

Suppose we wanted to capture part of our attitude towards the Bible via the sentence, 'The Bible is true.' What might we mean by this statement?

Let me begin with what I take to be three *desiderata* for a theory of 'the Bible is true,' that is, three things that such a theory must accomplish. First, such a theory must take note of our special human status as 'verbivores'.[1] Every living organism has certain needs that must be met in order for it to survive and thrive—food, shelter, a method of reproduction, and so on. But human beings are special among all the creatures in that we have an additional need, a need for words, particularly *words from God*. Thus in Deuteronomy 8: 3, Moses, speaking for God, says to the children of Israel, 'one does not live by bread alone, but by every word that comes from the mouth of the Lord'.[2] Secondly, such a theory must explain why Christians read the Bible as opposed to any other book. Why do we Christians hold the Bible to be unique among such classics as *The Iliad* or *The Koran* or *The Critique of Pure Reason*? Thirdly, such a theory must explain why Christians take the Bible to be normative or authoritative. Why is the Bible such that it is not only appropriate, but also mandatory for Christians to allow themselves to be formed as persons by it?

To tip my hand, I believe it will turn out that a strong factor in satisfying all three *desiderata* is the notion that in some important sense, *God speaks to us in the Bible*.

---

[1] I did not invent this term; so far as I know it was coined by Robert C. Roberts, 'Parameters of a Christian Psychology', in Robert C. Roberts (ed.), *Limning the Psyche: Explorations in Christian Psychology* (Grand Rapids, MI: Eerdmans, 1998).

[2] Notice also *Phaedo* 85d, where Plato has Simmias say: 'It is our duty to do one of two things, either to ascertain the facts, whether by seeking instruction or by personal discovery, or, if this is impossible, to select the best and most dependable theory which human intelligence can supply, and use it as a raft to ride the seas of life—that is, assuming that we cannot make our journey with greater confidence and security by the surer means of a divine revelation.' *The Collected Dialogues of Plato*, Edith Hamilton and Huntington Cairns (eds.) (New York: Pantheon Books, 1963), p. 68.

II

Now let us return to the statement, 'The Bible is true.' What might this statement mean? Well, for a philosopher this formulation presents some difficulties. Although we are well aware that there are several uses of the word *true*, philosophers normally think that the only sorts of things that can be true (or false) in the paradigmatic or realist sense of *true* are things like assertions, claims, statements, or propositions. This sense of *true* means 'having the truth-value true', that is, being in accord with what is the case. Thus Aquinas' justly famous claim that 'truth is the agreement between the idea and the thing.'[3]

Accordingly, rocks, trees, numbers, galaxies, quarks, and books (like the Bible) do not have truth-values and accordingly are neither true nor false. Of course if a given statement can be true, then surely a set of statements can be true, presumably if all the statements in the set are true. Thus we might speak of someone's testimony about a certain event being true, if all the statements made by the witness are true. Then perhaps even a book could be true if all the statements in it were true.

But this does not seem a helpful route to follow in trying to decide what we might mean by 'The Bible is true.' For one thing, to say that the Bible is true in *this* sense—all the statements in it are true—does not seem nearly enough to capture what orthodox Christians want to say about the Bible. To illustrate this point, imagine the following scenario: for a lark, I decide to write a book that contains nothing but true statements. It contains sentences whose truth I know by experience like, *Grass is green* and *San Francisco is north of Los Angeles*. It also contains mathematical or logical truths like, *7+5=12* and *All triangles have three sides*. It also contains true statements about the past like, *Lincoln was shot at Ford's Theatre* and *The Pirates were world champions in 1960*. Imagine that the book is three hundred pages long and consists of nothing but one true statement after another. Notice that we could call such a book 'true'. We might even call it 'inerrant'. But it would be a banal, pointless, virtually incoherent, religiously useless book—in other words, quite unlike the Bible.

Indeed, the Bible consists of far more than assertions. (I emphasize this point because those who hold conservative views of the Bible are sometimes caricatured as holding that the Bible consists only of a set of propositions.)

---

[3] *De Veritate*, 1, 3. See also William P. Alston's magisterial defence of realism on truth in his *A Realist Conception of Truth* (Ithaca, NY: Cornell University Press, 1996).

Everybody knows that the Bible contains all sorts of genres and linguistic elements—law codes, poetry, parables, songs, commands, questions, expressions of praise, exhortations, and many others—which seem incapable of being, in the paradigmatic sense, true (or false).

None of this is meant to deny the importance of there being true statements in the Bible. There are obviously many narrative sections in the Bible in which historical assertions are made; there are also many theological and moral assertions. Doubtless it is important that most or even all of these assertions be true. It does seem difficult to grasp how a book replete with false claims could be considered authoritative. Yet surely those Christians who want to express their attitude towards the Bible by the statement, 'The Bible is true,' must mean a great deal more than just, 'its assertions are all true'.

Of course the word *true* can be used in ways other than 'having the truth-value of true'. We sometimes use expressions like 'true to oneself', 'true blue', 'true north', 'true feelings', 'a true copy', and 'to come true', and such expressions seem not to have much to do with 'having the truth-value of true'. 'True' can mean things like loyal, sincere, trustworthy, having fidelity, giving helpful guidance, or proving accurate. And some of these usages are surely relevant to what we might mean by saying, 'The Bible is true.'

Still, I want to see whether we can make progress by sticking to something like the paradigmatic sense of true. Suppose we ask this question: What psychological attitude do we have towards assertions that we regard as true, statements such as

San Francisco is north of Los Angeles;
7 + 5 = 12;
My mother loves me;

and (if we are theists)

God exists?

And what psychological attitude do we have towards assertions that we regard as false? Part of the answer, as I suppose, is that with regard to statements which we take to be true, we commit ourselves to believe them (together with all propositions entailed by them), we accept their propositional content, we 'trust' them, we 'lay ourselves open' to them. That is, we allow our noetic structures and behaviour to be influenced by them. And we do not do any of that with statements that we regard as false.

Let me suggest that we mean something like this when we say, 'The Bible is true.' We mean that our attitude towards the Bible is such that we believe what it says, we trust it, we lay ourselves open to it. We allow our noetic structures and beliefs to be influenced by it. Such an attitude will include, but not by any means be limited to, accepting the truth (in the paradigmatic sense) of the assertions that we find in it. (What they are, obviously, will have to be interpreted.[4]) It also means taking questions in the Bible ('Should we sin the more that grace may abound?') as legitimate and probing questions addressed to us. It also means taking biblical exhortations ('Give thanks to the Lord, for He is good') as exhortations addressed to us that we must heed. It also means taking poetic sections from the Bible ('We are his people, and the sheep of his pasture') as powerful affective expressions of the way reality is.

If we take the Bible to be true, we trust it to guide our lives. We allow our lives to be influenced by it. We intend to listen where it speaks. We consider it normative. We look to it for comfort, encouragement, challenge, warning, guidance, and instruction. In short, we *submit* to the Bible. We place ourselves under its theological authority.

III

Notice that some of the things I believe to be true I believe more firmly than other things that I believe to be true. I believe the statement, *The dean of the faculty respects me*. After all, he and I have been friends and colleagues for years, and I think I know him and his opinions quite well. But I believe the statement, *My mother loves me*, much more firmly than I believe the statement, *The dean of the faculty respects me*. Now in fact I believe both statements; but I believe the one with a great deal more certainty than I believe the other. It will be much more difficult to convince me that my mother does not love me than to convince me that the dean does not respect me. Much more powerful defeaters will be needed.

Clearly, those who hold the Bible to be true in the sense we are considering—they trust it, listen to it, look to it, submit to it, consider it normative—believe the Bible to be true with a great deal of firmness or certainty. Their belief in it is not tentative. Their submission to it is not halting. The Bible is allowed to guide their lives, influence their behaviour, and form them as persons.

---

[4] Indeed, I should point out that in the present chapter I am abstracting away from all hermeneutical questions in a quite arbitrary way. I know well that judgements about the truth of an utterance—whatever notion of 'true' is envisaged—are parasitical on judgements about the meaning of that utterance. Although I do make a few hermeneutical comments in Section VI of the chapter, for the most part I am simply assuming that we know what various biblical utterances mean.

In one sense, this submission is quite voluntary. It is not as if somebody coerces Christians to submit to the Bible, like the way most people obey rather quickly when a policeman says, 'Put your hands behind your back!' But I do not want to give the impression that those folk who in some strong sense submit their lives to the Bible do so randomly or capriciously. It is not like flipping a coin or choosing one flavour of ice cream over another. It is not like one person saying to another, 'My holy book speaks to me but, somehow, yours leaves me cold.' Those who place themselves under the authority of the Bible do so precisely because they hold that the Bible is true. That is, they hold that the Bible is objectively authoritative. It is, as we might say, *worth* submitting to.

If I submit myself to the Bible, it has authority over me in one sense only because I take it as authoritative. (Note that it is possible for people to reject a given law—say, the law forbidding exceeding the speed limit—to regard it as having no authority over them.) But in another sense I take the Bible as authoritative over my life precisely because I regard it as objectively authoritative. (Similarly, even those who choose to ignore it are under the authority of the law forbidding speeding and can be ticketed and fined.) The Bible is objectively authoritative, then, in that people *ought* to accept its authority, whether they do so or not.

In philosophy we say that every assertion or proposition has certain truth-conditions, that is, the conditions that must be satisfied in order for the proposition to be true. The truth condition of 'San Francisco is north of Los Angeles' is simply San Francisco's being located north of Los Angeles. Maybe the linguistic utterances from the Bible that are not assertions (e.g. 'Honour your father and your mother', 'Pray without ceasing', 'Praise God in the sanctuary') also have (in an extended sense) truth conditions. Reality must be in a certain way, and not in other ways, in order for them to be objectively authoritative. It must be the case that it is morally obligatory to honour one's mother and father; it must be the case that God commands us to pray without ceasing; it must be the case that God deserves our praise and that the sanctuary is an appropriate place to express that praise.

IV

There is nothing in the theory of 'the Bible is true' that I am espousing that requires a defender of it to reject the theory known as biblical inerrancy. This is the theory that every properly interpreted assertion in the Bible—whether about theology, history, science, logic, sociology, geography, mathematics, or whatever—is true. Still, it is also perfectly possible to hold the theory without embracing inerrancy. To some folk, that indeed might amount to one of its strong points. Early in my career, I wrote a brief critique of biblical inerrancy in favour of what I called biblical infallibility.[5] Although I still embrace its overall approach, I now regard some of the arguments used in that book as unconvincing, and I am now familiar with more nuanced ways of understanding the concept of 'biblical inerrancy' than were available in 1977. Still, my basic problem with the doctrine of inerrancy, and the reason that I do not defend it, is that commitment to it seems to drive interpreters of the Bible at various points towards forced, awkward, and even ridiculous interpretations of the Bible in order to make problematic assertions come out true.

It is clear that a great many people do *not* regard the Bible as true in the sense just explained. (1) Some of them—atheists, religious sceptics, enemies of Christianity—explicitly disbelieve what the Bible says, or at least much of it. Certainly they reject the crucial bits. (2) Others in effect suspend judgement on what the Bible says until there exists a scholarly consensus. This latter seems to be the attitude of many Scripture scholars today; they consider the Bible to be no different in principle from any other ancient text—Plato's *Republic*, for example, or the Gospel of Peter. They believe what the Bible says only if historical-critical research substantiates what it says. In other words, their view is that it is a wholly human book, like any other book. (3) Many other people today have no idea what the Bible says, and don't seem to care. Anybody who has taught undergraduates in secular colleges or universities in recent years is familiar with such attitudes.

Those who hold that the Bible is true are in effect distancing themselves from all such views as this. They approach the Bible with a hermeneutic of trust. As Anselm said, 'I am sure that, if I say anything which plainly opposes the Holy Scriptures, it is false; and if I am aware of it, I will no longer hold it.'[6] Such folk take Scripture to be the source of religious truth above all other sources, the norm or guide to religious truth above all other norms or guides. As discussed in Chapter 15, the idea is that all sources of religious truth are subordinate to Scripture and should be tested by Scripture; Scripture has the last word or final say; whatever Scripture says (when it is correctly interpreted) goes. I take it that this is what the Westminster Divines were affirming when they wrote: 'The Supreme Judge, by whom all controversies of religion are to be determined, and all decrees of councils, opinions of ancient writers,

---

[5] Stephen T. Davis, *The Debate About the Bible: Inerrancy Versus Infallibility* (Philadelphia: Westminster Press, 1977).

[6] Anselm, *St Anselm: Basic Writings* (trans. S. N. Deane) (La Salle, IL: Open Court, 1962), p. 220 (*Cur Deus Homo*, I, xviii).

doctrines of men, and private spirits, are to be examined, and in whose sentence we are to rest, can be no other but the Holy Spirit speaking to us in the Scriptures.'[7]

The opinion that the Bible is true depends on a certain view of its character, so to speak. It is not just that *we take it* to be Scripture (although we do). (As if we could also take *Thus Spoke Zarathustra* or *The History of the Synoptic Tradition* to be Scripture if we wanted.) It depends on the view that the Bible is a special book, a book unlike all other books, a book in which in some strong sense *God speaks to us*. Those who hold that the Bible is true can never regard it as merely or simply a human product like the *Iliad* or the *Phaedo* or the works of Nietzsche or the works of Bultmann. They hold it to be the word of God. Despite their status as cultural or academic classics, God does not speak to us in the words of the *Iliad* or the *Phaedo* or *Thus Spoke Zarathustra* or *The History of the Synoptic Tradition*. Or at least, God does not do so in anything like the same way.

V

In this connection, it will be helpful to refer to the writings of two of my fellow philosophers who have recently written about the status of the Bible. Explaining what troubles me about their arguments—especially what they say about the various discrepancies and difficulties in the Bible—will help me develop my own view.

The first is Nicholas Wolterstorff's excellent and ground-breaking book, *Divine Discourse*.[8] I fully accept and presuppose much of his argument; the item I will mention constitutes the only major point where I demur. Wolterstorff wants to argue that the Bible constitutes, or can constitute, divinely appropriated human discourse (or that it can be rational to hold that it does). That is, in the Bible, God can be taken as speaking. Wolterstorff notes that there are discrepancies between different narrative accounts of the same events in the Bible. But since God cannot speak falsehoods, how can this be?[9]

One of Wolterstorff's strategies for dealing with this problem amounts to a suggestion that the Gospels can be seen as analogous in genre and intent to Simon Schama's book, *Dead Certainties*.[10] (I have not read this book and so

---

[7] The Westminster Confession, I, 10. See *The Constitution of the Presbyterian Church (USA)*, Part I (New York: Office of the General Assembly, 1983), 6.010.

[8] Nicholas Wolterstorff, *Divine Discourse: Philosophical Reflections on the Claim that God Speaks* (Cambridge: Cambridge University Press, 1995) (hereinafter *Divine Discourse*).

[9] *Divine Discourse* (n. 8 above), pp. 252–60.

[10] New York: Knopf, 1991.

will accept at face value everything Wolterstorff says about it.) Ostensibly a book of history—it is about the controversial death of British General James Wolfe in the battle of the Plains of Abraham near Quebec in 1759—it is actually a work of what might be called imaginative history. Schama offers several quite different and even mutually inconsistent perspectives on this event, some from wholly invented characters writing wholly imaginary accounts, but which are plausible given one way or another of looking at the actual historical evidence. Schama also makes invented, but again (according to him) plausible, claims about the inner thoughts and feelings of Wolfe at various points. Wolterstorff sees Schama as asserting not actuality but *plausibility*. In effect, Schama says that things might well have actually gone this way in 1759. Schama never suggests anything *contrary* to the available historical evidence, but he goes far beyond it at points. He offers something like artistic portraits of Wolfe.

Wolterstorff wants to suggest that the Gospels are something like this. They are *portraits* of Jesus. In places they suggest not what certainly happened, but what might well have happened. The evangelists agree on 'the identity and significance of Jesus', but they disagree, for example, on whether the cleansing of the temple occurred early or late in his ministry. In places the evangelists were claiming to report what actually happened, but in other places they were only claiming 'illuminating plausibility' for their accounts. This viewpoint, Wolterstorff suggests, explains why the early church, aware as it was of the discrepancies, was so little troubled by them.

Now perhaps I have misunderstood Wolterstorff, but, if I have caught his meaning, I cannot agree. I too am aware of, and to a certain extent troubled by, the discrepancies between various narrative accounts of the same events in the Gospels. But if the Gospels are viewed as similar in genre and intent to *Dead Certainties*, then I think that the Christian church faces an immense problem. Unlike Schama's book, almost nothing in the Gospels as individual texts makes us want to think of them in this way. (I say 'almost nothing' because I agree with Wolterstorff, Eusebius, and Papias that Mark was not much concerned with issues of chronology.) Indeed, I think it is about as clear as anything can be that the evangelists believed, and wanted us to believe, that *this is how things actually happened*. That is, they all seem to be making factual assertions about what Jesus said and did and what happened to him.

I suspect Wolterstorff feels moved to make his proposal not by looking at the individual Gospels or their pericopes, but by comparing the several Gospels. And of course there is nothing in the world wrong with doing that. But perhaps there are other and better responses to the discrepancies than this. One is to deny that they are there, that is, to try to harmonize the discrepant accounts. In the case of many of the discrepancies, I believe this enterprise can succeed. Another response is to deny that the discrepancies much matter, since none (or none of the discrepancies that cannot sensibly be harmonized) seems to affect any crucial area of Christian belief or practice. Another response is to affirm inspiration, infallibility, and maybe even inerrancy, but arrive at a way of understanding those notions that is not undermined by occasional discrepancies. Another response is to claim that the discrepant accounts mean different things, which is what Philo did with discrepancies in the Hebrew Bible, and certain Church Fathers of the Alexandrian school did with discrepancies in the New Testament.

I said that adopting Wolterstorff's proposal would present the Christian church with a big problem: his proposal requires a hermeneutic for distinguishing between those texts in the Gospels that are meant as actualities and those that are meant only as likely plausibilities. But surely radical interpreters of Christianity—to whom I, for one, want to give little ground—will claim, for example, that the resurrection of Jesus from the dead was not meant to be an actuality. How will we refute such people? I suppose by showing them that the chapters at the end of the Gospels simply do not read that way; the evangelists thought of themselves as reporting sober fact. But surely that is true of just about everything we find in the Gospels (again, with the possible exception of Mark's chronology, Luke's grouping together of episodes with similar themes, etc.). I do not see how the job can possibly be done.

Rather than offering a useful interpretive tool, Wolterstorff's distinction between those accounts that the Gospel writers intended as true and those that they intended only as plausible seems almost impossible to apply to individual texts. How will we be able to tell where a given text fits? Moreover, the distinction can easily play into the hands of those interpreters who deny the literal truth of points that I at least consider crucial to the Christian faith, for example, that Jesus really was God incarnate and really was raised from the dead.

VI

The second scholar whose views I want to explore briefly is Mark Wallace.[11] So far as I can tell, he and I are miles apart on several important philosophical issues. I am much more inclined to embrace realist notions of truth than he is.

---

[11] See his essay, 'The Rule of Love and the Testimony of the Spirit in Contemporary Biblical Hermeneutics', in A. Wiercinski (ed.), *Between the Human and the Divine: Philosophical and Theological Hermeneutics* (Toronto: The Hermeneutic Press, 2002), pp. 280–91.

And although I would never want to de-emphasize the interaction between the Bible and its reader, I see the act of interpretation primarily (not entirely) as the discovery of something that is there in the text, rather than the creation of something new.

To put the point crudely, Wallace is concerned that there is both good content and bad content in the Bible. The good content is constituted, presumably, by the teachings and example of Jesus and the high ethical teachings found elsewhere. The bad content consists of passages that picture God as capricious, taunting, violent, malicious, malevolent, and vengeful, for example, the stories of Job, the Passover, and Ananias and Sapphira. Wallace's sensitivity to this issue leads him to see 'truth' in relation to the Bible as something that is made or created (by the Bible *and* its reader), rather than something that is found in the Bible.

Wallace says: 'biblical truth is the ethical performance of what the Spirit's interior testimony is prompting the reader to do in the light of her encounter with the scriptural texts.' And: 'biblical truth consists in performing the Spirit's promptings to love God and neighbor.'[12] So it seems that according to Wallace, biblical truth exists (presumably exists *for* someone; let's eschew originality and call her Jones) when four conditions are satisfied:

(1) Jones reads biblical passage P.
(2) In reading P, Jones is prompted by the Spirit to do action A.
(3) Jones does A.

and

(4) A is ethical, that is, loving towards God and neighbour.

Notice that the definition of biblical truth that Wallace provides is not a characteristic of the Bible, but rather a result of interaction between the Bible and a reader. Accordingly, my central difficulty with Wallace's proposal is that it does little to preserve any sense of the Bible's uniqueness.[13] Notice that almost any other piece of writing can be true in this sense, for example, *The Republic* or *War and Peace* or the *Bhagavad-Gita*. As such, Wallace's notion is insufficient to preserve what I think the Christian community wants to say about the Bible. His definition of biblical truth leads him to a larger, but closely related, notion of theological truth. In theology, he says, a belief is true 'just insofar as it fosters a life of benevolent regard toward the "other" '. A theological judgement is valid, he says, 'whenever it enables compassionate engagement with the world in a manner that is enriching and transformative for self and other.'[14]

---

12 Wallace, ibid., pp. 283, 284.
13 Indeed, he denies that the Bible is unique in this regard. See p. 286.
14 Wallace (n. 11 above), p. 286.

Here I only want to point out the real possibility that false theological statements (false in the sense of not corresponding to reality) might be true in Wallace's sense. Indeed, two logically inconsistent theological statements might *both* be true in his sense. Indeed, it is entirely possible that some true (true in a realist sense) theological statements may be false in Wallace's sense because they never foster 'a life of benevolent regard for the "other"'. Take some abstruse and long-forgotten statement from, say, eighteenth-century Reformed theological anthropology, for example, *Adam was the federal head of the human race.* Now assuming, as I do, that the statement is coherent, it follows that either it or its negation must be true in a realist sense. But it is quite possible that the true one—whichever it is—has never fostered any particular ethical attitude in anyone and thus is false in Wallace's sense.

In short, even if we adopt Wallace's notion of truth and apply it to some biblical text, it is still an open question whether the claims made in that text (if any are made) are true in Aquinas' sense. In many cases, this is a question in which many Christians will be deeply interested. For example, I genuinely want to know whether Jesus' claim, 'I and the Father are one' (John 10: 30), is true in a realist sense, quite apart from whether the Spirit has ever used that text to induce anyone to act lovingly and non-violently.

What are the other available options for someone who wants to claim that the Bible is true but is as aware of and sensitive to the troubling texts in the Bible as Wallace is? Well, it seems that there are lots of possibilities. One has been mentioned already: (1) harmonization. Here the effort would be to try to show that the character of God as apparently presented in the 'bad content' texts is not really God's character; when properly understood, the bad content passages do not teach that God is violent or malevolent. Here are some others: (2) Two of my Claremont colleagues, John Roth and Frederick Sontag, simply grasp the nettle and embrace both the bad content and the good content; their view is that God is both evil and good; God has a demonic side.[15] (3) One might try to find a theological principle that allows one to subordinate the bad content to the good content, for example, some such notion as 'the progress of revelation'. The idea would be to argue that the bad content texts represent a lower or more primitive understanding of the character of God than the good content texts do; the good content texts accordingly are allowed to criticize and supersede the bad content texts. (4) One might engage in what might be called theodicy—argue that the bad content texts are not as bad as they look, argue that God was morally justified in killing Ananais and Sapphira, for example.

---

[15] See their respective essays in Stephen T. Davis, *Encountering Evil: Live Options in Theodicy,* 2nd edn. (Louisville KY: Westminster John Knox Press, 2001).

Most of us who are committed to some version of what Wallace calls 'the infallibilist model' engage in all three of (1), (3), and (4). We try to find a hermeneutic that allows us to emphasize the good content over the bad content (which in his own way is of course exactly what Wallace does). And I see no reason for his worry that people who follow that path will fail to listen to the voices of suffering people or fail to allow them space to struggle with God or express their anger with God.

The central point is that not all texts of Scripture are of equal theological importance or relevance to various religious issues. I believe that virtually all Christians—even those who believe in biblical inerrancy—at least implicitly recognize this fact. If proper hermeneutical principles simply entailed lining up various biblical texts and treating them all equally, there would be no sense in talking (as Wallace apparently does want to talk, given his notion of the 'supreme christological plot line' of the Bible[16]) about a unified theme or message in the Bible. More ominously, if we were simply to line up texts and treat them equally, then the Bible could fairly be said to teach things like the legitimacy of slavery, or the subordination of women, or the need to sacrifice animals at the altar of the temple in Jerusalem. Christians have always sensed that certain texts take hermeneutical and theological priority over others.

It is clear that there are places in the Bible where the Christian community has found it difficult to hear God's voice. What is needed, in the light of the murkier nooks and crannies of the Bible (among which I would include the divine command to slaughter all the Canaanites (Deut. 2: 31–5; 3: 1–8; 7: 2; Josh. 6: 15–21; 8: 25–6; 11: 12), as well as the conclusion of Psalm 137) is what I will call *theological exegesis*. This is exegesis in the light of what the early Fathers called 'the rule of faith', that is, the church's view of the overall message of the Bible. Any given text must be interpreted in the light of the Christian community's vision of the witness of the whole of Scripture. Of course such a vision must always be viewed as fallible and amendable by future exegesis. Otherwise, the Spirit's freedom to speak to us in Scripture is curtailed. Moreover, theological exegesis ought never amount to simply disregarding the clear and obvious sense of a text in favour of a reading that we like better. Nevertheless, that overall vision of the macro-meaning of Scripture can be seen as a canon against which to test various interpretations of various texts. In the end, Christians need to be open hearers of the word, expecting that even the less promising parts of Scripture will have something or even much to say to us.

Three hermeneutical principles help clarify (although they do not exhaust) what I mean by theological exegesis: (1) the Old Testament should be interpreted

---

[16] Wallace (n. 11 above), p. 289.

in terms of the New Testament; (2) obscure passages are to be interpreted in terms of clear passages; and (3) everything is to be interpreted christologically. Many of the psalms, the four Gospels, and certain of the Pauline epistles (especially Romans and Galatians) are taken to be hermeneutically founda-tional.[17] Are they 'more inspired' or 'more truly God's word' or even 'more true' than others texts? No. The claim is merely that they are more hermen-eutically foundational to Christian belief and practice. Nor is this an attempt to find something helpful or authoritative in a book which one largely rejects. I disassociate myself entirely from any view such as that (nor am I accusing Wallace of holding it).

I take it that Wallace thinks that some such procedure is acceptable as long as it is recognized that it is merely an act of interpretation, rather than a discovery of the Bible's 'original meaning'. Well, certainly discovering what one takes to be the rule of faith is an act of interpretation, one that in the early church involved strenuous effort, vigorous debate, and careful discernment. However, I do not accept the idea that any proposal as to the macro-meaning of the Bible must be imposed on the Bible. It is entirely possible that it is really there.

My own Reformed theological tradition has always placed great emphasis on the sovereignty of God. One aspect of this sovereignty is that, throughout redemptive history, God makes choices that are free, even (so far as we can tell) arbitrary. God chooses Abel over Cain, Jacob over Esau, the children of Israel over the Moabites or the Philistines. And God is not required to account for those choices. My fear is that the parts of the Bible that are *true* in Wallace's sense reveal a God that is too tame, too much under our control, not sovereign, not mysterious or 'wholly other'.

Moreover, as I argued in Chapter 12, the biblical concept of the wrath of God—an embarrassment to theology in the last century or more—is in my view an essential part of the Bible's message. Indeed, I would go so far as to say that the wrath of God is *our only hope* as human beings. (The grace of God is also our only hope, but that is another story.) Once when I was a child, the foreman of our family's ranch was showing me how to do something with a horse. He said, 'There are lots of wrong ways, and one right way, to do this.' I proceeded to do it in one of the wrong ways, and I had to pay for it with bruises, cuts, hurt pride, and some colourful language directed my way by the foreman. Similarly, there are lots of wrong ways and one right way to live a life, and if we live our lives in any of the wrong ways, we will have to pay for it. The wrath of God shows us clearly that it matters deeply how we live our lives.

---

[17] Several of these points were suggested years ago by E. J. Carnell in his *The Case for Orthodox Theology* (Philadelphia: Westminster Press, 1959), pp. 51–65.

Our contemporary folk wisdom is not true, for example, when it says that any way you choose to live your life is okay, as long as you are sincere and try hard not to hurt anybody.

My conclusion, then, is that we need a stronger notion of biblical truth than Wallace provides. We need to know why anybody should read the Bible as opposed to any other book. One has the feeling that Wallace thinks the Bible is a worthwhile book to read because we can take good things from it, or (more fairly) because the Spirit can use it to make us act compassionately. But can't the Spirit use other books too? Again, why then the Bible?

In the end, I need to admit quite frankly that not all biblical problems can be solved, at least not by me. No matter what moves are made or arguments are presented, we will still be deeply troubled by some of them. In places, our belief that the Bible is true will amount to an act of *trust*. There are texts that we will have to believe are true despite our inability to show that or how they are true. We may just have to *wait*. And perhaps that is not altogether a bad thing. As it says in one of the most troubling books in the Bible, 'It is good that one should wait quietly for the salvation of the Lord' (Lam. 3: 26).[18]

VII

I now return to my main argument. Discerning readers will have noticed that I have been saying two quite different things about the sentence, 'The Bible is true.' Let us summarize the trusting attitude towards the Bible that I have been discussing (submitting to it, considering it authoritative, holding it higher than all other sources or norms of religious truth, etc.) as 'submitting'. Now it is clear that I have been claiming both (1) when I say the sentence 'The Bible is true' I *mean* 'I submit to the Bible'; and (2) my belief that 'The Bible is true' *is caused by* my belief that 'The Bible is worthy of submission' (which ultimately is caused by the Holy Spirit). There is no inconsistency here. I am indeed saying both.

I have said little in this chapter until now about *how one comes to know or believe* that 'The Bible is true.' Some theologians have claimed that the Bible is 'self-authenticating'. I would prefer not to use this expression, primarily

---

[18] There is a version of biblical inerrancy, which I cannot honestly say that I hold, but which I have no desire whatsoever to oppose. We might call it 'eschatological inerrancy'. This would be the claim that in the eschaton, when we will 'know as we are known' (1 Cor. 13: 12), it will turn out that, properly interpreted, every claim that the Bible makes will turn out to have been true. But this theory is a long way from the here-and-now inerrancy that is widely defended in some circles today.

because, following Calvin, I think some things *do* authenticate the words of Scripture. Calvin lists, as I would, the testimony of the church (which he mentions but de-emphasizes), the admirable properties of the Bible itself, and (far and away the most important) the inward testimony of the Holy Spirit.[19] As noted in Chapter 1, I would define the inward testimony as that influence of the Holy Spirit on the minds of believers that they reach certainty that in the Bible God speaks to them and that, accordingly, they must submit to it.

What do we mean when we say, 'The Bible is true'? It is vital to note that the question is in the first person plural—'What do *we* mean?' I take the 'we' in this question to range over the whole of the Christian community, past and present. That is why I want to stress a notion of the Bible's truth that honours what the Fathers call the rule of faith, one that includes as many Christians as possible and as much of the past as possible. There are, of course, Christians with whom I cannot agree at various points, nor am I recommending slavish obedience to the Christian past.

But as a Christian academic who has spent his entire full-time career at secular institutions of higher education, this 'we' has always been important and comforting to me. In the face of opposition or, more often, indifference from my colleagues, I frequently need to remind myself that my affirmation that the Bible is true is not an affirmation made by me alone. It is an affirmation made by the community of which I am part, the Christian community, the Body of Christ.

We human beings are 'verbivores'. We live by the words that come from the mouth of the Lord. I have not committed myself to any particular theory of Biblical inspiration in this chapter. I have, however, affirmed that in the Bible we hear God speaking to us. We read the Scriptures expecting them to give us light and life. As we hear God's voice in them, the proper response is submission, wonder, and praise. That God speaks to us in the Bible and that we faithfully submit to those words is what we mean when we say 'The Bible is true.'[20]

---

[19] See *The Institutes of the Christian Religion* (Philadelphia: Westminster Press, 1960), I, vii, 4; III, ii, 34.

[20] I would like to thank Dale Tuggy for his helpful comments on an earlier version of this chapter.

Select Bibliography

Abbott, Walter M., S.J. (ed.), *The Documents of Vatican II* (New York: Guild Press, 1966).

Abraham, William, *Divine Revelation and the Limits of Historical Criticism* (New York: Oxford University Press, 1982).

Allen, Charlotte, *The Human Christ: The Search for the Historical Jesus* (New York: Free Press, 1998).

Alston, William P., *A Realist Conception of Truth* (Ithaca, NY: Cornell University Press, 1996).

Anglin, W. S., *Free Will and Christian Faith* (Oxford: Oxford University Press, 1990).

Anselm, *St. Anselm: Basic Writings* (trans. S. N. Deane) (LaSalle, IL: Open Court, 1962).

—— *Why God Became Man (Cur Deus Homo)*, (ed. and trans. Jasper Hopkins and Herbert Richardson) (Lewiston, NY: The Edwin Mellen Press, n.d.).

Aquinas, Thomas, *Summa Contra Gentiles* (trans. Charles J. O'Neil) Book IV (Notre Dame, IN: Notre Dame University Press, 1975).

—— *Summa Theologica* (trans. Fathers of the English Dominican Province) (New York: Benzinger Brothers, Inc., 1947).

Athenagoras, *Embassy for Christians and the Resurrection of the Dead* (trans. Joseph H. Crehan, S.J.) (London: Longmans, Green, 1956).

Augustine, *The Enchiridion on Faith, Hope, and Love* (trans. Henry Paolucci) (Chicago: Henry Regnery, 1961).

—— *On Christian Doctrine* (trans. D.W. Robertson, Jr.) (Indianapolis, IN: Bobbs-Merrill, 1958).

—— *The City of God* (trans. Marcus Dods) (Grand Rapids, MI: Eerdmans, 1956).

Badham, Paul, 'The Meaning of the Resurrection of Jesus', in P. Avis (ed.), *The Resurrection of Jesus Christ* (London: Dartman, Longman and Todd, 1993).

Baillie, Donald, *God Was in Christ: An Essay on Incarnation and Atonement* (New York: Scribner's, 1948).

Baillie, John, *The Idea of Revelation in Recent Thought* (New York: Columbia University Press, 1956).

Barnes, Michel Rene, 'Rereading Augustine's Theology of the Trinity', in Stephen T. Davis, Daniel Kendall, S.J., and Gerald O'Collins, S.J., *The Trinity: An Interdisciplinary Symposium on the Trinity* (Oxford: Oxford University Press, 1999).

Barr, James, 'Abba, Father', *Theology*, 91/741 (1988).

—— 'Abba Isn't "Daddy"', *Journal of Theological Studies*, 39 (1988).

—— *Holy Scripture: Canon, Authority, Criticism* (Philadelphia: Westminster Press, 1983).

Barth, Karl, *Church Dogmatics*, vol. I: 1 (trans. G. T. Thomson) (Edinburgh: T. and T. Clark, 1960).

Bauckham, Richard, 'Jesus, Worship of', *The Anchor Bible Dictionary*, vol. iii (New York: Doubleday, 1992).

—— 'Tradition in Relation to Scripture', in Richard Bauckham and Benjamin Drewery (eds.), *Scripture, Tradition, and Reason* (Edinburgh: T. and T. Clark, 1988).

Berkhof, Hendrikus, *Christian Faith: An Introduction to the Study of the Faith* (trans. Sierd Woudstra) (Grand Rapids, MI: Eerdmans, 1979).

Bettenson, Henry (ed.), *Documents of the Christian Church*, 2nd edn. (London: Oxford University Press, 1960).

Beversluis, John, *C. S. Lewis and the Search for Rational Religion* (Grand Rapids, MI: Eerdmans, 1985).

Boliek, Lynn, *Resurrection of the Flesh* (Grand Rapids, MI: Eerdmans, 1962).

Brown, David, 'Trinity', in Philip L. Quinn and Charles Taliaferro (eds.), *A Companion to the Philosophy of Religion* (Cambridge, MA: Blackwell, 1997).

Brown, Raymond E., *An Introduction to the New Testament* (New York: Doubleday, 1996).

—— *The Virginal Conception and Bodily Resurrection of Jesus* (New York: Paulist Press, 1973).

Brunner, Emil, *Revelation and Reason* (trans. Olive Wyon) (Philadelphia: Westminster Press, 1946).

Bultmann, Rudolf, *History of the Synoptic Tradition* (trans. John Marsh) (New York: Harper and Row, 1976).

—— *Jesus and the Word* (trans. Louise Pettibone Smith and Ermine Huntress Lantera) (New York: Scribner's, 1958).

—— *Jesus* (Tübingen: J. C. B. Mohr, 1951).

Burrill, Donald R. (ed.), *The Cosmological Arguments* (Garden City, NY: Anchor Books, 1967).

Calvin, John, *The Institutes of the Christian Religion* (ed. John T. McNeil; trans. Ford Lewis Battles), 2 vols. (Philadelphia: Westminster Press, 1960).

Carnell, E. J., *The Case for Orthodox Theology* (Philadelphia: Westminster Press, 1959).

Carnley, Peter, *The Structure of Resurrection Belief* (Oxford: Oxford University Press, 1987).

Cartlidge, David R. and Dungan, David, L. (eds.), *Documents for the Study of the Gospels* (Philadelphia: Fortress Press, 1980).

Charlesworth, M. J. (ed.), *St. Anselm's Proslogion* (Notre Dame, IN: Notre Dame University Press, 1979).

Clark, Kelly James, 'Trinity or Tritheism', *Religious Studies*, 32/4 (Dec., 1996).

Clarke, Samuel, selections from *A Demonstration of the Being and Attributes of God*, in D. Raphael (ed.), *British Moralists 1650–1800* (Oxford: Oxford University Press, 1969).

Clarkson, John, S.J., et al. (eds.), *The Church Teaches: Documents of the Church in English Translation* (St. Louis: B. Herder Book Co., 1955).

Coakley, Sarah, 'What Does Chalcedon Solve and What Does It Not? Some Reflections on the Status and Meaning of the Chalcedonian "Definition" ', in Stephen T. Davis, Daniel Kendall, S.J., and Gerald O'Collins, S.J. (eds.), *The Incarnation: An Interdisciplinary Symposium on the Incarnation of the Son of God* (Oxford: Oxford University Press, 2001).

—— ' "Persons" in the "Social" Doctrine of the Trinity: A Critique of Current Analytic Discussion', in Stephen T. Davis, Daniel Kendall, S.J., and Gerald O'Collins S.J. (eds.), *The Trinity: An Interdisciplinary Symposium on the Trinity* (Oxford: Oxford University Press, 1999).

Congar, Yves, *I Believe in the Holy Spirit*, I (London: Geoffrey Chapman, 1983).

Copan, Paul and Craig, William L., *Creation Out of Nothing* (Grand Rapids, MI: Baker Book House, 2004).

Craig, William L., 'Scientific Confirmation of the Cosmological Argument', in Louis P. Pojman. *Philosophy of Religion*, 4th edn. (Belmont, CA: Wadsworth, 2002).

—— *Assessing the New Testament Evidence for the Historicity of the Resurrection of Jesus* (Lewiston, NY: The Edwin Mellen Press, 1989).

—— *Reasonable Faith: Christian Truth and Apologetics* (Wheaton, IL: Crossway Books, 1984).

—— 'The Bodily Resurrection of Jesus', in R. T. France and D. Wenham (eds.), *Gospel Perspectives*, vol. i (Sheffield: JSOT Press, 1980).

—— (ed.), *The Cosmological Argument from Plato to Leibniz* (New York: Barnes and Noble, 1980).

Cupitt, Don, 'Professor Stanton on Incarnational Language in the New Testament', in Michael Goulder (ed.), *Incarnation and Myth: The Debate Continued* (Grand Rapids, MI: Eerdmans, 1979).

Davis, Stephen T., *Encountering Evil: Live Options in Theodicy*, 2nd edn. (Louisville, KY: Westminster John Knox Press, 2001).

—— 'A Somewhat Playful Proof of the Social Trinity in Five Easy Steps', *Philosophia Christi*, Series 2, 1/2 (1999).

—— *God, Reason, and Theistic Proofs* (Edinburgh: Edinburgh University Press, 1997).

—— *Risen Indeed: Making Sense of the Resurrection* (Grand Rapids, MI: Eerdmans, 1993).

—— 'Universalism, Hell, and the Fate of the Ignorant', *Modern Theology*, 6/2 (January, 1990).

—— *Logic and the Nature of God* (London: Macmillan, 1983).

—— 'Evangelicals and the Religions of the World', *The Reformed Journal*, 31 (June, 1981).

—— *Faith, Skepticism, and Evidence* (Lewisburgh, PA: Bucknell University Press, 1978).

—— *The Debate About the Bible: Inerrancy Versus Infallibility* (Philadelphia: Westminster Press, 1977).

Descartes, René, *Philosophical Writings*, vol. II (ed. John Cottingham, Robert Stoothoff, and Dugald Murdoch) (Cambridge: Cambridge University Press, 1984).

Dilley, Frank, 'Resurrection and the "Replica Objection"', *Religious Studies*, 19/4 (1983).

Dulles, Avery, S.J., *Models of Revelation* (Garden City, NY: Doubleday, 1983).

—— 'Scripture: Recent Protestant and Catholic Views', in Donald K. McKim (ed.), *The Authoritative Word* (Grand Rapids, MI: Eerdmans, 1983).

Edwards, Paul, *Reincarnation: A Critical Examination* (Amherst, NY: Prometheus Books, 1996).

—— 'Karmic Tribulations', in Paul Edwards (ed.), *Immortality* (New York: Macmillan, 1992).

Evans, C. Stephen, 'The Self-Emptying of Love: Some Thoughts on Kenotic Christology', in Stephen T. Davis, Daniel Kendall, S.J., and Gerald O'Collins, S.J. (eds.), *The Incarnation: An Interdisciplinary Symposium on the Incarnation of the Son of God* (Oxford: Oxford University Press, 2002).

—— 'Methodological Naturalism in Historical Biblical Scholarship', in Carey C. Newman (ed.), *Jesus and the Restoration of Israel* (Downers Grove, IL: Inter-Varsity Press, 1999).

—— *The Historical Christ and the Jesus of Faith* (Oxford: Oxford University Press, 1996).

Feenstra, Ronald J, 'Reconsidering Kenotic Christology', in Ronald J. Feenstra and Cornelius Plantinga (eds.), *Trinity, Incarnation, and Atonement: Philosophical and Theological Essays* (Notre Dame, IN: Notre Dame University Press, 1989).

Fitzmyer, Joseph A., S.J., *The Gospel According to Luke (X–XXIV)* (Garden City, NY: Doubleday, 1985).

Flew, Antony, *The Presumption of Atheism and Others Essays* (London: Elek/Pemberton, 1976).

—— 'Immortality', in Paul Edwards (ed,), *The Encyclopedia of Philosophy* (New York: Macmillan, 1967).

—— 'Can a Man Witness His Own Funeral?', *Hibbert Journal*, 54 (1956).

Fuller, Reginald, *The Formation of the Resurrection Narratives* (Philadelphia: Fortress Press, 1980).

Funk, Robert W., et al. (eds.), *The Five Gospels: The Search for the Authentic Words of Jesus* (New York: Macmillan, 1993).

Geach, P. T., *Providence and Evil* (Cambridge: Cambridge University Press, 1977).

—— *God and the Soul* (London: Routledge and Kegan Paul, 1969).

Geiselmann, Josef R., 'Scripture, Tradition, and the Church: An Ecumenical Problem', in D. Callahan, H. Oberman, and D. O'Hanlon, S.J. (eds.), *Christianity Divided* (New York: Sheed and Ward, 1961).

Geisler, Norman and MacKenzie, Ralph E., *Roman Catholics and Evangelicals: Agreements and Differences* (Grand Rapids, MI: Baker Books, 1995).

Gruenler, Royce Gordon, *New Approaches to Jesus and the Gospels: A Phenomenological and Exegetical Study of Synoptic Christology* (Grand Rapids, MI: Baker Book House, 1982).

Gundry, Robert H., 'The Essential Physicality of Jesus' Resurrection According to the New Testament', in Joel B. Green and Max Turner (eds.), *Jesus of Nazareth, Lord and*

Christ: Essays on the Historical Jesus and New Testament Christology (Grand Rapids, MI: Eerdmans, 1994).

—— *Soma in Biblical Theology: With Emphasis on Pauline Anthropology* (Cambridge: Cambridge University Press, 1976.

Hamann, Henry, *The Bible: Between Fundamentalism and Philosophy* (Minneapolis: Augsburgh Publishing Company, 1980).

Hampson, Daphne, 'On Autonomy and Heteronomy', in Daphne Hampson (ed.), *Swallowing a Fishbone? Feminist Theologians Debate* Christianity (London: SPCK: 1996).

Harris, Murray, *Raised Immortal* (Grand Rapids, MI: Eerdmans, 1983).

Hawthorne, Gerald F., *Philippians* (Waco, TX: Word Books, 1983).

Hebblethwaite, Brian, *The Incarnation: Collected Essays in Christology* (Cambridge: Cambridge University Press, 1987).

Helm, Paul, *The Divine Revelation* (Westchester, IL: Crossway Books, 1982).

—— 'A Theory of Disembodied Survival and Re-embodied Existence', *Religious Studies*, 14/1 (1978).

Hengel, Martin, *Between Jesus and Paul: Studies in the Earliest History of Christianity* (Philadelphia: Fortress Press, 1983).

—— *The Son of God: The Origin of Christology and the History of Jewish–Hellenistic Religion* (Philadelphia: Fortress Press, 1976).

Hick, John, *The Metaphor of God Incarnate: Christology in a Pluralistic Age* (Louisville, KY: Westminster John Knox Press, 1993).

—— 'A Response to Hebblethwaite', in Michael Goulder (ed.), *Incarnation and Myth: The Debate Continued* (Grand Rapids, MI: Eerdmans, 1979).

—— 'Is There a Doctrine of Incarnation?', in Michael Goulder (ed.), *Incarnation and Myth: The Debate Continued* (Grand Rapids, MI: Eerdmans, 1979).

—— (ed.), *The Myth of God Incarnate* (Philadelphia: Westminster Press, 1977).

—— *Death and Eternal Life* (New York: Harper and Row, 1976).

—— (ed.), *The Existence of God* (New York: Macmillan, 1964).

Hodgson, Peter and King, Robert (eds.), *Readings in Christian Theology* (Philadelphia: Fortress Press, 1985).

Horton, Michael S., 'What Still Keeps Us Apart?', in *Roman Catholicism: Evangelical Protestants Analyze What Divides and Unites Us* (Chicago: Moody Press, 1994).

Hurtado, Larry, *Lord Jesus Christ: Devotion to Jesus in Earliest Christianity* (Grand Rapids, MI: Eerdmans, 2003).

—— 'Pre-70 C.E. Jewish Opposition to Christ Devotion', *Journal of Theological Studies*, 50/1 (April, 1999).

Hyder, O. Quentin, 'On the Mental Health of Jesus Christ', *Journal of Psychology and Theology*, 5/1 (Winter, 1977).

Jeremias, Joachim, *The Central Message of the New Testament* (London: SCM Press, 1965).

Kahler, Martin, *The So-Called Historical Jesus and the Historic, Biblical Christ* (trans. Carl Braaten) (Philadelphia: Fortress Press, 1964).

Kasemann, Ernst, 'The Problem of the Historical Jesus', in Ernest Kasemann (ed.), *Essays on New Testament Themes* (Naperville, IL: Allenson, 1964).

Kaufman, Gordon, *Systematic Theology: A Historicist Perspective* (New York: Scribner's, 1958).

Kendall, Daniel, S.J. and O'Collins, Gerald, S.J., 'The Uniqueness of the Easter Appearances', *Catholic Biblical Quarterly*, 54/2 (April 1992).

Kierkegaard, Søren, *On Authority and Revelation* (trans. Walter Lowrie) (New York: Harper and Row, 1966).

Kreeft, Peter and Ronald K. Tacelli, *Handbook of Christian Apologetics* (Downers Grove: IL: Inter-Varsity Press, 1994).

Küng, Hans, *On Being a Christian* (trans. Edward Quinn) (New York: Pocket Books, 1970).

Kvanvig, Jonathan L., *The Problem of Hell* (Oxford: Oxford University Press, 1993).

Ladd, George E., *I Believe in the Resurrection of Jesus* (Grand Rapids, MI: Eerdmans, 1975).

Leftow, Brian, 'Anti Social Trinitarianism', in Stephen T. Davis, Daniel Kendall, S.J., and Gerald O'Collins, S.J. (eds.), *The Trinity: An Interdisciplinary Symposium on the Trinity* (Oxford: Oxford University Press, 1999).

Leibniz, Gottfried, 'On the Ultimate Nature of Things', in Philip P. Wiener (ed.), *Leibniz: Selections* (New York: Charles Scribner's Sons, 1951).

Lewis, C. S., *The Problem of Pain* (New York: Macmillan, 1973).

—— *Mere Christianity* (New York: Macmillan, 1960).

Lienhard, Joseph, T., S.J., '*Ousia* and *Hypostasis*: The Cappadocian Settlement and the Theology of "One *Hypostasis*"', in Stephen T. Davis. Daniel Kendall, S.J., and Gerald O'Collins, S.J. (eds.), *The Trinity: An Interdisciplinary Symposium on the Trinity* (Oxford: Oxford University Press, 1999).

Lovejoy, Arthur, *The Great Chain of Being* (Cambridge, MA: Harvard University Press, 1936).

MacDonald, Dennis, *The Homeric Epics and the Gospel of Mark* (New Haven, CT: Yale University Press, 2000).

MacGregor, Geddes, *Reincarnation As a Christian Hope* (London: Macmillan, 1982).

McGrath, Alister, *Studies in Doctrine* (Grand Rapids, MI: Zondervan, 1997).

Mackie, J. L., *The Miracle of Theism* (Oxford: Oxford University Press, 1982).

Manson, William, 'Grace in the New Testament', in William T. Whitley (ed.), *The Doctrine of Grace* (New York: Macmillan, 1932).

Martin, Ralph P. and Dodds, Brian (eds.), *Where Christology Began: Essays on Philippians 2* (Louisville, KY: Westminster John Knox Press, 1998).

Martyr, Justin, *First Apology*, XLIII, Alexander Roberts and James Davidson (eds.), *The Ante-Nicene Fathers*, vol. 1 (Edinburgh: T. and T. Clark, 1989).

Marxsen, Willi, *The Resurrection of Jesus of Nazareth* (trans. Margaret Kohl) (Philadelphia: Fortress Press, 1979).

Mavrodes, George, *Revelation in Religious Belief* (Philadelphia: Temple University Press, 1988).

Mitchell, Basil and Wiles, Maurice, 'Does Christianity Need a Revelation?', *Theology*, LXXXIII/692 (March, 1980).

Moffet, James, *The First Epistle of Paul to the Corinthians*, Moffet New Testament Commentary (New York: Harper, 1938).

Moreland, J. P. and Nielsen, Kai (eds.), *Does God Exist? The Great Debate* (Nashville, TN: Thomas Nelson, 1960).

Morris, Thomas V., *The Logic of God Incarnate* (Ithaca, NY: Cornell University Press, 1986).

—— 'Divinity, Humanity, and Death', *Religious Studies*, 19 (1983).

Moule, Charles, 'Three Points of Conflict in the Christological Debate', in Michael Goulder (ed.), *Incarnation and Myth: The Debate Continued* (Grand Rapids, MI: Eerdmans, 1979).

—— *The Origin of Christology* (Cambridge: Cambridge University Press, 1977).

—— 'St. Paul and Dualism: The Pauline Concept of Resurrection', *New Testament Studies*, 12/2 (1966).

Nash, Ronald H., *The Word of God and the Mind of Man* (Grand Rapids, MI: Zondervan, 1982).

Niebuhr, H. R., *The Meaning of Revelation* (New York: Macmillan, 1962).

Oakes, Robert, 'The Wrath of God', in David Shatz (ed.), *Philosophy and Faith: A Philosophy of Religion Reader* (Boston: McGraw-Hill, 2002).

O'Collins, Gerald, S.J., *Christology: A Biblical, Historical, and Systematic Study of Jesus* (Oxford: Oxford University Press, 1995).

—— *Jesus Risen* (New York: Paulist Press, 1987).

—— *What Are They Saying About the Resurrection?* (New York: Paulist Press, 1978).

—— *The Resurrection of Jesus Christ* (Valley Forge, PA: Judson Press, 1973).

Oden, Thomas, *The Word of Truth* (San Francisco: Harper, 1992).

Osborne, Grant, *The Resurrection Narratives: A Redactional Study* (Grand Rapids, MI: Baker, 1984).

Pannenberg, Wolfhart, *Jesus—God and Man* (Philadelphia: Westminster Press, 1977).

Parfit, Derek, *Reasons and Persons* (Oxford: Oxford University Press, 1986).

Penelhum, Terence, *Survival and Disembodied Existence* (New York: Humanities Press, 1970).

Perrin, Norman, *Rediscovering the Teaching of Jesus* (London: SCM Press, 1967).

Perry, John, *A Dialogue on Personal Identity and Immortality* (Indianapolis, IN: Hackett, 1978).

Phillips, D. Z., *Death and Immortality* (New York: St. Martin's Press, 1970).

Plantinga, Alvin, *The Nature of Necessity* (Oxford: Oxford University Press, 1974).

Plantinga, Cornelius, 'Social Trinity and Tritheism', in Ronald J. Feenstra and Cornelius Plantinga (eds.), *Trinity, Incarnation, and Atonement* (Notre Dame, IN: Notre Dame University Press, 1989).

Plato, *The Collected Dialogues of Plato* (ed. Edith Hamilton and Huntington Cairns) (New York: Pantheon, 1961).

Price, H. H., 'Survival and the Idea of "Another World"', in John Donnelly (ed.), *Language, Metaphysics, and Death* (New York: Fordham University Press, 1978).

Prior, A. N., 'Limited Indeterminism', in A.N. Prior, *Papers on Time and Tense* (Oxford: Clarendon Press, 1968).

Purtill, Richard L., 'The Intelligibility of Disembodied Survival', *Christian Scholars Review*, V/1 (1975).

Rahner, Karl, *Foundations of Christian Faith* (New York: Crossroad Publishing Co., 1984).

—— 'Scripture and Tradition', in Karl Rahner (ed.), *Encyclopedia of Theology: The Concise Sacramentum Mundi* (New York: The Seabury Press, 1975).

Ramm, Bernard, *The Witness of the Spirit* (Grand Rapids, MI: Eerdmans, 1959).

Ramsey, A. M., *The Resurrection of Christ* (London: Fontana Books, 1961).

Reichenbach, Bruce R., 'Justifying In-Principle Nonpredictive Theories: The Case of Evolution', *Christian Scholars Review*, 24/4 (May, 1995).

—— *The Law of Karma: A Philosophical Study* (Honolulu: University of Hawaii Press, 1990).

—— *Is Man the Phoenix? A Study of Immortality* (Washington, D.C.: University Press of America, 1983).

—— 'On Disembodied Resurrection Persons: A Reply', *Religious Studies*, 18/2 (1982).

Reid, John K. S., *The Authority of Scripture* (London: Methuen and Co., 1957).

Richardson, Cyril, *Early Christian Fathers* (Philadelphia: Westminster Press, 1953).

Roberts, Alexander and Donaldson, James (eds.), *The Ante Nicene Fathers*, vol. i (New York: Charles Scribner's Sons, 1899).

Roberts, Robert C., 'Parameters of a Christian Psychology', in Robert C. Roberts (ed.), *Limning the Psyche: Explorations in Christian Psychology* (Grand Rapids, MI: Eerdmans, 1998).

Robinson, J. A. T., *Can We Trust the New Testament?* (Grand Rapids, MI: Eerdmans, 1997).

Salvation and the Church: An Agreed Statement (London: Church House Publishing/ Catholic Truth Society, 1987).

Sanders, E.P., *Jesus and Judaism* (Philadelphia: Fortress Press, 1985).

Sider, Ronald J., 'The Pauline Conception of the Resurrection Body in I Corinthians XV: 35–54', *New Testament Studies*, 21/3 (1965).

Smart, James D., *The Interpretation of Scripture* (Philadelphia: Westminster Press, 1961).

Soskice, Janet Martin, 'Sight and Vision in Medieval Christian Thought', in Martin Jay and Teresa Brennan (eds.), *Vision in Context: Historical and Contemporary Perspectives on Sight* (London: Routledge, 1996).

Sproul, R. C., '*Sola Scriptura*: Crucial to Evangelicalism', in J. M. Boice (ed.), *The Foundation of Biblical Authority* (Grand Rapids, MI: Zondervans Publishing House, 1978).

Sturch, Richard, *The New Deism: Divine Intervention and the Human Condition* (New York: St. Martin's Press, 1990).

Swinburne, Richard, *The Resurrection of God Incarnate* (Oxford: Oxford University Press, 2003).

—— *The Christian God* (Oxford: Oxford University Press, 1994).

—— *Revelation: From Metaphor to Analogy* (Oxford: Oxford University Press, 1992).

—— *Responsibility and Atonement* (Oxford: Oxford University Press, 1989).

Tavard, George H., *Holy Writ or Holy Church* (New York: Harper and Brothers, 1959).

Taylor, Richard, *Metaphysics* 4th edn. (Englewood Cliffs, NJ: Prentice-Hall, 1992).

Tertullian, 'On the Resurrection of the Flesh', in Alexander Roberts and James Donaldson (eds.), *The Ante Nicene Fathers*, vol. iii (New York: Charles Scribner's Sons, 1899).

The Book of Confessions (New York: Office of the General Assembly of the Presbyterian Church (USA), 1984).

Trembath, Kern R., *Divine Revelation: Our Moral Relation With God* (New York: Oxford University Press, 1991).

van Inwagen, Peter, 'The Possibility of Resurrection', *International Journal for Philosophy of Religion*, IX/2 (1978).

Vermes, Geza, *The Changing Faces of Jesus* (London: Penguin, 2000).

Wainwright, Arthur, *Beyond Biblical Criticism: Encountering Jesus in Scripture* (Atlanta: John Knox Press, 1960).

Wallace, Mark, 'The Rule of Love and the Testimony of the Spirit in Contemporary Biblical Hermeneutics', in A. Wiercinski (ed.), *Between the Human and the Divine: Philosophical and Theological Hermeneutics* (Toronto: The Hermeneutic Press, 2002).

Webber, Robert E., 'An Evangelical and Catholic Methodology', in Robert K. Johnson (ed.), *The Use of the Bible in Theology: Evangelical Options* (Atlanta: John Knox Press, 1985).

Weigel, Gustave, S.J. and Brown, R. M., *An American Dialogue* (Garden City, NY: Anchor Books, 1960).

Welsh, Claude (ed. and trans.), *God and Incarnation in Mid-nineteenth Century German Theology* (New York: Oxford University Press, 1965.

Weston, Frank, *The One Christ: An Enquiry into the Manner of the Incarnation* (London: Longmans Green, 1907).

Williams, Bernard, *Problems of the Self* (Cambridge: Cambridge University Press, 1973).

Williams, C. J. F., 'Neither Confounding the Persons Nor Dividing the Substance', in Alan Padgett (ed.), *Reason and the Christian Religion* (New York: Oxford University Press, 1994).

Williams, Rowan, 'Looking for Jesus and Finding Christ', in D.Z. Phillips and Mario von der Ruhr (eds.), *Biblical Concepts and Our World* (London: Palgrave, 2004).

Witherington, Ben, *The Many Faces of the Christ* (New York: Crossroad, 1998).

—— *The Jesus Question* (Downers Grove, IL: Inter-Varsity Press, 1995).

—— *The Christology of Jesus* (Minneapolis, MN: Fortress Press, 1990).

Wolfson, Harry A., 'Immortality and Resurrection in the Philosophy of the Church Fathers', in Krister Stendahl (ed.), *Immortality and Resurrection* (New York: Macmillan, 1965).

Wolterstorff, Nicholas, *Divine Discourse: Philosophical Reflections on the Claim that God Speaks* (Cambridge: Cambridge University Press, 1995).

Wright, N. T., *The Resurrection of the Son of God* (Minneapolis, MN: Fortress Press, 2003).

—— 'Jesus and the Identity of God', *Ex Auditu*, 14 (1998).

—— *Jesus and the Victory of God* (Minneapolis: Fortress Press, 1996).

Young, Frances, 'The Finality of Christ', in Michael Goulder (ed.), *Incarnation and Myth: The Debate Continued* (Grand Rapids, MI: Eerdmans, 1979).

Index

Ingram Content Group UK Ltd.
Milton Keynes UK
UKHW022352130323
418540UK00004B/235